FRENCH REVOLUTIONS, 1815–1914

To
Ali Wardak
and
Masuda Sahil Wardak

FRENCH REVOLUTIONS, 1815–1914

An Introduction

SHARIF GEMIE

EDINBURGH UNIVERSITY PRESS

Edinburgh University Press
22 George Square, Edinburgh

Typeset in Bembo
by Norman Tilley Graphics, and
printed and bound in Great Britain
by Creative Print and Design,
Ebbw Vale, Wales

A CIP record for this book is available
from the British Library

ISBN 1 85331 214 2

Contents

Acknowledgements

I would like to acknowledge the assistance of the School of Humanities Research Fund in writing this book, and to thank Catherine Evans for designing the map.

Writing a history book is always a collective effort, even if only one person is named as author. I would like to thank all my friends and colleagues who have helped me in many different ways to complete this work:

To my colleagues, Penny Byrne, Andy Croll, Chris Evans, Patrick Hagopian, Beatrice Le Bihan, Margaret Majumdar, Ursula Masson, Peter Mercer, Ieuan Thomas and Neil Wynn, who have listened patiently to my ideas. I would like particularly to thank Gareth Pritchard for his co-operation and assistance.

To Charles Rearick, for his assistance in finding the cover picture.

To Pamela Pilbeam and my friends across the water, Elinor Accampo and Jo Burr Margadant in the USA, and Peter McPhee in Australia, for their encouragement and interest.

To Tom Cahill, Richard Cleminson, Ruth Kinna, Carl Levy, John Moore and Jon Purkis, for inspirations and ideas.

To Rob Southall, for introducing me to Malicorne.

To the Clarks and the Slapes, for book tokens and cakes. Particular thanks to Daniel Slape, for his calendar of 1848.

To my family, for refuges in south-east London.

To Roz and Tim for, once again, food, wine and a working model of emotional stability; plus, mellow non-Eurocentric music and good advice on how to cope with the fifth decade.

To Ali and Masuda: *soyez bienvenus*.

To Patricia, *mi compañera*.

Abbreviations

AD I&V: Archives départementales de l'Ille-et-Vilaine
ADR: Archives départementales du Rhône
ADV: Archives départementales de la Vendée
AML: Archives municipales de la ville de Lyon
AN: Archives nationales (Paris)
GOF: Grand Occident de la France
LAF: Ligue Antisémitique française; sometimes also labelled Ligue Anti-sémitique de la France
nd: no date (i.e., no date of publication has been given)
np: no place (i.e., no place of publication has been given)
UP: University Press

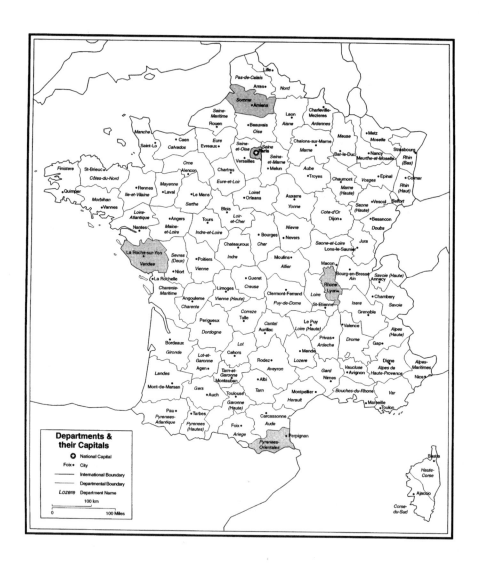

Departments & their Capitals

- ⊙ National Capital
- Foix • City
- International Boundary
- Departmental Boundary
- *Lozere* Department Name

100 km

0   100 Miles

CHAPTER 1

Introduction

– I. POLITICAL CULTURE –

It may seem strange to see these two words placed together. The most common image of 'politics' is probably the noisy, clumsy, point-scoring debates which we see or hear in the House of Commons; while 'culture' is still generally understood in the sense of 'great culture': the plays of Shakespeare, the opera of Mozart, the music of Beethoven. How can the two terms be united? The only possible combination would seem to be in something like the 'theatre of power' – the intricate ceremonials through which medieval monarchs expressed their dignity and status.

However, the two words have other meanings. The word 'politics' originates from the Ancient Greek word 'polis': a term normally applied to the small city-states of the pre-Christian era, and meaning something like our term 'community'. Often, in these communities, politics was not understood as something which stood above, or away, from the life of the citizens. An eloquent evocation of what it might mean was written by Aristotle, one of the most perceptive Ancient Greek philosophers.

> Man is by nature a political animal; it is his nature to live in a *polis*. He who by his nature ... has no city, no state, is ... either sub-human or super-human ... He is a non-cooperator like an isolated piece in a game of draughts. Nature ... does nothing without some purpose; and for the purpose of making man a political animal she has endowed him alone among the animals with the power of reasoned speech. Speech ... serves to indicate what is useful and what is harmful, and so also what is right and what is wrong. For the real difference between man and other animals is that humans alone have perception of good and evil, right and wrong, just and unjust. And it is the sharing of a common view in such matters that makes a household or a city.[1]

There are a number of problems with this passage. First, it has to be stressed that Classical Athens was not as 'democratic' as Aristotle's writing might imply. It was a deeply hierarchic society, based on slave labour, in which women, slaves, foreigners and children were denied the status of citizens and had no access to its democratic forms. Second, it must also be stressed that Aristotle was a critic of these early forms of democracy and not a supporter. Third, there are some rather more involved biological, anthropological and socio-linguistic problems with Aristotle's musings on the 'political animal': how, exactly, are politics transmitted from generation to generation? Is it inscribed in our DNA? Or is learnt through education?

Whatever its shortcomings, the above passage succeeds in evoking a challenging image of the nature of politics. As Cornelius Castoriadis notes: the Greek interpretation of politics was based on 'an explicit questioning' of the way in which a society was established.[2] It implied that nothing was accepted as 'above question': there was no area which was defined away as sacred, natural, or traditional, and so on. Politics, in this sense, is about power, and about its arrangement and distribution: it is (potentially) something wider and deeper than parliamentary politics, and includes issues such as sexual politics, local politics, cultural politics, and so on. Aristotle's sketch suggests that all people are, by their nature, political.

I find the passage by Aristotle a thought-provoking piece of writing. Reducing debate to its most basic, it could be said that, having made some qualifications, I have taken this as 'my definition' of politics. A more subtle formulation is possible: rather than attempting to conclude debate, once and for all, this book attempts to develop a discussion. Rather than saying 'this is politics', this book is based on a question: *'What if* politics works in the way that Aristotle and Castoriadis describe?'.

Just as we have questioned the meaning of the word 'politics', so something similar needs to be done for the term 'culture'. Here we are aided by a relatively new academic discipline, Cultural Studies. The starting point of this discipline is a rejection of the notion that culture is located in museums, theatres, opera houses and libraries, and the counter-proposal that everyone has a culture: as with our redefinition of politics, culture is to be found in everyday life, speech and relationships. Richard Johnson, a historian who turned to Cultural Studies, explains his new field of study thus:

> Cultural studies is about historical forms of consciousness or subjectivity, or the subjective forms we live by, or ... the subjective side of social relations ...
>
> Our project is to abstract, describe and reconstitute in concrete studies the social forms through which human beings 'live', become conscious, sustain themselves subjectively.[3]

Elsewhere in the same work Johnson considers whether the word 'consciousness' might be more appropriate than 'culture'.

What happens when we put these two terms together to form 'political culture'? It should now be obvious that we are not thinking of a study that will be centred on the pinnacles of power, but rather one which will gauge the relationship between the mass of the population and political ideas. There are some obvious problems here: for much of the nineteenth century most Frenchmen and all Frenchwomen were disenfranchised. Many people were illiterate and even those who were literate did not necessarily read. There were no opinion polls through which mass opinion was registered. And like it or not, it is easier to hear the voices of an articulate, literate minority who debate political questions in the press, in parliament and in books. Surely, it might be argued, it would make sense to focus our study on this minority? Their works are easily available; many are still in print in (relatively) cheap paperback editions. As for the majority ... how exactly does one study their politics?

However, it can (and will) be argued that it is only when the articulate political ideas of intellectuals and writers are reflected, echoed or expressed through the actions, beliefs or dreams of the mass of the population that they acquire some real power. Karl Marx once wrote that 'theory ... becomes a material force once it has gripped the masses'.[4] The point he is making here is a complex one, relating to the place of ideas within Marxist philosophy. However, we can take his words at face value, and note that 'theory' or 'political ideas' become noticeably different when they take the form of words or ideals expressed by a mass movement. The precise relationship between intellectual culture and popular culture is a complex question, and it is one to which we will return frequently.

Before leaving these questions of definitions and methods, perhaps it would be useful to distinguish 'the history of political culture' from the two other most common forms of historical writing on politics. The first can be identified as 'intellectual history' or the 'history of ideas', and Isaiah Berlin can be cited as a fine example of the strengths of this method.[5] Berlin considers the political writings of many intellectuals, and debates the coherence and logic of their arguments. While he certainly leaves the reader with a sense of greatly increased knowledge and understanding, Berlin rarely considers the political or social effects of political ideas; he concentrated on printed texts, perhaps on the assumption that these constitute the purest forms of political debate.

The second most common method is usually called 'political history', though perhaps 'history of political institutions' might be a more accurate title. Skilled political historians – for example, Carl E. Schorske – can produce detailed analyses of the development and decline of parties, and can debate the reasons for the rise and fall of particular factions or theories within parties.[6] While an integral part of such studies has to be the ability (or otherwise) of an organisation to gain popular support, the focus of political historians is usually on the great institutions: parliaments, parties, perhaps trade unions or political leagues.

To demonstrate how these approaches differ, let us take an example. In fact, this particular example pushes our approaches to their limit: it is the Party Political Broadcast (PPB). While Isaiah Berlin would probably shudder at the idea of considering such a vulgar form of political expression, the 'history of ideas' approach could certainly say something about the political ideas expressed within a PPB, and could show how these developed from other political ideas. However, within this perspective, little would be said about the viewer's reaction.

The political historian would be more willing to engage with the PPB, and could perhaps say whether it reflected the rise of one faction within a party, or the decline of another. He or she would also want to say something about reactions to a PPB, although probably only from the perspective of its effectiveness: did it win votes? Did it win the election? If not, why not?

Neither of these approaches would have much to say about the most common reaction to the PPB, which is for television watchers to get up, go to the kitchen, and make a cup of tea. (This is a serious point: Electricity Boards across the country are prepared for a massive power surge during PPBs, as hundreds of thousands of electric kettles are switched on.) For the historian of ideas, for the political historian, this point is at best 'negative evidence', at worst irrelevant. However, for the historian of political culture, it reveals an important aspect of the nature of political culture in contemporary Britain, for it indicates the deep apathy felt by the majority of the population for the dominant forms of political debate.

This book will study ten different examples of political culture. In all these cases – with the exception of Chapters 5 and 10 – our studies will centre on dramatic events in French history, when there was no doubt that illiterate, unprivileged people were participating in the making of history. Such moments are often termed 'revolutions'; for our purposes this means an explicit questioning of the dominant power structures in a society, coupled with an attempt by a substantial body of people to institute another form of power structure.[7]

– II. HISTORIANS' DEBATES –

A sense of crisis is developing among historians, particularly social historians. Historical journals regularly feature articles with worrying titles such as 'the End of Social History?'. In the 1960s and 1970s social history was understood to be setting the agenda for historical writing. It presented an exciting challenge to the 'old' political history, which was concerned with the lives of the great and the good. Political history produced narratives about monarchs, presidents, prime ministers and great leaders; it frequently resembled biography in its equation of a time with a person – 'the Victorian Age' – and, at its best, it could take the form of perhaps exciting, or at least relatively clear, stories about memorable people.

The 'new' social history challenged these assumptions. Rather than focusing on the lives of the great, social historians wrote about the masses. There was often a critical, radical edge to this writing, sometimes taking the form of an explicit commitment to socialist ideals, but more often infused with a gentle, humanist quality. This is nicely illustrated by the words of one of the greatest social historians, the English Marxist E. P. Thompson. 'I am seeking to rescue the poor stockinger, the Luddite cropper, the "obsolete" hand-loom weaver, the "utopian" artisan, and even the deluded follower of Joanna Southcott, from the enormous condescension of posterity.'[8] Rather than focusing on the 'headlines' of history, social historians attempted to get behind, or beneath, such dramatic events, and to write a history of the slow processes of change in the lives of the poor and powerless. This could involve a deliberate challenge to the notion of history as a story with a beginning, a middle and an end: some – for example, Emmanuel Le Roy Ladurie – wrote of 'immobile history'; in other words, histories of lives and conditions which did not change. At its best, social history could produce works which were as readable as the old political narratives, and which were – arguably – more intellectually and politically challenging. Why should this form of history now be in a state of crisis?

This is a difficult question, and one to which each individual historian would probably give a different answer. However, there seem to be at least three issues preoccupying historians. The first is an internal crisis within social history. In the 1950s and 1960s, one model of social history concentrated on long, centuries-wide, structures of evolution, based on long-term economic and social changes. This form of history is exemplified by the work of Fernand Braudel.[9] In opposition to this, other social historians insisted that the best way to understand the development of society was through examining what people thought, or even what they felt. Such social historians still wished to study the lives of the mass of the population: as, for much of history, the masses have been illiterate, this often meant that these social historians were studying small pockets of unusual written documentation rather than long seams of socio-economic evidence. Perhaps for this reason, their histories often concentrated on small case studies of identifiable communities, such as those written by Carlo Ginzburg and, sometimes, by Le Roy

Ladurie.[10] One aspect of 'the crisis of history' has been the swing from the study of 'hard', quantifiable, socio-economic history to 'soft', qualitative, intellectual and cultural history.

A second aspect has been the long-term effects of the development of women's history. While social historians tried to uncover the lives of the masses, these masses frequently seemed to be male peasants, male workers and male bourgeois. The concept of 'class' seemed to group people according to the position of the male head of the family. Feminists reminded historians that there was at least one other key concept which deserved to be considered, namely that of 'gender'. Through a number of breathtakingly original studies, they demonstrated that the simplistic and insulting assumption that men were the masters of history, women the servants, was – to put it mildly – invalid.[11] The long-term effects of this revolution are still being felt. Issues or approaches which had seemed self-evident no longer look so clear-cut. Once you recognise that half the human race is female, how do you write a history of the First World War? Of the French Revolution? Of housing?

Finally, the third aspect of this crisis has been the questions provoked by a form of thinking which originally developed among literary criticism, and which is usually known as 'post-modernism', or sometimes as 'post-structuralism'. One problem here is the basic difficulty in providing a simple definition of this mode of thinking. The most commonly traded definition is 'scepticism about grand narratives'. This means that post-modernists do not accept the idea that there is some identifiable story to be told about the human race, whether in the form of the Christian narrative which starts in the Garden of Eden and ends with the Second Coming, or the Marxist narrative of feudalism through capitalism to socialism, or any other version. However, while this short definition might tell us what post-modernists are *against*, it does little to explain what they are *for* – after all, there are many reasons for being 'sceptical' about 'grand narratives' besides those provided by post-modernists.

To complicate matters further, there are a number of 'soft' and 'hard' versions of post-modernist thinking. All these varieties place 'texts' (again, a word subject to a number of possible definitions) at the centre of their enquiries. Perhaps a concrete example might help at this point. Imagine that we find a note (or 'text') written by a secular schoolmistress in the 1880s which describes her experience of teaching. In this text there is a phrase which suggests that she was thinking of her work as being like a religious vocation. How would the 'soft', 'semi-soft' and 'hard' versions of post-modernist thought treat this point?

1. **'soft'**: The metaphors and images that people use are important: they do not simply register human experience, they also record the way in which they made sense of their lives. If we examine a series of documents written by schoolmistresses which make use of the same type of metaphor, then we could speak of a 'vocabulary', even a 'language', which was specific to schoolmistresses. Through analysing this language we can learn more about their lives and experiences, and this form of enquiry can tell us more about them than other forms of analysis of rates of pay, promotion, life expectancy, marriage rates, or maternity.

2. **'semi-soft'**: For the sake of argument, let us forget or ignore all other information that we might know (or be able to guess) about this schoolmistress. Let us concentrate on the words in this text alone; if we want to research more widely, let us compare her way of writing to other contemporary forms of writing. Information about schoolmistresses' rates of pay, promotion, life expectancy, marriage rates, or maternity are therefore irrelevant.

3. **'hard'**: All that we can be sure about are the words on the page. There is no 'reality' outside it, there is no wider context within which we can put it, beyond that furnished by other texts. (A dramatic way of making this point is to speak of 'the death of the author', meaning that we do not need to consider the author's intentions when he or she wrote a text, and also implying the liberation of the reader, who is now free – or freer – to interpret.) We can analyse the form of words used, but if we imagine that this allows us to understand something about their author, then we would fooling ourselves. Texts do not reflect reality, they constitute it.

One point to note here is that the techniques suggested in the 'soft' version of post-modernism easily merge with the forms of cultural and intellectual history previously discussed: this leads to some confusion about what really constitutes a distinctively post-modern history.

Each of these debates has influenced me while writing this work. As later chapters will show, despite discussing politics, I have followed the paths of the 'new' social history rather than the 'old' political history. While this is not a work of 'women's history', I hope that I have learnt several lessons from women's historians. The first is the basic one of recognising women's participation in political movements, rather than assuming that men's participation is more central, more politicised or more important. Second, when we come across a situation in which men debate political themes with only a few isolated female contributors present, we should ask *why* this is so, and question what this disparity says about sexual identities. Finally, while this is not a work of post-modern history, it does resemble post-modernists' works, particularly in the 'soft' version, in that we will be concerned with themes, metaphors and images found in texts.

– III. ON FRENCH HISTORY –

Debates concerning power and political cultures developed with unusual force in nineteenth-century France. We will return to this topic in my conclusion: at this point, I wish to present some preliminary information about the nature of French history.

In 1815 approximately thirty million people lived in France. Why should we consider them French? Perhaps the most obvious answer is to reply that they were French because they lived in France. This line of argument is an inadequate simplification of the nature of nationhood in modern nation states. In the place where I am writing, there are people who live in Britain but consider themselves to be Welsh. During the latter years of the period which we will be discussing, there were people in Alsace-Lorraine who were classified as German, but who considered themselves French, and who became recognised as French once more in 1919, following the Treaty of Versailles. Thus, the 'they're French because they live in France' argument cannot be taken as conclusive.

Let us briefly consider a few further arguments on this point.

1. **language**: if it could be shown that all thirty million people spoke approximately the same language, then it could be argued that this facet of their daily lives made them different from the other peoples of Europe. However, French was not always the dominant language. Eugen Weber has estimated that in 1863 French (and regional forms of the French language) was the first language of – at most – about four-fifths of the population.[12] At almost every point of the compass, French was challenged: in the north-east by Flemish, in the east by German and Swiss dialects, in the south-east by Italian dialects, in the south by Catalan, in the south-west by Basque, and in the west by Breton. Added to this linguistic complexity were divisions within the French language itself, of which the most important was the difference between the 'langue d'oïl' of north-central France and the 'langue d'oc' of the south. Furthermore, there were a vast range of local dialects and slangs. When travellers left Paris to go into the regions, they would automatically hire local guides: partly to assist them in their journeys, but also to act as interpreters with the local people. Of course, institutions such as the press, the railway and the primary school eventually helped to change this situation, but we cannot explain French national identity by a unified French linguistic identity.

2. **religion:** There is no doubt that the majority of French people thought of themselves as Catholics during the period that we will be discussing. However, it must be remembered that there were other forms of religious identity: in the 1870s there were also approximately six hundred thousand Protestants and forty thousand Jews living in France.[13] Were they any less 'French' than their Catholic neighbours? While monarchists often did connect monarchism, 'Frenchness' and Catholicism, the new political cultures of the nineteenth century asserted a *secular* French identity.

3. **government and law:** Prior to the Revolution of 1789, France, like most European countries, was a patchwork of competing law codes. One of the lasting achievements of the Revolution was the foundation of a single, relatively coherent, law code for the whole of France and, accompanying this, the establishment of coherent bureaucratic structures. The Revolution created the basic pattern of eighty-five departments, each divided into two, three or four *arrondissements*, these divided in turn into cantons, which grouped together approximately thirty-six thousand communes, the most basic administrative unit. During the Empire, this structure was supplemented by a non-elected administrative bureaucracy: within each department there was a prefect appointed by the head of state, with the task of ensuring that the state's policies were carried out; in turn, each *arrondissement* was directed by an appointed sub-prefect, and often the mayors of the more important towns were also appointed from above rather than elected from below.

Perhaps it was this political edifice which bound the varied populations of France together?[14] This is a strong argument, which certainly seems to make sense in, for example, August 1914, when call-up papers were sent to young men across the whole of France and, in almost 99 per cent of cases, they obeyed. However, one can question whether August 1914 is typical of the individual French person's relationship with the state. For much of our period, contact with agents of the state was rare. Schooling did not become compulsory until the 1880s; conscription was intermittently enforced but hated by the majority of conscripts (hardly a good lesson in nationhood); and while law might effect land sales and negotiations about property, it was hardly a *daily* presence in the lives of most French people. Indeed, the most visible sign of the state might be the annual visit of the tax collector.

What we are searching for is what Benedict Anderson has termed 'an imagined community'. By this term, Anderson meant that no concrete, biological, organic form linked French peoples together. Modern forms of nationhood are, despite the rhetoric about blood, soil and race, highly abstract.[15] In other circumstances, one could imagine a shared (if manipulated) sense of national history uniting these disparate peoples together, and allowing them to think of themselves as 'a nation'. However, following the Revolution of 1789, French history was more a source of division than unity.

My final response to the question 'what was "French-ness"?' is to reply that we are examining peoples with a weak and contested sense of national unity. Certainly, one can find examples of *nationalism*, which we could understand as the political assertion of national unity as the most important political goal of a party or movement. However, assertions of French nationhood generally only mobilised a minority, attracting sometimes genuine opposition, but more often apathy, from the majority.

What this means is that the political conflicts which we will be studying have another dimension: as well battles between left and right, republic and monarchy, new and old, they are also examples of the creation of a nationwide culture. Ultimately, the answer to the question of 'Frenchness' might lie in changing the question. Instead of looking for monolithic forms of unity, such as the 99.9 per cent majorities which Communist Parties used to win in the old Eastern Bloc, we should begin to accept that 'nationhood' might be constituted around a shared sense of conflict or, less violently, diversity. In other words, while monarchists and republicans might disagree about every element of their respective interpretations of the French past, they might still both agree about *which* moments constituted the crucial moments of division.

– IV. POLITICAL CONFLICTS –

One unusual aspect of nineteenth-century French history is the frequency of the violent political conflict. We will be studying ten examples of such conflicts in the course of the course of this work, but, with a little imagination, ten more examples could be found. Why was French society so frequently troubled by revolutionary conflict?

I will not give a full answer to this question here, but in the last pages of this chapter I want to signal some unusual aspects of French politics.

Our starting point is the legacy of the French Revolution. During the years from 1789 to 1815 at least three different models of rule were established:

1. monarchy
2. republic
3. empire

France, prior to 1789, had been a monarchy: during the first three years of the Revolution, Louis XVI remained head of the French state, and this period of his rule set a pattern of constitutional monarchy, involving representative (*not* democratic) political structures, which remained the model for the monarchical rule following the Restorations of 1814 and 1815.

In August 1792, as a result of further revolutionary action, France became a Republic, and remained officially republican until 1804. In September 1792 the Jacobins attempted to ratify the new Republic through elections, in which almost all men could vote. Given the atmosphere of panic and confusion, few made use of this opportunity: historians generally estimate that only between 10 per cent and 15 per cent actually voted. Following this unique episode, the Jacobins turned to rule by revolutionary dictatorship, and were then in turn replaced by the Directory (1795) which returned to the previous model of representative, but not democratic, republican government. In the nineteenth century, republicans usually accepted the principle of male-democracy.

Napoleon effectively seized power in 1799, but it was not until 1804 that he created the Empire. This can be understood as an attempt to construct a compromise between the republican and monarchist forms of government. In the Emperor, the Empire had a strong, powerful leader, like a king. The position was made hereditary – again, like a monarchy. But, unlike a monarchy, Napoleon always claimed to recognise the principle of popular sovereignty: in other words, that the right to rule could only be bestowed by the people. For republicans and liberal monarchists, popular sovereignty could only mean one thing: representative or democratic parliaments, chosen by the electorate. However, Napoleon made use of referendums to replace elections, and made a virtue of such practices, claiming that they were a more direct, more representative practice than the faction-ridden parliaments. In the Second Empire (1852–70), Napoleon's nephew, Louis-Napoleon, skirted parliamentary rule in a similar way.

The struggle between these three forms of rule resulted in the following regimes:

Table 1.1: Political regimes in France, 1789–1940

Date	Regime
1789	The French Revolution; constitutional monarchy.
1792	The Convention: creates the **First Republic**, based 'loosely' on manhood suffrage.
1795	The Directory: restricted suffrage, republican.
1799	Napoleon's coup d'état.
1804	**Empire** (based on irregular plebiscites).
1814	First **Restoration** (extremely restricted suffrage, constitutional monarchy).
1815	Napoleon's Hundred Days (political form undefined). Second **Restoration** (extremely restricted suffrage, constitutional monarchy).
1830	July Revolution, creating liberal **Orleanist** constitutional monarchy (restricted suffrage).
1848	**Second Republic** (manhood suffrage).
1852	**Second Empire** (pseudo-democratic).
1870	**Third Republic** (manhood suffrage; chamber of deputies and senate; weak, indirectly elected President).
1871	Paris **Commune**.
1940	Collapse of the Third Republic following defeat by German forces.

Much more could (and will) be said about each of these regimes, but for the moment I wish to stress one point. This list merely summarises the headlines. Many of these apparently catastrophic changes of regime were actually minor matters: after all, it was in France that the expression '*plus ça change, plus c'est la même chose*' (the more things change, the more they're the same) was devised. Most importantly, this list says nothing about the lived experience of the majority of the French people. Even in 1914, the majority of French people still lived in small villages and worked the land; and nothing resembled a village of 1814 as much as a village of 1914.

One way of understanding the course of this history is to think in terms of a 'two-speed' history. On the one hand there were the dramatic, exciting and sometimes important revolutionary changes; on the other hand there was the slow, step-by-step process of change among the ordinary people.

One further legacy of the Revolution needs to be stressed. During the early 1790s many of the new revolutionary groups began to aim their appeals at the mass population. Few responded, but none the less a new model of political organisation, the club, had been created. Governments were often worried by the implications of this model: from 1792 onwards, laws were passed to restrict both access to clubs and activities undertaken by clubs. These restrictions were codified in the Code Napoléon of 1804, which banned all associations of more than twenty people, unless they were specially authorised.[16] Even quite innocent organisations such as theatrical groups or gambling clubs had to apply for authorisations in order to hold meetings. With some qualifications, this legislation remained in force until July 1901 when the Law on Associations permitted certain forms of association to meet without seeking permission. This repressive legislation shaped the development of French political culture. The mass political party was not legally possible for most of the period we will examine. Political activists were either forced into illegality, or made to consider other means by which to co-ordinate political activities.

– CONCLUSION –

The Revolution of 1789 broke the aura of unthinking respect which had previously surrounded the French monarchy. However, it was not able to devise a stable regime which was accepted by the majority of French people in its place. In the nineteenth century, a profound and demanding debate on the nature of power developed. This debate lies at the centre of the issues raised by the chapters which follow.

– V. FURTHER READING –

– HISTORIANS' DEBATES –

There are a number of provocative and well-written books which explain the methods used by historians. My personal favourite is E. P. Thompson, *The Poverty of Theory* (Harmondsworth: Penguin, 1979), but it must be acknowledged that this is not a good starting-point for the beginner. E. H. Carr, *What is History?* (Harmondsworth: Penguin, 1964) is an 'oldie but goldie': hardly up-to-date, but still effective in introducing key concepts. John Tosh, *The Pursuit of History* (London: Longman, 1984), is still relevant. Keith Jenkins, *Re-thinking History* (London: Routledge, 1991) is sympathetic to recent post-modern thinking.

There are also many short essays: as a general comment, the more of these that you read, the more they make sense. Lynn Hunt, 'French History in the Last Twenty Years; the Rise and Fall of the *Annales* Paradigm', *Journal of Contemporary History* 21 (1986), 209–24; Patrick Joyce, 'The End of Social History?', *Social History* 20:1 (1995), 73–91; James F. McMillan, 'Social History, "New Cultural History" and the Rediscovery of Politics; Some Recent Works on Modern France', *Journal of Modern History* 66 (1994), 755–72; Gianne Pomata, 'History, Particular and Universal; On Reading Some Recent Women's History Textbooks', *Feminist Studies* 19:1 (1993), 7–50; William Sewell, 'Towards a post-materialist Rhetoric for Labor History' in L. R. Berlanstein (ed.), *Rethinking Labor History* (Urbana and Chicago, Illinois UP, 1993), pp. 15–38.

– POLITICAL CULTURE –

Interpretations on this area are still very fluid. I have found the following to be useful: Clifford Geertz, 'Ideology as a Cultural System' in his *The Interpretation of Cultures: Selected Essays* (London: Fontana, 1993). Geertz is an anthropologist who is being increasingly read by historians. Richard Johnson, *What is Cultural Studies Anyway?* (Birmingham: Centre for Contemporary Cultural Studies, 1983) provides a useful introduction. Interesting arguments can also be found in the introductions to: Robert Gildea, *The Past in French History* (New Haven: Yale UP, 1994) and Dena Goodman, *The Republic of Letters: A Cultural History of the French Enlightenment* (Ithaca: Cornell UP, 1994).

– FRENCH HISTORY –

There are a number of useful works on nineteenth-century French history: Roger Magraw, *France, 1815–1914: The Bourgeois Century* (London: Fontana, 1983) stresses the interplay between politics and society, and also provides useful commentaries on interpretations of particular issues. Roger Price, *A Social History of Nineteenth-Century France* (London: Hutchinson, 1987) and Peter McPhee, *A Social History of France, 1780–1880* (London: Routledge, 1992) are principally social histories. Robert Tombs, *France, 1814–1914* (London: Longman 1996) is more than six hundred pages long and is probably best used as a reference work.

On the specific issue of political organisations, Raymond Huard, *La Naissance du parti politique en France* (Paris: Presses de Sciences Po, 1996) is an extremely useful work.

– NOTES –

1. Aristotle, *The Politics*, trans. T. A. Sinclair (Harmondsworth: Penguin, 1979), pp. 28–9.
2. Cornelius Castoriadis, *Le Monde morcélé* (Paris: Seuil, 1990), p. 126.
3. Richard Johnson, *What is Cultural Studies Anyway?* (Birmingham: Centre for Contemporary Cultural Studies, 1983), pp. 11–13.
4. Karl Marx, *Early Writings*, trans. Rodney Livingstone and Gregor Benton (Harmondsworth: Penguin, 1977), p. 251.
5. The two studies by Berlin which are most relevant to this work are his essays on 'the Counter-Enlightenment' and 'Georges Sorel', in his *Against the Current* (London: Hogarth, 1979).
6. See Carl E. Schorske, *German Social Democracy, 1905–1917* (Cambridge, Mass.: Harvard University Press, 1955).
7. Castoriadis, *Monde Morcélé*, pp. 127 and 163.
8. E. P. Thompson, *The Making of the English Working Class* (Harmondsworth: Penguin, 1978), p. 13.
9. See, for example, Braudel's *The Mediterranean and the Mediterranean World in the Age of Philip II*, translated by Sîan Reynolds (London: Collins, 1976).
10. Carlo Ginzburg, *The Cheese and the Worms: the Cosmos of a Sixteenth Century Miller*, trans. J. and S. Tedeschi (New York: Dorset, 1980); Emmanuel Le Roy Ladurie, *Montaillou* (Harmondsworth: Penguin, 1978).
11. See, for example: Bonnie G. Smith, *Ladies of the Leisure Class: the Bourgeoises of Northern France in the Nineteenth Century* (Princeton: Princeton UP, 1981); Elinor A. Accampo, Rachel G. Fuchs and Mary Lynn Stewart (eds), *Gender and the Politics of Social Reform in France, 1870–1914* (Baltimore: Rutgers UP, 1995).
12. Eugen Weber, *Peasants into Frenchmen: the Modernization of Rural France, 1870–1914* (London: Chatto and Windus, 1979), pp. 67–9 and 498–501.
13. Weber, *Peasants*, p. 339.
14. This argument is put forward in Robert Tombs, *France, 1814–1914* (London: Longman, 1996).
15. See Benedict Anderson, *Imagined Communities: Reflections on the Origins and Spread of Nationalism*, second edition (London: Verso, 1991).
16. Raymond Huard, *La Naissance du parti politique en France* (Paris: Presses de Sciences Po, 1996), p. 44.

CHAPTER 2

1830, The Liberal Revolution

The Revolution of 1830 defies easy definition. To Victor Hugo, a royalist novelist, playwright and poet who converted to liberalism in the late 1820s, it was simply 'the people ... lashing out'.[1] To the Revolution's most recent historian, Pamela Pilbeam, 'the July Days were a mere incident in a long chain of events'.[2] An older study, discussing the Revolution's social consequences, argues that political power remained with the same groups – landowners, office holders and professional men – before and after 1830. 'In this respect the July Days had effected no revolution'.[3] On the other hand, François Chateaubriand, a distinguished, independent-minded royalist, argued that the Revolution 'had nothing to do with politics, properly speaking: it was a social revolution'.[4] These four descriptions clearly contradict each other. They argue that: the Revolution was a single explosion; it was part of a long, drawn-out process; it did not change class structures; it was a social revolution. However, there is a common theme to all four. They all belittle the import-ance of 1830. For Hugo, it was not a 'proper' revolution, merely an act of violence. For Pilbeam, it was not a turning-point, but simply a step along a longer path. For Pinkney, it was not an event which fundamentally changed French society. And for Chateaubriand, it did not raise any points of deep political principle. Both contemporary observers and modern historians find the Revolution of 1830 disappointing: it was a flat revolution, a hollow rebellion.

– I. Participants –

Before we can identify who the revolutionaries were, we need to consider when the Revolution of 1830 actually happened. A common-sense answer is to consider the three days of street-fighting in Paris, from 27–9 July 1830, as marking the climax of the Revolution. Some of the leading members of the government created by the Revolution did precisely this, and so devised the myth of the 'Three Glorious Days': days which, while glorious, were conveniently short-lived and clearly identifiable. In other words, according to this conservative interpretation, the Revolution ended, once and for all, on 29 July 1830.

Other observers had contrasting ideas. Many compared 1830 with past events: with the English 'Glorious Revolution' of 1688, with the Revolution of 1789, with the constitutional monarchy of 1791, with the restoration of the monarchy in 1814, and so on. But some did more than simply compare: they saw these past events – 1789, 1791 or 1814 – as marking the origins of the 1830 Revolution. In particular, liberals argued that the Revolution started in 1814, as a reaction against the Bourbon restoration of that year. This was the interpretation put forward by Guizot, a liberal prior to 1830, and a prominent conservative politician afterwards. He considered that 1830 was an 'explosion of all the angers, the political hopes and dreams which had been stored up for sixteen years'.[5]

In July 1830 the revolutionaries overthrew the Bourbon monarchy, which had been restored by the allies who defeated Napoleon in April 1814. Napoleon returned to France in March 1815, and seized power for a period usually termed the 'Hundred Days' (March–June 1815). The monarchy was restored for a second time in July 1815. Napoleon's brief return in 1815, coupled with the surprising surge of support for him, and the populist, anti-aristocratic, even (in a sense) 'democratic' image which he cultivated, was to change French politics profoundly. One result was to muddy the differences between republicanism and Bonapartism for thirty-five years (until 1851 – see Chapter 8). A second result was of more immediate importance. Napoleon's defeat in 1814, his exile on Elba, his return in March 1815 and his final defeat at Waterloo made an incredible story. It sounded like a medieval legend: the saviour of the country who remained hidden in his castle until the moment his kingdom needed him, when he returned, to the acclamation of his people. Following this incredible, fabulous episode, who could discount even the most unlikely of rumours?

The early Restoration became a golden age of political rumours. Many can be cited: for example, in July 1816 the Rédon sub-prefect (Ille-et-Vilaine) reported to his prefect that people were talking of pirates who had escaped from Cartagena in Spain, first flying the Spanish flag, then the Revolutionary tricolour. As these stories were retold, the pirates changed into Americans, carrying Bonaparte to the Spanish-American insurgents. The sub-prefect ended his letter 'those who've been educated a bit – or who think that they have – shape the story this way. You can imagine what form this rumour will take among the people.'[6]

One can laugh at the credulity of those who believed such stories, but before (metaphorically) throwing the document away, let us consider it more closely. One possibility is that this story had been created by Bonapartist agitators, perhaps seeking to unnerve the Restoration authorities, or hoping to create a 'snowball' effect, whereby if enough people started to talk about Bonaparte's second coming then, eventually, the stories would become true. A third possibility is that the story was invented spontaneously. If so, it still tells us something about the political culture of the rural people and, even as a political fairy-tale, it cannot be ignored.

Such stories would easily have been dismissed as nonsense in normal times. However, following the 'Hundred Days', it was difficult to dismiss anything. The fact that the sub-prefect informed the prefect about it shows how seriously such rumours were taken. Their persistence, and the authorities' concern about them, means that we must face difficult questions about the nature of political culture and the 1830 Revolution: what 'counts'? And what can be dismissed? Obviously, the articulate and measured 'addresses' which liberal deputies sent to the monarch in 1830 were important expressions of political principle. Another significant political debate took place within and between the new journals, which were often allied to the liberals. There were also the more polemical, sometimes more scurrilous, pamphlets and brochures which circulated alongside the journals. Most historians would agree that all these printed forms 'count' as expressions of political values.

However, there was another dimension to protest: aside from the printed word, there were handwritten posters, anonymous letters, words shouted in the streets and *cabarets*, that is, bars, and rumours which circulated from one end of France to the other. Historians have been dismissive of such protests. Pinkney writes of the revolutionary crowds of 1830: 'their political aims scarcely went beyond the popular cry of "A bas les Bourbons!" [Down with the Bourbons!]'.[7] Roger Magraw suggests, more tentatively, that working-class political culture was marked by an 'absence of coherent protest against growing extremes of wealth and poverty'.[8] Another response by historians has been to suggest 'layers' of politics, in which the better educated and more formally organised act to direct the confused and ignorant.[9] Is this correct? Were the street-fighters of 1830 and the rumour-mongers of 1816 just ignorant malcontents, permanently in need of the aid of élite, educated groups to form and direct their actions?

Such attitudes seem unnecessarily dismissive. No one is trying to argue that the gossips who spread rumours of Napoleon's return, or the carpenters and builders who tore down royalist symbols from the streets of Paris in 1830, were capable of giving a lecture in political philosophy. However, it should be recognised that a lively, articulate oppositional political culture grew among the poor, unschooled people of France. For fifteen years prior to 1830, anonymous, humble people had created a culture of protest. The research undertaken by Bernard Ménager allows us to be more precise about their identity.

Ménager's research concerns popular Bonapartism: it therefore ignores or underestimates other forms of anti-Bourbon protest, such as anti-clericalism, republicanism or liberalism. Ménager argues that Bonapartism was the central strand within popular protests, for Napoleon's Empire seemed 'the sole credible alternative' to the Bourbons.[10] Surveying some two thousand convictions for subversive activity, Ménager analyses the militants who appeared before the courts. Peasants were relatively under-represented, as were workers in big industries. Travelling people – tinkers, labourers looking for work, beggars and tramps – were over-represented, as were the artisanal trades: shoemakers, tailors, masons, and joiners. Lastly, perhaps a point unique to popular Bonapartism, soldiers were also likely to be active.[11]

Ménager's identification of Bonapartist activists during the Restoration seems similar to Pinkney's analysis of the revolutionary crowds of 1830. The bulk of the crowd were mature men who worked in skilled crafts: often fathers, and often also people who had benefited from some education, although this was more likely to have been a craft apprenticeship than a primary school. There are some differences between the groups identified by Ménager and Pinkney: Ménager identifies soldiers as a particularly active group, Pinkney highlights the specific role played by print-workers.[12] Yet our final impression is of the similarity of the two portraits. This suggests a long-running cycle of protest, which culminated in the three days of street-fighting, and – as will be shown in the next two chapters – continued into the early 1830s. It is difficult to be precise about who the revolutionaries were, for the simple reason that there were so many of them. As well Bonapartist protesters and street-fighters, artisans and journalists, there were millions who gave the Revolution their indirect or tacit consent. Chateaubriand's description of the Revolution's transmission from Paris is clearly hostile, but it does capture something of the manner in which it developed. 'The provinces are always like sheep; they are Paris's slaves. Each movement of the telegraph, or each tricolour flag stuck on top of a stage-coach, made them cry out "Long live [Louis-] Philippe!" or "Long live the Revolution!"'[13] Chateaubriand, a critic of the Revolution, portrays its acceptance as proof of the 'sheep-like' nature of the provinces.

Today, such explanations are unlikely to satisfy historians. In fact, 1830 is unique among French revolutions in that it aroused so little opposition. The actions of the Paris street-fighters made sense: as news of the revolt spread to waiting crowds in provincial cities, and then filtered out to towns and villages, it was normally greeted with joy, relief or, at the very least, acceptance.

Chateaubriand's analysis can be compared with that written by the liberal journalist and politician, Louis Adolphe Thiers. He also notes the rapid acceptance of the Revolution across France, and argues that this was evidence of a national consensus. 'There are times when an entire people, spread over millions of square miles, has only one thought, one wish, one cry: they know, they do, almost exactly what is known, seen and done thousands of miles away.'[14]

The 'participants' of this Revolution are, then, a wide group, arguably including the majority of the French population. Our task is to explain why this Revolution gained such widespread sympathy.

– II. EVENTS –

The 1830 Revolution started in April 1814, as Louis XVIII, exiled in Britain, considered the restoration of the monarchy. More than a decade of Napoleon's authoritarian rule and near-permanent warfare de-politicised France. The fighting which took place on French land during the spring of 1814 had disrupted administration, and left towns and communities isolated. The allied powers who defeated Napoleon needed someone with whom they could negotiate a peace settlement: under these peculiar circumstances they accepted a remnant of the Napoleonic power structure as a legitimate representative of French interests. This was the Senate, composed of 'old' nobles who had rallied to Napoleon, 'survivors' from the days of Jacobinism, and 'new' nobles created by Napoleon.

What form was the Restoration to take? Some expected a root-and-branch restoration of genuinely monarchist political culture, based on a romantic view of the Middle Ages: a caring, paternalistic king, aided by a strong Church and a virtuous aristocracy, ruling for his people. (See Chapter 4.) However, most people (including Louis XVIII) considered that this was impossible. Some gestures were made to appease conservatives: the red, white and blue tricolour of the Revolution and Empire was abolished, and replaced by the white flag and the fleur-de-lis emblem (a floral design representing a lily) of the Bourbon dynasty; but the largely unspoken assumption which guided the debates of 1814 was that a return to the pre-1789 monarchy was impossible. The conditions of the times forced most participants in this cautious, tiptoeing debate to accept pragmatic calculations. France was exhausted, divided, shattered ... any attempt to rouse reactionary passions would not solve these problems, it would merely re-ignite the violent cycle of revolution and counter-revolution.

All the participants in this debate were keen to conclude quickly. The longer the debate went on, the more permanent the presence of allied occupying forces seemed, and the greater the danger to French national independence. All the participants rejected Napoleon's Empire, and accepted that the Restoration should not initiate a settling of scores between political rivals. Furthermore, there was agreement that the nation needed liberty, usually understood as freedom of speech and representation. Another largely unspoken consensus grew around the acceptance of some of the basic administrative developments of the Revolution: France remained divided into eighty-six approximately equally sized departments, instead of returning to the pre-Revolutionary patchwork of irregular provinces. Other innovations also survived: the Université (a secular, semi-autonomous bureaucracy which regulated education) and the Concordat (the 1801 religious agreement between the Pope and Napoleon) were not abolished.

Following debates in April and May 1814, a seventy-six-article constitution was produced: a remarkably short document, when compared with 200 articles of the 1791 constitution and the 377 articles written by the Jacobins in 1793. It created a constitutional monarchy, with an elected lower Chamber of Deputies and a part-hereditary, part-appointed upper Chamber of Peers. The limits to the monarch's power were left vague: he had the right to call elections, to declare war and to choose ministers – but was he to choose ministers to represent the Chamber of Deputies, or to choose ministers to represent his will to the Chamber?

The one real debate in spring 1814 concerned the *form* of this constitution. Liberal constitutionalists understood it as a contract between monarch and nation, which imposed binding limits on the monarch's power. Monarchists rejected this interpretation: this was not a constitution, it was a 'Charter' – a medieval word which sounded old-fashioned even in 1814. Moreover, it had not been negotiated: it was *'octroyé'* – another medieval word which could be translated as 'granted' – by the monarch to the nation. However, liberal constitutionalists and monarchists did not disagree about the *content* of this document: in fact, 1814 and 1815 saw few sustained discussions on political philosophy in any form. Their two conceptions of the Charter – a contract binding the monarch, or a gift granted by the monarch – were significantly different, and became important in 1827–30.

The Charter created a tiny electorate. In a country of some thirty million people, only 110 000 men were allowed to vote in 1817 – a figure which shrank to less than eighty thousand in 1829, despite an increase in the population. The average department had somewhat more than a thousand voters in 1817, somewhat less by 1829. Voting was not only limited to the wealthy few, but was further restricted to those whose wealth came from land ownership. Before 1820 voting was organised on a department-wide basis, requiring voters to travel to the head town of each department in order to vote. This procedure changed in 1820: voting was organised by *arrondissement*, with a supplementary department–wide process which gave the richest quarter of the electorate a second vote.

Only small groups were involved. In 1824 almost a quarter of a million people lived in the eastern department of the Doubs: 585 voted. They were divided into two *arrondissement* colleges: 245 in Baume, 340 in Besançon.[15] More than a third of a million people lived in the western department of La Vendée. In its central *arrondissement* of Bourbon-Vendée, 266 people voted in 1820; in Fontenay, 346; and in the Sables-d'Olonne, 185.[16]

The meaning of voting was unclear. In 1817 the liberal writer Benjamin Constant offered some advice to this new electorate. In a memorable phrase, he noted: 'for the first time in seventeen years, I count for something in the State'[17] – words which capture both the sense of liberation offered by the Restoration's representative structures, and the strangeness of these new-found rights. Elections were quite different from today's processes. They frequently took up a whole day: time which busy electors might consider that they could not spare. The small numbers involved may have contributed to a strong sense of collective self-identity: it was possible that each elector might have some personal or family connection with all the others. Such conditions militated against strong national organisations. Elections were won through mobilising small, locally-based, inter-linked interest groups, not through national campaigns.

During the early Restoration, there were no formal party groupings, so it is difficult to estimate political trends. Most historians agree that from 1817 to 1820 the majority of deputies were liberal. This point is an important one: these elections were held in relative calm, and without significant pressure from government, church or press to persuade electors to vote for one tendency, or to frighten them against another. Tentatively, we could suggest that these elections show a 'natural' majority in favour of, loosely speaking, a liberal tradition, based around an acceptance of elements of the Revolutionary legacy (particularly of land settlements), a defence of constitutional government and freedom of speech.

After 1820 this 'natural' majority seemed to disappear. Again, accurate figures are not available, but liberals certainly lost elections, and ultra-royalists were winning them. (We will investigate the ultras' political culture in Chapter 4. For the moment, let us note a common definition of their politics: they were more monarchist than the monarch.) The 1824 election represented an all-time low for the liberals. However, they made a comeback in the December 1827 election (see table 2.1).

Table 2.1: Liberal deputies in the Chamber of Deputies[18]

Date	Liberal deputies
1824	40 Liberals (out of 430 deputies)
1827	180 Liberals, 180 'ministerials', 60–80 Ultras

('Ministerials' were usually office-holders who owed their position to one of the major ministers. They voted steadily for the government.) The figures above are approximate. Deputies did not belong to organised parties, and there were significant groupings of 'independents', such as the twenty or so deputies who followed Chateaubriand. While profoundly, passionately royalist, they opposed the conservative governments of the mid-1820s, and voted with the liberals on issues such as freedom of the press.

Why did the liberals lose votes in the early 1820s? One reason was the government's organised hostility to them. In these small constituencies, where almost everyone knew everyone else, it was easy to influence electors. However, it still comes as a shock to see how keenly administrators threw themselves into this task. For example, a list drawn up by the Prefect of the Haute-Garonne in June 1820 identifies the 327 electors in his department. They are listed by name, and neatly divided into five categories: definite liberal voters, probable liberals, uncertain, probable royalists, and definite royalists. The Prefect calculated that 168 royalist voters would confront 152 liberals.[19] This was not an opinion poll, but rather a chart which was used to plan a campaign by officials to influence the forthcoming elections.

In 1824 attempts to fix the elections grew more blatant. The Interior Minister wrote to prefects, asking them to identify which electors had 'voted badly' (that is, voted liberal) in the last elections. Those who were employed by the legal administration were to be reminded by the Justice Minister of the necessity of conforming to the government's wishes.[20] Sylvia Neely, examining the Sarthe, to the west of Paris, has calculated that about a fifth of the electorate experienced this type of pressure.[21] Even more seriously, state employees were denied the right to vote in secrecy: their employers knew how they had voted. Another tactic used frequently by prefects was to fail to register liberals as voters – hence the drop in the number of registered voters from 110000 in 1817 to less than eighty thousand in 1829.

When we hear of these practices, probably the first word that will come to mind is 'corruption'. This may well be anachronistic. Bureaucrats such as the Prefect of the Haute-Garonne or the Interior Minister did not see themselves as 'fixing' elections of behalf of an unrepresentative minority. Instead, they used a highly moral language, speaking of their paternal duty to guide the more excitable, and the less well-informed among their voters. We can note a similarity between such justifications, and the 'monarchist' interpretation of the Charter as a gift from a generous monarch his obedient subjects.

Such tactics worked well in the early 1820s. Fearing revolution, confused about the liberals' intentions, voters backed ultra-royalist candidates. However, in the long-term, these tactics worked against the government and against the ultra-royalists, giving disparate, isolated, local groups a single national issue around which they could unite in opposition to the government.

To make matters worse for the government, an economic depression in the late 1820s demonstrated its failure to provide for the very poor, or to encourage the wealthy and ambitious. A British financial crisis in 1826 triggered a credit crisis in France, leading to a wave of bankruptcies. Through an unlucky coincidence, this was followed by a series of disastrous harvests, lasting from 1828 until 1832. Such events provoked the classic symptoms of economic distress: the increasing number of tramps and beggars, who suggested to each passer-by poignant, troubling or threatening symbols of economic disorder. In itself, poverty did not create a revolutionary movement: however, rural and urban workers had good reason to feel resentment towards their government.

Following the disastrous electoral results of 1824, the liberal opposition presented a more unified platform in 1827. They also organised a type of para-political organisation, named Aide-toi, which encouraged voter registration and monitored the administration's actions.[22] Liberals won perhaps half the parliamentary seats. They were sometimes supported by the independent royalists grouped around Chateaubriand. Throughout 1828, 1829 and the first five months of 1830, a series of complex parliamentary conflicts developed, which revealed the contradictions inherent in the 1814 Charter. One key issue was the status of ministers: were they to represent the views of the majority of the deputies? Or were they to represent the views of the monarch, now the reactionary Charles X, to the deputies?

Charles X clearly took the second view, and in August 1829 imposed a cabinet headed by Polignac. In March 1830, 221 deputies signed an address to the King which, while composed in the polite language of courtly exchange, clearly indicated their disquiet concerning his ministers. Charles X's response was to dissolve the Chamber and call new elections. Every effort was made by the government to push voters into supporting 'governmental' candidates. However, the elections in late June and early July 1830 returned a liberal majority: Pinkney estimates that 270 deputies sympathised with the opposition and 145 with the government. Of the 221 deputies who signed the address of March 1830, 201 were re-elected.[23]

Rather than accepting the will of the electorate, Charles X dismissed the new Chamber. On 26 July 1830, taking advantage of another rather vague article in the 1814 Charter, he issued a set of ordinances (that is, laws passed without parliamentary sanction). If implemented, these would have dramatically changed the nature of French politics. They would have deprived almost three-quarters of the already tiny electorate of their vote, halved the number of deputies and severely curtailed press freedoms. They reveal the logic of the monarchist interpretation of the Charter: if it was granted by the monarch, then it could be taken away by him. Charles X, relying on police reports and ministers' opinions, was confident that his ordinances would be accepted without opposition.

Instead, they caused widespread consternation. Chateaubriand recorded the shock he felt on reading them on 27 July: 'I could not believe my eyes … [the ordinances showed] a total ignorance about the present state of society.'[24] Their most immediate effect was the new restrictions on newspapers, which were expected to pass a rigorous authorisation procedure before they could print another edition. This made printshops reluctant to publish further copies of the liberal press. Instead, they preferred to lay off their workers. There were approximately five thousand print-workers in Paris. Most of them had experienced police harassment of printshops during the 1820s; many were naturally hostile to the ordinances.

On Monday 26 July central Paris seemed calm, but there were signs of unrest. It was hot: 90° at midday. During the day, print-workers told other workers about the ordinances. Many workers had followed the customary habit of taking Monday off, and as evening drew in, they walked in the parks, where people discussed the ordinances. The crowds seemed larger than the normal number of early evening strollers.

Thiers, a handful of opposition deputies and a couple of dozen journalists met to discuss the ordinances. Forty-three signed a petition drafted by Thiers which called on papers to ignore the ordinances and to continue to publish. Their proclamation contained a number of dramatic, radical phrases: 'the government has violated legality. We are no longer required to obey it.'[25] However, their declaration was not a call for a revolution, but a demand for press freedom. The first flicker of violence concerned a printshop. At eight p.m. police arrived to shut down forcibly a printing press in central Paris. It was locked: they broke in and made arrests. A crowd gathered to watch this contest; many sympathised with the printers, and scuffles developed between the crowd and the police. However, by midnight, central Paris was calm.

On the next day, 27 July, further scuffles developed as police attempted to implement the ordinances by closing down printshops, arresting journalists and editors, and even closing reading rooms (early forms of libraries). Illegally printed papers were circulated and discussed. Troops were posted to guard the ministries in central Paris. The first deaths occurred at about four p.m. as mounted policemen, trying to clear roads, charged demonstrators.

The Duke de Raguse, newly charged with security in Paris, did some rapid calculations. He had the following forces at his immediate disposal.

Table 2.2: Forces available in Paris, July 1830[26]

Royal Guard:	infantry	3 800
	cavalry	800
Regular Infantry		4 400–5 400
Police:	mounted	600
	foot	800
Total		10 300–11 500

About fifteen hundred soldiers were occupied in guarding public buildings. Thus, there were at most some ten thousand soldiers and policemen to control a city of three-quarters of a million people. Calling in reinforcements was not easy as many French soldiers were on a military expedition to Algeria.

By the morning of Wednesday 28 July, some four thousand barricades had been built across Paris. During the night, gunshops had been broken into, and in many households improvised cartridges were being made with marbles and gunpowder. Some old soldiers from Napoleon's armies emerged to direct preparations and to command the revolutionary forces. There were even a few members of the old middle-class municipal militia, the National Guard, on the streets in uniform. (The National Guard had been banned in 1827: Charles X's governments considered it a source of liberal subversion.)

A particular form of symbolic vandalism developed: fleur-de-lis on walls and posters were torn down and destroyed. Postmen tore them off their uniforms, coach-drivers took them off their jackets and hats. The word 'royal', where it was written on public buildings, was either scraped off, or covered in mud. White Bourbon flags were torn from the outside of municipal buildings and thrown into ditches.

During 28 and 29 July full-scale military clashes developed. A number of factors favoured the revolutionaries. First, they were fighting on their home-ground: they knew every inch of the narrow, winding, still-medieval streets of early nineteenth-century Paris. Few soldiers had fought on this type of terrain as most military engagements took place in open countryside. Second, while the soldiers were armed, they were poorly provisioned. In the July heat they were often left for hours without food or water. Third, by chance, the Parisians adopted the classic tactics of guerrilla warfare. When the military columns advanced, they retreated. Their improvised barricades were incapable of halting full-scale military offensives, but they were effective in slowing them down. As soldiers queued to cross barricades, their position became dangerous. The barricades were built across narrow roads, between high, four- or five-storey houses. These houses were often divided vertically by class: the richest occupied the ground floor, the quite rich the first floor, the comfortable the second floor, and so on. This meant that soldiers met, and talked to, respectable bourgeois, who would at least appear to be supporting the forces of law and order, and who might offer them food and much-needed drinks. However, as the column stopped, the reaction of the higher floor inhabitants could be quite different. Snipers would shoot down, and in the glare of the midday sun it was difficult to see from where the shots were coming. In other quarters, columns were met with a hail of tiles, chairs and pots as they passed. Again, it was impossible to work out who was throwing these objects. If the column then retreated, the revolutionaries would re-emerge, and rebuild their barricades. Night-time operations proved particularly hazardous, as the revolutionaries smashed streetlamps, and military columns became lost in the maze of darkened streets.

Soldiers quickly became disillusioned. Charles X had left Paris for his summer residence at St-Cloud, leaving the soldiers to defend empty royal apartments. They were not used to confronting French people and were uncomfortable when revolutionary crowds appealed for their sympathy. Some were moved by Bonapartist slogans which were shouted. Their officers were ill-prepared and confused. The army could not win a battle against this massive, shifting, omnipresent enemy. Under these circumstances, the decision to withdraw the army from Paris on 29 July was a happy one, for which many soldiers must have been grateful. Thiers's summing-up captures some of the conflicting emotions of these days. 'A heroic people, and a demoralized government, gave our cause an unexpected victory.'[27] Within Paris itself there was an atmosphere of celebration: radical posters were pasted on the walls (see document 2.1) and crowds of young revolutionaries cheered anti-Bourbon politicians (see document 2.2). By then, approximately two thousand people had died: two hundred soldiers and eighteen hundred revolutionaries. Over five thousand had been seriously wounded: eight hundred soldiers and four and a half thousand revolutionaries.[28]

Charles X held on to power until 2 August, when he abdicated in favour of his grandson. Meanwhile, Louis-Philippe, the leading member of the Orleanist branch of the royal family, had been invited by politicians to take the post of Lieutenant-General. This position was supposed to maintain government during the regency of a young prince: in theory, Louis-Philippe should in turn have given the throne to Henri, the Duke of Bordeaux, Charles X's grandson. This never happened: Louis-Philippe was crowned King on 9 August 1830.

– III. POLITICAL CULTURE –

The revolutionary ideas of July 1830, and the critical ideas which preceded the Revolution, form a very broad spectrum of ideas. These currents of thinking are normally divided by historians into two, with an articulate, 'politicised', stream of liberal ideas being identified with journalists and deputies, and an inarticulate, more emotional stream of ideas coming from the crowds, street-fighters and protesters. A left-wing variant of this division speaks of the *'révolution escamotée'* – the stolen revolution. Here it is argued that the workers of Paris fought for their own revolution, but were then tricked into accepting Louis-Philippe. One problem with these interpretations is explaining *why* the Parisian workers revolted in 1830: if liberal ideas were so different from the themes and issues which motivated the working class, why did the workers act? Historians following this type of argument usually rely upon weak ideas such as the 'tricking' of the workers.

To understand these issues better, let us return to the popular protest of the Restoration. We will start by citing a few examples.

Marie-Anne Toussaint lived in the department of the Meurthe, in eastern France. She was the wife of a retired soldier. In July 1817 she was convicted on the charge of spreading rumours about Napoleon's return.[29]

In the town of Beaune (Côte-d'Or), in eastern France, a primitive type of slide-show attracted a big audience on 3 August 1817. When an image of the royal family was shown, members of the audience shouted out 'down with them!'. Pictures of the future Charles X, then still merely Louis XVIII's brother, attracted shouts of 'down with the Prussian, down with the Austrian!' – presumably references to the foreign connections that Charles had made while in exile during the Revolution. Supporters of the government tried to drown out these shouts by cheering and clapping, but their efforts just added to the volume of noise. As the room was dark, it was impossible to identify the anti-royalists.[30]

Jean-Baptiste Richard came to court in the eastern department of the Vosges on 8 March 1822. His trial summary is worth quoting in full:

> Richard, unemployed, without fixed abode, born in Remiremont, is found guilty of having, on 8 December 1821, in the streets of the said town, shouted out loud, several times, 'Long Live Napoleon! Down with the Bourbons!', and of having followed these shouts with seditious songs.[31]

In the south-eastern department of the Basses-Alpes, the inhabitants of Sisteron were shocked when, on the evening of 16 March 1826, they discovered subversive messages scattered across their town's streets. The messages were to be found attached to the door of the King's Prosecutor, in front of shops, outside a gentlemen's club, outside a café, and even at the church door. Most of these messages were short and sharp:

> Open your eyes, French men! You're being placed in chains! Arm yourselves! Long live Napoleon and Liberty!
> Long live Napoleon! Shit to the Bourbons!
> Frenchmen, the nation is threatened! Let each man cry: death to the infamous Bourbons! Death to the priests! Death to the Royalists![32]

French archives are packed with these sorts of records relating to incidents during the Restoration. Their volume ebbs and flows, but do these changes indicate the changing strengths of oppositional movements or a shift in the degree of police interest in rumours and shouts? One pattern within the documents is readily explained: the month of March – the month in which Napoleon returned to France in 1815 – was usually marked by a resurgence of Bonapartist agitation.

The evidence preserved does not allow us to comment on the agitators' motivations. Predictably, the accused usually deny all political connotations to their actions, claim that their accusers are lying, or – the usual last resort – say they were drunk. The reactions of the authorities is more interesting. For example, in the case of the shouts at the slide-show discussed above, the local authorities were clearly as appalled by the development of political debate in the form of opposing cries of 'long live the red rose!' (that is, the Revolution) and 'long live the white rose!' (that is, the monarchy), as they were by the expression of opposition to the monarchy. This simple shouting was far from the dignified, proper ethic of monarchist political behaviour which the Restoration authorities wished to encourage.

In Sisteron, the anonymous messages affected a wide section of the town's population, including illiterates. On 7 June 1826 Sisteron's police lieutenant interviewed an illiterate woman. She explained how she had seen a piece of paper in the street and had immediately remarked to her friend 'I bet that this bit of paper is like those which were scattered about the town two months ago.'[33] When the postmistress received a message, she wrote the following comment to her employer. 'This is the inevitable result of the poison which has been spread across France by the lampoons and pamphlets sold so cleverly by secret agents.'[34] Her comment links together a whole range of protest activities to suggest a single movement.

The key issue in this contest between government and opposition was the control of 'public space'. For Restoration authorities, an (allegedly) drunk man shouting 'long live Napoleon!' on the high street was not simply a problem because he represented a form of defiance to the King: he was also a problem because his action was *public*. Why did this matter? First, and most obviously, he might act as an example to others. But more than this: this mass of messages, shouts, rumours and gossip was coming to form a counter-authority to the cultural authority of the Restoration itself.

We come back to the great themes of Restoration political culture: the Charter was granted from above by a generous monarch. People, nation and monarch were to be linked by moral bonds, which were expected to inform behaviour and to guide political expression. Such ideas can be seen operating on a macro level when we examine how the Charter was presented; however, they also work on a micro level, in villages and cabarets. As we have seen, administrators and officials could insist that their employees had a moral duty of political loyalty to Restoration authorities. The key point here is not so much that the explicit content of the Restoration's political culture was obviously monarchist, but that this political culture took hierarchical and paternalistic forms which demanded respect and obedience from below.

Under these circumstances, the most apparently innocent of activities could assume a political dimension. To explain this point more fully, let us consider subversive tobacco pouches. During the Restoration there were a series of arrests of pedlars and stall-holders for selling tobacco pouches decorated with pictures of Napoleon, or of scenes connected with Napoleon's life. One, for example, showed a military tomb, and underneath the sentence 'he will live for ever in our hearts'.[35] Was this subversion? There seem to be many reasons why someone might want to buy a Bonapartist tobacco pouch. One reason might be to commemorate a dramatic period of French history, during which many people had lost friends, fathers, husbands, sons and neighbours. Another reason might be the cult of the anti-hero. In medieval times there were stories of Robin Hood-style bandits, in the late twentieth-century we watch horror movies – why should Napoleon not be celebrated in the same fantastic but anodyne way?

However, there is more evidence for the subversive quality of the tobacco pouches. Some had double covers: when the first innocent, Catholic picture was removed, a picture of Napoleon was then revealed. But the really conclusive evidence comes from the department of the Haute-Garonne, near the Spanish border. In 1822 and 1823 a strong anti-royalist movement harassed efforts to build a military presence along the border, in preparation for the short French military intervention in Spain in 1823. During the first days of December 1822 a colonel stopped for a drink in an inn near the border. There he met Tournon, a cloth worker. They drank some hot punch together. Then Tournon pulled a tobacco pouch from his pocket, on which was a picture of Bonaparte's tomb, surrounded by an officer, a woman and three children, all grieving. There was also a slogan: 'Here lies a great man'. As he fiddled with the pouch, Tournon began to sing a Bonapartist song.[36]

Tournon was charged with incitement to desertion: there seems little doubt that his actions were leading to an attempt to persuade the colonel to refuse service in Spain. However, the important point here is the form of actions which Tournon chose. He did not put forward an articulate political case relating to the legitimacy of the French intervention in Spain. Instead, he manipulated symbols: what soldier could deny that Napoleon was 'a great man'? What soldier could not recognise a Bonapartist song? Yet in using these symbols, Tournon was not explicitly demanding any clear action from the colonel. Such forms of verbally inarticulate, but none the less eloquent, agitation were typical of popular politics during this period. Just as Tournon presented a picture of Napoleon to sum up his political aspirations, so the Parisian revolutionaries of July 1830 turned their anger on the symbols of monarchy: the white flag, the fleur-de-lis, and even just the word 'royal'. In turn, they cheered revolutionary symbols such as the tricolour.

It is easy to dismiss such political manoeuvres as ignorant. Guizot presents this argument: 'The mass of the population cannot act by themselves: their desires and their projects must be personified in great figures who march ahead of them.'[37] For him, the cult of Napoleon was nothing more than a form of leader-worship. However, another interpretation is possible: the *symbol* of Napoleon was being used by uneducated and politically inexperienced people to articulate their political wishes.

So far in this section I have referred to the most simple forms of political culture: the cry, the song, the rumour – and the tobacco-pouch. Let us now turn to more articulate forms of opposition. The fascinating point here is that the fundamental issues seem remarkably similar.

Once again, we are dependent on the reports of hostile Restoration officials for information. We need to note how these reports develop. The golden age of the rumour is 1817–22, when the memory of Napoleon's return in 1815 is still alive, and when a series of rather farcical Bonapartist military conspiracies suggested a real possibility of civil war. These were sometimes linked to a secret network: the *charbonnerie*. Approximately 60 000 people may have joined this liberal organisation.[38] During the period from 1823 to 1827 there is less evidence of discontent: perhaps the repression of the early years of the Restoration has done its job or – more likely – authorities are feeling more confident and therefore more inclined to ignore a drunkard's shout or gossip's rumour. Then, from 1827 to 1830, there is a renewal of protest: fewer absurd rumours, but more economic protest related to bread prices, wages and jobs. More protest seems to be obviously political: some concerning the fiercely disputed elections of 1827 and 1830, and much concerning the press, pamphlets and books.

Throughout the Restoration various forms of press censorship had been loosely implemented. However, the royal ordinance of 24 June 1827 threatened to establish a more substantial form of censorship, with a censorship committee in each department. This caused some government embarrassment. The Restoration of the monarchy had supposedly liberated France from Napoleon's dictatorship. Why was this 'liberating' regime going back to the techniques of dictatorship? The best answer to this point was given in the first report issued by the Parisian Censor's Office: this was a different sort of censorship, which did not seek to clash with public opinion, but rather to guide journals along the right track. They even hoped that this sort of censorship would be welcomed by public opinion. The Office accepted that political principles could and should be debated – however, there were limits, and these were set by the principles of religion, monarchy and the constitution, which were all above criticism.[39]

The arguments were not convincing, and public opinion was not grateful for the censors' actions. Censorship was so unpopular that in some departments – such as the Aisne, to the east of Paris – no one would act as censor and Prefects were forced to take on this responsibility themselves.[40] Alongside these not-very-convincing arguments proposing a 'gentle' censorship, there was another theme present in the letters and circulars issued by the Restoration administration. Let us survey a few reports from the late 1820s by officials, concerning the political situation.

The Prefect of the Gard saw a close connection between a form of politics and the press. 'In the towns and in all the communes ... where there are cafés and circles [that is, clubs] which subscribe to papers, there is a class of men who are almost exclusively concerned with politics everyday.'[41]

The Prefect of the western department of the Ille-et-Vilaine was largely content with the political situation in the spring of 1827. The 'people' were largely religious and monarchist, as were the 'electoral class'. However, the Prefect had some worries about the latter as they were more educated and therefore more under the influence of the press.[42]

In Sisteron, as authorities struggled to find the author of the anonymous messages which had astonished the town, the sub-prefect drew up a report for the Prefect. He described 'the people who make opinion in this land [pays], that is to say the idle men of the cafés, the judges, the lawyers'.[43]

The Prefect of the Haute-Garonne was depressed about the political situation of his department in 1826. He used an interesting expression for the opposition: 'les hommes de parti', the party men, suggesting a division between the simple, 'natural' politics of the Restoration authorities, and the artificial politics of these malicious agitators. The Restoration authorities did not claim to represent a party, their politics were simply the natural politics of France. 'Party' was a dirty word, an insult to be flung at this opposition. The key means by which the party expressed itself was through journalists and through 'allusions' at the theatre.[44] Often cafés only took out subscriptions to liberal papers such as the *Constitutionnel* and the *Courrier*: 'they are in all the reading rooms'.[45] Following the introduction of censorship in June 1827, the Prefect felt more secure.

> The effect of press censorship has been felt in a most satisfactory manner. Public places and salons are calmer: from this it is easy to see the amount of harm that was done by their appeals to emotion and by the lies which they spread every day.[46]

Prefects were extremely suspicious of the press: partly, of course, because many papers were liberal. The top-selling paper in 1828 was the liberal *Constitutionnel*, which had twenty thousand subscribers. Chateaubriand's *Journal des Débats* had eleven thousand, while the biggest selling progovernment paper was the *Gazette de France*, with only ten thousand subscribers.[47] However, once again, it is clear that prefects were not only worried by liberal papers, but by the growing authority of the press itself. It led to a new type of political culture, which developed in networks of papers, cafés and theatres: another counter-authority to the government's power.

By 1830 this had become a central political issue. Polignac, the leading member of Charles X's last government, singled out the press as his key concern: 'the press is the principal centre of corruption which grows more serious each day, and the principal source of the dangers which threaten the kingdom.'[48] This line of attack does not suggest a division between a monarchist right and a liberal left. Polignac is, on the contrary, suggesting the existence of a legitimate and an illegitimate political culture. One is morally correct, and therefore should be dominant; the other is corrupt, and therefore should be eradicated.

Here we begin to see the true nature of the coalition created by the liberals. The movement of 1830 was not based around a distinct political programme, nor was it led by a party. However, liberal politicians and writers were able to identify some common experiences which were shared by the humble Bonapartist drinker, the journalist and the opposition deputy. All three were faced with a state which simply refused to accept the legitimacy of certain forms of protest. The fullest expression of their coalition is not to be found in the articulate writing of liberal philosophers such as Benjamin Constant, but in more informal works such as the pamphlets of Jean-Paul Courier and the songs of Béranger.

Courier merits our attention here. A minor bureaucrat under Napoleon, a small landowner during the Restoration, tragically and mysteriously murdered in 1825, he sums up both the glories and the weaknesses of

Restoration liberalism. He pioneered a new type of politicised literature: fiery, no-nonsense, common-sense pamphleteering, set among the daily realities of the small traders and farmers in his department, the Indre-et-Loire, south-west of Paris. Throughout his brief literary career, he wrote of the plight of the poor. His first Restoration pamphlet was written in December 1816; it concerned what happened when François Fouquet met a funeral procession on a narrow track. Courier acknowledged that a polite man would have stopped his horse, taken off his hat, and stood by one side to allow the hearse to pass. Fouquet did none of these things: his behaviour was certainly impolite, but who would have expected that, three days later, he would be arrested by four policemen and held for two months in jail, alongside two thieves? His family, utterly dependent on him for their livelihood, were then reliant on charity.[49] Courier went on to give other examples of arbitrary arrest, and made a number of well-aimed points about the nature of political power.

> Do you get on with so-and-so? If you're a good subject, they'll let you live. But have you been involved in a trial with such-and-such, have you failed to greet him, have you quarrelled with his maid, or thrown a stone at his dog? Then you're a bad subject, even a subversive: they'll set the law on you, and sometimes they'll be a bit rough.
>
> Courier, 1936: 55

This was coarse, knock-about stuff. Courier did not debate the nature of sovereignty; he said little about the monarch's power, and refrained from rehearsing the standard anti-clerical arguments about the Church. However, he did reduce political arguments to a form which anyone could understand. He noted how secular and religious bigotry seemed to work hand-in-hand, and he pinpointed the hypocrisy, the arrogance and the unpleasant urge to repress which seemed to motivate Restoration authorities.

He also pointed out exactly who was arresting these people on the charge of being Bonapartists: it was the same magistrate who, a few years ago, had arrested the same people on a quite different charge: that of being too critical of Bonaparte (Courier, 1936: 58). Who were the real subversives?

> The real subversives can be found everywhere. They are those who, holding power, always see their enemies as the king's enemies, and who try to make them act this way by constantly harassing them; those who find in Luynes [Courier's commune] ten men to arrest, ten families to wreck, to ruin in the name of the King – these are the enemies of the King.
>
> Courier, 1936: 59

Another issue which he made his own was a conflict which was replicated many times over France. New priests, who had been hurriedly taught a censorious, small-minded Catholicism, arrived in villages in which often no active priest had served for years. In the absence of a priest, the nature of popular Catholicism had changed: it had adapted to the rural people's daily needs. One thing they needed above all else was a chance for a festival, and they seized on the holy days of the religious calendar as reasons for dancing, drinking, romance and a more-than-generous amount of illicit sexuality. The new priests condemned such practices. Often such conflicts centred on peasants' dances: at *the* moment when these naïve, pleasure-seeking peasants were seeking the priest's blessing for their celebrations, the new priest would condemn them, would tell them that they were not good Catholics and would often cancel the celebrations altogether. Courier mocked the po-faced seriousness of a government which was so suspicious of its own people that it supported priests who refused to allow them to dance. 'Do you want to turn a happy village into a sombre Trappist convent?' (Courier, 1936: 169). He countered the government's suspiciousness with his faith: 'the people are good, whatever is said in secret reports' (Courier, 1936: 163). Courier publicised this sort of daily, banal authoritarianism, and argued that the liberal deputies would end such practices.

During the 1820 general elections he noted the unfair balance of forces which weighed against the liberals, but remained confident of their victory.

> Prefects, telegraphs, policemen, censorship, political repression: nothing works. Missionaries, Jesuits, and chaplains are wasting their Latin. They can preach, threaten, flatter, promise, and ruin all they like. As soon as we get to the elections, we'll choose men … The ministers can laugh at us, but our arguments are better than theirs.
>
> Courier, 1936: 90

Courier's strengths as a pamphleteer are obvious: he had the knack of seizing the issue, of deftly mixing irony and polemic, of picking the telling example, and of discussing complex issues with a perfect rhetorical clarity. However, was there a coherent political vision within his writing? Our answer has to be positive. One issue which reveals some more substantial aspects of Courier's thinking is his discussion of the so-called 'black band', who were buying up the old châteaux of ruined aristocrats and turning them into farms. For some, such as the young (and royalist) Victor Hugo, this was a tragedy. They were ignoble speculators; their success showed that 'we no longer have the spirit of those centuries. Industry has replaced art.'[50] Courier saw a quite different dilemma: it was a choice between monuments and industry. Monuments stood for superstitions, ruins and medieval dungeons: the speculators stood for activity, energy and economic expansion.

Such thoughts are almost textbook examples of the classic themes of nineteenth-century liberalism: its faith in economic expansion, with perhaps the proviso that liberals such as Courier were imagining a people's capitalism; a little economy, based around small family farms, family firms and small traders. The limits of Courier's thought need to be stressed. He stood for fair elections, but not for a widening of the suffrage. Even when he spoke in terms of the 'people' – which he did frequently – the idea of giving them political power was not in his mind. He also showed sympathy for the poor, but he certainly did not argue for a programme of wealth redistribution. Instead, he promised a new form of moral contract, which would bind forward-looking, generous-minded, enlightened, permissive liberals to an independent-minded stratum of small property-owners.

The central promise made by liberals to the population related to the issue of authority. They promised to undo the links which wove together the extra-parliamentary power of the priest, the aristocrat and the king. In some ways this can be understood as a lofty, liberal ideal of political freedom, and it can certainly be linked to the thought of philosophers such as Benjamin Constant. However, such ideas also had an immediate, concrete application: they meant that François Fouquet would not be imprisoned for two months for failing to take his hat off to a priest; they meant that workers and peasants could be free to talk about Bonaparte without being spied on or threatened. Within this programme, there was little clear discussion of economics. The focus was on civil liberties. Liberalism, in this form, could be supported by people from all classes: by labourers, peasants and landlords, and by workers and bosses.

Another theme within liberal thinking was its masculine nature. In some families – such as that of Victor Hugo – this was reproduced in the personalities of the parents. 'In general, our fathers are bonapartists, our mothers are royalists.'[51] There was an obvious reason for this: fathers had been recruited to serve in Bonaparte's armies, and it was through the male line that stories of Bonaparte's glory were most likely to circulate. In the excitement of the Revolution, in its explosion of political energies and debates, women were increasingly pushed to the sidelines. It therefore comes as no surprise to learn of their 'return' to the Church, initiating the 'femininisation' of French Catholicism.

Liberal writers often took delight in emphasising the masculine quality of their thought, which they contrasted with the feminine qualities of their rivals. Pierre Béranger who, like Courier, could dress liberalism in the clothes of the people, was once asked whether he did not think that his poems and songs went a bit too far, whether they were not a bit too rude. 'My book isn't supposed to serve for the education of young ladies' was his prompt reply.[52] Here was a point which everyone could understand. Béranger had a predilection for telling smutty stories with an anti-clerical twist, including variations on the old theme of the priest and his (nudge-nudge) maid. Of course, such stories were seen as being unsuitable for respectable women but – more importantly – what business did women have interesting themselves in politics anyway?

The liberals sought, ideally, a society where the laws were fair, where power was transparent, where the degrading pseudo-medieval rituals of the Restoration monarchs would be abolished once and for all. They rejected the stiff ceremonial behaviour which the ultras admired (see document 1.3): they wanted France to turn its back on the Middle Ages. The nineteenth century, liberal, rational and progressive should be allowed to grow. All these terms were code words which warned against female power. In the past, women had held power: the queen-regents of the sixteenth and seventeenth centuries had decided France's future; the aristocratic and bourgeois women who ran salons in the eighteenth century had practically shaped the culture of the Enlightenment; and the 'women of the people' had run workshops and small businesses. Most notorious of all, prostitutes (or, more politely, courtisanes) had wheeled, dealed and manoeuvred in the royal courts. All these forms of power represented precisely what the liberals were fighting against: they were never formalised or submitted to rational examination. Thus, as in the case of Béranger's quip, female power became almost in itself *the* symbol of the political culture which the liberals opposed.

– IV. LEGACY –

If the '*révolution escamotée*' argument makes any sense at all, it is understanding the days after July 1830. There were a few journalists and students among those killed and wounded in July 1830, but the vast majority were working class. They were drawn principally from the skilled workers of Paris who, if not literate, were at least in contact with political ideas, and who sought to push forward their own political projects, sometimes loosely based around trade organisations. Many of them produced petitions for their collective rights, which they sent with formal, dignified processions to the new government. They got a cold response. The new government treated them 'more like children than rational adults'.[53] Both workers and liberal politicians exposed the patronising authoritarianism of the Restoration authorities: but the liberals wished to replace it with a clear, rational, individualistic form of authority, in which collective interests should not be allowed to hold back the individual entrepreneur. The workers' collective liberty had no place in the new liberal society. (See Chapter 3.)

Did the July Revolution fundamentally change France? Honoré de Balzac, a liberal in 1830, and a royalist by 1832, gave an affirmative answer to this question.

> The July Revolution has completely changed the relationship between authority and the people, between the governors and the governed. On 1 July 1830, we were the subjects of a king, on 30 July, we were all citizens. Before, we were only a people, afterwards, a nation.[54]

Balzac is probably correct to stress that this was a *political* revolution, which did not directly address issues of the economic power or class relations. However, a number of provisos need to be made. First, it must be remembered that the Revolution was political in the broadest sense of the word, including parliamentarians' procedures, anti-clericals' jokes and drinkers' talk. All could hope to benefit from the anti-authoritarian principles proclaimed in 1830.

Our second proviso is to warn against counterposing 'the political' and 'the economic' as if they belong to different worlds. While political issues were stressed in 1830, they unfolded in an economic context: the economic crisis of the late 1820s, the widespread perception that the Restoration governments did nothing to encourage economic expansion, and the 'popular' version of small capitalism propounded by liberals like Courier were all factors which encouraged support for the Revolution. Therefore, yes, this was a political revolution, but it certainly had an economic dimension.

The revolution produced some reforms. The electorate was increased from about ninety thousand to about one hundred and sixty thousand voters, and local elections drew in a still wider electorate. Schooling was encouraged by a law passed in 1833; child labour was limited and regulated by a law of 1840; the Church was less likely to be used as a secondary arm of government. However, there was much that did not change significantly: elections continued to be fixed, although perhaps less clumsily than before 1830. Papers continued to be harassed, although less strictly than before. There was little help for the poor, although it could be said that the government was more active in encouraging economic expansion.

This was not a great revolutionary change, but it still amounted to a shutting-off of one political option. Ultra-royalism never returned as the dominant political culture in France. The consequences of the Revolution are eloquently evoked in a work by Ernest Renan, a prominent liberal philosopher in mid-nineteenth-century France. He was born in the heart of the conservative west, in Brittany, and his memoirs record the lives and ideas of people from that old-fashioned region. He tells of the reactions of an old priest to the Revolution of 1830. 'One day, he saw on the horizon something strange. It was a tricolour flag, floating from a steeple … The July Revolution had just finished. When he learnt that the king [Charles X] had left, he realized quite clearly that this was the end of a world.'[55] Perhaps 1830 was only a little revolution, but it had a deep significance. It ended, once and for all, any chance of a return to the pre-1789 *ancien régime*; it initiated the long cycle of revolutions which erupted throughout the nineteenth century.

– V. DOCUMENTS –

– DOCUMENT 2.1: STREET POSTER IN PARIS –

The following poster appeared on the walls of Paris on 30 July 1830. It shows how the single issue of resistance to Bourbon rule could be the basis for a wide-ranging programme of political and social reform, often based on nationalist themes.

NO MORE BOURBONS!

The foreigners' party has been beaten. But while the presence of a single Bourbon still defiles our nation, foreigners will find a spy and an accomplice. No agreement is possible between them and us.

For forty years we have struggled to rid ourselves of this untrustworthy, odious race. Yesterday, we tore the crown from their head at bayonet point. The people did everything: from now on let the government be for the people, not for the priests, the aristocrats and the foreigners. We have bought the tricolour with our blood. We want to keep it: we want municipal councillors and National Guard officers to be elected by us. We don't want any more indirect taxes, we don't want any more monopolies ... We don't want any more Bourbons, as we have everything: grandeur, calm, public prosperity, freedom.

Source: Louessard, p. 172

– DOCUMENT 2.2: CHATEAUBRIAND AND REVOLUTIONARY YOUTH –

Chateaubriand had ambivalent feelings about the July Revolution. He was a convinced, passionate monarchist, but he despaired of the political tactics used by the Restoration monarchs, and felt some sympathy for the ideals for which the July revolutionaries were fighting. The following passage describes his experiences on 30 July 1830.

A ditch had been dug in front of the Louvre. A priest ... was saying prayers by the side of the ditch in which corpses were being placed. I took off my hat and made the sign of the cross. A silent crowd looked respectfully at this ceremony... So many memories and thoughts came to me, that I remained motionless. All at once I was pushed: a cry went up: 'Long live the defender of freedom of the press!' They had recognized me by my hair. Young people grabbed me and said to me: 'Where are you going? We're going to carry you.' I did not know what to say: I thanked them, I talked to them, I begged them to leave me alone... These young people kept on shouting 'Where are you going? Where are you going?'. Without thinking, I said 'Well, to the Palais-Royal!'. Straight away I was taken there with shouts of 'Long live the Charter! Long live the liberty of the press! Long live Chateau-briand!' ...

We arrived at the Palais-Royal. They rushed me into a café under a wooden gallery. I was dying of heat. I begged them to forget my glory. It was out of the question, none of these young people would let me go. In this crowd there was a man with his sleeves rolled up. He had dark hands and a sinister expression, with glowing eyes – the sort of man who I had seen often since the beginning of the revolution. He kept trying to get close to me, but these young people pushed him away. I never found out what he was called or what he wanted.

In the end I had to say that I was going to the Chamber of Peers. We left the café; the shouts started again. In the courtyard of the Louvre different cries were heard ... People ran alongside us; others opened their windows. So much honour hurt me, as they kept pulling at my arms. One of these young people who was pushing me from behind suddenly dipped beneath me and lifted me up on his shoulders. There were more shouts: they cried to the on-lookers in the street and at their windows: 'Hats off! Long live the Charter!' to which I replied, 'Yes, gentlemen, long live the Charter! But long live the King!' No one repeated my cry, but they did not get angry.

Source: Chateaubriand, pp. 191–2

– DOCUMENT 2.3: STENDHAL VISITS A SALON –

Stendhal was one of the greatest French novelists of the nineteenth century. His novel *Le Rouge et le Noir* (the Scarlet and Black) is a grimly comic tale of a young man's rise during the Restoration. In this passage Stendhal satirises one of the aristocracy's key social institutions: the salons. In the eighteenth century these informal gatherings had been liberating, providing a space for innovative debates and political networking. By the nineteenth century, they had decayed into mere ritual.

In this passage, Stendhal summarises the rules which his hero learnt about the correct behaviour to adopt.

As long as you did not tell jokes about God, priests, the King, or the people in power, or the artists that were protected by the Court, or about anything that was official; as long as you did not say anything good about Béranger, about opposition newspapers, about Voltaire, about Rousseau, or about anyone who was a bit outspoken; as long as you never discussed politics, you could speak freely about anything.

Neither great wealth nor prestigious decorations could fight against such a Charter of the Salon. A lively idea was seen as obscene. Despite elegance, perfect politeness, and the desire to be friendly, you could see just how bored everyone was. Young people only turned up because they had to. As they were scared of saying anything which might suggest they were capable of thinking, or which would betray their reading of some forbidden work, they would keep quiet after saying a few polite words about Rossini or about the weather.

Stendhal, *Le Rouge et le Noir* (Paris: 1964 [1830]), pp. 264–5

– VI. FURTHER READING –

Introductory works: André Jardin and André-Jean Tudesq, *Restoration and Reaction, 1815–1848* (Cambridge: Cambridge UP, 1980): well-written and informative account. Divided into a central political narrative, and a series of surveys of different regions. Laurent Louessard, *La révolution de juillet 1830* (Paris: Spartacus, 1990): committed left-wing history based on the '*révolution escamotée*' argument. Extremely valuable for its many quotations from contemporary documents; some vivid descriptions of events. John Merriman (ed.), *1830 in France* (New York: New Viewpoints, 1975): collection of well-researched essays discussing the social and economic results of the Revolution across the whole of France. Pamela Pilbeam, *The 1830 Revolution in France* (London: Macmillan, 1994): combines a narrative account of the Revolution with a wider social, political and economic analysis. Contains a particularly forceful conclusion. David H. Pinkney, *The French Revolution of 1830* (Princeton: Princeton UP, 1972): a well-written narrative account of events in Paris.

There are many very useful contemporary accounts. Chateaubriand's *Mémoires d'Outre-Tombe / Memoirs from Beyond the Grave* (various editions): immensely egotistical and not always trustworthy as a record of events, but packed with insights into the passions of this period. F. Guizot, *Mémoires pour servir à l'histoire de mon temps,* seven vols (Paris: Librarie Nouvelle, 1870): detached, cool memoirs of a liberal-conservative. Victor Hugo, *Les Misérables* (various editions): over-sentimental novel with various social concern themes; includes a description of the Revolution. A. Thiers, *La Monarchie de 1830* (Paris: Mesnier, 1831): after the event, justification of revolution; tries to establish its legitimacy.

The following works provide analyses of particular themes.

On the Hundred Days and the political mobilisations they provoke, see R. S. Alexander, *Bonapartism and Revolutionary Tradition in France; the Fédérés of 1815* (Cambridge: Cambridge UP, 1991). Bernard Ménager, *Les Napoléon du Peuple* (Paris: Aubier, 1988) discusses Bonapartism after the death of Napoleon: a useful and imaginative work.

On the political struggles during the Restoration see G. de Bertier de Sauvigny, *The Restoration* (several editions) – imaginatively written if a little dated. Sylvia Neely, 'Rural Politics in the Early Restoration: Charles Guyot and the Liberals of the Sarthe', *European History Quarterly* 16:3 (1986), 313–42: useful case study of a particular department. Edgar L. Newman, 'The Blouse and the Frock Coat: the Alliance of the Common People of Paris with the Liberal Leadership ...', *Journal of Modern History* 46:1 (1974), 26–59. Ingenious argument which stresses the role of anti-clericalism. Pamela Pilbeam, 'The Growth of Liberalism and the Crisis of the Bourbon Resto-

ration', *Historical Journal* 25:2 (1982), 351–66; 'The "Three Glorious Days":
the Revolution in Provincial France', *Historical Journal* 26 (1983), 831–44;
'The "Liberal" Revolution of 1830', *Historical Research* 63 (1990), 162–77 –
useful studies of specific themes. Daniel L. Rader, *The Journalists and the July
Revolution in France* (The Hague: Martinus Nijhoff, 1973): studies the important issue of the press. Alan Spitzer, 'The Elections of 1824 and 1827 in
the Department of the Doubs', *French History* 3:2 (1989), 153–76: a statistical
analysis.

On political theory: Pierre Rosanvallon, *La Monarchie impossible: les chartes
de 1814 et de 1830* (Paris: Fayard, 1994): contains a valuable selection of
contemporary documents; an essential work. Paul Bénichou, *Les temps de
prophètes; doctrines de l'âge romantique* (Paris: Gallimard, 1977: useful on connections between philosophical, political and literary ideas. Stendhal, *Le
Rouge et le Noir/The Scarlet and the Black* (various editions): cynical, sometimes
funny novel set in the last years of the Restoration. Some astonishing insights
into class and political culture.

On Guizot: Douglas Johnson, *Guizot: Aspects of French History* (London:
RKP, 1963): well-written biography. Pierre Rosanvallon, *Le moment Guizot*
(Paris, Gallimard, 1985): detailed, imaginative analysis of Guizot's political
thinking.

On the legacy of the Revolution: Honoré de Balzac, *La Peau de Chagrin/
The Wild Ass's Skin* (various editions, originally published in 1831): novel set
among the students who had been delighted by the revolutionary movement;
vivid, poignant descriptions of their disillusion.

– NOTES –

1. Victor Hugo, *Littérature et Philosophie mêlées* (Paris: Nelson, nd), p. 177.
2. Pamela Pilbeam, *The 1830 Revolution in France* (London: Macmillan, 1994), p. 174.
3. David Pinkney, *The French Revolution of 1830* (Princeton, Princeton UP, 1972), p. 367.
4. François Chateaubriand, *Mémoires d'Outre-Tombe*, Vol. III, ed. P. Clarac (Paris: Livre de Poche, 1973), p. 252.
5. François Guizot, *Mémoires pour servir à l'histoire de mon temps*, Vol. II (Paris: Librarie Nouvelle, 1870), p. 3.
6. AD I&V, 1.M.93, 9 July 1816.
7. Pinkney, *Revolution*, p. 145.
8. Roger Magraw, *A History of the French Working Class, Vol. I* (Oxford: Blackwell, 1992), p. 44.
9. Pilbeam, *1830 Revolution*, p. 190.
10. Bernard Ménager, *Les Napoléon du peuple* (Paris: Aubier, 1988), p. 15.
11. Ménager, *Les Napoléon*, pp. 41–3.
12. Pinkney, *Revolution*, pp. 252–73.

13. Chateaubriand, *Mémoires*, p. 218.
14. A. Thiers, *La Monarchie de 1830* (Paris: Mesnier, 1831), p. 39.
15. Alan Spitzer, 'The Elections of 1824 and 1827 in the Department of the Doubs', *French History* 3:2 (1989), 153–76.
16. Figures from ADV, 3.M.25.
17. Benjamin Constant, *Polémiste*, ed. Olivier Pozzo di Borgio (Utrecht: Pauvert, 1965), p. 79.
18. Pamela Pilbeam, 'The Growth of Liberalism and the Crisis of the Bourbon Restoration', *Historical Journal* 25:2 (1982), 351–66 (p. 351).
19. AN/F/1cIII/Garonne-Haute/6 June 1820.
20. AN/BB/30/261, Interior Minister to Justice Minister, 20 January 1824.
21. Sylvia Neely, 'Rural Politics in the Early Restoration: Charles Goyet and the Liberals of the Sarthe', *European History Quarterly* 16:3 (1986), 313–42 (p. 331).
22. '*Aide-toi*' ('help yourself') were the first words of the French saying 'God helps those who help themselves', coined by La Fontaine (1621–95) in his *Fables*, book 6, no.18 (Paris: Hachette, 1925).
23. Pinkney, *Revolution*, p. 37.
24. Chateaubriand, *Mémoires*, p. 159.
25. Pierre Rosanvallon (ed.), *La Monarchie impossible* (Paris: Fayard, 1994), p. 298.
26. Pinkney, *Revolution*, p. 102.
27. Thiers, *Monarchie*, p. 17.
28. Pilbeam, *1830 Revolution*, p. 62.
29. AN/BB/18/975.
30. AN/BB/18/976.
31. AN/BB/18/1010.
32. AN/F/7/6704.
33. AN/F/7/6704, report dated 7 June 1826.
34. AN/F/7/6704, letter dated 20 March 1826.
35. AN/F/7/6704, police report dated 1 May 1822.
36. AN/BB/30/245, Prosecutor's report dated 7 December 1822.
37. Guizot, *Mémoires*, Vol. I, p. 237.
38. Pilbeam, *1830 Revolution*, p. 21.
39. AN/BB/30/269, report dated 2 July 1827.
40. AN/BB/30/269, letter dated 30 August 1827.
41. AN/F/7/6769, letter dated 12 June 1828.
42. AN/F/7/6769, letter dated 4 March 1827.
43. AN/F/7/6704, letter dated 28 June 1826.
44. AN/F/7/6769, letter dated 2 May 1826.
45. AN/F/7/6769, letter dated [30?] March 1826.
46. AN/F/7/6704, Prefect's letter dated 27 July 1827.
47. Figures from Daniel Rader, *The Journalists and the July Revolution* (The Hague: Martinus Nijhoff, 1973), pp. 19–30.
48. Rosanvallon, *Monarchie impossible*, p. 284.
49. All details from Courier's pamphlets are taken from his *Oeuvres choisies*, ed. J. Giraud (Paris: Delagrave, 1936).
50. Hugo, *Littérature et philosophie*, p. 307.
51. Hugo, *Littérature et philosophie*, p. 166.
52. P. J. Béranger, *Oeuvres complètes* (Paris: Charpentier, 1858), p. xi.

53. William Sewell, *Work and Revolution in France* (Cambridge: Cambridge UP, 1980), pp. 195–7.
54. Honoré de Balzac, *Oeuvres Diverses*, Vol. II, eds P.-G. Castex, R. Cholland, C. and R. Guize (Paris: Gallimard, 1996), p. 983.
55. Ernest Renan, *Souvenirs d'enfance et de jeunesse* (Paris: Nelson, nd), p. 56.

CHAPTER 3

Lyon, 1831: Working-class Protest

The new Orleanist politicians of 1830 hoped that the July Revolution had ended the cycle of violence, revolution and counter-revolution which had begun in 1789. However, in the months following the July Revolution, France seemed as turbulent as ever. One significant challenge to the government came from a new quarter: the working class of Lyon.

– I. PARTICIPANTS –

Lyon is the second city of France, situated about three hundred miles southeast of Paris and about one hundred miles from France's eastern border. It lies on a natural crossroads: on the internal communications routes which connect Paris to the south-east, and on the international routes which link France to Switzerland and Italy. There were good communications between Lyon and Paris in the 1830s: the express mail arrived within about two days, and there was also a semaphore telegraph service which worked on clear days. Jérôme Lippomano, a Venetian ambassador visited the city in 1579. 'Lyon's antiquity, its greatness, its position and its commerce,' he wrote, 'make it not just one of the principal towns of the France, but also one of the most celebrated towns of Europe.' The ambassador noted that the Saône and Rhône rivers, which met at the city, carried goods from England, Flanders, Germany and Switzerland: they were taken by mule to Savoy, or by river to the Mediterranean, to the southern regions of France and even to Spain.[1] Lyon was a major economic centre, holding fairs, which sold cloth and exchanged money for traders from the whole of Europe. The city's connection with weaving began in the early sixteenth century, when the first looms were imported from Italy.

By 1789, 143 000 people lived in the city or in its suburbs. Almost half of them depended on the silk industry. Three hundred and eight rich silk merchants traded in finished cloth and – increasingly – attempted to organise silk production. Another thirty-five thousand people were employed in weaving silk, and still more were involved in its preparation and trading.[2] Lyon was an unusual city: few other European cities had such a high concentration of workers employed in a single trade and, because of this, the decay of guild structures operated here with particular force.

During the Middle Ages guilds developed in all European cities. Guilds were urban organisations for skilled trades such as jewellery, carpentry, weaving, brewing, and so on. They enforced high standards of work, and attempted to unite masters, workers and apprentices within a moral community, bound by rules of honour. In theory, guild structures guaranteed an internal structure of promotion: young men – and some women – entered guilds as apprentices, then served as journeymen, before gaining full membership as masters. In practice, by the eighteenth century there were many obstacles to this line of progress. One was set by the high fees which were charged at each point of transition: from apprentice to journeyman, and from journeyman to master. Another obstacle was the growing tendency for masters' sons to be placed on a 'fast track', which allowed them to complete their training more quickly than others. Such developments meant that guilds were becoming stratified. Many workers were stuck at the stage of journeyman with little chance of promotion.

The 1791 Chapelier Law enforced the principle of economic individualism, whereby workers and employers negotiated issues such as rates of pay and conditions of work as individuals. It banned all forms of trade coalitions, whether by workers or employers. At first sight, one would expect this law to result in the complete disappearance of all guilds and guild-like structures. However, the historical record suggests a different picture. Skilled workers, particularly those working in small workshops which they owned, showed a lasting respect for the ethics of honour and pride in work expressed by guild culture.

In Lyon, the decay of the guilds took an unusual form. Instead of the masters as a group rising above the apprentices and journeymen, a split took place among the masters. Some of them became specialist *fabricants*, or merchants, responsible for selling finished cloth and arranging orders for new cloth; others became master-weavers, usually weaving themselves, and also directing perhaps two, three or four other looms. The two groups were under the formal authority of the Grande Fabrique, which assumed the guild-like functions of assuring quality, and setting rates of pay and prices. However, the old ideal of a moral, united work community was no longer respected, and masters and merchants battled for control of the Fabrique. From the mid-seventeenth century onwards, it was dominated by merchants. The master-weavers fought a centuries-long rearguard action. At times their disputes could result in street violence: in 1744 and 1786 there were major weavers' riots in Lyon. The silk-weavers grew more politically sophisticated. As well as rioting, they appealed to local and national authorities. In this context, guild-like ideals of honour in work were important in inspiring silk-weavers to defend their status.

The revolutionary decade of the 1790s was difficult for the Lyonnais. Silk clothes were associated with the old royal court, and so became unfashionable. The new ideal was republican simplicity, expressed in clothes made from imported muslin. Moreover, revolutionary violence disrupted markets and caused difficulties for commerce. Lastly, Lyon fell into a bitter dispute with Jacobin Paris in the summer of 1793, which resulted in a full-scale military siege of the city and, following the Jacobins' victory, months of bloody repression. Almost two thousand people were executed.[3] Following these events, the number of looms fell to about two thousand.[4] One legacy of the Revolution was a widespread fear of Republicanism in Lyon.

The city fared better under Napoleon. The Continental Blockade, directed by Britain, produced a boom in the continental silk industry. Workers flocked to Lyon, and the pressure of increased population meant that new working-class quarters grew, first to the north, just within the city walls, but gradually, in the 1820s, outside the city walls, into the old village of the Croix-Rousse which, in 1818, was reclassed as a town. As it was outside the city walls, it was free of urban taxes and therefore a cheaper, if less prestigious, place in which to live. Tall, south-facing apartments were built there. These were suited to the new Jacquard looms, which were usually nine foot high, and which allowed weavers to produce complex woven patterns cheaply and quickly.

Despite their close proximity, the Croix-Rousse and Lyon were separate from each other. In part, this was created by the steep slopes which ran up to the Croix-Rousse. It was difficult for horses to pull carriages up these hills, and the few roads connecting the town to the city soon acquired the nickname of 'horse-killers'. But there was another type of gap between the two: a social and cultural division. Most urban areas were still organised on the basis of 'vertical' class divisions, whereby the same building was inhabited by people from different classes, with the richest occupying the biggest apartments at the bottom. The Croix-Rousse was one of the first working-class suburbs, distinctively different from the central city.

Its population increased rapidly in the early 1830s: 16 210 people were registered as living there in 1831.[5] They were the object of some curiosity, for the weavers of the Croix-Rousse seemed unusually well-off. Villermé, a leading Catholic social commentator, noted how well-dressed they were on Sundays and holidays: smart enough to resemble middle-class people. They also seemed more hard-working, more sober and more intelligent than most other French workers.[6] Bunet, a Lyonnais writer, applauded their morality and respectability. 'The Croix-Rousse is like a giant hive' he said: in its houses the orderly silk-weavers, gathered together in family groups, worked hard, behaved properly and respected moral values. These *canuts* (a slang word for silk-weaver) were quite different from the demoralised, impoverished proletarians of Birmingham, Manchester, Rouen or Mulhouse.[7] Similar points were made by another Lyonnais writer. 'The Lyonnais worker has the advantage that he possesses his loom, which links him directly with order and with respect for property.'[8] The male silk-weaver was seen as distinctively different from the proletarianised worker of the industrial slums: his education, relative wealth, and status as a property-owning artisan and a father marked him out as natural conservative.

However, there was another image of Lyon's workers, which was expressed in the *Journal du Commerce*, Lyon's leading liberal paper in the 1820s and early 1830s. (It took its name from a better-known Parisian liberal newspaper with the same title.) This paper often reported on working-class activities. Sometimes its articles portrayed the workers as respectable: they attended traditional Catholic festivals and processions, but other reports introduced another theme. If we examine articles from 1828, we find that it reported a fight between apprentice locksmiths on 8 February, an outbreak of machine-breaking in the Croix-Rousse on 19 March, the formation of illegal trade unions among hat-makers on 11 April, a fight following a worker's funeral on 18 June, fights between bakers on 10 August and 5 September, a riot by ribbon-makers on 14 November in the town of Tarare (to the west of Lyon), and a fight among shoemakers on 12 December. Often these violent clashes involved *compagnons* – members of journeymen's organisations. While the *Journal* says little about weavers, it gives the impression that working-class culture was primitive, mysterious and violent. After the November 1831 revolt, a local liberal writer summed up this line of thinking: he claimed that the silk-weavers' apprentices 'smash things during riots out of a simple love of noise'.[9] In these writings little distinction was made between worker, hooligan and beggar: all were regarded with hostility. Such attitudes were common among the silk merchants and some local officials.

In July 1830, Lyon did not *follow* the Parisian revolution. Rather, Lyonnais revolutionaries independently launched their own anti-Bourbon insurrection. A contemporary source describes these activists as belonging 'to the intermediary class which has always protected the people from the attacks of the aristocracy, and protected the aristocracy from the outbursts of popular anarchy. They were merchants, workshop owners, bankers, doctors, young clerks.'[10] In other words, this was a bourgeois coalition of property-owners and professionals, involving the middle-class National Guard and perhaps including a working-class élite, but quite different from the largely working-class crowds of revolutionary Paris.

In the weeks after the 1830 Revolution, there was little immediate sign of independent working-class politics. The *Journal du Commerce* was dominated by other concerns. One was the defenders of the old Bourbon monarchy, who were labelled 'Carlists'. The *Journal* claimed that they were trying to subvert the silk-workers, but without success. The second concern was the danger of the spread of cholera to Lyon: while this epidemic affected many French towns, including Paris, in 1830–1, Lyon escaped.

In the eighteenth century weavers had agitated within the structures of the Fabrique in order to preserve their status and standard of living. In 1804, following the revolutionary hiatus, the Fabrique was replaced by the Conseil des Prud'hommes, which also tried to draw together merchants and weavers to discuss common concerns, and which over-represented the merchants. Lyon was the first French town to have such a Conseil although they were eventually set up in all French towns. Collective agreements – or 'tariffs' – concerning payments were agreed in 1807, 1811 and 1818. Following the Revolution of 1830, a depression resulted in a drop in the rates offered to silk-weavers. Some responded by emigrating, but others looked to the new government to sponsor another round of negotiations which would produce a new, higher tariff. This would be a difficult process: by 1830 there were approximately eight hundred merchants, eight thousand master-weavers, and thirty thousand silk-workers in Lyon.[11]

There were some new factors in play now. In 1827 the Society of Mutual Duty had been founded by a group of weavers. This was not a guild, and it does not seem to have imitated either the archaic ritual or the ready violence of the journeymen's *compagnonnages*. Instead, its first role was as a mutual aid society. All members paid a franc each month, and in return gained some limited social insurance against accidents and illness, and the right to a dignified funeral. Like the guilds, it stressed moral themes: it campaigned against drunkenness and swearing, and it encouraged marriage and orderly households. Lastly, some of these 'mutualists' prepared for a conflict with the silk merchants. Prior to 1830, at most a couple of hundred weavers belonged to the Society. After 1830, its membership began to grow: perhaps to twelve hundred in 1833, and even to three thousand by 1834.[12] The Society anticipated conflict between the merchants and weavers taking place *outside* the structures of the Conseil des Prud'hommes.

Another new factor was the formation of the 'Volunteers of the Rhône' during the winter of 1830–1. They aimed to fight in the north-western regions of Italy – in Savoy and Piedmont – against the Austrian forces which prevented the unification of Italy. Between seven hundred and one thousand men enrolled.[13] In part, they were mercenaries, recruited among unemployed workers. However, some were motivated by idealist, patriotic, even republican, ideas. During the winter of 1830–1 they underwent military training which gave them a collective psychological preparation to face danger. Initially the Volunteers were tolerated by the July Monarchy. However, when they set off to march to Italy in February 1831, the government had second thoughts, and their organisation was officially dissolved. Many Volunteers kept in contact with each other during 1831.

– II. EVENTS –

Following the 1830 Revolution, Lyon's local authorities feared political subversion. They watched the silk-weavers carefully, but there was little cause for concern. Republicans were slow to organise in Lyon. Police reports stressed divisions among the Carlists, and their inability to gain support from the *canuts*.[14] There was a third possible source of subversion: in June 1831 a 'mission' from the utopian socialist Saint-Simonians arrived in Lyon. (See Chapter 5.) The Prefect considered banning them, but finally judged that they represented peaceful – if unusual – religious values, rather than subversive politics.

Local authorities carefully monitored signs of economic discontent. One silk-weavers' initiative which confused them was a petition drawn up by two master weavers in March 1831, and directed to the Chamber of Deputies.[15] It noted the effects of the economic crisis on the silk trade, called for a new tariff and criticised the merchants' domination of the Conseil des Prud'hommes. Was this petition illegal? One police commissar considered that it 'contains nothing which is hostile to the government, and its only aims are to make justice respected, to guarantee the workers' interests which … have been compromised, and to obtain a new organization of the Conseil des Prud'hommes.'[16] None the less, the petition's authors were arrested in April 1831, and initially charged with fraud, only to be released later without trial. Nothing came of their petition, but throughout the summer of 1831 there were further signs of discontent in the Croix-Rousse. In the evenings, silk-weavers would gather in cafés to debate. On more than one occasion they marched through the streets, sometimes singing the Marseillaise, the republican song which was later to become the national anthem.[17] By October, the silk-weavers had elected a new Commission to represent them.

Police and local authorities were confused about these activities. On the one hand, they understood the silk-weavers as 'good', property-owning artisans, not as anarchic proletarians. The *canuts* were clearly suffering as a result of the economic crisis and, under these circumstances, it was difficult to refuse them the right to voice their discontent. Officials' reports and letters often show this sympathetic attitude. For example, one police official visited a silk-weavers' meeting on 13 October 1831 – 150 were gathered in a café, and another group waited outside. The official recognised that their meeting was illegal, 'but did not believe that he ought to prevent it, for it is quite possible to meet peacefully and calmly, to discuss matters of common interest.'[18] On the other hand, there were worrying aspects of the weavers' agitation, particularly their demonstrations. 'This will worry our orderly citizens, if the authorities do not do something to repress these audacious young people. Carlism could well make use of these actions and will want to turn them to its profit.'[19]

Official indecision was exacerbated by division and rivalry within the administration. For Prunelle, Lyon's mayor, 1830 was the start of a process of decentralisation. He was keen to assert Lyon's independence from central control, represented by the Rhône's prefect. His policy had some concrete effects: he defended incompetent officials against dismissal and attempted to control the appointment of prefects. As a result, there was a rapid turnover of prefects. Following the 1830 Revolution, Paulze d'Ivoy was appointed prefect. Partly because of Prunelle's pressure, he was then replaced by Bouvier Dumoulart in May 1831. Dumoulart had been one of Napoleon's prefects during the Empire and the Hundred Days. He had retired during the Restoration, but returned following 1830. It should be remembered that he had only been prefect for six months when confronted with the November events.

Prunelle argued with prefects, but was not able to provide an alternative focus of leadership. As well as being mayor of Lyon, he was also a deputy for the neighbouring department of the Isère, to the east of Lyon, and was in Paris throughout November 1831.

On 18 October 1831 Dumoulart received a petition from the silk-weavers' Commission. They called on him to act for them, invoked his 'paternal care' and requested that he arrange a new tariff. Dumoulart had to think quickly. Silk was an extremely successful French export: in 1830 money earned by silk exported from Lyon represented no less than one-third of the value of all French exports for that year.[20] Lyon was effectively dominated by this single industry: impoverished silk-weavers would find few other sources of employment. Dumoulart might have considered how past prefects had acted: there were several occasion on which they had facilitated discussions, as in 1812 and 1817. Political considerations may also have influenced him: as an official with Bonapartist sympathies, Dumoulart may have noted the actions of past Imperial prefects. An orderly, respectable section of the working class was asking for his help: how could he refuse?

From 18 to 25 October 1831 Dumoulart chaired a series of discussions. The merchants were initially reluctant to participate, but did not refuse a direct invitation from the Prefect. On 25 October, six thousand silk-weavers marched into the Place des Terreaux in central Lyon, the site of the Prefecture. Their discipline and order was noted by observers. They waited silently while the last discussions took place. When they heard that agreement had at last been reached between their Commission, the merchants and the Prefect, they were overjoyed. 'Long live the King!' they shouted. Dumoulart considered that he had achieved his political objective: by facilitating the discussions which had produced a new tariff, he had won the Lyonnais working class to the July Monarchy.

When Dumoulart reported back to the head of the government, Casimir Périer, he met a different reaction. Périer had believed that the silk-weavers' petition proposed reforms to the silk industry, not a new tariff.[21] Communications between the Minister and the Prefect had been interrupted; fog had prevented the use of semaphore-telegraph. When it became clear that Dumoulart had accepted a price-fixing arrangement, Périer was horrified. The scene on 25 October particularly shocked him: in his opinion, free discussion could not take place when six thousand silk-weavers were watching the participants.

In Lyon, the silk-weavers were overjoyed. Their efforts to bypass the structures of the Conseil des Prud'hommes had succeeded. A symbol of their new-found confidence was the publication of a new paper, *L'Echo de la Fabrique*. Aimed at the silk-weavers, it was the first workers' paper in France. It published the new rates, and soon they were posted up in every workshop in Lyon.

The merchants were less enthusiastic. Many argued that in the face of English competition, they could not afford to pay higher rates. News of the disagreement between the Prefect and Périer leaked out, encouraging merchants to dissent. On 5 November they organised a petition which protested against the new rates. Périer was later to argue that this proved his case: the agreement had not been freely entered into, and therefore could not be enforced. When weavers objected to the low rates which they were being offered, merchants refused to compromise, and instead closed their warehouses.

Dumoulart was now in an extremely difficult position. Could he simply renounce the discussions which he had chaired? Could he oppose Périer? His compromise was to redefine the nature of the tariff. It did not establish legally-binding rates on silk-weavers and merchants; instead it merely recommended rates which merchants should aim to honour, circumstances allowing. Predictably, this compromise satisfied no one.

Once again, there were mass meetings in the Croix-Rousse. The mayor grew concerned: as he noted to the Prefect, it only took a moment to gather together all the town's workers in a single place.[22] Rumours spread. 'Words of attack, devastation, pillage circulated from mouth to mouth, and should have caught the authorities' attention.'[23] On the other hand, some police reports noted the Croix-Rousse's calm and suggested that the danger had passed.[24]

Late in the evening of 20 November 1831, a police report was sent to the Prefect. 'The silk-weavers of the Croix-Rousse have decided that tomorrow they will go down to Lyon, carrying a black flag, calling for work or death.'[25] The next morning, at about seven a.m., 'commissioners' visited all the workshops in the Croix-Rousse, calling on the weavers to demonstrate. Many readily followed; those that did not were intimidated and threatened. They were formed into groups: some carried drums, suggesting that they would march in military file. Barricades were built to prevent entry into the Croix-Rousse. Lacombe, the old commander of the Volunteers of the Rhône arrived in the Croix-Rousse at about nine a.m.

The Prefect called out Lyon's National Guard. By an unfortunate coincidence, the first battalion to arrive at the Croix-Rousse was largely composed of silk merchants. When the Guardsmen met the rebels, at first they talked, then they argued. Stones were thrown. According to one account, at that point the leader of Guardsmen, a merchant named Firmin Gentelet, shouted 'My friends, sweep these bastards away!'[26] Shots ran out, but it was the Guardsmen who retreated under a hail of stones. The weavers were now the masters of the Croix-Rousse. They seized guard posts and their weapons, and then met to discuss their plans.

> [There were] young men, young workers, men armed with shovels, picks, hammers, sticks and similar instruments, some carrying guns, plus a large number of women and children gathered together … Their mood was one of exasperation. They were led by several speakers who tried to inspire the timid to be brave, and who told the brave of the duties they had to fulfil.[27]

Meanwhile, in Lyon, there was a general mobilisation of the National Guard. In theory, this should have called out some fifteen thousand Guardsmen: in reality, only two thousand responded on 21 November, and only five hundred on 22 November. In the Croix-Rousse, and in other working-class suburbs, many Guardsmen fought on the silk-weavers' side.

At eleven a.m. the silk-weavers' columns descended the slopes of the Croix-Rousse. Some carried black flags, the colour of mourning and a reminder of their economic distress. Others pushed loaves of bread on the bayonets of their guns and held them aloft. The symbolic force of this action was reinforced by a repeatedly-shouted slogan: 'bread or lead!': in other words, if they were not given bread which they could afford, then they were prepared to face bullets. At some point during the rebellion, a more eloquent expression was devised: 'Vivre en travaillant ou mourir en combattant!' – 'Live working or die by fighting!'. Some witnesses report seeing this painted on a black flag.

A curious situation developed in the city over the next three days (21–3 November). As in Paris in 1830, the regular army was ill-prepared for the concentrated, street-by-street conflicts which developed. Caught by surprise, they were pushed back by the silk-weavers, who gathered support from other groups of workers. There was some bloody fighting: about six hundred people were either killed or seriously wounded, with the casualties evenly distributed between workers and soldiers.[28] At two a.m. on 23 November the army pulled out of Lyon, leaving it in the hands of the weavers. They continued to respect the Prefect who, after briefly being held hostage on 21 November, was allowed to remain in the Prefecture. Both Carlists and republicans tried to agitate among the rebels. While some rebel leaders identified with one or other of these traditions, neither really influenced the crowds. It was noticeable that while the silk-weavers would readily listen to fiery speeches, their attentions wandered when the speaker turned to Henri V, the Carlist Pretender, or to the Republic. A similar observation can be made about the crowd's Bonapartism: there were a few shouts praising the Emperor, but no sustained commitment. Instead, there was an unusual apolitical quality to the revolt. A telling example is cited by François Rude. During the fighting a group of weavers ran into an arcade. The shopkeepers began to close their doors. The weavers, seeing this, shouted out: 'Don't close your doors! We don't want to do any damage, we're not going to steal anything, all we want is the Tariff.'[29]

The clearest expression of their aims was a poster issued on 23 November (see document 3.1). This calls for a root-and-branch reform of local government, which would create a new form of political power in which the silk-workers would no longer be subordinate. However, there are some strange aspects to this poster. It makes no mention of the tariff, which other evidence suggests was at the centre of silk-weavers' concerns. Rude suggests that its rather mysterious reference to 'corporations' is drawn from Carlist politics, and that the poster's authors were Carlists trying to adapt their agenda to the silk-weavers' concerns. After the poster was printed, the militants who were listed as its authors denied any involvement.

Considering this strange apolitical revolt, one hostile witness commented:

Amazed by their victory, [the workers] did not know what to do, nor what direction to take.

In the middle of these disasters, no political or seditious symbol was raised. No flag other than the tricolour was raised. A group shouted in the streets 'Long live the Republic!'. No other cry was heard.[30]

Another illustration of the same point comes from the Prefect. On the afternoon of 23 November the Prefect in Marseilles telegraphed the Rhône prefect, asking him for news. Dumoulart's reply read:

The situation is serious. The infantry have been forced to retreat. The National Guard has defected. Civil authorities have stayed at their posts, and I hope to re-establish order. Blood has flowed for two days. A disagreement between the merchants and workers has caused this deplorable event: it has nothing to do with politics.[31]

During the period of the workers domination, theft was forbidden and armed workers' patrols kept order. But there were few signs of a wider political project: the weavers seemed concerned about the tariff, and little else.

The revolt ended on 29 November, when the Dumoulart, backed by reinforced military forces, returned to full power in Lyon.

– III. POLITICAL CULTURE –

The account of events given above leaves us with a number of intriguing questions. We can identify the immediate causes of the revolt: however, it is more difficult to define its *nature*. Many sensitive, observant witnesses stress its non-political nature. What does this mean? Should we accept this judgement? If not, how should we classify the revolt? A second set of questions relates to the authorities: why was Dumoulart willing to co-operate with the weavers' commission, while Périer was so critical of their demands?

The events of November 1831 are a bewildering mixture of old and new. A medieval historian, conversant with the history of urban guilds, could easily point out similarities between medieval conflicts and those of 1831. Furthermore, the rebels brought with them their memories of previous rounds of negotiation between apprentices, weavers and merchants: their knowledge of past events gave them certain expectations. In a sense, the innovators were not the weavers, who expected the old rules to apply, but the merchants, who only reluctantly joined the process of negotiation and refused to recognise the new tariff.

Many of the weavers' actions echoed older traditions of corporate bargaining within guild-like structures. When negotiations proved difficult, there were a number of established tactics for the weavers to use. 'Bread or lead!' was a centuries-old slogan which crowds in bread riots had screamed at bakers and police in marketplaces across Europe. Its significance is that it defined the crowd as *consumers*, as buyers of bread whose first concern was its price, and not as *workers* contesting the level of wages.

The other established tactic was that of appealing to alternative authorities. In this case, the weavers turned to the Prefect. Significantly, in talking to him they explicitly made use of a paternalist vocabulary. Lacombe, writing to the Prefect on 24 November, reminded him 'the workers have called you their father; you replied that you would only be the father of good children'.[32] The Prefect himself referred to this theme in a poster distributed on the same day: 'Good workers, you called me your father, help me to save the City from the misfortunes which still threaten it.'[33] This type of language defines the weavers as junior partners in a process of corporate negotiation and appeals for the sympathy of élite groups.

However, in 1831 the old patterns of negotiation were no longer accepted by the merchants or the government. While the weavers' first response was to try to revive them, their revolt is truly significant for their later attempts to transcend them. Their movement was moving out of the old structures and mentalities set by guilds, and into the new structures of the Society of Mutual Duty. Weavers were attempting to find their own, independent voice, separate from, and opposed to, that of the merchants. Their paper, *L'Echo de la Fabrique*, was an important aspect of this process.

The division of forces was noticeably different from an old guild dispute. This was not one faction fighting another, but a broad majority of unskilled and skilled workers, apprentices and masters, fighting a small minority of merchants. More interesting still, this majority identified itself in class terms, as working-class, even if this identification was arguably more emotional than economic. This is the genuinely original aspect of the weavers' other slogan – 'Live by working or die fighting!'. It defined the rebels as *workers*, not as *consumers*, insisting on their right to control the work process and to participate collectively in negotiations. As a slogan, it can be faulted for its vagueness: does the call to 'live working' mean simply that the weavers wanted enough money to protect them from starvation? Or does it imply something else: a call for dignity, to be more than just hands at a loom? Whatever its implications, its originality is indisputable. Just as *L'Echo de la Fabrique* was the first workers' paper in France, so this may well be the first occasion in which a rebellious crowd defined themselves as working-class, rather than as consumers, anti-clericals, Bonapartists, or so on. This innovation marks the entry of a class-based vocabulary into the culture of popular politics.

Concepts such as 'working-class' or 'proletarian' are problematic, and at times discussions about them can sound like hair-splitting dissections of abstract issues. However, even apparently minor points can be vital in shaping political strategies. One issue here is the meaning of the term 'proletarian'. Consider Marx's description:

> Owing to the extensive use of machinery and to the division of labour, the work of the proletarians has lost all individual character, and, consequently, all charm for the workman. He becomes an appendage of the machine, and it is only the most simple, most monotonous, and most easily acquired knack, that is required of him ... Modern industry has converted the little workshop of the patriarchal master into the great factory of the industrial capitalist. Masses of labourers, crowded into the factory, are organised like soldiers. As privates of the industrial army they are placed under the command of a perfect hierarchy of officers and sergeants.[34]

One can debate exactly how accurately Marx has described the new industrial labour. However, one point is clear: these are definitely *not* the conditions under which the silk-weavers worked. Perhaps there are similarities. It could be argued that work discipline had grown harsher, and that the Croix-Rousse, that 'vast hive' of workers, did constitute a 'virtual factory', in which contracts and sub-contracts pulled the whole community into one economic unit. But these points are mere qualifications to our principal argument: the silk-weavers were not proletarians. In the case of the masters, they were small property-owners, while the apprentices were workers who had some reasonable expectation of eventually becoming property-owners.

And yet ... the silk-weavers identified themselves as proletarians. As Roger Magraw notes, 'when J. Benoît, a small master-weaver and future socialist deputy for Lyon in 1848, came to write his autobiography, he called it *Confessions d'un prolétaire* even if, by some definitions, he might be categorised as a small businessman.'[35] Lyon's silk-weavers were not alone in this misidentification. Barraud, a Parisian print-worker, writing in the aftermath of the revolt, labelled himself 'a proletarian', while most modern sociologists would classify him as a skilled worker.[36]

How do we explain this strange disparity?

On the one hand, there were significant economic and technological developments, principally the widespread adoption of the Jacquard loom and the massive growth of an export-orientated trade. These developments were not equivalent to an 'Industrial Revolution', and certainly did not result in the proletarianisation of the silk-trade. Alongside these economic shifts, there were also important political changes, principally the government's and merchants' repudiation of the collective negotiation of tariffs. This can be seen as a de-politicisation of the issue of rates: political authorities (the government, prefect, mayor) were no longer involved in this process; paternalistic relations between employers and workers were rejected. Henceforth negotiations over prices would be a 'private' matter between individual merchants and individual weavers, who were supposedly equal.

One of the silk-weavers' responses was to try to turn the clock back: to appeal to the prefect to act as their father. Their other response was to re-politicise the whole issue. By using the language of class, they were refusing to accept that the issue of the tariff could be resolved through private negotiations between 'equal' individuals. They insisted that unequal and collective interests were involved and that these had to be represented in negotiations. Terms such as 'working-class' and 'proletarian' present a distorted description of the weavers' economic position, but capture an essential aspect of their experience. Once denied their political right to collective representation in negotiations, their collective identity was based solely on their economic status. Another way of making the same point would be to say that while the weavers were not (yet) proletarians, they feared proletarianisation: in this sense they made the term meaningful (see document 3.2). It was the weavers' stark assertion of their *economic* identity which at once shocked and confused contemporary observers, unused to this form of political culture.

As has been seen, the Prefect himself considered that the revolt 'has nothing to do with politics'. (This comment can be compared with Chateaubriand's statement, quoted at the start of the last chapter, that the 1830 Revolution was social, not political.) At first sight, this comment seems mystifying: what were three days of rioting and six hundred casualties, if they were not political? There is a simple explanation for the Prefect's observation: he meant that the revolt was not caused by political groups like the Carlists and republicans. However, there is another implication. Politics, for men like the Prefect, had to be the activity of élite groups. There were legitimate forms of political culture, represented by the July Monarchy itself. There were illegitimate forms, represented by the Carlists and Republicans. The activities of sub-ordinate groups like silk-weavers might or might not be legitimate, but they did not merit the title 'political'.

One curious consequence of this line of thinking was sometimes to absolve the weavers of blame for the revolt: as non-political beings they were not seen as capable of such acts. Instead, the administration was captivated by fears of underground conspiracies of republicans, Carlists, utopian socialists, Italian nationalists, and so on. Dumoulart's replacement, Gasparin, was almost permanently searching for such plots. A list which he wrote in approximately 1833 identifies no less than thirteen different conspiracies.[37]

Other Orleanists developed a more pessimistic argument. Ideally, workers were not supposed to be involved in politics. However, 'one of the worst results of the November events will be to make the Lyonnais workers a political class.'[38] Orleanists did not call for the democratisation of politics: they wished to oppose the development of working-class politics. Instead, they considered other ways of integrating the working class into society *without* encouraging their politicisation. One characteristic solution was the expansion of schooling, which was expected to teach the working class to accept its subordinate position.

– IV. LEGACY –

Within the terms of Orleanist politics, Dumoulart (the Prefect) was the exception, Périer (the Prime Minister) the norm. On 17 December 1831, the Count d'Argout, the Minister of Commerce in Périer's government, sent out a circular to all the prefects, summing up the government's attitude. No new law was propounded, but he made it clear how the government interpreted existing legislation, particularly the Chapelier Law of 1791. Collective meetings of workers and collective petitions by workers were illegal.

> Neither workers nor merchants are allowed to form corporations. No treaty established between them can be compulsory for the whole profession. Each individual is free to negotiate a contract as he wishes, but even the agreement of the majority [of those in a trade] cannot make a law binding on the minority.[39]

Despite the letter of the law, no group of merchants or employers was ever prosecuted for 'coalition', while there were numerous examples of workers' organisations being judged illegal. These harsh conditions governing trade organisations were modified in 1864, but were not finally abolished until 1884.

In February 1834 a new law made working-class and republican organisation still more difficult. All political associations had to seek authorisation. Any member of an illegal association could be subject to a year in prison and a one thousand franc fine. Such policies alienated working-class activists, and contributed to the July Monarchy's image as an uncaring, 'bourgeois' regime.

The events of November 1831 show the difficulties which the July Monarchy experienced in trying to integrate the working class into society. They point to a new form of political culture, based on concepts of economic class, which would eventually lead to socialist thinking. The peculiar 'apolitical' character of the weavers' revolt was not an expression of their political neutrality, but an indication that the form of political culture which they represented could not be accommodated within the structures of the July Monarchy.

–V. DOCUMENTS –

– DOCUMENT 3.1: THE SILK-WEAVERS' PROCLAMATION –

This poster, printed on 23 November 1831, is discussed in section III, Political culture.

Lyonnais!

Treacherous officials have lost their right to public confidence. A barricade of corpses has been built between them and us. All compromise has therefore become impossible and Lyon, gloriously liberated by its children, must have officials of its own choice: officials whose clothes are not stained with the blood of our brothers! Our defenders will name delegates, and they will preside, alongside all the respective corporations, over the representation of the town and the department of the Rhône. Lyon will have meetings or primary assemblies. The needs of the provincial people will finally be heard, and a new citizens' guard will be organised. No more ministerial trickery will impose it on us. Soldiers, you have been misled: come to us, your wounded will tell you that we are your brothers! National Guards, you have been given orders by treacherous men with special interests; they have compromised your uniform. Your hearts must be French: join us to maintain order ... All good citizens will hurry to re-establish confidence by re-opening their shops. The rainbow of true freedom will shine this morning on our town: may its light never be obscured. Long live true liberty!

Lyon, 23 November 1831

Source: Mazon, *Evénemens*, p. 25

– DOCUMENT 3.2: DESTITUTION –

Flora Tristan, a pioneering socialist-feminist, toured France in 1843–4. In May 1843 she visited the Croix-Rousse. Her description is written in the sentimental, heavily emotional style which was often favoured by early socialists. It presents a vivid picture of the silk-weavers' sense of destitution.

We entered a room which was at once a bedroom, a kitchen and a workshop. A woman was at one loom, a man at another. When he saw me, the man blushed: he was surprised. The woman also seemed very shocked. At first I did not understand why they were upset, and I tried to re-assure them about the purpose of my visit. The man got up, and I realised that he was almost naked. The poor man tried to cover his shoulders and neck with a vest which was the only thing he wore, and mumbled excuses. After a moment his wife, who was frowning, said to me in a despairing tone:

'My God, madame, how you surprised us ... My husband has just come back from the shop, where he delivered his work. His shirt was wet with sweat – it's there, drying on the window, and ... Well, madame, he can't put on another because ... because he hasn't got another one.'

As she finished speaking her voiced altered, as she strangled the sobs in her throat. She grasped her hands, gripped by the blackest despair. A moment of silent, poignant pain passed. The husband did not want me to see that he was crying, so he hid in the corner where the bed lay. Two or three neighbours came in, and were seized by a feeling which it is impossible to describe. As for me, I have that sense of calm which a wartime surgeon has to have, but I was shaken to my very being. My eyes filled with tears, despite my efforts to master my emotions.

For more than five minutes there was a silence that I must call terrifying. None of us spoke.

What could be said in front of such desperate poverty! Such pain! All at once the woman stepped into a little alcove, and drew out twenty or thirty pieces of yellowing paper. They were receipts from a pawn-shop.

'Look, madame,' she said in a stifled and trembling voice, 'look.'

'Why show this lady the proofs of our misery?' asked the husband in a voice which meant: what can she do?

'I want to show this lady,' shouted the wife, 'that we weren't always so poor, that this isn't our fault, that in the time when good workers could earn their living we had shirts, and underclothes, but since then it's been impossible for good, hard-working people to earn more than their bread, even if they work eighteen hours a day. We pawned our shirts to pay the rent, to buy coal, and so on.'

This women drew herself up. She was no longer crying, but in a threatening and terrifying voice she cried:

'Madame, things can't go on like this. We'd prefer to die fighting rather than to die of famine.'

The husband found his breath, and said to me in the same tone:

'I'm not scared of dying,' he said, 'I want to save my brothers from this dreadful poverty that's killing them, even if it means losing my life. I'm ready to go into the square and fight.'

Source: Flora Tristan, *Le Tour de France* [1843–4], Vol. I (Paris, 1980), pp. 156–8

– VI. FURTHER READING –

There are few English-language works on the silk-workers' revolt. The most useful is Robert J. Bezucha, *The Lyon Uprising of 1834: Social and Political Conflict in the early July Monarchy* (Cambridge, Massachusetts: Harvard UP, 1974) which, while concentrating on the April 1834 revolt, does discuss the 1831 revolt. W. D. Edmonds, *Jacobinism and the Revolt of Lyon, 1789–93* (Oxford: Oxford UP, 1990) provides useful information on the preceding decades. Georges Ribe, *L'Opinion publique et la vie politique à Lyon ... (1815–1822)*, (Paris: Sirey, 1957) is a useful guide to the early Restoration in Lyon. Fernand Rude has written several full-length studies of the November revolt. I have found his *C'est nous les canuts* (Paris: Maspero, 1977) the most useful: it presents a clear narrative of events.

There are many studies on working-class history and socialism in this period. Roger Magraw, *A History of the French Working Class, Vol. I: The Age of Artisan Revolution* (Oxford: Blackwell, 1992) provides a detailed overview. William H. Sewell, *Work and revolution in France: the language of labor from the old regime to 1848* (Cambridge: Cambridge UP, 1980) is a challenging discussion of the origins of socialism. See also Tony Judt's essay 'The French Labour Movement in the Nineteenth Century' in his *Marxism and the French Left* (Oxford: Oxford UP, 1986), and Bernard H. Moss, *The Origins of the French Labor Movement, 1830–1914* (Berkeley: California UP, 1976). Alain

Faure and Jacques Rancière (eds), *La Parole Ouvrière, 1830–51* (Paris: Bourgeois, 1976) is a valuable collection of primary texts. Mark Traugott (ed.), *The French Worker: Autobiographies from the early Industrial Era* (Berkeley and Los Angeles: California UP, 1993) is an extremely useful selection from a wide range of working-class autobiographies. Francophone readers should also listen to Malicorne's CD, *L'Extraordinaire Tour de France d'Adélard Rousseau* (BP9301 – 082301 – WM322): a spirited attempt to recreate the world of the *compagnonnage*. Alain Cottereau, 'La gestion du travail, entre utilitarisme heureux et éthique malheureuse', *Mouvement social* 175 (1996), 7–31 and 'Justice et injustice ordinaire sur les lieux de travail … (1806–66)', *Mouvement social* 141 (1987), 25–59 are detailed studies of the new work relations.

Tessie P. Liu's *The Weaver's Knot: the Contradictions of Class Struggle and Family Solidarity in Western France, 1750–1914* (Ithaca, New York: Cornell UP, 1994) contains only one reference to Lyon, but is still a thoughtful examination of weaving families and includes a far fuller consideration of gender than I have been able to present here. To this should be added E. P. Thompson, 'The Moral Economy of the English Crowd in the Eighteenth Century' in his *Customs in Common* (Harmondsworth: Penguin, 1993) which also makes no mention of Lyon, but does contain some extremely lucid thoughts about pre-industrial forms of social protest.

The 1832 cholera epidemic intensified class tensions across France. A useful study of its effects is: François Delaporte, *Le Savoir de la maladie: essai sur le choléra de 1832 à Paris* (Paris: PUF, 1990). Orleanist schooling policy is discussed in my 'What is a School? – Defining and Controlling Primary Schooling in early nineteenth century France', *History of Education* 21 (1992), 129–47.

– NOTES –

1. *Voyage de Jérôme Lippomano, ambassadeur de Venise en France en 1577*, in Jean Goulemot, Paul Lidsky and Didier Masseau (eds), *Le Voyage en France, Vol. I* (Paris: Bouquins, 1995), pp. 109–33 (p. 124).
2. Robert J. Bezucha, *The Lyon Uprising of 1834: Social and Political Conflict in the Early July Monarchy* (Cambridge, Mass.: Harvard UP, 1974), p. 7.
3. W. D. Edmonds, *Jacobinism and the Revolt of Lyon, 1789–93* (Oxford: Oxford UP, 1990), p. 300.
4. Bezucha, *Lyon Uprising*, p. 13.
5. Bezucha, *Lyon Uprising*, p. 242.
6. Villermé, *Tableau de l'état physique et moral des ouvriers* (Paris: Renouard, 1840), pp. 363–5.
7. J.-F. Bunet, *Tableau historique, administratif et industriel de la ville de la Croix-Rousse* (La Croix-Rousse: Lepagnez, 1842), p. 22.
8. Anon., 'Statistique: Revue politique de Lyon', *Archives historiques et statistiques du département du Rhône* 13 (1830–1), pp. 81–92 (p. 82).

9. J.-B. Monfalcon, *La Révolte des canuts* (Toulouse: Eché, 1979), p. 32.

10. Mornard, *Une Semaine de révolution: ou, Lyon en 1830* (Lyon: Idt, 1831), p. 6.

11. Fernand Rude, *C'est nous les canuts* (Paris: Maspero, 1977), pp. 9–10.

12. Bezucha, *Lyon Uprising*, p. 101.

13. Bezucha, *Lyon Uprising*, p. 59.

14. For example, ADR, 4.M.209, report dated 27 March 1831.

15. Petition in ADR, 4.M.209.

16. ADR, 4.M.209, letter, 16 March 1831.

17. ADR, 4.M.209, police report, 18 October 1831.

18. ADR, 4.M.209, police report, 13 October 1831.

19. ADR, 4.M.209, police report, 22 October 1831.

20. Bezucha, *Lyon Uprising*, p. 25.

21. Casimir Périer's interpretation of the events was given in his speech to the Chamber of Deputies in December 1831 and subsequently printed as *Discours prononcés à la Chambre de Députés* (Paris: Imprimerie Royale, 1831).

22. ADR 4.M.209, letter dated 4 November 1831.

23. J. F. R. Mazon, *Evénemens de Lyon, ou les trois journées de novembre 1831* (Lyon: Guyot, 1831), p. 7.

24. ADR, 4.M.209, letters dated 5 November 1831.

25. ADR, 4.M.209, letter, 20 November 1831.

26. Rude, *C'est nous*, p. 30.

27. Mazon, *Evénemens*, p. 8.

28. Rude, *C'est nous*, p. 77.

29. Quoted in Rude, *C'est nous*, p. 63.

30. Mazon, *Evénemens*, p. 23.

31. Telegram in ADR, 4.M.209.

32. ADR, 4.M.209, letter, 24 November 1831.

33. ADR, 4.M.209, 24 November 1831.

34. Karl Marx, 'The Manifesto of the Communist Party' in *Selected Works in Three Volumes*, Vol. I (Moscow: Progress, 1977), pp. 114–15.

35. Roger Magraw, *A History of the French Working Class, Vol. I* (Oxford: Blackwell, 1992), p. 65.

36. J. F. Barraud, 'Etrennes d'un prolétaire' in Alain Faure and Jacques Rancière (eds), *La Parole ouvrière* (Paris: Bourgeois, 1976), pp. 56–73.

37. Undated list in the AML, Documents Gasparin, Vol. X.

38. Monfalcon, *La Révolte*, p. 99.

39. Circular in ADR, 4.M.209.

CHAPTER 4

La Vendée, 1832: Monarchy and Revolution

The *bocage* stretches across western France: it is a gentle, rolling countryside, criss-crossed by streams, low hills and hedges. When Dumouriez, a prominent republican general, toured this area in 1792, he remarked that this would be the best region in France for a civil war.[1] The *bocage* was too irregular to allow the use of cavalry or artillery, and its valleys and hedges provided ample hiding spaces. Rapid movement of troops was difficult, for there were few roads. In the decades which followed, the accuracy of Dumouriez's observation was proved several times over.

Bazoges-en-Pailliers was a small commune in the *bocage*. There was nothing remarkable about it: about six hundred people lived there in the 1830s, some in a central village, many in the small hamlets characteristic of this region. Rather than searching for its special features, it is easier to list what Bazoges did not possess: it had no school, no priest, no tax office, no lawyer and no policeman. There was a church, but even this was only a *surcursale*: a part-time church opened irregularly by a visiting priest. However, even in this little commune, there was economic development. Many of the inhabitants were both farmers and artisans, and the commune had two annual fairs, held on the third Thursdays of April and June.[2]

Something extraordinary happened here on 6 June 1832. At mid-morning, around nine or ten a.m., thirty armed men arrived. They entered the church and sounded the *toscin* – the repeated ringing of the church bell which signalled an emergency. When the villagers gathered in the square, the armed men selected the younger males. Some were given old guns, others were told to bring hunting weapons. The villagers remained in the main square, while the armed men toured the surrounding hamlets, bursting into cottages, looking for young men, and then forcing them at gunpoint or swordpoint to follow. They went into the mayor's house, threatened him and smashed his statue of Louis-Philippe.

At least six men went with them.[3] Later, when questioned by a judge, each claimed that he had been forced to follow. The six were:

René Boudard, 42 years old, a carpenter
Pierre Chapeleau, 21, a weaver
Pierre Chauvrière, 37, a shoemaker
Antoine Congnon, 32, a weaver
Pierre Gaillard, 22, a grocer
Henri Guiberd, 22, a baker.

They left Bazoges around midday. Gaillard carried a stick, Congnon an old gun, Boudard a hunting gun. The mayor remembered 'they looked sad' as they left. The band then called on the neighbouring commune of Beaupaire and went through the same procedure of ordering out the young men.

By the afternoon their group was two hundred strong. Sentries patrolled, preventing the unwilling from leaving. At no point were they told why they had been gathered together: were they to fight the National Guard? Was there a connection with the debarkation of the Duchess of Berry in Marseille? Some shouted 'long live Henry V!' as they marched northwards, but most were silent. In the evening they reached St Aubin, where they were lodged in an inn, given food and drink and more arms were distributed. Some of the reluctant rebels slipped away during the night.

The next morning they were drawn up in two lines. As Boudard was later to put it, 'someone I didn't recognise inspected us'. Then they marched out to face the National Guard.

What was happening here? Was this a revolution? The answer is found in one word: this happened in La Vendée.

– I. PARTICIPANTS –

On hearing the word 'Vendée', most French people would have thought that they understood these events. It was a term loaded with memories, passions and much bitterness; it evoked a legend to be related by grandparents to their grandchildren.

The term 'Vendée' was used at different times to refer to three separate areas. Prior to 1789, La Vendée was a sub-province of the western province of 'Poitou'; it possessed a cluster of administrative institutions which gave it some distinct political identity. In 1790, when the old patchwork of provinces and regions was reorganised into eighty-five new departments, La Vendée was the name given to a western coastal department, south of the Loire river and the city of Nantes. This use of the same name for a pre-Revolutionary province and a department is unusual: none of the other new departments recycled old names. Lastly, the third meaning of this word refers to what historians have termed the 'military Vendée': the area which revolted against the conscription organised by Jacobin Paris in 1793. The rebels were to be found in the eastern and north-western parts of the Vendée department; there were also major rebellions in the neighbouring departments of Deux-Sèvres, Maine-et-Loire and the Loire-Inférieure, and violent incidents across Brittany.

In the 'military Vendée' the rebellion of 1793 initially took the form of battles between peasant militias and republican armies. To the north, over the Loire river, and in the western departments of Brittany, resistance took another form, termed 'chouannerie'. This word originated from the rebels' signals, which imitated the calls of owls. The Chouans realised that battles with professional armies would be disastrous: instead, they acted as guerrillas, harassing republican authorities. As the rebellion persisted, the Vendéens' military confrontations tended to be replaced in all twelve rebel departments by the Chouans' scattered violence, which soon became barely distinguishable from ordinary brigandage.

Jacobin Paris never forgave the west for this rebellion. Following the military defeat of the Vendéens in 1794, military forces exacted revenge. This resulted in some of the worst savagery seen during the Revolution. Armed soldiers, organised in columns, stormed through the defeated and largely unarmed areas, engaged in deliberate, systematic destruction: burning houses and crops, killing old people and children, raping women, stealing food and drink. The effects of such actions were traumatic. Even simple population figures give a grim indication of the force of this revenge. In 1791, 305 381 people lived in the department of La Vendée; by 1806 there were only 268 646. At least thirty-six thousand died because of the repression: the final total may have been as high as forty-four thousand.[4]

This revolt remains mysterious. Initial explanations were emotionally charged. Republicans argued that it was an act of treachery, organised by conspiratorial minorities of priests and aristocrats, who exploited the peasants' naïvety and ignorance. Counter-revolutionary historians produced a mirror-image of such interpretations: the Vendéens were noble, idealistic Catholics who, horrified with the Revolution, revolted for Church and King. A pamphlet published by Chateaubriand in 1822 popularised this idea of the 'holy' Vendée. During the Revolution

> La Vendée stayed Christian and Catholic; therefore, the monarchist spirit still lived in this corner of France. God seemed to have preserved this model of society to teach us how a people to whom God has given laws is stronger than a people who legislate for themselves.[5]

During the nineteenth century, the debate about the rebellion was fixed along these lines, with republicans and monarchists trading insults. In the twentieth century, with the development of social history, new interpretations emerged (see Further reading).

Social historians noted that the priests and nobles were barely involved in the start of the rebellion. The controversial religious reforms initiated by the Revolutionary assemblies in 1791, which were rejected by about half the priests of France, did not initiate the rebellion. The amateurish aristocratic conspiracies of 1792 aroused little popular sympathy. It was the conscription of 1793 which ignited the rebellion. Social historians also stressed that this was essentially a rural rebellion against the towns. In the whole of the west, not a single town sided with the rebels. A new interpretation emerged: according to social historians, the rebellion was not a holy crusade for Church and King, nor an example of mass ignorance, but a popular anti-bourgeois movement, motivated by a deep hatred of the relatively rich urban people who stole the promised benefits of the Revolution from the rural people.

During Napoleon's Empire, censorship prevented debate about the rebellion, and Napoleon took steps to encourage the 'rallying' of the Vendée to the Imperial cause. In other words, during the 1800s, the department's image as a monarchist Holy Land was not fixed. After the Restorations of 1814 and 1815, a flood of memoirs and histories were published. They established the legend of the Catholic and monarchist rebellion. In the department itself, priests encouraged this interpretation. An informal network of memorials and pilgrimage places developed to commemorate the rebellion.[6]

The Vendée had suffered after the rebellion, and the hard-pressed Empire was unable to take effective measures to encourage its revival. The number of priests in the department gives an indication of its condition: there had been around eight hundred in 1790, by 1815 there were only 194[7] – the Empire's one significant gesture to establish a new departmental capital. The broken village of La Roche-sur-Yon was chosen in 1804, and was slowly built up in the following decades. Its municipal council requested – and was granted – a new name: Napoléon-Ville. However, few rural people benefited. In the countryside there were still impoverished Chouans who felt a strong emotional loyalty to their cause, and who passed their political passions on to their children. They demonstrated their loyalty by taking up arms against Napoleon in 1813 (as a new mass conscription drive was launched) and in 1815 (during the Hundred Days).

Such Vendéens expected much from the Restoration. They wanted the monarchy to restore the department's economic position, but more importantly they also wanted redress for the violence they had suffered following 1793.

Louis XVIII promised pensions to all who had contributed to the royalist cause during the Revolution, and to their families, widows and orphans. By the 1820s many Vendéens were receiving some form of state allowance. In 1815 Napoléon-Ville was renamed Bourbon-Vendée, but such gestures were not enough to satisfy the Vendéens. What else could the Restoration do to integrate this department into the body of France? There were two principal instruments available: the Church and the monarchy.

The Church did not recover from the Revolution until the mid-nineteenth century. In the early Restoration, Catholic orders pioneered a new Catholic faith: condemnatory of the Revolution, pessimistic about the human condition and hostile to social and cultural progress. This new faith was spearheaded by aggressive missions which toured France, supplementing the efforts of hard-pressed priests to win the population back to Catholicism. When a mission arrived in town, theatres were closed and dances cancelled. Processions marched through the town, and adults were encouraged to attend dramatic sermons, in which prayers were said for the conversion of Protestants, usury condemned and the Inquisition defended. Preachers aimed to create an emotional effect, sometimes, for example, holding their sermons in cemeteries at sunset, in order to encourage a 'collective repentance for the sins of the French Revolution'.[8] The climax of the missions' visit was the construction of huge oak crosses, forty or fifty feet high, which were carried by a procession, and placed opposite the homes of those who had bought Church property during the Revolution.

These missions could be seen as 'educational', for they sought to re-educate people who had not received religious instruction during the Revolution. However, they were suspicious of all learning and literacy. In some missions, books were publicly burnt. Such ideas were typical of Restoration Catholicism, which opposed faith (represented by the Church) to reason (represented by the Enlightenment and Revolution). The Count de Bonald, a prominent ultra-royalist philosopher, raged against 'the growing number of impious books, seditious books, obscene books. They are printed, advertised, sold, lent, given *even to kitchenmaids*.'[9]

This type of repressive thinking was applied in the Vendée. For example, in 1826 its General Council expressed concern about the poor salaries paid to priests, and called for the establishment of a women's teaching congregation. Furthermore, 'the Council, concerned by the ever-growing propagation of evil books [*mauvais livres*] which will ... cause the dissolution of social order, asks the Government for efficient actions to end this flood.'[10] In the context of the Vendée, this pronouncement is rather strange. This was supposedly the department which, according to Chateaubriand, had been created by God as an example to the rest of France. The words of the General Council suggest that, notwithstanding the myth of the Catholic and royalist crusade of 1793, there was the same hostility shown by élites to popular culture here as elsewhere. In other words, Catholicism did not reintegrate the people of the Vendée into the mainstream of French political culture. What of the monarchy?

The Restoration monarchy seemed to accept the department's special status. While Louis XVIII never visited it, there were five separate visits by members of the royal family between 1814 and 1830. Most of these were disappointing. After more than twenty years of exile, royal visitors were disarmingly incompetent when faced by a crowd, even a sympathetic one. When the Duke of Angoulême, the King's nephew, visited in July 1815, he forbade all processions by armed Chouans. In other words, he refused to see precisely the people who most wanted to demonstrate their loyalty! His speeches reflected Louis XVIII's priorities: he spoke of the need to forget the past, to reconcile enemies and to avoid political passions. This careful approach provoked a devastating response from one priest: 'Vive le roi, quand même!' or 'long live the King, all the same'. In other words, a half-hearted, moderate monarch would only attract half-hearted, moderate support. The priest's words summed up the mixed feelings of many ultra-royalists and Vendéens, and were repeated by disillusioned ultras across France.

There was a gap between the cautious ideals of the restored monarchy and the rough, memory-sodden, political culture of the Vendéens. The visits by these nervous, prudent princes only deepened this division. However, one visit by a member of the royal family was a success: a visit by the Duchess of Berry in 1828.

Marie-Caroline de Berry was twenty-nine in 1828, and already a controversial figure.[11] Unlike her royal relations, she had not experienced any deep personal trauma during the Revolution and Empire. Her marriage to the Duke of Berry, Louis XVIII's younger nephew, was arranged by their respective families in 1816: she was seventeen, he was thirty-eight. Their marriage initially conformed to the pre-Revolutionary view of marriage, uniting as it did two households, rather than joining two individuals. Her principal duty was to provide the ageing Bourbon monarchy with a male heir. She arrived in the south of France in 1816, and began her slow, ceremonial journey from Marseille to Paris to meet her bridegroom. Her journey introduced her to two cultures. One was the old, revived culture of formal public display. Each town on her route would welcome her as a new member of the royal family. However, at the same time, she was receiving love letters from her husband-to-be, written in the new language of romantic love.

Following their marriage, the Berrys briefly acquired a reputation similar to that of some of the British royal family in the 1980s: they were modern royals, willing to break with stuffy traditions. In a court of ageing aristocrats, loyal to a half-remembered pre-Revolutionary culture, they were rebels against convention. Their public behaviour was particularly shocking: they held hands and spoke to each other using the intimate '*tu*' form, instead of the formal '*vous*'. All these gestures suggested a romantic, loving marriage, in the new nineteenth-century pattern. They attended the theatre and dances together, and the Duchess wore fashionable clothes. Such behaviour attracted attention and criticism. For example, in 1818 the Duchess gave birth to a son who died quickly afterwards. Some courtiers blamed her behaviour, and in particular her dancing, for his early death. The birth of a daughter, in September 1819, was a disappointment to monarchists who longed for a male heir.

The Berrys' cultural rebellion ended in 1820. On 12 February the Duke was stabbed as he left the Opéra. His wife leapt from her carriage when she saw his plight. He died in her arms the next day. The image of the Duchess running to help him was widely reproduced: it made a poignant picture and won her much sympathy. However, what of her political role? How could she now supply a legitimate male heir? The Duchess was already pregnant when her husband was killed. She gave birth to a boy in September 1820. This accumulation of images – the fun-loving wife, the tragic widow and the fortuitous mother – meant that the Duchess was fast becoming the most-noticed member of the Bourbon family. Her son was termed 'the child of the miracle', and her giving birth to him seemed to save the Bourbon monarchy from extinction.

After the Duke's death she remained in mourning and was rarely seen in public. Following Bourbon tradition, she had little contact with her children. Their future role as members of the royal family was judged more important than any emotional link with their mother. Under these circumstances, one might have expected that the Duchess would quietly retire into respectable obscurity.

However, the Duchess had other plans. She was a politically ambitious woman who intended to make the most of her position as mother of the future king. By 1824 she was once again seen frequently in public. She attended theatres, hosted dances and followed the new fashion of visiting the seaside. By 1826 she had effectively built a counter-court to the grave, formal court of Charles X. She even became a trendsetter, and accepted a position of patron to one of the first French fashion magazines, *La Mode*. In 1829 Liberal journalists began to cite her as an example of a 'new royal', representative of the type of monarchy which France needed in the nineteenth century. (See document 4.1.)

In July 1828 the Duchess visited La Vendée, the fifth member of the royal family to tour the department since 1814. By 1828, many Vendéens had grown disillusioned with the restored monarchy. They could see all too plainly how uneasy the Duke and Duchess d'Angoulême felt before a crowd of Chouans, they had heard their disappointing message of conciliation and there was widespread disillusion at the low level of pensions distributed to the old warriors. To their delight, the Duchess of Berry was different. She ignored protocol, and conducted what we might term 'walkabouts'. She was relaxed when talking to ordinary people, and seemed not only interested in their lives, but genuinely respectful of their history. At one point, as the Duchess was meeting a crowd, a woman said 'she's not very pretty'. The Duchess looked up, and retorted 'that's right, but she's good.' As she spoke, she threw her purse to her critic. The crowd cheered her action.[12] Perhaps this gesture does not seem very special, particularly when compared with the PR spectacles of the 1990s, but the key point is that no other member of the royal family would have been capable of such wit, such deftness, in front of an excited crowd.

It was clear that many Vendéens enjoyed her visit, and felt that at last their department had received the recognition it deserved. The department's general council expressed its sympathy for her: they approved plans to build a monument to commemorate her visit.[13] She herself carried away a deeper emotion. Compared to the cold formality of Charles X's court, or to the hostility which liberal Parisians were beginning to show the monarchy, the Vendée seemed quite different. She accepted at face value the Catholic and royalist myth of the crusade of 1793; she thought of the Vendée as the heartland of the French monarchy. On 31 July 1830, as the despairing Charles X watched the Bourbon monarchy collapse, the Duchess urged him to flee to the Vendée to raise an army.

– II. Events –

After the July 1830 Revolution, the Orleanists expected opposition from many quarters. As was seen in Chapter 3, police action was taken to prevent republican and working-class agitation in the cities. However, Orleanists were also concerned about opposition from the supporters of the old monarchy. Two regions in particular worried them. First, in the south, towns such as Toulouse and Nîmes were considered to be likely bases for opposition.[14] In these towns, rich aristocrats exerted strong powers of patronage over workers and peasants. They had watched the civil wars unfold in Spain during the 1820s, which opposed an absolutist monarchist faction – the Carlists – against a constitutional monarchy. Some southern ultra-royalists adopted the name of 'Carlists' to indicate their approval of violent methods of opposition.

Orleanists were also aware of the danger from the west. Pamphlets such as that written by Chateaubriand, which popularised the myth of a Catholic and royalist sanctuary, aroused Orleanist suspicions about the Vendée. However, there was little sign of opposition after July 1830. The biggest city in the region – Nantes, in the Loire-Inférieure – had revolted against the Bourbons independently of Paris. Soldiers were quickly transferred to the region; frequent and visible patrols seemed to intimidate opposition. In the words of the Vendée's prefect, the Orleanists' opponents were dominated by a 'healthy fear'.[15] As has been noted, the Vendéens had been disappointed by the Restoration monarchy: why should they defend it? Many ultra aristocrats were hostile to the new regime, but they expressed their opposition by resigning from official positions, rather than by sedition. Their actions followed the decision taken by the last supporters of Charles X in the Chamber of Deputies: approximately one hundred refused to take the new oath of loyalty to Louis-Philippe and so resigned their posts.[16]

The new local authorities in the Vendée effaced the fleur-de-lis from churches and flew tricolour flags from town halls. Following the calm summer, the first hint of trouble came with the enrolment of conscripts in the autumn of 1830. Because of the invasion of Algeria undertaken in the last weeks of Charles X's reign, and growing international tension, more young soldiers than usual were called up. Sixty-nine Vendéens refused conscription in 1830; 179 in 1831.[17] In November 1830 a sub-prefect reported to the Prefect: 'The conscripts' attitudes are less favourable that we had thought. There is a lot of movement, a lot of coming and going during the night … [It is rumoured that] the conscripts from the marshes are determined not to go.'[18] Local authorities began to note hostility to the new monarchy. As yet, these were only isolated incidents: there were no signs of mass rebellion.

The old dynasty had powerful supporters, but they were poorly organised. The first issue for the legitimists (as the supporters of the Bourbons were now known) to discuss was the parliamentary elections of July 1831. Should they put up candidates for election? Their debate on this question proved difficult: one problem was *how* to discuss it. Who was the proper representative of the Bourbons, and how was his (or her) opinion to be expressed? Such problems were exacerbated by Charles X's silence. There was no organised Legitimist Party, and no formal structure for debate. Legitimism was organised around an informal network of families and salons. Their political principles were based on a simple loyalty to the king, not a coherent programme (see document 4.2).

Their debate unfolded in papers which presented themselves as representatives of legitimist opinion. The *Quotidienne* resolutely opposed participation in elections; the *Gazette de France* expressed some limited sympathy; while only the *Courrier de l'Europe* was fully in favour. Following this inconclusive debate, there was no sustained legitimist campaign during the July 1831 parliamentary elections. Only two legitimists were elected: Berryer in Marseilles, and the Marquis de Gras-Béville for the Haute-Loire.[19]

The Duchess of Berry had followed Charles X into exile in Britain in August 1830. His court settled in Edinburgh. While his advisers advised caution, the Duchess argued for action. Potentially, she was in an extremely powerful position. Charles X had abdicated in favour of her son, now known to legitimists as Henry V. The Duchess proposed an insurrection, inspired by her romantic image of the Vendéen rebellion of 1793. In June 1831 she secretly left Scotland and travelled across Europe to Italy. There she contacted several minor Italian royal families, trying to raise support for her venture, and received visitors from France. The Austrian court expressed some sympathy for her cause: like many conservative monarchies of eastern Europe, they were concerned that the July 1830 Revolution might ignite revolutions across Europe, and disturbances in Belgium and the Netherlands seemed to prove their case.

French legitimist opinion was, once again, divided. Berryer, the Legitimist deputy from Marseilles, visited the Vendée in June 1831 to act as lawyer in defence of a deserter. He had noted the strength of feeling against the July Monarchy, and was won over to the idea of a revolt. There seemed to be some support for a rebellion in the department: aristocratic families, old Vendéen leaders, and sometimes the children of the leaders from 1793, all expressed sympathy. However, many prominent legitimists were critical: Chateaubriand, Fitz-James, and other Paris-based politicians all warned against civil war. During the first months of 1832 some legitimists had tried to organise a conspiracy in Paris, and had even contacted Bonapartists and republicans. Their plot had been uncovered, and the resulting publicity, which seemed to reveal that the legitimists were unprincipled agitators, had done their cause no favours.

The Duchess continued with her plans. On 28 April 1832 she sailed from north Italy to southern France. She had believed that the south was ready for a legitimist rising, and expected two thousand soldiers to serve her. In reality, only sixty unarmed men arrived. In a farcical gesture, this tiny group marched on Marseille and were promptly dispersed after the arrest of their leader.[20] Instead of calling off her venture, the Duchess decided to cross France, and to attempt a second rising in the Vendée.

A network of conspirators helped her travel. She announced a date for the uprising: the night of 23–4 May. On 17 May she reached the Vendée. Twenty thousand proclamations had been printed by sympathisers (see document 4.3); arms and ammunition had been stored. However, the Vendéens' reactions were disappointing. The Duchess found that trustworthy legitimists and Vendéen chiefs were reluctant to join her rebellion. One point that was frequently made was that in 1793 the peasants had demanded that aristocrats lead them; in 1832, it was aristocrats who were calling the peasants to rise. Berryer arrived from Paris. He was undecided about the revolt, but the message from the Parisian legitimist leaders was clear: they were against it. By 22 May this disillusionment was reaching the Duchess herself. She reluctantly agreed to follow Berryer's advice. The insurrection was called off.

On 24 May the Duchess changed her mind.[21] She rediscovered her faith in the Vendée, and she may have believed that legitimists in the south had revolted. She announced that the uprising was to start on the night of 3–4 June.

The previous signal to cancel the uprising planned for 23–4 May had not reached all the Vendéen chiefs. There were some disturbances in the department: not enough to damage the July Monarchy, but enough to alert the police and army. On 4 June a few thousand peasants responded to the Duchess's call. More were raised in the following days, by the methods described in the first pages of this chapter. Astonishingly, the men drafted in Bazoges won a battle. Despite being met at St Aubin by a large contingent of the National Guard, they fixed bayonets in their muskets and charged. The National Guard scattered. Their panic in the face of this improvised band is difficult to understand: perhaps memories of 1793 were enough to terrify them. The Duchess remained in hiding until 7 November, when she was arrested in Nantes. It seemed that Louis-Philippe had won; the last battle of the Chouans was over.

Although the forces led by the Duchess were unable to win a sustained campaign, the Orleanist monarchy was not yet safe. Family traditions, royalist memories and simple hostility to the new monarchy remained strong in the Vendée. Feelings ran particularly high in the rural, agricultural canton of Pouzauges, which lay on the department's eastern border, and had suffered some of the worst fighting during 1793–4. Although there was little military activity in this canton during the revolt of May–June 1832, there was persistent unrest throughout the early years of the July Monarchy. The Prefect's 1833 report noted that in Pouzauges 'acts of brigandage are so common that a week rarely goes by without three or four reports being sent to the authorities'.[22]

Opposition to the July Monarchy was based around deserters. A group of young men refusing conscription had gathered in Pouzauges canton during 1831.[23] Often local people, including parents and relatives, sympathised with them and gave them food and clothes.[24] They would also alert deserters when soldiers approached. For example, a group of eighteen soldiers called at the farm of La Brosse in January 1833. As they approached, dogs started to bark. Jean Jadant, a sixty-nine year old peasant, looked up. When he saw the soldiers, he whistled loudly. Two men came out of a farm building, put their clogs on, and ran off. When Jadant was questioned by the soldiers, he told them that he had seen nothing.[25]

Even before the Duchess's expedition, many in the canton were hostile to the July Monarchy. In March 1831 young royalists gathered in a cabaret to sing a song with a chorus of 'Louis-Philippe is a pig'. Then they shouted 'long live the king!' with all their force.[26] Ordinary farm labourers voiced similar opinions. They would tell conscripts: 'ordinary soldiers don't even get a *sou* a day, while the Chouans, they're properly armed and they earn twenty *sous* a day.'[27] New Orleanist officials were also targets. In January 1831, Louis Batrand was arrested after uttering threats in a cabaret about the new Mayor of Pouzauges.[28]

The Orleanist authorities' solution was to billet soldiers in problem areas. In Pouzauges, this often had the opposite effect from that desired. Soldiers posted in Boupère commune were approached by Chouan sympathisers. A woman who owned a tavern would stand soldiers free drinks, and would offer to buy their uniforms and to supply them with other clothes if they would desert. Even a local aristocrat tried to persuade soldiers to desert. He offered them wine and then asked detailed questions about the army.[29] Significantly, while there is no evidence that the Church actively supported these men, priests did not help the authorities. One deserter was considering joining a band of Chouans. He went to confession, and asked the priest his advice. 'Do want you want' was the reply.[30]

Having refused conscription, or deserted, these men would join Chouan bands who did not simply hide from the authorities, but actively attempted to subvert the area. They would disguise themselves as hunters, and then tour the countryside, seeking to indoctrinate 'the poor rural people'.[31] The roads were unsafe, particularly for officials. The cantonal postman was stopped in September 1832 by a band of Chouans who robbed him of seven francs and his boots.[32] A local tax-collector suffered worse: he lost six hundred francs.[33] Three hunters met a group of five armed Chouans in the canton: they were chased by the Chouans, who stole one of their guns.[34] Chouans picked on other targets: when someone shot at a Protestant in Boupère, Chouans were immediately suspected.[35] Most sinister of all, Chouans would break into the houses of isolated officials. The Mayor of Meilleraie-la-Tilley suffered this in September 1833: in the middle of the night, gunshots rang out and fists hammered on his front door. Eight armed Chouans burst in. They smashed his goods, drank his wine, ate his bread, ham, cheese and butter, and stole 299 francs.[36] Three Chouans broke into the house of Mayor of St Michel-

Mont-Mercure in August 1833: they wrecked his garden and beat up his servant.[37]

Under such circumstances, the authorities grew suspicious of anyone who might have Chouan sympathies. The National Guard claimed that Grenon, a carpenter, deliberately wore clothes in Chouan colours (usually green and white), and that he had shouted subversive slogans in a cabaret. Grenon's defence was that he had been drunk, and could not remember what he had said. He said people mistook him for a Chouan because he wore a big hat.[38]

Such factors made Pouzauges a difficult canton for Orleanists to live in. Many felt intimidated. After he was robbed, the tax-collector felt so scared that he wanted to resign.[39] Mayors were reluctant to ask for police protection 'for fear of assassination. This panic which is caused by the mere mention of the word "Chouan" makes it impossible to crack down on these thefts. This panic is more than justified by the cruel revenge attacks that they carry out.'[40] Such pressures placed severe strains on local administration. In 1833, the Prefect had to cancel one in ten local elections, because of the intimidation which voters and candidates experienced.[41] Posting small groups of soldiers in each problem commune could end open resistance, but such soldiers could not be everywhere at once.[42]

How was such a cycle of violence to be ended? The authorities, faced with this long-running feud, called for strict punishments. However, this in itself could merely perpetuate the resistance. Deserters were reluctant to give themselves up for fear of punishment.[43] Priests and mayors were often awkward intermediaries in a difficult process of negotiation between the central departmental authorities in Bourbon-Vendée, and the deserters and bands who hid in the hamlets and woods.

Pouzauges is perhaps not typical of the department, and is certainly not typical of western France. None the less, its history does identify some of the difficulties which the Orleanist administration faced. While the Duchess's attempt at outright rebellion was a laughable failure, her perception that there was something distinctive about the department was not so foolish. The Vendée did sustain movements of deep, widespread hostility to the July Monarchy. Some figures from January 1833 demonstrate this point. The Prefect estimated that over the previous twelve months there had been four assassinations, seven attacks resulting in severe wounds, twenty-six cases of armed break-ins, and twenty-six thousand francs stolen: in each incident Chouans were suspected.[44] People throughout the department were scared. When one policeman was ordered to investigate a Chouan crime, he wearily warned his superior 'don't expect us to find a single witness'.[45]

In Pouzauges, confrontation with the July Monarchy often took the form of violent clashes. Elsewhere in the department, anti-Orleanist sentiment was a more diffuse matter, centred on symbols and rumours. For example, the National Guardsmen of La Brussière were worried by the new Orleanist administration's actions. In March 1831, thirteen of them discussed the matter, and then resigned en masse. They claimed that the last straw was the effacing of fleurs-de-lis from a local monument. The Mayor was puzzled by their actions, and told the Prefect: 'these are weak men, who have been provoked and excited by their wives and their sisters ... This is the result of what they have been told at confession, joined with the deadly advice of the white [Chouan] bands.'[46] When the Luçon bishop visited Dompierre in June 1836, the procession which greeted him carried a large silver cross, decorated with fleurs-de-lis. Was this a deliberate act of provocation by the priest? Or was he simply using his best cross? The local police force were certainly suspicious: 'such acts only serve to encourage vain hopes among the peasantry'.[47] Another common signal of Chouan sympathies was the white flag. In November 1833, one appeared in the night, set up opposite the Mayor's house in Bernadière.[48] Bearing in mind the Chouans' attacks on officials' homes, it was easy to see what this implied.

One of the most mysterious aspects of the Chouans' revolt was the minting of what may have been counterfeit coins with Henry V's insignia, or simply commemorative medals which resembled coins. They were certainly circulating in the department: in June 1836 Reveiller attended a fair at Bourbon-Vendée. When he returned home and examined his change, he found one of these strange coins, which he reported to the police.[49] In July 1838 a tobacconist was interviewed by the police when one was found in the money he gave the tax-collector.[50] He claimed that he had not noticed it. It is difficult to know why these coins were circulated: were they intended to make naïve country people think that Henry V had become king? Or were they a form of 'economic warfare' which was designed to disconcert the Orleanist businessmen?

One last example shows how intensely politicised the department became. One night in March 1831 a National Guard unit was on patrol in Châtaigneraie. They saw two men walking along a street. 'Who goes there?' they cried out, several times. Eventually an answer came back: 'shit!'[51] They were arrested, and accused of Chouan sympathies. In the Vendée, even a common swearword seemed to carry political connotations.

These examples suggest a quite different form of political culture from the glorious crusade which the Duchess of Berry had hoped to lead. Legitimism in the Vendée was an aggressive movement, based on threats, rumours and physical clashes. An informal political culture connected legitimist agitators, deserters, Chouan bands and the wider population – the farmhands, parents, gossips – in a common movement of hostility to the July Monarchy.

– III. Political culture –

Did any political principle unite these thieves, gossips and political romantics? One response can be found in the interrogations of witnesses and sympathisers, when they were asked direct questions about their political perceptions. For example, in December 1831 Jeanne Mertet was accused of supplying her son, a deserter, with bread, butter, clean shirts and well-darned socks. She protested that she had not acted for any political motive. The judge then asked her 'Isn't your son a Chouan?'. Her hesitant reply was 'Yes, if by that you mean that he is a deserter.'[52] Jean Faucheron was arrested in June 1832 after shouting rebel slogans in a cabaret. His defence was the usual one: he was drunk, and could not remember what he had said. The Judge then asked what he understood by the words 'Carlist' and 'liberal'. 'Carlists go to church often,' he replied, 'and liberals are people like you, who join the National Guard.'[53]

These simple replies suggest how closely the rebel Chouan culture had become merged into the 'normal' popular culture of the countryside. No sophisticated political arguments emerge, just a sense of separation of the rural people from 'people like you'. First, attitudes to the Church and then, second, ideals about the monarchy had become the dividing line between the villages and the towns. Such simple ideas of 'us and them' probably existed in most rural departments. What made the Vendée different was that this perception was articulated through Chouannerie. Significantly, legitimist propaganda often emphasised simple themes like taxes and trade – 'the poor will be happy' – rather than attempting to put forward ethical or philosophical arguments. (See document 4.4.) Such crude expressions of political culture are light-years away from the sophisticated writing of Berryer and Chateaubriand. None the less, is it possible to identify any common themes?

Chateaubriand did not understand the basis of the July Monarchy. He had lived through the Jacobins' rule, and while he opposed democracy, he recognised that the Jacobins had created a government. But what was the July Monarchy?

> What we have today is not a republic, nor a monarchy; not legitimacy, nor illegitimacy; it is a half-thing which takes in everything and nothing, which does not live and does not die; it is a theft without a thief, a day without a dusk and without a tomorrow.[54]

The July Monarchy, he argued, was the reign of eunuchs, of amphibians, of creatures who belonged to no coherent political tradition.[55] As it had no consistency, it would not be able to survive. Such arguments denied the need for an organised legitimist opposition, for the July Monarchy would be pulled down by its own internal contradictions.

Many shared these doubts. Some far-sighted legitimists were particularly concerned about social cohesion; events such as the November 1831 revolt in Lyon seemed to be a warning. Sometimes, their ideas almost anticipated socialist thinking. According to Villeneuve-Bargemont, the society created by the July Monarchy lacked human feeling: it ignored the plight of the factory workers who were suffering from what Villeneuve-Bargemont termed the 'deadly influence of the English political and industrial system'. The only cure was a revival of Christian values. 'A new phase of Christianity is needed. Only Christian charity, put into practice in politics, laws, institutions, and customs can save the social order.'[56] Villeneuve-Bargemont criticised the new industrial spirit, but his solution was not to empower the working class. Instead, he appealed to the conscience of factory-owners and political leaders. A hierarchy of orders was part of the great order of the universe. It could not be abolished, but it could work so that the rich took better care of the poor.

This type of thinking was quite different from the censorious, repressive Catholicism of the missions. It appealed to humanitarian feelings, it spoke of love, of caring; it was termed 'Social Catholicism'. Many prominent thinkers were influenced by it. However, it was very different from the violence of Chouannerie. One could argue that both streams of thought shared a common allegiance to a 'closed', backward-looking society without an industrial bourgeoisie, bound by tight communal controls over economic and cultural activities. However, beyond this basic similarity, the two movements were quite distinct.

The Parisian legitimists found it difficult to support the Duchess's revolt. Chateaubriand repudiated all conspiracies, pointing out that after forty years of political turmoil, not a single conspiracy had ever succeeded. Rather than seeing the Vendée as the vanguard of monarchism, he argued, it should be understood as an 'armed camp at rest'.[57] This careful phrase speaks volumes. Legitimists simply could not imagine their leadership of a peasant rebellion, let alone the idea of a restoration of the monarchy being produced by an insurrection. During the Restoration they had popularised the *image* of the Vendée as a holy land for the monarchy, but they were horrified by a real uprising. They preferred to present the Vendée of 1793 as an ideal, comfortably far away in space and time, rather than to accept the Vendée of 1832 as a real political force.

Early in 1833 the final divorce between legitimist leaders and the Duchess took place. While she was held in prison, it became obvious that she was pregnant. Wild rumours circulated as to the father of the child and it was finally revealed that she had married a minor Italian aristocrat before returning to France. While this man was a noble, he was too obscure to be acceptable to the rank-conscious legitimists.

– IV. Legacy –

As an ideal, legitimism lingered on for a remarkably long time. Legitimist thinking experienced a revival in the 1870s, influenced movements in the Third Republic (see Chapter 11), and was arguably a force within the Vichy government of 1940–4. Legitimists were largely unable to influence government policies; however, their ideal guided and instructed many people. Legitimism's great strength was that it suggested solutions to social problems.

One reason for this lingering influence was a type of quasi-feminism. Legitimists did not campaign for women's political rights, but they often adopted positive attitudes to female activism. The 1832 revolt had a woman as its leader, even if she was acting in her son's name. The Duchess's appeal was heard by many aristocratic women who acted as recruiting agents and, sometimes, leaders. Among the rural people, women sustained the movement: mothers and wives like Jeanne Mertet were needed to provide food and to carry messages. Often it was these women who sustained the memories of previous struggles, and who passed them down the generations. There was even a distinct women's history of 1793, in which women had played an active part in fighting.

While the Revolution had opened up enormous political possibilities for men, largely through the institutionalisation of representative, if not democratic, politics, it actually closed down female forms of politics. In response to this, many women turned (rather than 'returned') to the Church as the institution to represent their interests. While organisational power remained firmly in the hands of male ecclesiastical officials, the tone of religious culture changed: paternalism replaced patriarchy. A religion which spoke of love and redemption replaced the hellfire preaching of the missions. Philosophers increasingly claimed the language of rationality and individualism as masculine; therefore, when the church began to talk in terms of community, charity and care, it could be seen as 'feminine'.

This point also applies to recruitment patterns. Table 4.1 shows that male recruitment into the priesthood was severely damaged by the Revolution. However, female recruitment into 'congregations', which worked in areas such as hospitals, schools and prisons, continued to grow, and expanded massively during the nineteenth century. These figures suggest that women wanted to enter the Church and were more willing to do so than men. Such tendencies can also be found in church attendance: the majority of churchgoers were women.[59]

Table 4.1: Comparative numbers of priests and members of female
congregations in France[58]

	Priests	Female Congregations
1789	60 000	*c.*8 000
1808–09	32 000	12 343
1830–31	32 580	31 000
1848	39 025	
1851		35 000★

★ probably an underestimate

The combination of a 'femininised' Church culture, and widespread female participation in Catholic institutions, created a longlasting alternative to the eventually dominant republican political culture.

Another general point can be gained from our study of the Vendée. The July Monarchy is often referred to in disparaging terms. According to legend, it was a 'bourgeois monarchy', ruled by a king who carried an umbrella, and it initiated the rule of a caste of uncaring, money-obsessed industrialists. This study has shown a different aspect of Orleanism: in cantons like Pouzauges it took real courage to be an Orleanist. It meant being prepared to face Chouan aggression; it meant living with constant intimidation from bandits, aristocrats and, sometimes, priests. Such Orleanists adopted a distinctive radical political culture of their own: not the social radicalism associated with the quasi-socialist republican left, but a militant hostility against the Church and aristocracy.

This form of radicalism remained strong in the western towns throughout the nineteenth century: not socialist, not even necessarily democratic, but vigorously republican. It is often called 'blue' radicalism, from the colour of the republican soldiers' uniforms in the 1790s. One example can be cited from Bourbon-Vendée itself. In 1830, when its total population was about three thousand, no less than five hundred men enrolled in the town's National Guard.[60]

Most of the Vendée's towns followed this pattern: they were 'blue' islands in a sea of legitimist white. Throughout the July Monarchy they successfully resisted the legitimists. If one examines the Vendée's bigger towns, one gains the misleading impression that this was a radical department: in 1834, the radical opposition won thirty-nine per cent of seats on the bigger municipal councils, and it actually gained support during the succeeding years, winning no less than forty-nine per cent of these seats in 1846.[61]

Following the failure of the Duchess's revolt, her son was left to represent legitimism. In 1844, after the Duke d'Angoulême died, he adopted the title of the Count de Chambord, and claimed the throne. However, he repudiated the strategy of the Duchess of Berry. For the next thirty years, he attempted to strike a difficult balance. On the one hand, he wanted the French people to remember the monarchy, and so issued irregular manifestos and letters on diverse topics. On the other hand, he wanted to avoid any appearance of seditious conspiracy or popular rebellion. His solution was to adopt a 'providential' attitude: the monarchy would return when God wanted it.

Chambord's semi-public letters showed that he followed Social Catholic thinking. He declared that 'I do not wish to be the king of one class or one party, but the king of all.' He was interested in the labour movement, and advised his followers 'to march at its head'.[62] His thinking was paternalistic. He understood France as a fatherless nation and he waited for his unruly children to come to their senses. In the 1850s and 1860s he developed something closer to a political programme, promising decentralisation, the return to the pre-Revolutionary provinces, some form of universal suffrage and charity.

Many thought that he might return as king in the 1870s. Chambord himself may have believed this. However, in his years of exile, he never learnt the art of tactical compromise. His argument was the one which he had presented in the 1840s: his return would come when God willed it. When Orleanist monarchist groups asked for compromise, in particular requesting that he accept the tricolour flag, he understood this to mean that the time was not yet right. If God wanted his return, then his children would accept the entirety of his programme, without negotiation or qualification. He refused all compromise, and the last chance of a monarchist restoration melted away.

There are clearly some similarities between the Vendée in the 1830s and liberal departments during the Restoration. In both situations, the micro-élites of mayors and municipal officials who supported the government were lonely minorities in hostile areas. In both cases the suspicion and aggression of the government often served to exacerbate the situation and to politicise actions which could have been ignored or discounted as trivial. In both cases, there was a subversive popular culture engaged in 'symbolic warfare' to ridicule the government and to assert their own culture. Both sides made abundant use of political symbols – the Bonapartist tobacco-pouch and the legitimist medal. Are we to conclude that one was simply the mirror-image of the other?

While acknowledging similarities, it is also important to notice their differences. Liberal oppositions consistently praised the value of learning, and eventually made the principle of press freedom into their own cause.

While there was a legitimist press, it did not have the same centrality in the monarchist political culture. There were also some obvious differences in the contents of these cultures: the Chouans were sympathetic to the Church, and never robbed priests or bishops. The liberals saw the Church as the model of the type of society which they opposed. Their ideal was an expanding sphere of education and culture, although they might disagree over how far and how fast this sphere should be extended. This clearly differentiated them from the psychological and physical intimidation of the missions and the Chouans. Another important difference relates to political structures: while there were legitimist and liberal intellectuals, and legitimist and liberal popular movements, only among the liberals can one find an intermediate stratum of mediating intellectuals: pamphleteers and poets like Courier and Béranger who could both read intellectuals' books *and* speak to the people. Lastly, Chouans, legitimists and Social Catholics all thought in terms of paternalistic rule from above, for the benefit of the nation, while liberals, Bonapartists and republicans had a far stronger commitment to the ideals of equality and popular sovereignty – even if they found this difficult to put into practice.

While the 1832 rebellion failed, it did create a powerful language of political opposition. Part of this measured success was the use of a female-orientated vocabulary, based on values of faith and community. If the Duchess was unable to direct a rebellion, she did succeed in creating a long-running tradition of female support for the monarchist cause.

– V. DOCUMENTS –

– DOCUMENT 4.1: A NOBLEWOMAN'S IMPRESSIONS OF THE DUCHESS OF BERRY –

At first sight, Boigne's comments might seem to be a positive appreciation of the Duchess's merits. In fact, it was precisely these qualities which alarmed conservative critics.

> [The Duchess of Berry] was cheerful, natural, and of a gay and clever disposition; she was a good mistress, and was adored at Rosny [her country house], where her bounty was intelligently distributed. She also enjoyed a certain popularity among the middle class of Paris. Her chief merit consisted in the fact that she differed from the rest of the [royal] family. She was fond of art, liked the theatre, and gave entertainments. She used to walk in the streets, indulged her fancies, and went into shops. She paid much attention to dress, and brought a little movement into court life; this was sufficient to secure the affection of the shopkeeping class. The banking class liked her because she would appear in public and be present at every small festivity without etiquette. She would have been less disposed than the Dauphine [the Duchess of Angoulême] to insist upon distinctions of rank. The artists she

employed, and whose work she appreciated with the intelligent tact of an Italian woman, also praised her and contributed to increase her popularity.

Source: *The Memoirs of the Comtesse de Boigne (1820–1830)*, edited and translated by Charles Nicoullaud (London, 1908), p. 125

– Document 4.2: Berryer's speech to the electors of the Haute-Loire, 4 July 1830 –

Berryer was one of the leading Legitimist politicians of the 1830s and 1840s. This text shows how powerful the simple image of the King as father-figure was to the Legitimists.

Berryer first read out Charles X's address to all electors, and then commented:

Gentlemen,

What can I possibly add to the words that you've just heard? An offended King, a distressed father has sent you the most serious exhortations, and the most caring advice. He remembers his duties, he says that he knows how to fulfil them, and he calls on us to fulfil ours. These duties of a loyal subject, which are always sacred and dear to our hearts, the duties which a Frenchman owes to his land, these duties are more needed than ever in the present circumstances.

Our King's intentions have been misunderstood, the privileges of the Crown have been attacked, he has been refused the co-operation which he expected to help him do the good which his heart desired! The enemies of order are spreading false fears and unworthy suspicions. They plot to make the future an accomplice of the crimes of the past, they want the new generations to carry the burden of their old hatreds. So they propagate these vague worries about our liberties, about the return of an order which no longer exists and which cannot be revived, so they spread these threats of some violent attack on the kingdom's laws, on the institutions created by the constitutional Charter, so they separate the King's interests from those of his people, and so they throw into us deadly defiance and disorder!

Voters of the Haute-Loire, reject these dreadful insinuations! Let nothing stop our legitimate attachment to civil liberties, let nothing shake our devotion to the King, our trust in this loyal and good monarch!

Source: Berryer, *Discours parlementaires* I (Paris: Didier, 1872), pp. 14–15

– Documents 4.3: Two proclamations issued by the Duchess of Berry in the name of Henry V in May–June 1832 –

These proclamations show the Duchess's confidence in the special nature of the Vendée, and her certainty that a revolt can succeed in this department.

Vendéens! Bretons! All inhabitants of the loyal provinces of the West! Having debarked in the south, I was not afraid to cross France, in the face of danger, to fulfil my sacred vow: that of returning to my brave friends, and to join them in their dangers and their tasks. I have finally arrived among this people of heroes. Bring fortune to France!

Frenchmen! For forty years [since 1789] men who called themselves my friends have constantly tricked you. For fifteen years [during the Restoration], their projects were frustrated. Tax-payers of all ranks, of all classes, arise! Aren't your taxes double what they were under the Restoration? Tradesmen, industrialists, merchants, haven't your profits turned into losses? Frenchmen, you want glory, you want liberty. Only Legitimacy can bring them to you.

Source: Gabory, Les Guerres, p. 985

– DOCUMENTS 4.4: CHOUAN EPHEMERA FROM THE VENDÉE –

The authors of these posters are unknown. Their writing gives an indication of the simple faith which ordinary Legitimists and Chouans had in the benevolence of Henry V, and of the violence which they invoked.

Handwritten poster stuck on the door of the town hall of Fontenay, July 1832

Long Live Henry V, king of France!
Greetings!
Arise, immediately, my brave comrades! It's time that we killed these infamous people. The English will help us. They will send us arms. Arise, our friends are fighting and they are winning everywhere. Soon there'll be many of us, and we will have our beloved princes.
    Taxes will be lower.
    Indirect taxes will be abolished.
    The poor will be happy.
    The workers will be satisfied.
HV HV HV HV HV

Source: ADV/1.Z.312

Handwritten poster found in Magnis-Regnier, March 1832

Vendéens!
An army of 6,000 thousand [sic] men is going to cross your lands to put Henry 5 on his throne, to bring back trade and peace which the revolution has destroyed. Long Live Henry 5.

Source: ADV/3.U.2/624

Handwritten poster stuck on the JP's door in Bourbon-Vendée, August 1832

Woe! Yes, woe to them who called the troops in. Woe to the authorities of this town; woe to all the Liberals; yes, woe, the day of vengeance isn't far!

Source: ADV/3.U.1/636

– VI. FURTHER READING –

To my knowledge, there is no English-language account of the 1832 revolt. However, there are two excellent short essays on relevant themes. Jo B. Margadant, 'The Duchesse de Berry and Royalist Political Culture in Post-revolutionary France', *History Workshop* 43 (1997), 23–52 is an incisive and original analysis of monarchism and political culture. John M. Merriman, *The Margins of City Life: Explorations of the French Urban Frontier, 1815–51* (Oxford: Oxford UP, 1991): chapter four contains a fascinating description of the creation of the new capital of La Vendée.

A number of studies discuss legitimism in 1832. Roger Price, 'Legitimist Opposition to the Revolution of 1830 in the French Provinces', *Historical Journal* 17:4 (1974), 755–78 is a useful study which sets the political context. Hagues de Changy, *Le Soulèvement de la Duchesse de Berry, 1830–1832* (Paris: DUC/Albatros, 1986) primarily considers Legimitist politics during the early 1830s. Jean-Clément Martin, *La Vendée de la Mémoire, 1800–1980* (Paris: Seuil, 1989) discusses the changing memories and interpretations of the Vendéen revolt of 1793, and puts forward a fascinating analysis concerning historical identity. Emile Gabory, *Les Guerres de Vendée* (Paris: Bouquins, 1989) is an older work, written between 1912 and 1923: it presents an exhaustive study of events, and includes a long study of the 1832 revolt. Brian Fitz-patrick, *Catholic Royalism in the Department of the Gard, 1814–1852* (Cambridge: Cambridge UP, 1983) is a useful study of another stronghold of French legitimism.

There is no full-scale work on the royal visits during the Restoration; however, Landric Raillat, 'Les manifestations publiques à l'occasion du sacre du Charles X' in A. Corbin, N. Gérôme and D. Tartakowsky (eds), *Les Usages politiques des fêtes* (Paris: Publications de la Sorbonne, 1994), 53–62, does consider the problems which the Restoration faced in presenting a public face.

The revolt of 1793 has attracted many historians. A good starting-point is Claude Petitfrère, 'The Origins of the Civil War in the Vendée', *French History* 2:2 (1988), 187–207. Another good introduction is the novel by Balzac, *The Chouans* (Harmondsworth: Penguin, 1976): the first third of this work is some of the most exciting writing about the Chouan revolts. Jean-Clément Martin, 'Femmes et guerre civile; l'exemple de la Vendée', *Clio* 5 (1997), 97–115 considers gendered representations of 1793. However, it is weak on sociological issues. Charles Tilly, *The Vendée* (Harvard UP, 1964) is perhaps the definitive work which demonstrated the usefulness of a social history approach. Paul Bois, *Paysans de l'Ouest* (Paris: Flammarion, 1971) is another very powerfully argued work, centred on the Sarthe. Donald

Sutherland, *The Chouans: the Social Origins of Popular Counter-revolution in Upper Brittany, 1770–96* (Oxford: Oxford UP, 1982) should also be consulted. Jacques Godechot, *The Counter-Revolution: Doctrine and Power, 1789–1804* translated by Salvator Attanasio (London: Fertig, 1972) considers the ideas and actions of the counter-revolutionaries.

Legitimist politics are considered in a number of works. Robert Gildea, *The Past in French History* (New Haven: Yale UP, 1994): chapters five and seven are useful analyses of nineteenth-century right-wing thinking. Isaiah Berlin, 'The Counter-Enlightenment' in his *Against the Current* (London: Hogarth, 1979), pp. 1–24 presents a brilliant analysis of the philosophy of the counter-Revolution; D. K. Cohen, 'The Vicomte de Bonald's Critique of Industrialism', *Journal of Modern History* 41:4 (1969), 475–84 and W. Jay Reedy, 'The Traditionalist Critique of Individualism in post-Revolutionary France', *History of Political Thought* 16:1 (1995), 49–75 are useful studies of the most influential of the counter-Revolutionary philosophers. J.-J. Oeschlin, *Le mouvement ultra-royaliste sous la Restauration* (Paris: PUF, 1960) is an older study, but still useful in analysing the origins of Legitimism. Steven Kale, 'The Monarchy according to the King: the ideological content of the *Drapeau Blanc*, 1871–1873', *French History* 2:4 (1988), 399–426 is a well-written analysis of Chambord's failure to lead the Third Restoration in the 1870s.

There have been a number of good studies of Catholicism. Ralph Gibson, *A Social History of French Catholicism, 1789–1914* (London: Routledge, 1989) is a lively and up-to-date study. Martyn Lyons, 'Fires of Expiation; Book-Burnings and Catholic Missions in Restoration France', *French History* 10:2 (1996), 240–66 is a vivid study of the missions. J.-B. Duroselle, *Les Débuts du Catholicisme social en France (1822–70)* (Paris: PUF, 1951), is an older study, but still useful. Claude Langlois, *Le Catholicisme au féminin* (Paris: Cerf, 1984), an exhaustive study of women's participation in Catholicism. Yvonne Turin, *Femmes et religieuses au XIXe siècle; le féminisme 'en religion'* (Paris: Nouvelle Cité, 1989) is a more approachable book on the same subject. Bonnie G. Smith, *Ladies of the Leisure Class: the Bourgeoises of Northern France* (Princeton: Princeton UP, 1981) is an imaginative study of female cultures.

– NOTES –

1. Emile Gabory, *Les Guerres de Vendée* (Paris: Bouquins, 1989), p. 9.
2. J. A. Cavoleau, *Statistique ou description générale du département de la Vendée, augmentée par A.-D. de la Fontenelle de Vaudoré* (Marseilles: Lafitte, 1978 [originally published 1809 and 1844]), pp. 747–8.
3. Judge's interviews, ADV, 3.U.1/636.
4. Gabory, *Les Guerres*, p. 573.
5. Chateaubriand, *De la Vendée* (La Rochelle: Rumeur des Ages, 1990 [1819]), p. 31.

6. Jean-Clément Martin, *La Vendée de la Mémoire, 1800–1980* (Paris: Seuil, 1989), pp. 165–86.

7. Martin, *La Vendée*, p. 28.

8. Martyn Lyons, 'Fires of Expiation: Book-burnings and Catholic Missions in Restoration France', *French History* 10:2 (1996), 240–66 (p. 246).

9. Comte de Bonald, *Oeuvres complètes* III (Paris: Migue, 1864), p. 823.

10. ADV/1.N.4, 7 August 1826.

11. The information concerning the Duchess of Berry in the following paragraphs has been drawn from the excellent study by Jo Burr Margadant, 'The Duchesse de Berry and Royalist Political Culture in post-Revolutionary France', *History Workshop* 43 (1997), 23–52.

12. Gabory, *Les Guerres*, p. 898.

13. ADV/1.N.419 (bis), Prefect's letter, 27 August 1829.

14. Thiers, *Discours parlementaires*, Vol. I (Paris: Calman Lévy, 1879), pp. 121–3.

15. Paulze d'Ivoy, *Rapport du préfet … au ministre de l'Intérieur sur les troubles en Vendée (juillet 1833)*, (La Roche-sur-Yon: Archives Départementales de la Vendée, 1958 [originally written 1833]) p. 3.

16. Hugues de Changy, *Le Soulèvement de la Duchesse de Berry, 1830–32* (Paris: DUC/Albatros, 1986), pp. 21–2.

17. d'Ivoy, *Rapport*, p. 8.

18. ADV/4.M.443, 22 November 1830.

19. Changy, *Soulèvement*, pp. 33–4 and 72–80.

20. Gabory, *Les Guerres*, pp. 976–7.

21. The reasons for this are still not clear. See Gabory, *Les Guerres*, p. 991.

22. d'Ivoy, *Rapport*, p. 18.

23. ADV/3.U.2/624, Bernard's confession, 8 October 1831.

24. See, for example, ADV/3.U.2/624, Jeanne Mertet, December 1831.

25. ADV/3.U.2/624, 7 January 1833.

26. ADV/3.U.2/624, 12 March 1831.

27. ADV/3.U.2/624, police report, 17 August 1832.

28. ADV/3.U.2/624, police report, 8 January 1831.

29. ADV/3.U.2/624, Bret's declaration, 25 January 1832.

30. ADV/3.U.2/624, Pignon, 6 February 1832.

31. ADV/4.M.449, 15 September 1833.

32. ADV/4.M.444, police report, 14 September 1832.

33. ADV/4.M.444, sub-prefect, 26 November 1833.

34. ADV/4.M.444, police report, 21 September 1833.

35. ADV/4.M.444, sub-prefect, 13 December 1833.

36. ADV/4.M.444, mayor, 1 September 1833.

37. ADV/4.M.444, sub-prefect, 6 August 1833.

38. ADV/3.U.2/624, 11 June and 8 August 1832.

39. ADV/4.M.444, sub-prefect, 26 November 1833.

40. ADV/4.M.444, sub-prefect, 6 August 1833.

41. Christine Guionnet, *L'apprentissage de la politique moderne* (Paris: L'Harmattan, 1997), p. 233.

42. ADV/4.M.449, mayor, 15 September 1833.

43. ADV/4.M.446, mayor, 25 October 1833.

44. ADV/1.N.5, General Council, January 1833.

45. ADV/3.U.1/636, police report, 21 June 1832.

46. ADV/4.M/444, Mayor, 2 April 1831.

47. ADV/4.M.394, police report, 12 June 1836.

48. ADV/4.M.444, police report, 18 November 1833.

49. ADV/4.M.394, police report, 22 June 1836.

50. ADV/4.M.394, police report, 5 July 1838.

51. ADV/3.U.2/624, JP's report, 27 March 1831.

52. ADV/3.U.2/624, interrogation, 6 December 1831.

53. ADV/3.U.2/624, interrogation, 11 June 1832.

54. François-René de Chateaubriand, *Grands Écrits politiques*, Vol. II (Paris: Imprimerie nationale, 1993), p. 629.

55. Chateaubriand, *Mémoires d'Outre-Tombe*, Vol. III (Paris: Livres de poche, 1973), pp. 301–2.

56. Le vicomte Alban de Villeneuve-Bargemont, *Economie politique chrétienne*, Vol. I (Paris: Paulin, 1834), p. 22.

57. Chateaubriand, *Mémoires*, Vol. III, pp. 299–300.

58. Figures from Claude Langlois, *Le catholicisme au féminin; les congrégations françaises* (Paris: Cerf, 1984) and Charles Pouthas, 'Le Clergé sous la monarchie constitutionnelle', *Revue d'histoire de l'Eglise de France 29* (1943), 19–53.

59. Ralph Gibson, *A Social History of French Catholicism, 1789–1914* (London: Routledge, 1989), p. 181.

60. Gabory, *Les Guerres*, p. 962.

61. Guionnet, *L'apprentissage*, pp. 154–5.

62. Henri, comte de Chambord, *Textes politiques* (Paris: Communication et Tradition, 1995), pp. 12–14.

CHAPTER 5

Utopian Socialism

The utopian socialists were cultural revolutionaries. Most of them were pacifists; they did not think of 'revolution' as a violent rebellion but as a mental, even spiritual, transformation. Among their number were social visionaries, sexual radicals, mystics, eccentrics and technocratic planners. Echoes of their thinking were present throughout the nineteenth century. They can be heard in 1830, in its youth activism, in 1848, in the Provisional Government's non-violent republicanism (see Chapter 6); and in many of the projects of the Second Empire (1852–70), such as the Paris–Lyon–Marseilles railway, the Crédit Mobilier Bank, and the Suez Canal.

One word of warning is needed before we investigate these visionaries and planners. They were called many names by their contemporaries, but no single, generally acceptable term was ever devised. Marx and Engels used the term 'critical-utopian socialism' for them in their *Communist Manifesto* (written in 1847). This label was shortened to 'utopian socialist' by Engels in 1875, and since then it has been applied so many times that it has stuck. Like many labels, it is not very accurate. It could be said that the utopian socialists were neither utopians nor socialists and that the term muddies the differences between particular thinkers and movements. I will continue to use it as it is the best term available, but readers should be aware of its limitations.

– I. PARTICIPANTS –

The revolutionary experiences of the 1790s bewildered and terrified many people, but they were also a tremendous stimulus to confront complex political questions: what was the meaning of the Revolution? Had it determined France's future? One reactionary response was to admire the past: thinkers such as de Bonald, de Maistre and Lamennais followed this line of argument. Another response was to applaud the Revolution: an attitude which usually meant ignoring the tragedies it caused. A third current, including the utopian socialists, wished to avoid both these paths. They sought a new politics which would respond to the issues raised by the Revolution, while avoiding both nostalgic idealisation of pre-Revolutionary hierarchies, and apologies for the chaotic violence of Revolution. Such musings must have seemed obscure: what audience would listen to them?

Rather than defining the utopian socialists' audience in terms of class, it makes more sense to think in terms of generations. Young people – in particular, young male students – suffered many problems during the Restoration, including 'a massive deprivation of believable ideals'.[1] Their parents did not leave them a solid core of political beliefs, but a mass of fragmented, contradictory ideas. Real faith in the old certainties of Church and King was, frankly, difficult: recall the Vendéen priest's weary comment: 'Long live the king, all the same' (see Chapter 4). But could one support the enemies of monarchy? The shadows of the Terror, the guillotine and the Bonapartist dictatorship fell heavily over these young people. The priests, the missions and most political leaders vigorously repudiated the Revolutionary legacy, and even gifted polemicists such as Courier and Béranger only presented oblique defences of its legacy, using irony and humour to disguise their political commitments.

Another factor had a still more corrosive effect on these young people. This was the 'weather-vanes': those politicians who were Bonapartists in 1813, royalists during the Restoration of 1814, Bonapartists again in March 1815 when Napoleon returned to France, and then royalists after his defeat. A whole stratum of French politicians, from noted philosophers such as Benjamin Constant to humble mayors with one eye on their prospects for reappointment, followed this empty strategy of turning whichever way the political wind blew. Who could believe in any political cause after seeing this spectacle?

A common response was to withdraw from political commitment. The term '*mal du siècle*' (the sickness of the century) was coined to describe the mood of this apathetic, pessimistic, inward-looking generation. According to Alfred de Musset, a gifted spokesman for the young, this was caused by the conflict between the glory of which they had dreamt in Bonapartist colleges, and the sad reality of the Restoration.[2] These dilemmas were of particular importance to Parisian students. The Restoration authorities were suspicious of students from liberal or Bonapartist families, and of those from Bonapartist schools. A strict disciplinary code was enforced, and any protest or complaint was treated as an attempt to subvert the state. From 1815–22, no less than sixteen of the thirty-two élite royal colleges of Paris experienced serious discipline problems.[3]

Students did not rally to the Restoration, but withdrew their faith in the educational system. Some formed informal study groups, called *cénacles*, outside the colleges. Students felt betrayed by their elders: the ultra-royalists were seen as merely legitimating repression, the liberals as dogmatic and partisan, and the 'weather-vanes' as cowardly. The most ambitious student leaders saw their protests as the beginning of a new political movement, representing the cause of 'youth', which sought to repair the damage which the older generations had done. Student agitation became concerned with larger issues than university regulations. For example, in June 1820 Parisian students led a full-scale riot over the changes in the voting system which gave the richest quarter of the electorate a second vote.

Two prominent radicals in these circles were Pierre Leroux and Paul-François Dubois. In 1824 Leroux was twenty-seven and Dubois thirty-one. Both had been expelled from university; Leroux worked in a printshop. They decided to create a journal to give a voice to the new generation. Their ambitions were reflected in the title they chose: the *Globe*. It survived for eight years, and was widely recognised as an extraordinary contribution to French journalism. The *Globe* evaded Restoration censorship by downplaying its political ambitions. It did not follow liberal journalists in grubby, muck-raking innuendo, but adopted an 'uncompromisingly highbrow, remorselessly didactic' tone.[4] Its editors took scrupulous care to give exact, fair reviews of books and even, on occasion, praised their enemies' works and criticised their friends – a practice unheard of at that time in French journalism. By following this strategy, they attempted to introduce a new political ethic: their battle was not a sectarian conflict, but a constructive initiative. Perhaps inevitably, the *Globe's* sympathies were with the liberals, who at least talked of freedom of speech and educational reform, but there was always a distance between the scrupulously fair *Globe* and the liberals' point-scoring pamphleteering.

Such ideals led many students to identify with the July 1830 Revolution, although few were present during the street-fighting. Following the Revolution, these young men suffered the deepest disillusion. They realised that the Orleanists' ultra-cautious reformism was not leading to the new France of which they had dreamt. They devised a new term in their criticism of the Orleanists, arguing that France had become a 'gerontocracy' – a society ruled by the old. Rather than ending this monopoly on power, the Orleanists had intensified it. Old bureaucrats and officials from the Empire rushed to rally to the new monarchy – another generation of 'weather-vanes'! – and the idealistic youth were once again excluded.

It was in this context that the utopian socialists first found an audience. Three thinkers in particular will concern us: Henri de Saint-Simon (1760–

1825), Charles Fourier (1772–1837) and Etienne Cabet (1788–1856). In each case, the movements and organisations they inspired often differed significantly from their leader's ideas.

– II. POLITICAL CULTURE –

Utopias have haunted history. Even before the invention of writing, there were folk utopias. Often humorous, these told of impossibly hospitable lands: the land of milk and honey, the Big Rock Candy Mountain, Cockayne … Their dominant theme was the satisfaction of physical needs: first, the end of hunger, but also sexual fulfilment. Some suggested the collapse of social hierarchies. All were dreamt before political philosophers turned to consider utopias.

Thomas More coined the term 'utopia' in 1516. The word was a pun, based on the English translation of two Greek terms. 'Eu-topia', in Greek, meant 'good place', while 'ou-topia' meant 'no place'. Both terms sounded the same in English, and in his work *Utopia* More intrigued his readers by deliberately leaving unclear which sense he intended. Was his work a verbatim account of a traveller's experience in the South Seas? Or was it a fantasy which was designed to provoke? Most sixteenth-century readers realised it was the latter, but there were a few who thought that it was a genuine account. More's work created a new instrument for the expression of political ideas. It inspired many Catholic, Protestant and humanist utopias in the sixteenth and seventeen centuries. All rejected the hedonistic, physical pleasures of the older folk utopias. Their dominant political cultures were austere, improving and even dictatorial. However, even in these serious works, there often remained comic sub-themes, which satirised existing norms.

A major innovation in utopian thinking was devised by Louis Sébastien Mercier, who wrote his utopia in 1768. The contents of his work were undistinguished, but its plot was astonishingly new. Rather than setting his work on a distant island, Mercier set his work – *2440* – in the future. Instead of a u-topia (good place/no place) Mercier had written a 'u-chronia' (good time/no time). This was more than finding a new setting: it linked utopian thinking with the analysis of social development. Utopias were no longer free-floating visions of alternative ways of life, they were also forecasts of the future.

The French Revolution encouraged – and sometimes forced – many people to confront history. Ideas about progress and better worlds became common currency. At the same time, the Revolution prevented open political organisation or discussion. Under the Terror, the Empire and, to a lesser extent, the Restoration, political organisations were driven underground. This combination of intense intellectual activity and a near absence of legitimate political movements formed the fertile ground in which utopias grew.

Like their sixteenth- and seventeenth-century ancestors, the utopian thinkers of the early nineteenth century had no intention of creating mass movements, let alone of planning revolutions. Saint-Simon, Fourier and Cabet thought their schemes were so obvious, so desirable, that they could not imagine any government actually refusing them. All three understood the need for effective propaganda, and all battled with Parisian publishers and journals in efforts to ensure that their ideas were heard, but none of them actually aimed to create a political movement.

Count Claude-Henri de Rouvroy de Saint-Simon had served as an officer prior to 1789, and had fought alongside Washington against the British. In the first years of the Revolution he was an enthusiastic supporter of the new regime, working hard to propagate revolutionary ideas, and investing in the Revolution by buying Church property. However, in November 1793 he was arrested, probably by mistake. Protesting his innocence, he survived the Terror, but lost his fortune. For the next decade he was involved in further financial dealings, but was penniless again by 1805.

Saint-Simon was left with a lasting impression of the chaos of the Revolution. So much energy had been spent, but nothing permanent had been constructed. His response was to imagine a form of stable progress, organised by a benevolent, scientific élite. His first political work, *Letter of an Inhabitant of Geneva* (1803), suggested a way forward: a scientific élite should be formed and, financed by public subscription, it should devise social schemes in the common interest. This first pamphlet attracted little interest, but Saint-Simon developed his ideas in the following years.

Saint-Simon intended to devise a scientific analysis of society, but his social categories were ill-defined. He divided society into three groups. There was an intellectual élite, the scientists, engineers and artists; a conservative property-owning élite, usually opposed to new ideas; and the group which he initially termed 'the surplus', or the mass of workers and peasants.[5] The three sectors were in conflict with each other. The intellectual élite had no political power of their own, but they were capable of arousing the masses to violent, destructive activity, as had happened in the Revolution.

As his writing developed, Saint-Simon grew more interested in the differences between the old and new élites, describing them as 'idle' and 'productive'. The 'productive' people were those brought to prominence by the new industrial and commercial forms. The idle were the old élites of pre-Revolutionary France: the nobles, the clergy and those who lived off investments, the *rentiers*. In his later writings, Saint-Simon often included military leaders in this category. Often he made no distinction between factory-owners and factory-workers: Saint-Simon thought in terms of a single 'industrial sector'. His model of industry was the small workshop, as among the Lyonnais weavers, where there was no great distance between worker and owner.

Saint-Simon believed that the new industrial forms represented a new ethic, which had the capacity to remake French society, and to replace the feudal social organisation which had lasted for some eight centuries. To some extent, his ideas were similar to those of Adam Smith, who also believed that the business of buying and selling contained an implicit set of values.[6] However, unlike Smith, Saint-Simon was always more interested in the *collective* actions of the new élite, rather than in their individual choices. According to Saint-Simon, the new industrial forms were liberating: where the people had been subjects, they became shareholders (see document 5.1). The true purpose of modern government, argued Saint-Simon, was to support this new 'industrial' sector. However, France was a 'back-to-front society'.[7] Old-fashioned governments, still based on the feudal landowning class, failed to understand the importance of social progress.

There were two important developments in Saint-Simon's thinking during the Restoration. First, he took note of the working class. Never an egalitarian, Saint-Simon believed in rule by rational élites. However, he was concerned that the misery of the poor might produce another social crisis like the Revolution. Moreover, he began to consider the possibility that the workers could act as a type of lobbying group, putting pressure on owners to promote co-ordinated, industrial forms of organisation.[8]

The second development in his work reflected his concern to see his message more widely accepted. During the last decade of his life (1815–25) he began to realise that other forms of persuasion were needed to win people over. He showed a renewed interest in techniques and ethics of Catholicism, and his last essay was entitled *A New Christianity*. Here he suggested that all religions could be stripped of their particular dogmas, and reduced to a universal ethic of fraternity. Such intellectual themes were not new in Saint-Simon's writing: what was innovative was the *form* he considered for them. His belated appreciation of the psychological power of religion suggested that he had realised that an appeal to reason alone was not enough to gain success. His sympathisers felt uncertain about this work. Prosper Enfantin, who was later to become the leader of the Saint-Simonian movement, said of the *New Christianity* 'I feel little disposition to follow Saint-Simon'.[9]

During his lifetime, Saint-Simon won few converts. However, shortly after his death, a new journal named the *Producteur*, which cautiously discussed Saint-Simonian themes, began to attract student idealists. This group would later gain more support.

François-Marie-Charles Fourier came from the Franche-Comté, in eastern France. His father, and several of his relations, worked as cloth merchants; some were rich; and Fourier's family expected him to follow his father into the textile trade. In the 1780s he attended Besançon college, studying the standard curriculum of classical and religious texts. His essays won several prizes, for he was a gifted student. His father's trade did not attract him, but, despite his horror at the widespread use of fraud by merchants, he had to follow in his footsteps. The Revolution changed little: in 1791 he was sent to Lyon as a commercial apprentice. In 1793 he inherited enough money to become an independent trader. By an unlucky coincidence, this was also the year in which Federalist Lyon fought Jacobin Paris (see Chapter 3). Fourier lost his property and was threatened with execution. He spent a few months in prison, and was then conscripted into a cavalry regiment, serving for eighteen months. In 1796 he returned to commerce, and travelled across France. In 1797 he had an experience which fixed his attitude to commerce: he was employed to supervise the dumping of a large store of rice which had rotted while being stored by a merchant waiting for the price to rise. Fourier drew two conclusions from this experience: not only were existing economic arrangements immoral, they were also inefficient.

Fourier interpreted the violence of the Terror as the culmination of twenty-five centuries of philosophical debate.[10] What alternative was there? He refused any idealisation of pre-Revolutionary hierarchy but, unlike Saint-Simon, he could not accept that commerce represented a social or moral alternative. On inheriting money once more, Fourier went to Paris to study. He did not engage in exhaustive research, but he did have first-hand knowledge of the working of the economy, and he had travelled widely across Revolutionary France, seeing with his own eyes the Republic's successes and failures. He seemed to have the knack of getting people to talk. He had few close male friends but, while travelling in coaches, he would fall into conversation with other voyagers. He never married, but throughout his life he had many close relationships – and possibly affairs – with female friends. This wide social experience made Fourier a reasonably knowledgeable and sensitive commentator. Marx and Engels would later criticise him for his 'mysticism' and 'extravagance', but they did note the coherence of his thinking. Engels commented that his writing was 'scientific research, cool, unbiased, systematic thought; in short, *social philosophy*'.[11] Fourier's most prominent follower, Victor Considérant, made the same claim, arguing that

Fourier was a scientist like Columbus, Copernicus or Galileo. In his writing, nothing was arbitrary, 'everything is scientific'.[12]

By 1808 Fourier had devised a challenging and reasonably coherent analysis not only of French society, but of the human species. He believed that there was a basic human nature which was benign. The key problem afflicting modern society was that it denied this human nature. There were deep, natural needs for pleasure, in a wide variety of forms, but priests and atheists, monarchs and republicans had devised systems which repressed these needs. In arguing along these lines, Fourier was refusing the strict, austere thinking which had dominated utopian thinking since More, and was returning to the physical and sensual pleasures of the older folk utopias. Another unusual quality of Fourier's utopian thinking is his humanism: this is manifested in his refusal to set his system above the everyday needs of ordinary human beings. Rather than preaching at people, he made a genuine attempt to understand the impulses which motivated them.

The resulting scheme was extraordinarily wide-ranging. Fourier did not see the world as divided into two camps, one good, one bad: instead he saw a society which had been constructed '*à rebours*' (back-to-front), within which the young were set against the old, the poor against the rich, the ugly against the good-looking, the women against the men. Because of these divisions, there was little co-operation: individuals rebelled against repression through thousands of petty gestures. Fourier's consideration of women's status was particularly sensitive. Men had imposed a monogamous, powerless condition on them through the institution of marriage: they therefore had no right to complain when women responded by lying to their husbands, by making their marriages miserable, or by having affairs. (See document 5.2.) Politicians and public speakers constantly praised the virtues of 'pure love': it had become 'a universal mask', worn by all people, but in reality it existed nowhere.[13] Fourier felt contempt for politicians who ignored these vital issues. He predicted that in the future 'there will no longer be debates on charters, budgets, conquests and monopolies; there will only be two points to discuss: work and pleasure.'[14]

Fourier proposed that medium-sized communities of approximately eighteen hundred people, capable of managing their own industrial and agricultural activities, should replace the free market. He termed these units '*Phalanstères*'. He specified the figure of eighteen hundred as, he calculated, this was the number of the different sorts of personalities. In 'civilisation' they were thrown into competition with each other, in his *Phalanstères* they would act in harmony. Planning would replace the free market, but this was not socialism in the accepted sense of the word: while extremes of wealth and poverty were to be avoided, there would still be a limited form of private property, and even a system of investment. During the 1820s and 1830s, his thinking did not develop conceptually. He analysed new topics, considering how work could be made attractive, and how schooling could be transformed into a pleasure-driven process.

Should we term Fourier a utopian? Some of his works, such as the *New Amorous World* (which was not published in his lifetime), contained some extended, semi-fictional descriptions of 'Harmony', the future new world. These sketches may have been intended as satires, rather than as predictions – for example, he proposed giving medals to great lovers and cooks rather than to generals – but the bulk of his works are concerned with the analysis of the present. His first entry into political culture was in reaction against the Jacobins, who he saw as obsessed with ideals, and whose relentless, bloodthirsty efforts to implement them resulted in the tragedy of the Terror. Fourier wanted his ideas to be based on a different sort of thinking. 'Let us forget about what *ought to be*,' he argued, 'let us forget about duty, and let us analyse *that which is*.'[15] He certainly attempted to ground his work in the historical reality of his time, and in the drives which he saw dominating human nature.

Fourier's works were largely ignored in the 1810s and 1820s. They received few reviews, most of which were scathing and hostile. However, following the 1830 Revolution, a small Fourierist network developed.

Etienne Cabet is the last of our three thinkers. His father was a barrel-maker, but Cabet was unable to follow this trade due to his poor eyesight. Instead he went to university, and graduated in 1812 with a law degree. During the Restoration he joined a semi-secret *Charbonnerie* assocation. At this stage, his political sympathies lay with the reformist, liberal Orleanists rather than with the Bonapartist or republican revolutionaries. Following the 1830 Revolution, he retained his faith in the new dynasty, and was elected as a deputy in Dijon in 1831. However, during the social tensions of 1831 and 1832 he rethought his ideas. He became a republican, and edited one of the first large circulation weeklies in France: *Le Populaire*. Over twelve thousand copies were sold in Paris alone.[16] The Orleanist regime, worried by this success, campaigned against the paper, and eventually brought Cabet to trial in 1834. Instead of going to prison, Cabet chose to go into exile, and travelled in Belgium and Britain, where he met Robert Owen, the social reformer. He returned to France in March 1839.

During his exile, his ideas had developed. Rather than assuming that political reform would solve social problems such as poverty, he argued that radical social reform was needed. In particular, he condemned private property. His argument on this point was simple enough: free market capitalism did not lead to a balanced economy, in which all participated in social and economic advances. Instead, it encouraged the accumulation of wealth in the hands of a few. In its place he proposed a type of communism.

He presented his ideas in a utopian text, similar in structure to More's *Utopia*. There was little tension in the plot: Lord Carisdall arrived in Icaria, and was overjoyed to see a society in which the technical facilities of modern industry were used to provide 'an equal abundance' for all.[17] For over four hundred pages he reports on Icaria's wonders. Everyone, boys and girls, receives an equal basic instruction in co-educational schools, in which each child learns off by heart the Icarian constitution. Each has an advanced apprenticeship in a particular trade. The family is strongly supported. There is training for midwifes and compulsory maternity courses for mothers. Motherhood is given high status. 'The first feeling which a mother seeks to develop in her child is filial love, ... a blind trust, which the mother herself will prevent from going too far.'[18] The whole of this society forms 'a single vast machine, in which each cog regularly carries out its function.'[19] There are no cafés, no cabarets, no naughty books or rude songs.

Its political system is curiously old fashioned: Icaria is ruled by the great Icar, who appears to be a benevolent despot. Late twentieth century readers may grow suspicious at this point: is this not a recipe for another Stalin or Hitler? Is Cabet glorifying totalitarianism? Christopher Johnson's remarks on this point are pertinent:

> Icarian political life, unreal as it may appear, is not totalitarian. Cabet simply *makes* it democratic. It may involve total regulation, but no coercion is present because the individual regulates himself, through the medium of society and for his own good. Cabet's system is obviously riven with authoritarian implications, but with a series of outrageous over-simplifications, he just blots them out.[20]

In the simplest, most literal way, Cabet had studied the problems which working-class families faced, and produced almost a mirror image of their lives: a society in which their every need was satisfied. He took care to include specific responses to women's problems: hence the references to midwives and respectable domesticity. Moreover, beyond some criticism of the very rich, Cabet made sure that his message was socially inclusive. Icaria was open to the workshop-owner, shopkeeper, and merchant as well to the worker.

– III. LEGACY –

Of our three thinkers, Cabet was the only one to actually lead a political movement. Saint-Simon and Fourier both unwittingly stimulated networks which were inspired by their ideas.

Cabet's intention was to appeal to a bourgeois sense of conscience. He hoped that his *Voyage* would stimulate paternalistic social reform. However, the middle classes largely ignored his book. In the early 1840s some working-class readers came across it and were clearly entranced. As had been the case with More's *Utopia*, there were even a few who were naïve enough to believe that Icaria was a real place, and who asked for instructions on how to get there! Cabet had not anticipated a working-class readership, but was able to respond. Using the *Populaire* as a vehicle for his politics, he began to transform Icarian Communism into an effective political ideology. He broke with the conspiratorial tactics of the republican secret societies of the 1820s and 1830s, and pulled together diverse political strands: a sentimental nostalgia for the Revolution of 1789, and even for Robespierre; a sensitive reponse to a working-class desire for respectability and class dignity; and, in the late 1840s, an increasingly religious tone, as Cabet took the title *père* [father]. As an ideologist, Cabet was a subtle and imaginative thinker. His *Populaire* had a print-run of 4 500 in 1846, at a time when most prestigious dailies survived with a circulation of a thousand, and the majority of its readers were working-class.[21] Individual copies were read out aloud in cabarets, and circulated from family to family in the working-class suburbs.

Cabet's strongest support came from the skilled workers, like the Lyonnais silk-weavers. The peak of his support was probably in 1844, when approximately one or two hundred thousand workers may have considered themselves to be Icarians.[22] They were grouped together in the old manufacturing towns – Lyon, Toulouse, and, to a lesser extent, Vienne and Paris. Rural labourers and the urban petty-bourgeoisie resisted his appeal. As well as noting his social appeal, we must also note its chronological context: the 1840s were a sad, dispirited decade, in which the hopes of 1830 had finally dissolved, and in which new efforts to revive hope and forms of political agitation had been crushed. The revolt in Lyon in 1831 had not stopped the decline in working-class standards of living. In other words, Cabet found a response among weak, disorganised and disappointed sections of the working class, people who could not find any other voice.

Icarian Communism had one great flaw: it was unable to guide its followers into any meaningful form of political activity. Marx and Engels were surely correct to observe that Cabet was 'the most superficial representative of communism'.[23] Other contemporary observers, such as Flora Tristan, made similar criticisms (see document 5.3). Icarians did not engage in conspiracies, nor did they found trade unions. While some Fourierists turned their efforts into founding *Phalanstères*, Cabet refused this sort of experiment until, in a gesture of desperation, in May 1847 he encouraged his followers to emigrate to a colony in the USA. Throughout the 1840s, the principal strategy which Cabet recommended to his followers was a quasi-religious appeal to the conscience of the ruling class.

After Saint-Simon's death in 1825, a group of nine disciples published the *Producteur* journal. Like the editors of the *Globe*, they were young. Their average age in 1825 was thirty.[24] They included Olinde Rodrigues (aged thirty-one in 1825), Saint-Amand Bazard (aged thirty-four), and Prosper Enfantin (aged twenty-nine). The *Producteur* started publication in October 1825. Initially it adopted a technocratic and apolitical tone, in the hope that the cause of scientific social reorganisation would unite 'liberal bankers and businessmen, radical political revolutionaries and state-trained engineers'.[25]

In summer 1826, the *Producteur* assumed an explicitly Saint-Simonian tone, stressing the ideal of a moral regeneration. Its articles called for a new spiritual power to reconcile the conflicting demands of masters and workers. The *Producteur* appealed to the same sort of young student idealists who read the *Globe*. However, during 1826, differences between liberals and Saint-Simonians became clear: liberals, like Courier (see Chapter 2), tended to see free-market capitalism as a liberating force; Saint-Simonians tended to talk of collective forces and organised industry. Liberals were vigorously anti-clerical; Saint-Simonians increasingly talked of spiritual values. The leading liberal political philosopher, Benjamin Constant, noted these differences, and publicly denounced the Saint-Simonians' ideas. The *Producteur* collapsed in December 1826, and many thought that this was the end of Saint-Simonianism.

However, a small network survived. Their pacifism attracted supporters from those worried about the violent rhetoric of the republican or Carbonari conspiracies, particularly among students from the technocratic and forward-looking Ecole Polytechnique. Bazard and Enfantin became their leaders. Bazard – who came out of the *Charbonnerie* – stressed the rationalist, social-scientific aspects of the Saint-Simonian doctrine, while Enfantin developed an increasingly mystic frame of mind. Both travelled across France, giving lectures to sympathisers. The main group remained in Paris, and by 1829 a group of forty convinced Saint-Simonians lived together communally in the city. They were divided into three grades and met privately to discuss the doctrine three times a week.[26] Occasionally visitors were allowed to enter, and they often came away with a curious impression. Rather than resembling a study-group, the Saint-Simonians' meetings seemed more like religious ceremonies.

Enfantin had moved far from the rationalistic, scientific spirit of Saint-Simon. He studied the *New Christianity* closely, and placed far greater emphasis on sentiment and feeling. He began to consider that artists were of greater importance than scientists in expounding the doctrine. The key turning-point came in December 1829 when Enfantin declared that Saint-Simonism was a religion, and he and Bazard were elected as 'fathers' of the movement. Bazard was increasingly eclipsed by Enfantin, and in November 1831 he left the movement.

The Revolution of 1830 surprised the Saint-Simonians. The 'fathers' recommended abstention: they were worried by political violence. Following the Revolution, there was a more open atmosphere, and some real interest in the Saint-Simonians' ideas. Saint-Simonian groups toured provincial France, giving lectures to explain their ideas. Interest increased as many of the young enthusiasts of 1830 grew disillusioned with the Revolution's meagre results and the continuing reign of 'gerontocracy'. The Saint-Simonians' greatest victory was to win over Pierre Leroux, still editor of the *Globe*, to their ideas. In December 1830 it became explicitly Saint-Simonian, and was published as a daily until April 1832, when it was suspended. Its maximum circulation was probably about 4 200 copies, some of which were given away free.[27]

Under Enfantin's direction, the Saint-Simonians were growing more theatrical. Enfantin, with his long hair and full beard, deliberately tried to resemble an Old Testament prophet, and prints of him emphasised this aspect of his appearance. Meetings were marked by 'exaltation and religiosity rather than reason and restraint'.[28] As this religious dimension expanded, Saint-Simonism grew increasingly concerned with the reconciliation of antagonisms: not simply between master and worker, but also between flesh and spirit, male and female, east and west, reason and sentiment. The most difficult debates concerned sexuality and gender.

While the Saint-Simonian doctrine had never promised working-class self-emancipation, it none the less encouraged consideration of the poor. Following the 1830 Revolution, they gained some following among working-class women in Paris. Some women – perhaps a hundred – went further and tried to gain full entry into the movement. Initially, there were separate hierarchies for male and female elites, but in 1831 the two were fused, and twelve women adepts were integrated into the same hierarchy as sixty-seven men.[29] Enfantin justified this change as part of the larger Saint-Simonian debate on the values of emotion and reason. If the Saint-Simonians were no longer simply scientists, if they recognised the powers of emotion and sentiment, this meant, argued Enfantin, that they must accept women as equals, representing the female virtues of feeling and emotion. This suggested a commitment to sexual equality. However, men still dominated the meetings. The retreats organised in a large house in Menilmontant, in eastern Paris, were only open to men.

The Saint-Simonians also discussed marriage and sexuality. Like many groups which stressed the ethics of community, they were suspicious about lifelong marriage, which seemed to be an institution which could conflict with a stronger commitment to the community. On economic grounds, they criticised an institution which functioned to transmit property and wealth from one generation to another, with little consideration of the managerial ability of the inheritor. They also criticised the traditional Catholic attitude to marriage, which proposed marriage as a poor alternative to chastity. Enfantin made the most far-reaching criticisms of marriage: he suggested that members of the movement should no longer be constrained by monogamous marriages, that they should feel no shame about their sexual desires, and that they should change sexual partners as they wished, while maintaining their commitment to the Saint-Simonian community. Perhaps such ideas could have been implemented in a responsible and organised manner: however, conservative group members were horrified. They were aware that their community was attracting press attention, and such ideas would be sensationalised and caricatured by hostile critics. It was these proposals, alongside other personal disputes, which led to Bazard's resignation.

The conflict between ideals and practices placed Enfantin in a difficult position, which he resolved with a characteristically theatrical gesture. While refuting criticisms, he accepted that it was impractical to implement his ideas immediately. He proposed a change in the Saint-Simonian hierarchy: while he remained 'father', there would also be a 'mother', to represent female virtues. At present, no women members were suitable for this post, but Enfantin was convinced that such a woman existed somewhere. He invited members to search for her, and some went to Britain, the USA, Germany and even to Turkey and Egypt, looking for her. Until her arrival, when Enfantin spoke at meetings, he had an empty chair next to him to represent the absence of the female leader.

As disagreements grew within the movement, Saint-Simonian women began to organise separately. In 1831 the cities of Lyon and Paris each contained approximately one hundred female Saint-Simonians, many of them single working-class women. Saint-Simonian 'missionaries' were active in setting up medical services and seamstresses' co-operatives.[30] In August 1832 two Saint-Simonian seamstresses launched their own paper, which was eventually entitled *La Tribune des Femmes*. Although the editors were Saint-Simonians, they explicitly invited all women to contribute, whatever their political ideas. All articles were written by women, who signed using only their first names, so rejecting male-orientated family surnames. Many articles and letters concerned practical issues such as female employment and economic independence, rather than the intricacies of Saint-Simonian doctrine. The *Tribune* had a print-run of about one thousand: no doubt it had many more readers, as copies were shared among sympathisers.[31] Within its columns were many eloquent and forthright assertions of female political autonomy. Claire Moses argues that this paper constituted 'the first female collective venture in history whose purpose was specifically and exclusively feminist'.[32] The Saint-Simonian doctrine of different but reciprocal male and female natures clearly shaped this early feminism. For example, one writer argued that women, as distinct from men, were 'people of feeling and inspiration' who 'leap over rules and traditions that men deviate from only with great difficulty'.[33] Such arguments, based on the premise of the basic difference between male and female natures, were to dominate French nineteenth-century feminist thought.

Many Saint-Simonians were disillusioned by the argument between Enfantin and Bazard, and the number of supporters declined. The final blow to the movement came in 1832, when police repression first closed their meeting rooms and residences, and then arrested Enfantin himself in December 1832.

In the months after 1830, the Saint-Simonians had attracted considerable public and media attention. Attending their meetings even became fashionable, but, as can be seen in document 5.4, many who listened went for amusement rather than out of sympathy for their ideas. To hostile critics such as Balzac, Saint-Simonianism seemed a laughable caricature of Catholicism, rather than a serious political movement.

The movement changed radically during its brief years, and was skilled at drawing in people from different sectors of society. Probably, as is the case with modern religious cults, its great attraction was its ability to rationalise individual failure, to help isolated or depressed people cope with feelings of marginality, and to offer hope – usually fallaciously – for the future. Analysing letters written by Saint-Simonians, Neil McWilliam comments: 'Saint-Simonianism is perceived as offering a sense of purpose in life, where previously only self-doubt existed.'[34] This source of hope had a different meaning for the student, the seamstress, or the philosopher.

While Saint-Simonians were involved in some of the first attempts at working-class self-organisation, their most lasting legacy was to create a collective ideal of solidarity for a forward-looking, technocratic section of the French bourgeoisie: an ideal which was to retain its power in the 1850s and beyond.

By comparison, Fourier's ideas never gained a wide hearing. Fourier initially tried to debate with the Saint-Simonians but, in 1831, perhaps motivated by jealousy for their apparent success, he published an angry polemic, arguing that they were charlatans and hypocrites. To compete with the *Globe*,

Fourierists raised money for a weekly publication entitled *Le Phalanstère*, which started in June 1832. Initially about a third of its contents were by Fourier himself. Its maximum circulation was about a thousand.[35] The journal's editors, disappointed by its lack of success, argued for opening up its columns to wider debates and a more diverse readership but Fourier was alarmed by this proposal. Arguments about contents exhausted the team, and by August 1833 the *Phalanstère* had to be converted into a monthly. While never acquiring the readership that the *Globe* had gained, it did succeed it making contacts across France, including the Lyon silk-weavers' *Echo de la Fabrique*.

Fourier's most gifted follower was Victor Considérant, who edited the more successful *Démocratie Pacifique* in the 1840s, and who was elected as a deputy in 1848. Considérant converted Fourierism into a doctrine of practical social reform, downplaying the themes of sexual liberation and female emancipation. Perhaps the one real success of the Fourierist tradition was in its appeal to writers and artists. Whereas the Saint-Simonians had proposed a narrowly moralistic approach to art, through which the artist was essentially understood as a gifted propagandist, the Fourierists suggested a far more libertarian approach to culture: art was to express the values of harmony.[36]

These writers, groups, sects and cults came to form a semi-permanent political underground in the 1840s. How effective were they? What sort of people did they attract? One person who attempted to evaluate the utopian socialists was the socialist-feminist, Flora Tristan, who toured France in 1843 and 1844.

Tristan had had an exciting life prior to 1844: she was unmarried and pregnant when she was fifteen, had married and then divorced, lived in Britain and Peru, and had written on the difficulties encountered by women travellers, on the death penalty, and on divorce. Her visits to London in 1828–31 and 1835–40 allowed her to study the beginnings of industrial capitalism. She was particularly concerned by the contraction of the public activity of women in this new society. Like her near-contemporary Friedrich Engels, she also saw the potential power of working-class resistance to industrial capitalism. Her *Workers' Union*, published in 1843, called for a unified working-class movement to oppose capitalism and to create a society in which women would be men's equals.

Tristan was a brave, tough-minded woman. She noted that everybody was speaking '*about the workers*, but nobody has tried to speak *to the workers*'.[37] Following the publication of her *Workers' Union,* she put her words into practice by touring France, partly to publicise her book, but more importantly to encourage workers to form their own class-based organisations. This strategy was, of course, very different from that of the utopian socialists.

Her tour took place in 1843 and early 1844. She died shortly after its completion, but the journal she kept has been preserved. It makes fascinating reading. In each town, Tristan made contact with groups she considered might be sympathetic. These included dissident priests, members of the old-fashioned *compagnonnages* and utopian socialists.

She started in Paris, noting the difficulties that she had in debating with the Saint-Simonians: 'their hobby-horse is authority ... for which they cannot give the slightest definition'.[38] By April 1843 she reached Dijon, to the south of Paris. There she found 'a lot of Phalansteriens [followers of Fourier] who, like all the others, are only good for talking' (Tristan, 1980, I: 81). Later in April she met more Phalansteriens in Chalon. These seemed different. They were 'a group of young people ... perhaps not very bright or scientific, but with a great deal of faith, and above all with heart and fraternity. They have a quality which their age usually refuses: they are reasonable, they have faith and warmth, but no exaltation' (Tristan, 1980, I: 98).

Lyon was disappointing: here Tristan found workers and socialists were divided among themselves. 'One is for Cabet, the other for Fourier, and they spend their time in arguing' (Tristan, 1980, I: 131). She had a conversation with a female Icarian, who told her, 'Madame, I thought your little book was quite good, but us communists, we've got something much better as we've got a complete plan ... I want my Icar and to live in Icarie, and that's all.' Tristan reflected ruefully 'Cabet has done a lot of harm to the workers. He has paralysed them ... today all they think about is the kingdom of Icarie' (Tristan, 1980, I: 134). On the other hand, even she conceded Cabet's success in appealing to previously de-politicised workers (see documents 5.3). Later she met some Fourierists. 'I met some Phalansterien workers. They were the first, and they seemed very stupid. Some Phalansterien women also visited, and they were just as stupid' (Tristan, 1980, I: 135). She noted the differences between her socialism, based on working-class action, and the social reform schemes of these Fourierists. 'Counting on the bourgeoisie is a stupidity which I can leave to the Fourierists,' she commented bitterly (Tristan, 1980, I: 143). In Lyon, the majority of Fourierists seemed to be middle class, and followed Considérant in interpreting Fourier as a defender of property rights (Tristan, 1980, I: 167).

Tristan is dismissive of these little groups and, in turn, her doctrine of working-class power got little response from them. However, we can gain some other points from her tour. Her diary gives an intriguing glimpse of a political underground, and shows that these groups had acquired some lasting presence in many towns. They were often no more than discussion groups, but some were involved in publishing and, sometimes, more practical politics. To many observers their ideas seemed to be a source of needless division, but we should be careful not to dismiss them: even utopian speculations could be the stimulus through which isolated militants and thinkers learnt how to discuss issues which were not on the government's agenda.

The language of utopian socialism took its revenge on Tristan. She had a very mixed reception, ranging from outright hostility, through incredulity ('I didn't realise she was a *woman*' was said more than once as she got off the coach), to some interest and sympathy. One reason for this sympathy was the old Saint-Simonian quest for 'the Mother'. This superwoman, who was prepared to travel across France by herself, to lecture priests and harangue social scientists, to visit the poor and to talk to workers, surely she could not be just an ordinary woman! She had to be *the* Mother whom Enfantin had searched for ...

– CONCLUSION –

These visionaries and planners began some of the most important political movements of the nineteenth century, arguably constituting the first feminist grouping and the first 'genuine socialist "party" with a working-class base', not only in French history, but in the history of the world.[39]

Their 'socialism' was a vague and ill-defined belief. The first modern use of the word socialism was to be found in the title of an essay by Pierre Leroux, 'Individualism and Socialism'.[40] Leroux's aim was to contrast two undesirable models of society: one in which individuals were always placed above social needs, and the second in which social needs always dominated individuals. However, it seems that many people never got further than reading the title. 'Socialism', seen as the opposite of the Orleanists' individualism, began to attract attention.

The utopian socialists can be credited with giving a voice to those who were normally silent. Issues such as the status of women, sexual identity, the treatment of children and the nature of work often seemed ridiculous to contemporaries, and were easy targets for caricaturists' scorn. However, they have returned again and again to our attention.

– IV. DOCUMENTS –

– DOCUMENT 5.1: SAINT-SIMON AND INDUSTRY –

This passage is taken from one of Saint-Simon's later writings. It shows his confidence in the ability of modern industry to reform social relations.

> In the old system, the people were *commanded* [enrégimentées] by their leaders; in the new system they are *combined* with them. Military leaders *commanded*, but industrial leaders only *direct*. In the first case, the people were subjects, in the second

they are share-holders. This is the marvellous point about industrial organizations: all who are involved are, in reality, collaborators, associates, from the simplest labourer to the richest manufacturer or the cleverest engineer.

When men enter a society without bringing some skill, or some stake, there will inevitably be masters and slaves. The workers would not be silly enough to agree to such an arrangement if they could avoid it. One can only conceive of such a society as being based on force. But in a co-operative society, into which everyone brings either a skill or a stake, there is true association, and the only inequality which exists is that of skills or interests, which are both necessary and inevitable, and which it would be absurd, ridiculous and dangerous to try to make disappear.

Each gains the status and the benefits proportional to his capacity and his stake: this constitutes the fullest form of equality which is desirable and possible. This is the basic character of industrial societies, and this is what the people have gained by organizing themselves with leaders of trades and crafts. No command is exercised over them by their new leaders, except that which is strictly necessary to maintain good order in work – which is a very minor matter. Industrial capacity is by its nature as unwilling to exercise despotic power as it is to accept it.

Source: Claude-Henri de Saint-Simon, 'L'Organisateur' (1820), in *Oeuvres*, Vol. II, part IV (Paris, 1966), pp. 150–2

– DOCUMENT 5.2: FOURIER AND MARRIAGE –

Fourier was particularly sensitive to the psychological tensions created by the new bourgeois ideals concerning marriage: his barbed comments spoke eloquently about the domestic unhappiness of men and women.

They say that in politics, it is the strongest that make the laws. It is not the same in domestic matters. The male sex, although it is the strongest, has not created a law to its advantage by creating isolated households and permanent marriages. You would think that such an order was the work of a third sex which wanted to condemn the other two to boredom. Who could think of anything better than isolated households and permanent marriages as a way to create boredom, venality, and dishonesty in matters of love and pleasure?

Marriage seems to have been invented to reward the depraved. The more a man is crafty and seductive, the easier it is for him to gain wealth and public respect by marriage. The same can be said for women. Use the worst tactics to get a rich partner: as soon as you have married you become a little saint, a loving spouse, a model of virtue. To suddenly win an immense fortune by exploiting a young lady is such a marvellous thing, that public opinion will forgive a lad everything he had done to succeed. Everyone declares that he is a good husband, a good son, a good brother, a good son-in-law, a good parent, a good friend, a good neighbour, a good citizen, a good republican … Public opinion acts in the same way with the captain of industry who manages to marry a lot of money … In 'civilization'*, fathers and mothers cannot do better than persuading their children to try any means, fair or foul, to get a rich spouse, for marriage, that civil baptism, wipes out all sins in the eyes of public opinion. It is not so tolerant towards other upwardly mobile people: it reminds them for a long time of their previous sins.

For each man who finds happiness in a rich marriage, how many others find this bond to be a form of torture! They may well recognize that women's enslavement is of no advantage at all to men. The male sex is tricked into carrying these chains which become an object of terror, and how men are punished, by the troubles of this bond, for having turned women into slaves.

★ 'Civilization' was a pejorative term in Fourier's vocabulary.

Source: Fourier, *Quatre Mouvements*, p. 136

– DOCUMENT 5.3: FLORA TRISTAN AND THE ICARIANS –

This is an extract from the private diary which Tristan kept as she toured France in 1843–4. It concerns her visit to Lyon in May 1843. Tristan was annoyed when, after she arrived half an hour late for a meeting, she found that the Icarians she had hoped to meet had left without waiting.

Poor old Father Cabet: he's got the disciples which he deserved. Such a man, such a monstrously vain, empty person could only create such ridiculous things ... All the pure Icarians are the same. However, I must be fair to this man, and acknowledge that he's done some good. With his novel about Icarie, whose form and content is enough to make any worker with a bit of sensitivity grit their teeth, he's motivated those basically ignorant, unmoving workers who wouldn't be touched by any other ideas. Mr Cabet's racket [*affaire*] is an organized form of narrow and inward-looking self-interest: the type of ideas which suit these workers. He shows them each a tidy and comfortable flat, a little garden, while keeping the father's and mother's authority intact, while giving them their own country, better than all the others, a leader (an Icar) chosen by them and so belonging to them. He was sure to please and to attract that section of the working class which is still blind or at least short-sighted, and which can't see further then their own narrow self-interest. This is so true that the strong, intelligent, generous part of the working class has rejected Icarie with disgust, and sometimes with a deep sense of pity. Everyday I'm happy to hear workers come up to me and say, with a sort of pity, 'What's this old man Icar jabbering on to us about? "Do we all want our own little garden, wouldn't that be nice?" We want the whole earth to be one great, magnificent garden for everyone, we want all humanity to be one great big family, in which each can live according to their desires and receive according to their needs.' All the intelligent Communists (and they're the great majority) think this way. They should not be confused with the Icarians of Father Cabet.

Source: Flora Tristan, *Le Tour de France*, 2 Vols (Paris, 1980), Vol. I, pp. 146–7

– DOCUMENT 5.4: BALZAC VISITS THE SAINT-SIMONIANS –

This passage is taken from an article published in the wake of the July 1830 Revolution, in which Balzac explained the effects of the Revolution to a provincial readership. During this period, Balzac was rethinking his own politics: having been a liberal supporter of the Revolution, he was growing disillusioned. His deep hostility to the Saint-Simonians' imitation of religion was indicative of his growing respect for Catholicism.

You could not imagine a more curious sight than the Saint-Simonians. They confirm all Voltaire's fears. Over the last few days we have found a little religion that we can laugh about. The Saint-Simonian sect already has a temple where some of their priests preach a comic gospel. There must be a few talented people in this school, because it is no small matter to seek to replace the fanaticism of mystery with the fanaticism of ideas, or to say, like Oven [sic: 'Owen'] and the methodists, that anyone can just turn up and make themselves a priest or a teacher, or to introduce a religion into politics. Unfortunately, the Saint-Simonian attack the sovereigns [*écus*] which you provincials love to horde ... They want all society's property to be controlled, and to prevent us from inheriting from our fathers. For the moment, the tax inspectors have left them alone, but the administration is so cunning! ... In fact, I would be annoyed if [the Saint-Simonians] get too stupid, because the pleasure which they give us would not last for much longer. These days, we go to the Saint-Simonians like we go to the Variétés [theatre]. Potier* never spoke such incomprehensible phrases with such dignity as these gentlemen preach their funeral sermons on inheritance rights. The director of the troupe is as clever as Mr Poirson**, because he pays some people to listen, some to understand. He has found women who have ecstatic experiences. Their pope has been enthroned, and I expect that this Sunday he will announce that Saint-Simon has been appointed a member of the Holy Trinity, replacing the Holy Spirit.

* an actor at the Variétés
** director of the Gymnase theatre

Source: Honoré de Balzac, second 'Lettre sur Paris', 9 October 1830,
in *Oeuvres diverses*, edited by Pierre-Georges Castex, Roland Chollet,
René Guise and Christiane Guise (Paris, 1996), pp. 877–8

– V. FURTHER READING –

The utopian socialists have been studied by a wide variety of scholars, including historians, political scientists and philosophers. A number of works survey the utopians' ideas. Paul Bénichou, *Les temps des prophètes: doctrines de l'âge romantique* (Paris: Gallimard, 1977) sets the intellectual context in which their ideas developed. Frank and Fritzie Manuel, *Utopian Thought in the Western World* (Oxford: Blackwell, 1979) is a quite encyclopedic review of utopias, but its centre of gravity is the sixteenth, seventeenth and eighteenth centuries. Frank Manuel, *The Prophets of Paris* (Cambridge, Mass., Harvard UP, 1962) considers the nineteenth-century utopians in more detail. All these works say little about the social context of utopian ideas, or about the movements they inspired. Friedrich Engels, 'Socialism: Utopian and Scientific' (various editions) is a clearly argued essay which clarifies the differences between Marxism and utopian socialism.

Neil McWilliam, *Dreams of Happiness: Social Art and the French Left, 1830–1850* (Princeton: Princeton UP, 1993) considers the specific relationship between artists and utopians in a lively and readable manner. Susan F. Grogan,

French Socialism and Sexual Difference: Women and the New Society, 1803–44 (Basingstoke: Macmillan, 1992) discusses the utopians' contribution to the development of feminism. Bruno Viard (ed.), *Pierre Leroux; A la source perdue de socialisme français* (Paris: Desclée de Brouwer, 1997) is a useful collection of texts by a unfairly ignored thinker and activist.

Jonathan Beecher, *Charles Fourier: the Visionary and his World* (London: California UP, 1986) is a wonderfully evocative biography and critical study of Fourier. It is essential reading for anyone seriously interested in studying this topic. Beecher has also written a shorter study – 'Parody and Liberation in the New Amorous World of Charles Fourier', *History Workshop* 20 (1985), 125–33 – and has edited *The Utopian Vision of Charles Fourier* (London: Cape, 1972), a collection of texts by Fourier. Joan Roelofs, 'Fourier and Computer Dating', *Telos* 65 (1985), 127–36, is a short, witty study, fully in the spirit of her subject.

Christopher H. Johnson, *Utopian Communism in France: Cabet and the Icarians, 1839–1851* (Cornell: Cornell UP, 1974) is the only full-length English-language study of the Icarians: it explores the social context in which they developed. 'Communism and the Working-Class before Marx: the Icarian Experience', *American Historical Review* 76 (1971), 642–89 is a shorter study by the same author.

There have been many studies of the Saint-Simonians. Robert B. Carlisle, *The Proffered Crown: Saint-Simonianism and the Doctrine of Hope* (Baltimore: John Hopkins UP, 1987) is the only recent full-length study in English: it is an eloquent defence of their ideas, but is weak on their social context. 'Saint-Simonian Radicalism: A Definition and a Direction', *French Historical Studies* 5:4 (1968), 430–45 is a shorter study by the same author. Sébastien Charléty, *Histoire du Saint-Simonisme (1825–1864),* (Paris: Gonthier, nd) is an older study, but still useful in following the varying forms of Saint-Simonianism. Jean-Paul Frick, 'L'Utopie de Saint-Simon', *Revue française de science politique* 38 (1988), 387–401 examines their relationship with capitalist political economy. Claire G. Moses, 'Saint-Simonian Men/Saint-Simonian Women; the Transformation of Feminist Thought in 1830s France', *Journal of Modern History* 54 (1982), 240–67 is a well-written study of feminism and Saint-Simonianism. Mary Pickering, 'Auguste Comte and the Saint-Simonians', *French Historical Studies* 18:1 (1993), 211–36: analyses the opposition of the philosopher Comte to the Saint-Simonians, while Bruce Tolley, 'Balzac et les Saint-Simoniens', *L'Année Balzacienne* (1966), 49–66 does the same for Balzac.

Tristan was not a utopian socialist, but the links between her thinking and the utopians has been discussed in several works. Maíre Cross and Tim Gray, *The Feminism of Flora Tristan* (Oxford: Berg, 1992), S. Joan Moon, 'Feminism and Socialism: the utopian synthesis of Flora Tristan' in M. J. Boxer and J. H. Quataert (eds), *Socialist Women* (New York: Elsevier, 1978), and Margaret Talbot, 'An Emancipated Voice; Flora Tristan and Utopian Allegory', *Feminist Studies* 17 (1991), 219–40 consider her political legacy. Felicia Gordon and Maíre Cross (eds), *Early French Feminisms, 1830–1940* (Cheltenham: Edward Elgar, 1996) is a useful collection of texts, which includes some of Tristan's writings.

Alan B. Spitzer, *The French Generation of 1820* (Princeton: Princeton UP, 1987) explores the experience of young people, and notes the attraction of utopian ideas. Maurice Agulhon, *Une ville ouvrière au temps du socialisme utopique: Toulon de 1815 à 1848* (Paris: Plon, 1970) is a case study of early working-class politics, which considers the effects of utopian ideas.

– NOTES –

1. Antony Esler, 'Youth in Revolt; the French Generation of 1830' in R. J. Bezucha (ed.), *Modern European Social History* (Lexington, Mass: Heath, 1972), pp. 301–34 (p. 308).
2. See Alfred de Musset, *La Confession d'un enfant du siècle* (Paris: Colin, 1962 [1834–6]).
3. Alan B. Spitzer, *The French Generation of 1820* (Princeton: Princeton UP, 1987), pp. 42–3. The next paragraphs owe much to Spitzer's work.
4. Spitzer, *Generation*, p. 109.
5. Saint-Simon, 'Lettre d'un habitant de Genève à ses contemporains', *Oeuvres*, Vol. I (Paris: Anthropos, 1966), part I, p. 26.
6. A. Hirschman, *The Passions and the Interests: Political Arguments for Capitalism before its Triumph* (Princeton: Princeton UP, 1977).
7. Saint-Simon, 'L'Organisateur', *Oeuvres*, Vol. II, part IV, p. 24.
8. Saint-Simon, 'Lettre de Henry Saint-Simon à messieurs les ouvriers', *Oeuvres* VI, pp. 436–44.
9. Quoted in Robert B. Carlisle, *The Proffered Crown: Saint-Simonianism and the Doctrine of Hope* (Baltimore: John Hopkins UP, 1987), p. 41.
10. Charles Fourier, *Les Quatre mouvements* (Paris: Pauvert, 1967), p. 74.
11. Friedrich Engels, 'The Progress of Social Reform on the Continent', in Marx and Engels, *Collected Works*, Vol. 3 (London: Lawrence and Wishart, 1975), p. 394.
12. Victor Considérant, *Description du Phalanstère* (Paris: Ressources, 1980), pp. 20–1.
13. Charles Fourier, *Le Nouveau monde amoureux*, ed. Simone Debout-Oleszkiewicz (Paris: Anthropos, 1984), p. 70.
14. Fourier, *Nouveau monde*, p. 137.
15. Fourier, *Quatre mouvements*, p. 114 (original emphases).
16. Christopher H. Johnson, *Utopian Communism in France: Cabet and the Icarians, 1839–1851* (Cornell: Cornell UP, 1974), p. 37.
17. Etienne Cabet, *Voyage en Icarie* (Geneva: Slatkine, 1979), p. iii.
18. Cabet, *Voyage*, p. 87.
19. Cabet, *Voyage*, p. 105.
20. Johnson, *Communism*, p. 56.
21. Johnson, *Communism*, p. 83.

22. Johnson, *Communism*, p. 145.
23. Karl Marx and Friedrich Engels, *The Holy Family, or Critique of Critical Criticism* (London: Lawrence and Wishart, 1980), pp. 162–3.
24. Spitzer, *Generation*, p. 153.
25. Carlisle, *Crown*, p. 48.
26. Sebastien Charléty, *Histoire du Saint-Simonisme (1825–1864)* (Paris: Gonthier, nd), pp. 65–6.
27. Charléty, *Histoire*, p. 127.
28. Neil McWilliam, *Dreams of Happiness: Social Art and the French Left, 1830–50* (Princeton: Princeton UP, 1993) p. 86.
29. Claire Moses, 'Saint-Simonian Men/Saint-Simonian Women: The transformation of feminist thought in 1830s France', *Journal of Modern History* 54 (1982), 240–67 (pp. 248, 255).
30. Claire Goldberg Moses, *French Feminism in the Nineteenth Century* (New York, State University of New York Press, 1984), pp. 52–3.
31. Moses, *French Feminism*, p. 66.
32. Moses, 'Saint-Simonian Men/Saint-Simonian Women', p. 252.
33. Claire Goldberg Moses and Leslie Wahl Rabine (eds), *Feminism, Socialism and French Romanticism* (Bloomington: Indiana UP, 1993), p. 296.
34. McWilliam, *Dreams*, p. 97.
35. Jonathan Beecher, *Charles Fourier: the Visionary and His World* (London: California UP, 1986), pp. 418–20, p. 435.
36. One example of this is Théophile Gautier's 'Preface' to his novel *Mademoiselle de Maupin*, published in 1835–6.
37. Flora Tristan, *Union ouvrière*, eds Daniel Armogathe and Jacques Grandjonc (Paris: Des femmes, 1986), p. 197 (original emphases).
38. Flora Tristan, *Le Tour de France*, 2 Vols (Paris: Maspero, 1980), Vol. I, p. 38.
39. Roger Magraw, *A History of the French Working Class Vol. I: The Age of Artisan Revolution* (Oxford: Blackwell, 1992), p. 66.
40. A copy of this essay can be found in Bruno Viard (ed.), *Pierre Leroux: A la source perdue de socialisme français* (Paris: Desclée de Brouwer, 1997).

CHAPTER 6

1848: The Republican Utopia

The Orleanists of 1830 had hoped that by proclaiming their moderation, by steering a path between Jacobinism and monarchism, by accepting the red, white and blue tricolour flag but refusing republicanism, they could create a compromise regime which would unite France. However, eighteen years after the 1830 Revolution, a full-scale social revolution erupted. This new revolution rejected Orleanist compromises and proclaimed republican principles. In returning to republicanism, the revolutionaries of 1848 had to overcome the deep hostility to the First Republic (1792–1804) expressed by counter-revolutionary and monarchist historians. Lamartine, one of the greatest republican orators and briefly President of France in 1848, recognised this fear. For many people, he observed, 1789 evoked images of violence, anarchy, terror, civil war, dictatorial laws, the confiscation of property and the guillotine.[1] Given these conditions, how did the revolutionaries of 1848 win widespread sympathy for their movement?

Chapters 6, 7 and 8 will discuss three episodes from the 1848 Revolution, with this chapter considering the collapse of the July Monarchy, and the ideals of social harmony which circulated in March and April 1848. The focus will be on Paris. The next chapter will examine the socialist left of 1848–51 and will draw examples from the southern department of the Pyrénées-Orientales. Chapter 8 will examine a quite different by-product of 1848: a new type of right-wing movement – Bonapartism – which made use of Revolutionary images and democratic tactics, even when it disagreed with democratic principles. Examples will be drawn from the northern department of the Somme.

– I. PARTICIPANTS –

The July Monarchy faced two challenges in the late 1840s. One was an age-old social problem: famine. The second was a new protest movement: the banquet campaign of 1847–8.

Orleanist governments seemed uncaring toward the poor. Ministers could defend their record by pointing to many measures: their commitment to economic expansion would – supposedly – lead to a better standard of living for the mass of the population. Their reform of popular schooling would eventually empower the ignorant and excluded. They also encouraged institutions such as savings-banks, which would help the poor to weather downturns in economic cycles. However, when it came to providing immediate relief for poverty, such policies seemed worthless. A small-minded, mean-spirited attitude gripped Orleanist ideologues, who sank to mouthing simple platitudes about the need to respect private property and the free market, while the poor took their last possessions to the pawnshops, and then resorted to almost medieval measures: begging on the streets, prostitution, tramping the countryside in search of work or charity, or rioting in the markets, calling for cheap bread and immediate economic assistance.

Signs of poverty were everywhere. Peter Amann notes that in 1846 almost three-quarters of tenants living in Paris were so poor that they were excused from paying rent-tax.[2] Examining the period from 1838 to 1846, Roger Magraw calculates that on average approximately ten million francs were spent each year on welfare. However, in 1847 this figure shot up to twenty million.[3] Peter McPhee finds another startling indication of social crisis: surveying marriage rates, he estimates that in seventy per cent of departments, marriage rates for the year 1847 were the lowest for the whole decade of the 1840s.[4]

This depression started in 1845 with the spread of a potato fungus, similar to that which later devastated the Irish potato crop. The shortage of potatoes, coupled with bad grain harvests, made grain prices double in 1845–7. This meant that the bulk of the population were spending a large part of their income on bread and were consequently less able to buy consumer goods. This in turn created a crisis in the manufacturing sector, resulting in over four thousand bankruptcies in 1847. In the autumn of 1847 there was finally an abundant grain harvest, but while bread prices fell, there was no economic and commercial revival. Gold reserves were exhausted and interest rates remained high.

The depression led to increased social polarisation. Victor Hugo recorded in his diary a scene from 1846. A rich lady passed by a beggar without looking at him.

> To me, this man is not simply a man, he is the very symbol of misery. He is a gloomy, deformed apparition which appears in the light of day, evoking a revolution which is still in the shadows, but which will come. Once the poor man rubbed shoulders with the rich … but now [the two] do not look at each other. They pass by. This could go on for a long time. But from the moment that this man

realizes that this woman exists, while this woman does not notice that this man is there, then a catastrophe is inevitable.[5]

In Hugo's account, the poor man represents a social reality which is ignored by the lady, who seems to stand for an arrogant, uncaring society. Such scenes grew more common in the months before the Revolution. Moreover, the poor did not always remain passive, as table 6.1 demonstrates. Bread riots and other forms of collective violence increased.

Table 6.1: Acts of violence by fifty or more people, directed against property or persons[6]

Year	Number of incidents	Number of participants (in thousands)
1845	4	1
1846	27	41
1847	33	11

Sometimes these were almost 'traditional' marketplace riots; in other areas convoys of grain carriages were attacked by angry crowds who resented the export of foodstuffs during periods of near-starvation, while forests were invaded by poachers and people stealing wood for fuel.

Local authorities became suspicious of all gatherings of workers or peasants. For example, in Roanne (Loire) in October 1846, workers were employed to rebuild the banks of the River Loire following its flooding. An official commented that 'the large number of workers needed for these repair works and the unhappy state of the poor classes could have led to disorders which it was wise to prevent'[7] and he recommended that troops should be stationed close to them. The first response of many local authorities to any social problem was to call out troops, to the point where the Minister of War began to protest at this misuse of resources. For example, in February 1848 the Bishop of Corsica noted that when highwaymen were arrested, juries were extremely reluctant to convict because, he argued, they felt intimidated. His solution? Call out the army. The Minister of War replied 'soldiers are not going make jurors more confident, they will not relieve their consciences of fear, nor put their impartiality above their passions.'[8]

This combination of high-sounding rhetoric about social reform with simple-minded repression served the July Monarchy well for most of its eighteen years and guaranteed its survival. However, it could not silence an articulate minority who developed an eloquent *moral* critique of the regime. For example, in March 1834 a law limited the right of meeting by associations, in order to stop republican and labour protest. Lamartine spoke against this law in the Chamber of Deputies. His scorn for this blindly repressive measure can still be felt almost one hundred and seventy years later.

> Society's falling apart? – [Pass] a law against public gatherings. Public spirit is changing, is growing corrupt? – [Pass] a press law. Sixty thousand workers seize Lyon and unveil the powderkeg on which industry rests? – [Pass] a law on coalitions. Brave young people who have nothing to employ their over-abundant powers dream of the republic, anarchy, disorder? – [Pass] a law on associations! ...
>
> [And what about] laws based on foresight, on the future, on tomorrow? Not a thing![9]

Government policy, argued Lamartine, could be summed up in one word: 'repress!'.

Critics of the Orleanists hoped that the elections of August 1846 would create an energetic new government which would tackle these issues. However, following the election, the government's majority remained as solid as ever.

Table 6.2: Proportion of seats won in general elections, 1834–46[10]

Date	Orleanists %	Democrats %	Legitimists %
1834	68.3	19.2	12.5
1837	68.6	18.2	13.2
1843	70.3	19.8	9.9
1846	70	20.1	9.9

Table 6.2 helps us understand the reformers' frustration. While, as ever, we must include the proviso that any estimate of deputies' loyalty to a particular political grouping in this period is at best an approximation, few historians would seriously disagree with these figures. By the 1840s, Orleanist politicians had learnt how to 'organise' their vote; a certain degree of low-level corruption had become commonplace in elections. Voters would be fed terrifying images of the revolution which the democrats would bring about, or seduced into supporting the government's preferred candidate with promises of railways, canals, tax-breaks, jobs or new economic policies for their regions. Such practices secured enough votes for government candidates to guarantee the survival of the Orleanist majority. Perhaps the most serious criticism of the government's political practices was that it encouraged civil servants to stand for election: such men were extremely unlikely to oppose government policies if they were elected.

There was no great scandal to be uncovered here. Guizot, the man who dominated French politics in the 1840s was fundamentally honest, but many felt alienated from his governments. A comment by Hugo in his diary on 20 June 1847 neatly expresses this feeling: 'Guizot is personally incorruptible, and [yet] he governs by corruption. To me, he looks like an honest woman running a brothel.'[11] Pierre Joseph Proudhon, a working-class political writer, made the same point more bluntly: Guizot was 'the great corruptor'.[12]

People who were dismayed by this apparent corruption faced a difficult choice. How do you oppose a corrupt system? There seemed a great danger that anyone entering parliamentary politics would be sucked into the vicious circle of deals, threats and promises. On the other hand, was it possible to organise outside the parliament? The July Monarchy's legislation made it difficult to hold public meetings. Moreover, there remained the abiding fear of revolution: if the opposition revived this anxiety, there was a great danger that they would push voters back to the Orleanists.

The parliamentary opposition tried again to introduce social and political reforms in the spring of 1847. Following the predictable defeat of their proposals, they then discussed other methods of opposition, which raised some problems. The opposition was not a united party: a number of contradictory themes aroused their passions. Many were concerned about political corruption: but was this to be solved by adjusting the franchise, or would nothing less than full-scale male democracy solve the problem? Was republicanism preferable to constitutional monarchy? Some were concerned by the government's weak foreign policy, and looked admiringly at the imperialist record of Napoleon's Empire (1806–14). A few – although probably not many – wanted economic action to help the destitute. One or two may have been influenced by the utopian socialists, or by labour movement activists. These discussions were potentially dangerous for the parliamentary opposition: rather than producing a strong movement, they might instead isolate the various strands of opposition politics, and shatter them into competing fragments.

Following the discussions in April and May 1847, it was suggested that banquets should be held to publicise the cause. This tactic proved extremely successful: the image of people gathering for a meal seemed quite different from the violent images associated with the 1789 Revolution. Entry to these banquets was restricted to men who could afford to pay: in this way their 'respectable' character was preserved, and the organisers were safe from the charge of rabble-rousing. Moreover, a banquet was far less likely to arouse police opposition than a public meeting. It provided proof of the calm, collective will of French citizens, united in their rejection of the distorted image of their sovereignty represented by Orleanist governments. In the words of one speaker, the banquets expressed 'the movement which has begun to awaken the land'.[13] Their gatherings would give greater moral force to opposition proposals in the next parliamentary session, which would start in January 1848.

The climax of these banquets was the lengthy toasts to the cause of reform offered by visiting deputies and local political enthusiasts. These would meet with collective acclamations from the assembled banqueteers. Local papers – and sometimes even the national press – would often publish the speeches, thus allowing a wider community of readers to identify with and, in a sense, to participate in the campaign.

The police grew concerned about the banquets. The results of their inquiries have been preserved in a file held in the Archives Nationales. It lists some fifty-two banquets held in thirty-two departments between July and December 1847.[14] This is not a complete list; it concentrates on the most prestigious meetings attended by the best-known deputies. Most of these were significant gatherings, with an average of 414 people attending. During the last months of 1847, more banquets were being held, and, in general, more people attended.

Table 6.3: Reform banquets held July–December 1847, based on list held in AN, BB/30/296[15]

Month	Number of banquets	Average number attending
July 1847	2	300
August 1847	4	112.5
September 1847	8	437.5
October 1847	9	251.5
November 1847	15	432
December 1847	14	595.5

The figures in table 6.3 suggest that the campaign developed successfully. This is misleading. Predictably, splits divided the reformers. Initially, the democratic and republican strand among the opposition, led by Ledru-Rollin, had been sceptical about the campaign, and so few of their speakers participated. Instead, Odilon Barrot became its leading speaker. He represented a grouping which has been labelled the 'dynastic opposition'. They campaigned for the renovation of the Orleanist monarchy, not for its replacement. Barrot and his followers argued that the key fault of the 1831 electoral law was that it isolated voters in small groups in each *arrondissement*, where they could be easily intimidated by the prefect. The solution, they suggested, was to gather together all the voters of each department in the main town for department-wide elections.[16] By November, Ledru-Rollin was growing interested in the campaign, and wished to propose democratic reforms. He agreed to speak at the same banquet as Barrot on 7 November

1847, in Lille. (See document 6.1.) When Barrot heard this, he became suspicious, and insisted that the banquet's toasts should include an oath of loyalty to constitutional monarchy. The organising committee proposed a compromise: there would be a toast 'to the purity, to the sincerity of the institutions founded in July 1830'.[17] Barrot refused this formulation, and left. Of the twelve hundred expected guests, some sixty followed Barrot in boycotting the dinner.

The importance of the split between radical and dynastic oppositions should not be overestimated: they did not form formal parties. They shared ideas which prefigured the themes of the 1848 Revolution. Dynastic and radical oppositions both portrayed the government as a ruthless, parasitic grouping which perverted and ruined the society it dominated. The deputies of the 1840s had betrayed the trust that was placed in them in 1830. Duverger de Hauranne asked whether the representative government was created so that 230 000 voters and 459 deputies could conduct their private affairs at the expense of the country.[18] Good Frenchmen were at the mercy of these 'corrupting ministers'.[19] In Compiègne (Oise), guests listened appreciatively to a polemic which claimed that 'corrupting the voter, corrupting the deputy is all that the administration thinks about',[20] while in Chartres (Eure-et-Loir) they cheered the lines: 'let's hunt out corruption in its twin lairs: in the electoral college and in Parliament!'.[21] Occasionally nationalist themes crept in: a Limoges banquet was told that this government, in its quest for profitable investments, had 'sacrificed everything' to England.[22] The banquet campaign would restore France to her rightful place.

The campaign was presented by its speakers as a conservative movement which defended a moral code violated by the July Monarchy. The basis of this morality was recognisably masculine: it was due to the Orleanists' corruption that men had lost their independence and honour, and had been reduced to a servile position. The speakers' references to prostitution are significant: it was a symbol (even *the* symbol) for a failed family, in which the father could no longer provide for his daughters and, perhaps, was no longer able to control them. (See document 6.1.) Other observers compared the banquet campaign to that other great male ritual: the duel. For example, Barrot wrote 'challenges had been exchanged, and it was inevitable that a duel should follow' to describe a parliamentary debate on the banquets.[23]

The campaign presented a counter-model of political sociability. The opposition deputies were living symbols of a different political culture.

Look at the different reception with which the nation greets the deputies of the [governmental] majority and those of the opposition. The former go by with a forced, embarrassed look, through cold and silent people. Even the hands which are held out to them for favours are gaunt and begging, and these hands are ashamed, and seem to fear some compromising contact. But look … how the deputies of the opposition are greeted, with warm sympathy. With nothing up their sleeves, they shake the hands which are offered to them.[24]

What were these opposition deputies offering France?

During the campaign, two different interpretations of their role were put forward. The first, which could be termed constitutional, suggested that the campaign was taking some political quality from Paris to the provinces. Crémieux told an audience in Orléans, 'we're going from town to town, from arrondissement to arrondissement, from commune to commune, carrying our flag into the darkness in which you're kept.'[25] His words suggested that the centre of political power lay in Paris, and that political debates had to carried into the provinces. A municipal councillor in Rouen (Seine-Maritime) had a similar message for his audience: 'soon a more serious struggle will follow this extra-parliamentary struggle: the [parliamentary] session will begin'.[26] Such comments suggested that the banquet campaign was a supplement to the real parliamentary struggle.

Other themes were proclaimed by the radicals. Consider these descriptions of the banquets and their guests. 'We're a Senate of honest men', Huré told his audience in Lille.[27] In Castres (Tarn) a speaker suggested they form an almost utopian community: they were 'voters and potential parliamentary candidates, doctors and lawyers, farmers and industrialists, intelligent workingmen of all classes … the true friends of order and liberty'.[28] After the split between the dynastic and radical oppositions in Lille, radical deputies began to make their interpretation of the banquet movement clearer. Flocon argued that the 'most eloquent argument' against the adulterated postures of Barrot's dynastic politics was 'your meeting, citizens. It is this meeting of free men, carrying in their hearts … the cult of truth.'[29] In other words, this was no longer a movement to *support* opposition deputies, but rather a representation of the nation which had the power to *replace* existing political structures. Lamartine summed up such radical thinking when he intervened in a parliamentary debate on a law to ban the banquets. He reminded the deputies that there was a political power which was superior to the Chamber: 'That's the country! That's [public] opinion!'[30] The banquet campaign represented this rival authority.

During the banquets there was a striking absence of references to the plight of the poor or to economic exploitation. Indeed, the simple act of holding a banquet in a time of starvation hardly suggests great sympathy with the poor. However, some speakers did raise social issues. Dupont de l'Eure, a radical deputy, told his audience at Neubourg (Seine-Inférieure) that the government 'was making money from the worker's sweat, from the food of the poor, instead of helping relieve their misery'.[31] Another speaker referred to the suffering of the proletariat, and proposed the following solution: 'there is only one remedy for these evils, gentlemen, and that remedy is reform'.[32]

Some used socio-economic terms, including an anti-bourgeois rhetoric, to identify the exploiters.

> Bourgeois! Look at what you're doing to us! You're letting yourself be paralysed by fear; you've betrayed all your natural alliances by following the egoist motto: 'everyone by themselves, everyone for themselves' [*chacun chez soi, chacun pour soi*] ... Your role is over. You've lost the people's trust; don't try to put yourselves at their head.[33]

Such references do not present a coherent analysis of economic exploitation. They make use of an economic vocabulary to raise *moral* themes. The workers' situation was only referred to as an example of a form of oppression suffered under the July Monarchy: exactly how this was to be ended by the opposition's anti-corruption reforms was never made clear. Rather than supporting the new class-based politics associated with the labour movement, speakers stressed the need to integrate the working class into the national community. (See document 6.1.) Once again, the utopian community suggested by the banquets provided the model for social progress: just as workers could (sometimes) sit alongside bourgeois at a banquet, and could cheer the same slogans, so France could be reorganised to allow the integration of the proletariat into a moral national community.

This balanced, harmonious moral community created a new political confidence, and allowed the banqueteers to rebuff the counter-revolutionary image of the French Revolution. Lamartine's research on the Girondins (a republican political grouping during the 1790s) was crucial to this process. At a banquet held to celebrate his work, Lamartine reminded his guests of the lesson of his research. There was a power above the government: 'that's the sovereignty of ideas, the kingdom of the mind! That's the Republic! That's the real Republic!'[34] 'Daniel Stern' (the pseudonym of Marie d'Agoult) noted the effectiveness of Lamartine's rewriting of Revolutionary history. Lamartine presented 'a revolution dressed up in the golden clouds of poetry ... with nothing frightening in it ... He renovated the revolutionary tradition by distancing it from bloody images.'[35] Following such historical revisions, banqueteers were willing to cheer Ledru-Rollin when he told them they were 'the children of the French Revolution'.[36]

During the second half of 1847 these fierce, idealistic speeches had been declaimed in perhaps half the departments, and most newspaper readers had become familiar with their rhetoric. Their ideas may look vague, but they were effective. The opposition's great strength was that it publicly challenged the July Monarchy to debate its principles. The Orleanists' great weakness was that, after eighteen years in power, they still had no effective public vocabulary: their festivals, celebrations and meetings were marked by 'hesitation, reticence and fear'.[37] In other words, what made the July Monarchy different from the preceding regimes was not that it was more corrupt, but that it was less able to defend itself politically.

– II. EVENTS –

A massive banquet was held in Rouen (Seine-Inférieure) on 25 December 1847, gathering some eighteen hundred guests and eighteen speakers. Following this, most opposition deputies considered that the campaign was over. The Chamber of Deputies was due to open, and, in the words of Barrot, 'as the tribune [of parliament] was open to us, it was best that the demonstrations outside should end'.[38]

However, in late December 1847, members of the National Guard and voters from the south-eastern 12th *arrondissement* in Paris began to discuss a new banquet. This move was unusual. Most banquets had hitherto been organised by 'notables', men in positions of power. This new banquet was proposed by carpenters, engineers and minor officers in the National Guard. Their aims were unclear. Some stressed their desire to represent all currents of the opposition. Others asserted their loyalty to constitutional principles. A third strand wanted to demonstrate support for deep, radical reform, not simply a change in government. It soon became clear that the Prefect might ban the event: only then did the radicals reluctantly approach opposition deputies.[39] Some deputies advised them to wait until after the parliamentary session, but the organisers pressed ahead with their plans. Several thousand were invited to attend a banquet and the admission price, at three francs, was significantly lower than previous banquets. Some five or six hundred tickets had been sold by 14 January 1848, when the organisers were told by the Prefect of Police that the event they were planning was illegal.[40]

In February 1848 a new committee of opposition deputies and journalists began once more to plan a Parisian banquet, this time anticipating a smaller number of guests – perhaps one or two thousand – and a higher ticket price of six francs. Instead of being held in the working-class 12th *arrondissement*, it was to be held in the bourgeois east of Paris, in the 1st *arrondissement*, 'as far away as possible from the working-class centres'.[41] Guests were to be invited from all the Parisian *arrondissements*. Initially it was suggested that only voters and National Guardsmen would be admitted, although this requirement was later dropped.[42] There was no specific appeal to either students or workers (both seen as potentially disruptive), but named delegates from both these groups were accepted. The opposition's unity was stressed. There was to be a single toast: 'to the right to hold meetings, and to reform'.[43] Some radical organisers of the previously planned banquet were dismayed by these signs of adherence to the dynastic opposition's principles.

The banquets of 1847 had been held while the Chamber of Deputies was closed: they were a temporary replacement to 'ordinary' politics. Both the planned Parisian banquets were to be held during parliamentary debates. This suggested that they might form a rival centre of political representation to that provided by the Chamber.

On 18 February 1848 a circular from the Ministry of Justice reminded legal officials of the existing laws concerning public order which allowed authorities to ban banquets.[44] On 20 February, the Prefect declared this second banquet to be illegal. Opposition deputies were uncertain how to react: the majority seemed inclined to accept his judgement, but some argued that while he could ban a planned procession of guests to the banquet, he could not ban the meal itself. Some National Guards, annoyed by the deputies' timidity, arranged to meet in the Place de la Madeleine, near the site chosen for the second banquet, on the day it should have been held (22 February).[45] Details of a demonstration to protest about the ban were published in the opposition paper Le National.

By the last week of February 1848 a class coalition for revolutionary action had been formed. Some sophisticated sociological analyses of this grouping have been written, but the brief summary provided by Tilly and Lees is clear enough: it brought together 'a sprinkling of intellectuals, of journalists, of lawyers and other members of the liberal professions, some shopkeepers, and many artisans from the old organized trades.'[46]

On the evening of 21 February a proclamation by the Prefect was printed and posted up across Paris. It denounced the planned banquet as 'a government opposed to the true government'.[47] The authorities had finally noted the implications of the banquet campaign. Late in the evening of 22 February the Prefect wrote a long letter to Guizot, then Foreign Minister, describing the day's troubling events.[48]

During the night of the 21–2 February, a group of workers had set up a tent on the site of the forbidden banquet. It was dismantled with little trouble at eight a.m.: a dozen onlookers watched without reacting. Between eight a.m. and ten a.m. Paris seemed peaceful. A few groups gathered round the new posters to read and discuss them, but they showed no signs of anger.

The first flickers of trouble started at ten a.m. Some workers, dressed in their smocks, and a group of armed National Guards emerged from the east-central quarter of La Bastille, and gathered in the western Place de la Madeleine. Another group of about a thousand students and young workers gathered south of the Seine, near the Pantheon. They marched north, over the Pont-Neuf bridge at eleven a.m., shouting 'Long live reform! Down with Guizot!'. They too arrived in the Place de la Madeleine. The square was now so crowded that carriages could not drive through it. Shopkeepers began to take fright, and pulled down the blinds on their shops.

At noon about a thousand workers and students left the Place de la Madeleine. They marched southwards, singing a song from the French Revolution, over the Seine, to the Chamber of Deputies. They shouted 'Long live reform! Long live Odilon Barrot! Down with Guizot!'. They reached the steps of the Chamber of Deputies, but were prevented from entering. Then they dispersed, some of them marching east to the Ecole Polytechnique, where they spoke to the students, others heading for the working-class suburbs.

Meanwhile, in the Place de la Madeleine, police had been deployed against the demonstrators. Fourteen people were arrested. Another group split away to demonstrate outside the Foreign Ministry, where they shouted 'Long live the Infantry! Down with Guizot!'. Despite their appeals to the soldiers, the demonstrators were charged by both infantrymen and cavalry. They dispersed, but gathered again and returned to the Ministry. Stones were thrown at the soldiers and, more seriously, a group turned back into central Paris and began to break into gunshops.

New groups gathered in the west of Paris, at the Champs-Elysées – then still open ground – and in the nearby Place de la Concorde. They set up barricades made from chairs and carriages. A sentry post was besieged by some three hundred demonstrators who were dispersed by the municipal police and soldiers at four p.m.

Barricades were built outside the Ministry of Finance. The municipal police and infantry were deployed and these barricades taken at six p.m. The demonstrators now gathered in the central market district of Les Halles. They still shouted their appeals to the infantry: 'Long live the Infantry! Down with the Municipal Guards!' More gunshops were raided. Soldiers were posted to guard the bridges across the Seine and the public squares during the night.

Throughout 22 February, attempts were made by the authorities to mobilise the National Guard. Roinville, a master carpenter, later recalled that drums beat the appeal for his unit between five and six a.m. on 22 February. Where two thousand might have been expected, only 150 responded. Roinville recalled: 'I was among them; my political friends were also there. We expressed our opinion out loud, by crying "Long live reform! Down with Guizot!" The people joined in.' Their commander understandably decided not to send them into action. They were called out the next day, and responded in the same way, adding insults to the colonel. Two days later, on

24 February, they would gather together once again and occupy themselves in seizing army barracks, then distributing arms to the people.

On the evening of 22 February, some National Guards were mobilised. Joint patrols of National Guardsmen and soldiers marched through the 12th *arrondissement*. They were met with cries of 'Long live reform! Long live the National Guard! Long live the Infantry! Down with Guizot!' Across Paris, most of the National Guards joined the people, and began to shout their slogans and sing their songs. Early on 23 February, Louis-Philippe was told that of 384 National Guard companies in Paris, only six or seven were loyal to the regime.[49] If the bulk of the National Guard had remained loyal, the Revolution could easily have been stamped out. Without them, Louis-Philippe was in a precarious position.

Guizot announced his resignation from the government at 4.30 p.m. on 23 February. The news was greeted with joy across Paris. Hubert Lannette, a cabinet-maker from the 12th *arrondissement*, and Jean Schumacher, an engineer, later recalled how they had marched at the head of a column of several thousand 'citizens and National Guards' to the *National*, to insist that they print an article applauding Guizot's fall. 'We sang the *Marseillaise*, the *Chant du Départ*, and other patriotic tunes. The shouts we cried were "Long live Reform! Down with the System! Down with Guizot!" ... Many people cheered as we marched by ... the houses were lit up and it all looked like a holiday.' Marching in wide ranks, they took up the whole of the road.[50] This sense of jubilation was felt by many sympathetic observers. 'The streets were rocking with the cries and joy of the crowd', wrote Hugo, 'it was like a festival.'[51]

The dynastic opposition, represented by Barrot and Thiers, considered that the Revolution was now over, and that soon they would form a cabinet. However, a procession marched out from the eastern working-class Saint-Antoine quarter to the western Place de la Madeleine. Close to the Place, it passed through the Boulevard des Capucines. Near the Foreign Ministry, someone started shooting. The soldiers guarding the Ministry then fired on the crowd. Perhaps forty, maybe fifty, were killed. On the evening of 23 February a low, open carriage transported the corpses of demonstrators through Paris. It stopped outside the offices of the *National* paper. 'It was surrounded by a vast crowd, who cried "To arms! Vengeance! We've been betrayed!"'[52] When Louis-Philippe heard of this massacre, he finally called on Thiers to form a new government.

Thiers agreed to head a government at 2.30 a.m. on 24 February. According to Hugo, by then there were 1 574 barricades on the streets of Paris.[53] Thiers still hoped that concerted military action could save the monarchy. However, regular army troops had begun to fraternise with the rebels: near the Ecole Polytechnique, Parisians gave soldiers bread and wine, and then walked through their ranks. A little later the colonel gave the order to fix bayonets, but it was impossible to make the soldiers obey.[54] At 10.30 a.m. Louis-Philippe reviewed soldiers and National Guards around the Tuileries palace in the centre of Paris. At first, some cheered him, but one National Guard unit shouted 'Long live reform!'. This incident may finally have persuaded Louis-Philippe that his situation was hopeless. He began to consider his abdication. At eleven a.m. the Hôtel-de-Ville (town hall) was taken by students from the Ecole Polytechnique and the National Guard: the infantry soldiers did not resist them. Later in the afternoon, the Tuileries palace was invaded. (See document 6.2.)

On the evening of 24 February an excited crowd gathered round the Hôtel-de-Ville. Dupont de l'Eure read out a list of members of a Provisional Government, which had been compiled in the offices of the *National*. Lamartine was chosen as President, and six out of the seven cabinet members were either journalists or editors linked to the paper. The seventh member was Ledru-Rollin. The *National* wanted to avoid committing this new authority to republicanism, but there was great pressure from the crowd. 'Long live the Republic! We don't want any more dynasties', they cried.[55] Lamartine bowed to their wishes, and proclaimed the Republic. One reason for the crowd's intransigence was their memory of the 1830 Revolution, which they saw as an occasion on which wily Orleanists had hoodwinked 'the people'. This time, the Parisian crowd insisted on clear evidence of the new government's willingness to share its victory with the rebels who had fought on the barricades. Soon, new names were added to the *National* list. Three were drawn from the more social reform-orientated *Réforme* paper: Louis Blanc, a republican utopian socialist, 'Albert' (the pseudonym of Alexandre Martin, a republican worker-militant), and Flocon (the editor of the *Réforme*).

Monarchy had finally collapsed in France. While members of the dynastic opposition had argued for the renovation of constitutional monarchy, the majority of the revolutionaries saw clear alternatives: monarchy or Republic. Having destroyed the monarchy, they must now build the Republic. Lamartine was determined that this Republic was not to be a bloody dictatorship on the model of Robespierre's Terror of 1794–5. On 26 February, capital punishment for political offences was abolished. In a typical gesture, he then applauded his own wisdom: 'this spontaneous cry from the soul of the government reveals the nature of the French nation'.[56]

The Fourierist paper, *Démocratie pacifique*, edited by Victor Considérant, was also concerned that the Revolution might be stolen. In order to guarantee that the working class would benefit, it drew up a petition for 'the Right to

Work', which was presented to the Provisional Government on 25 February.[57] The Provisional Government responded to workers' demands by recognising the right to work, and – on 28 February – by creating a type of subsidiary parliament, the Luxemburg Commission. This was chaired by Blanc and Albert, and was to discuss the organisation of work under the Republic.

Before concluding this section on the Revolution, let us note one key innovation. What did the first group of demonstrators shout as they marched into central Paris? – 'Long live reform! Down with Guizot!'. What did demonstrators shout when confronted by the infantry? – 'Long live the Infantry! Down with Guizot!'. How did National Guards respond when their colonel tried to mobilise against the demonstrators? They shouted: 'Long live reform! Down with Guizot!'. Almost every crucial moment of the Revolution seems to be associated with slogans. This point has two possible explanations: either crowds were more disciplined and, once alerted to such slogans, shouted them in a regular manner; or, observers were sensitive to such cries, and took care to record them when writing their descriptions of revolutionary action. Whichever explanation is correct, we have come a long way from the Bonapartist tobacco pouches described in Chapter 2.

– III. POLITICAL CULTURE –

Three new political institutions were created by the 1848 Revolution. These were the Luxemburg Commission, the National Workshops and the political clubs. Of these three, the clubs made the greatest contribution to the development of political culture. However, before discussing them, I will give brief descriptions of the Luxemburg Commission and the National Workshops.

The Luxemburg Commission represented the Parisian trades; that is, the old skilled trades which were quickest in electing delegates to it. It aimed to overcome the disunity which had divided workers, and to end trade rivalries. In March and April approximately 730 delegates attended its nightly meetings.[58] Prior to the April elections, the Commission was the only significant representative body in France: many workers thought of it as the beginning of a working-class parliament. While it sponsored some important investigations and debates, it was ignominiously dissolved by conservatives after their victory in the April 1848 elections.

Many proposals were made in these discussions. One persistent theme was a refusal of the practice of sub-contracting, through which work teams were made to compete with another. However, the most important economic measure introduced by the Provisional Government was the creation of the National Workshops on 26 February, which drew their title from a proposal in Blanc's *The Organization of Labour* (1840), but which based their practice on the traditional charity workshops created during crises. About one hundred thousand male workers were enrolled by June 1848; women were not admitted. Many were disappointed by the National Workshops' low wages and the basic manual labour they were given. Conservative critics resented the mere existence of the National Workshops, whose name alone seemed like a permanent reminder of a socialist threat.

The clubs were livelier institutions. The first was created by Auguste Blanqui, the veteran republican conspirator, after his release from jail on 25 February 1848; and, as the table below shows, they grew rapidly in number.

Table 6.4: Number of political clubs in Paris in 1848[59]

Date	No. of clubs
1 March	5
10 March	36
15 March	59
Mid–April	203

Their total membership may have totalled some fifty thousand, perhaps even one hundred thousand.[60] Peter Amann provides a colourful example of their popularity: in March 1848 the novelist George Sand was locked out of her Parisian home. She went in search of a locksmith and found that the nearest one was attending a club meeting. Arriving at a second locksmith's house, she found that he too was at a club. The third, also, was at a club. To her amazement she realised that, due to the clubs, there was not a single locksmith available!

The clubs were hybrid organisations. Their inspiration was drawn from memories of 1793–5, when clubs had effectively taken over Parisian municipal organisation. However, the clubs of 1848 performed different roles: they were part debating society, part activists' organisation, part political party. Their first promoters were often either conspirators from the 1830s or utopians from the 1840s, but they rapidly drew in a wider audience. While the Luxemburg Commission largely drew support from the skilled trades, the clubs attracted a more varied membership, including middle–class republicans and unskilled workers, and sometimes even accepting (or encouraging) female participation. Many clubs sponsored their own paper, often carrying the same name as the club. During the interregnum between the fall of the July Monarchy and the first elections of the Second Republic, Parisian local authorities were intimidated by the clubs, allowing them free, or at least cheap, access to public buildings for their meetings.

During March and April the clubs met two or three times a week. Their meetings varied enormously. Cabet's Central Fraternal Society offered orderly, quasi-religious sermons. Raspail, at his Society of the Friends of the People, gave a detailed weekly lecture to his audience of middle-class republicans. In most clubs, there was a cult of enthusiasm and spontaneity. Untrained, inexperienced speakers strained to make themselves heard without the benefit of public address systems: in the clubs' 'habitual disorder' they fell into using heart-rending, emotional appeals to hold their audiences' attention.[61]

In 1886, a veteran of 1848 looked back at his political education in the clubs. 'Some people were attracted by simple curiosity and a desire to see something new, others went to study methods of revolutionary action, or to get a clearer idea of the Republic, of how it really differed from monarchist government.'[62] The clubs managed to broaden and perhaps deepen the appeal of the sentimental republicanism of 1848; to a certain extent, they may also have performed an educational function, forcing both listeners and speakers to consider arguments and to debate questions. Proudhon, probably over-optimistically, saw them as the beginning for a true popular democracy, sensitive to the needs of the people.[63] Where they proved weak was in organising effective action; as Amann points out: 'club audiences were fatally attracted to symbolic acts'.[64] Audiences were easy to sway and proved unable to work consistently on a particular issue over a period of weeks.

In mid-March, the issue which gripped most clubs was the forthcoming National Guard elections. Clubs worked to prevent old, conservative, middle-class officers from retaining control. On 15 March, club delegates petitioned the Provisional Government to postpone the elections for three months in order to give them more time to prepare democratic candidates and pro-grammes. On 16 March, élite officers from the National Guard demonstrated for the retention of their privileged positions. During this demonstration right-wing slogans were shouted. This, in turn, provoked the giant demon-stration of 17 March. Originally intended to address the specific issue of the National Guard, the demonstration was transformed into a broader ex-pression of loyalty to the Republic. Between 150 000 and 200 000 people attended.[65] For many observers, such demonstrations seemed living proof of the new spirit in France (see document 6.3). However, in the National Guard elections held on 5–7 April, moderate and conservative candidates won the majority of posts. The clubs' first campaign was a clear failure.

While the clubs campaigned about the National Guard elections, they ignored the economic issues which were traumatising working-class families. Unemployment was occasionally discussed in their meetings, but issues such as bankruptcies and rent arrears were not addressed.

The next big test was the general election of 23 April 1848. Via a collective grouping known as the 'Club of Clubs', delegates tried to draw up agreed lists of candidates for all constituencies. The effort of sending delegates out into the departments, taking stock of the situation, analysing possibilities and then recommending candidates proved too much for these amateur bureaucrats. Few constituency lists were completed in time. Even in Paris, club candidates only won six out of thirty-four seats.[66]

The clubs declined rapidly after the elections. In June 1848, when workers rebelled against the Republic, there were only sixty active clubs left in Paris.[67] In July 1848 the National Assembly debated the nature of the clubs. Some still felt a lingering affection for 'these schools of mutual education'. However, the great majority were determined to abolish the 'bad clubs', which were 'usurping government', or which tried to impose 'the government of the streets' on to France.[68] A law limiting the freedoms of the clubs was passed on 28 July 1848.

The ideas which motivated the revolutionaries of 1848 clearly centred on masculine concepts of honour, provoked by the sense of outrage they felt about the Orleanist governments. Could such ideas be translated into a female political culture?

The female utopian groups of the 1830s and 1840s formed the basis for a new wave of female activism in 1848. While the utopian groups had tended to appeal to young single women, the female activists of 1848 were usually older, often asserting the legitimacy of their political activities by referring to their status as mothers. Like their male counterparts, female militants upheld concepts of moral respectability. They discussed the problems faced by single women workers employed in the new industries, and by those working at home, for the extension of market-driven production into the home was seen as corrupting settled family life and disrupting marital harmony.[69] Feminist activists sought to restore dignity to women, whether through the social reform of work or through political reform. Many shared the general belief that the Revolution represented 'the dawn of a new era'.[70] They formed a number of political clubs for women, including the Emancipation of Women and the Women's Voice clubs. A journal entitled *La Voix des Femmes* was attached to the second. The other example of women's political militancy which caught observers' attention was an attempt to form a female militia.

These feminist initiatives met with a very hostile response from male activists. Only Pierre Leroux and Victor Considérant spoke in favour of female suffrage. Considérant raised the issue in the Chamber of Deputies in April 1848 but his proposal that women should be enfranchised was voted down by 899 to one.[71] In the same vein, when the Assembly considered curbing the clubs, it also discussed banning women from them. The proposal that 'a woman's proper and correct place is in domestic life, not in political life; she loses something by leaving the first for the second' was accepted without opposition.[72] The logic of radical politics worked against feminism and women's rights: like the banqueteers, republicans such as Ledru-Rollin characterised the Orleanist regime as marked by corruption, and opposed it to the masculine values of the Republic's 'virile teaching'.[73] It is no co-incidence that Proudhon's rise to political prominence took place during the Second Republic: he was vigorously anti-feminist. His manifesto for the by-elections of June 1848 declared that 'woman's kingdom is in the home', refused the principle of divorce and called for a strengthening of paternal power in the family.[74]

Many feminist activists were intimidated by this hostility. In April 1848 George Sand (the pseudonym of a prominent female republican) was invited to stand as a deputy by a feminist group. She refused, referring to the concept of 'respectability'. 'Social conditions are such that women cannot honourably and loyally carry out political tasks.'[75] Daniel Stern, a moderate republican feminist, dismissed the idea of women's clubs as 'cranky'.[76] By accepting the language of honour initiated by the male revolutionaries, feminists found themselves prevented from participating fully in political life.

The key political concept developed by the banqueteers and the republican revolutionaries of 1848 was 'the people'. To put it mildly, this was an am-biguous term. 'The people' was not an economically coherent group: it could include labourers, peasants, artisans, small shopkeepers, petty investors, small businessmen, journalists, even lawyers and teachers. The term's great strength was its promise of social unity to a divided society. Lamartine captured this constructive potential when he proclaimed 'there are no more bourgeois and proletarians, there is only a people'.[77] Hugo put forward similar arguments: 'I don't understand how anyone can be scared of popular sovereignty. The people are all of us; it's like being scared of yourself.'[78]

In French, the word 'people' [*peuple*] is always singular. Thus Hugo wrote that the mind [*esprit*] of the people was like 'the mind of a child'.[79] He most certainly would not have written 'the minds of the people are like the minds of children'. 'The people' were thought of as a single mass, thinking and act-ing collectively, not as the union of disparate social and regional groups. This concept is difficult to match with current ideas of parliamentary democracy, which take for granted a plurality of opinions. The republican utopians ex-pected 'the people' to pronounce as one in the elections of April 1848, and therefore to guarantee the social and political unity of France.

Despite having made their revolution in the name of the people, and despite having accepted the principle of male democracy, republican poli-ticians felt nervous about the actual practice of the first parliamentary elections based on this concept.[80] They were uncertain about the uses that 'the people' would make of the vote: they were torn between their 'pride in having given the word to the people, and their worries about what the people would do'.[81]

– IV. LEGACY –

Like the Orleanists of 1830, the republicans of 1848 hoped that their revolution would end social conflict in France. Such hopes rapidly seemed foolish. In March 1848, Garnier-Pagès, the Provisional Finance Minister, acted to end the economic crisis which threatened the state. Because of the continuing economic depression, tax revenue remained low. Garnier-Pagès attempted to boost state income by an immediate forty-five per cent rise in all direct taxes: the so-called 'forty-five centimes' imposition. The principal direct tax was the land tax. While this measure caused some disquiet, the Provisional Government argued that aristocratic landowners would be most affected. They made a fundamental error: the group hit hardest by the new tax were the millions of small peasant farmers. This tax rise destroyed the Republic's reputation in many rural areas.

The elections took place on 23 April 1848. As was the case in the July Monarchy, it is difficult to be certain about deputies' precise political loyalties. The approximate results were: [82]

600 conservatives
200 moderate republicans
100 radical republicans or socialists.

However, these figures mask an important problem. Nearly all the candidates declared themselves to be republicans, but it is clear that most were merely playing lip-service to the Republic. Therefore, the precise political sympathies of the broad mass of deputies are unclear. In May 1848 the majority were probably prepared to work with republican institutions, although it is unlikely that they shared the political enthusiasm of a Lamartine or a Sand.

Any trace of republican optimism came to an end in June 1848. The legitimist Falloux proposed measures to close down the National Workshops, and to offer their workers the alternatives of conscription or emigration to provincial France. By 22 June one thousand barricades had been constructed in Paris.[83] Between forty and fifty thousand rebels, largely workers from the National Workshops, faced over fifty thousand soldiers and municipal guards. The National Guards once again refused to repress a rebellion. Fourteen hundred rebels were killed; over eight hundred soldiers and guards died. Following the rebellion, almost fifteen thousand people were arrested. [84]

According to Hugo, the most important legacy of the Second Republic was that it took terror out of republican political culture.[85] This idealistic, forward-looking, utopian strand of republicanism, which reached out to 'the People', was certainly different from the militant conspiracies of the 1820s and 1830s. It was a theme which would reappear in republicanism in the 1870s (see Chapter 10). Moreover, the dramatic use of slogans as a way of enforcing a political message, of presenting it publicly, certainly helped to build bridges between republican political groups and popular movements. However, one can question whether Hugo's observation is correct. Fear of the Republic remained strong in April 1848: many conservative voters were convinced that republican politicians were going to lead France into a new Terror; many rural farmers had been alienated by the forty-five centimes tax. The Republic did not yet represent majority opinion in France.

– V. Documents –

–Document 6.1: Ledru-Rollin speaks at Lille –

This is the speech which Ledru-Rollin gave in Lille on 7 November 1847, at the banquet which Barrot refused to attend. It is clearly the work of a master orator, who is able to 'play' his audience with great skill. Note also the continual question and answer form, through which the speech grows to resemble a dialogue with the audience.

My fellow citizens! Yes! To the workers! To their undeniable rights, to their sacred interests, which have been ignored up to the present! Their rights! After two revolutions, they have won them, no-one today can deny that principle, but their implementation has been indefinitely delayed. (*That's true! that's true!*) 'The people?' they say, 'what rights do you want to give them? They're incapable, they're ignorant. It would be anarchy, chaos, revolution, blood.' (*Long disturbance.*)

Gentlemen, you know the people of this industrial town. (*Yes, yes, and we love them.*) Do you think that this image is true? (*No, no.*) Well, of course, if we went to rich writers, we'd find that this was the people. (*Bravo, bravo.*) Of course, if we glanced over the pages written by well-paid novelists, they'd say this image was true. But where do they get this from? From Paris, where the police gather together those they've arrested. They're looking for dramatic effects in the fantastic and the horrific, and – through an amazing effort of their imaginations – they say to you 'these degraded, hideous beings who haunt these refuges, these are the people!' (*Great sensation – prolonged cheering.*)

Well, no, gentlemen, they aren't the people. You won't see them on that stage! (*no! no!*) You need to go to the manufacturing towns, where the masters, squeezed by capital, by fierce competition (*that's right*) no longer have any vacant positions because all the markets are closed to them, and because our flag is trodden on everywhere (*sensation*). The masters, I say, are forced to cut wages! It's not them that you ought to be blaming, it's those in power ... (*yes! yes!*) It's those in power who don't find [the masters] work for their trade. In these towns, the people suffer. What do they see? They see their daughters prostituting themselves to find a supplement for the wages they're not earning! (*Great sensation.*) They see their children crying when their fathers can't give them bread! (*Long agitation.*) Well, gentlemen, these men suffer with calm, with resignation. If disease, if rickets don't ruin them, they'll still be ready when their country needs to be defended! (*yes! yes!*) This is the people of the towns. (*That's good! That's very good!*)

Now you can see that all governments, which do not accept the principle that the people have the right to represent themselves, are false. I say that whoever pays his taxes with his blood, his sweat and his pride has the right to join the government which makes use of his wealth. This is fair. (*Agreement.*)

What do they say to this?

(*A voice shouts out 'nothing, nothing'. Laughter.*)

What do they say? That you must wait until the people are enlightened, and yet day by day more and more light is obscured. (*Agreement.*)

Source: AN, BB/30/296

– DOCUMENT 6.2: THE SACKING OF THE TUILERIES –

Gustave Flaubert was one of the most celebrated French novelists of the nineteenth century. His *L'Education sentimentale* is partly autobiographical. It includes a scene in which the hero, Frédéric, meets his friend Hussonnet, and the two wander around the Tuileries Palace on 24 February 1848. Frédéric's calm curiosity – he seems like a tourist – contrasts with the day's political passions. Flaubert's own mixed emotions are obvious: while amazed by the Revolution, he was unable to identify with it.

[Hussonnet and Frédéric] reached the Hall of the Marshals. The portraits of great men still hung there, intact, except for that of Bugeaud [charged with organising order in Paris], whose stomach had been pierced. [In their portraits] they stood up, leaning on their sabres, with lines of cannon behind them, striking attitudes which clashed with the situation they were in. It was 1.20pm, according to a large clock.

All at once the *Marseillaise* rang out. Hussonnet and Frédéric leaned over the banisters. It was the people. They rushed up the staircase, in waves of bare heads, helmets, red hats, bayonets and shoulders, moving so wildly that their faces disappeared into a whirling mass which climbed up, further and further, like a river pushed on by a spring tide, howling a great roar, with unstoppable force. At the top, they spread out, and the song ended.

All that could be heard now was their footsteps and their shouts. This harmless crowd was happy just to look. But, now and again, an elbow which was cramped for room, bumped through a window, or a vase, or a statue was knocked from its pedestal and fell to the floor. The panelling began to crack. Their faces were red and dripped large drops of sweat. Hussonnet said:

'These heroes don't smell too good.'

'Ah! Don't fuss,' replied Frédéric.

Pushed despite themselves, they went into a room in which a red velvet canopy was stretched along the ceiling. Beneath it, on the throne, sat a black-bearded proletarian, his shirt half-open, as stupid and as happy as an ape. Others climbed up to sit in his place.

'What a spectacle!' said Hussonnet. 'That's the sovereignty of the people!'

The chair was lifted up, and then carried, wobbling, across the room.

'Good grief! Look at it swaying! The ship of state is being rocked by a stormy sea. Look at it dance! Look at it dance!'

It was taken to a window and, as the audience booed, it was thrown out.

'Poor old thing!' said Hussonnet as he watched it fall into the garden, where it was quickly picked up to be taken to the Bastille, where it was burnt.

Then a joyful frenzy erupted as if, now the throne was gone, a future of limitless happiness had appeared. Less out of a spirit of revenge than out of simple desire to demonstrate their possession, they smashed and tore up mirrors, curtains, chandeliers, candlesticks, tables, chairs, stools, all the furnishings, even the sketch books, even the needlework baskets. Now that they had won, they ought to be happy! The mob dressed themselves up in lace and cashmere. Gold fringes were wound round smock sleeves, feathered hats were worn by blacksmiths, and the ribbons of the Légion d'Honneur decorated prostitutes' bosoms. Everyone indulged their whims; some danced, others drank. In the Queen's bedroom, a woman put pomade on her hair; behind a screen, two card-players gambled. Hussonet pointed out to Frédéric a man smoking his old pipe on the balcony. The madness deepened with the noises made by porcelain smashing and pieces of crystal falling, which rang out like a harmonica.

Things got worse. An obscene curiosity made them open up all the cupboards, alcoves and drawers. Jailbirds stretched out in the princesses' bed, and rolled about on it as they were unable to rape them. A few people, with sinister faces, looked for something to steal, but there were too many people about. Through the doors, all that could be seen was the dark mass of the people between the gilt carvings, under a cloud of dust. Everyone gasped for air. The heat grew worse and worse. The two friends, worried about being stifled, left.

In the antechamber, on a pile of clothes, was a prostitute standing like a statue of Liberty – still, with great staring eyes, terrifying.

Source: Gustave Flaubert, *L'Education sentimentale*, ed. S. de Sacy (Paris: Bouquins, 1965), pp. 316–18

– DOCUMENT 6.3: THE PROCESSIONS OF PARIS –

George Sand was a female journalist and novelist who briefly worked in Ledru-Rollin's Interior Ministry. She was an enthusiastic supporter of the Second Republic, and her joy at the sight of the transformations in Paris is clear. Unfortunately, the Mobile Guard to which she refers in this extract is now remembered most for its role in putting down the June 1848 uprising. This extract was first published on 9 April 1848, in Sand's journal *La Cause du Peuple*.

The street and the public square are the liveliest places in France today. All French people who were keen and willing to welcome the arrival of the Republic, run to see each new sight in this strange town which is nothing like what it was before, nothing like what it has ever been ...

A strange procession comes down the middle of the road. They do not march with that military discipline that turns each man into a perfect machine, but with the freedom, the relaxed quality of the volunteer who thinks of himself as a free man, a happy man, ready for action. Yet there is order in the ranks of this young militia who look after themselves, willing to accept an improvised discipline. An Englishman who lived next to us looked at everything; one day he asked where was the Mobile Guard.

'They're in front you, you can see them pass.'

'What, those little children?'

'Yes, sir, they would be ready to help you plant liberty trees in the all the corners of the universe, and even on the banks of the Thames, if your heart was in it.'

In fact, they are children who, for the most part, seem small and weak. They are the children of Paris, miraculous children, who were born in misery, who grew up in poverty, and who live deprived ... They are easily excited, subject to violent reactions; they are complex beings, as you have seen, and so very rich in emotions, in thoughts and in their actions ... Their bodies are weak, but their hearts are so strong! There are no giants who could take on this adolescent militia ...

The procession continues. The priests march to the sound of the drum; they walk in step without noticing. The crucifix floats over the crowd next to the flag of the Republic, a natural and logical alliance ...

Then come the workers, mixed in with the students, the delegates from the schools [the University colleges], the members of the [workers'] corporations; the smock, the military uniform, the bourgeois suit, and the jacket are mixed together; their crossed arms proclaim 'Fraternization', the seizure of power by fraternal equality ...

[Here are] the road-pavers, the navvies, the woodcutters ... Behind them, fifty others carry an enormous pinetree on their shoulders. Its green leaves are safe from the dirt of pavements: it is the Liberty Tree, the symbol of the Republic, which is passing.

Source: Sand, *Politique et polémiques*, pp. 336–41

– VI. FURTHER READING –

Two historians have produced excellent introductions to the Second Republic. These are Maurice Agulhon, *The Republican Experiment, 1848-1852*, trans. Janet Lloyd (Cambridge: Cambridge UP, 1983) and Roger Price, *The French Second Republic: A Social History* (London: Batsford, 1972). Both authors have also edited valuable collections of primary documents: Agulhon's is *Les Quarante-Huitards* (Paris: Folio, 1992), while Price has edited *1848 in France* (London: Thames and Hudon, 1975). All four of these books concentrate on the Second Republic rather than on the Revolution of February 1848.

The emerging radical opposition movement within the July Monarchy is studied in Christine Guionnet, *L'apprentissage de la politique moderne* (Paris: L'Harmattan, 1997), while disillusionment in the structures of the July Monarchy is marvellously evoked in Stendhal's novel, *Lucien Leuwen* (various editions). There have also been two important studies of public relations under the July Monarchy: Alain Corbin, 'L'impossible présence du roi: fêtes politiques et mises en scènes du pouvoir sous la Monarchie de Juillet' in A. Corbin, N. Gérôme and D. Tartakowsky (eds), *Les Usages politiques des fêtes* (Paris: Presses de la Sorbonne, 1994), pp. 77–116; and Mathilde Larrère, 'Ainsi paradait le roi des barricades: les grandes revues de la garde nationale à Paris', *Mouvement Social* 179 (1997), 9–32. Robert A. Nye, *Masculinity and Male Codes of Honor in Modern France* (Oxford: Oxford UP, 1993): does not consider the banquet movement, but his research is clearly relevant to its themes. The only detailed published account of the banquet campaign is John J. Baughman, 'The French Banquet Campaign of 1847–48', *Journal of Modern History* 31:1 (1959), 1–15.

The best study of February 1848 is Georges Duveau, *1848: the Making of a Revolution*, trans. Anne Carter (London: RKP, 1967), which presents a genuinely dramatic account of events. There have also been many useful short studies of the revolution: George Fasel, 'The Wrong Revolution: French Republicanism in 1848', *French Historical Studies* 8 (1973–4), 654–80 considers the effects of the republicans' ignorance about rural life; O. E. and C. M. Heywood, 'Rethinking the 1848 Revolution', *History* 79 (1994), 394–411 suggests some new lines of enquiry; Robert Bezucha, 'The French Revolution of 1848 and the Social History of Work', *Theory and Society* 12 (1983), 469–84 analyses forms of labour radicalism; and Mark Traugott, 'The Crowd in the French Revolution of February 1848', *American Historical Review* 93 (1988), 638–52 presents a detailed sociological profile of the revolutionaries.

Peter H. Amann, *Revolution and Mass Democracy: the Paris Club Movement in 1848* (Princeton: Princeton UP, 1975), is a detailed, well-researched study of the lively political culture of the Parisian clubs. T. J. Clark, *The Absolute Bourgeois: Artists and Politics in France, 1848–1851* (London: Thames and Hudson, 1988) is a valuable and original study of the social and political context of the history of art.

There are several important studies of June 1848. Charles Tilly and Lynn Lees, 'Le Peuple de juin 1848', *Annales ESC* 29:5 (1974), 1061–92, presents a sociological analysis of those arrested. Pierre Caspard looks at the intriguing question of why the largely working-class Garde Mobile fought against the rebels: 'Aspects de la lutte des classes en 1848; le recrutement de la garde nationale mobile', *Revue historique* 511 (1974), 81–106. His conclusions are re-examined in Mark Traugott, 'The Mobile Guard in the Revolution of

1848', *Theory and Society* 9:5 (1980), 683–720. Roger Gould, *Insurgent Identities: Class, Community and Protest from 1848 to the Commune* (Chicago: Chicago UP, 1995) presents a challenging argument about the nature of working-class radicalism in this period; it is primarily concerned with the Commune. Casey Harison, 'An Organization of Labor: Laissez-faire and *Marchandage* in the Paris Building Trades Through 1848', *French Historical Studies* 20:3 (1997), 356–80 considers a theme in working-class radicalism.

There are a number of good studies on women's history and gender relations in 1848. Unfortunately, no published work yet integrates women's history into the 'orthodox' political narrative. Louis Devance, 'Femme, famille, travail et morale sexuelle dans l'idéologie de 1848', *Romantisme* 13–14 (1976), 79–103 is still useful as an overview on sexual politics. Felicia Gordon and Máire Cross (eds), *Early French Feminisms* (Cheltenham: Edward Elgar, 1996) includes extracts from the writings of feminist militants in 1848. Joan W. Scott, *Gender and the Politics of History* (New York: Columbia UP, 1988), contains several valuable essays on the social history of work. Laura Strumingher, 'The Vésuviennes; images of women warriors in 1848', *History of European Ideas* 8:4/5 (1987), 451–88 is a well-written account of male journalists' hostility to a female militia, worth examining for the pictures alone. Whitney Walton, 'Writing the 1848 Revolution: Politics, Gender, Feminism in the Works of French Women of Letters', *French Historical Studies* 18:4 (1994), 1001–24 considers the topic of middle-class women's reactions.

The Revolution stimulated contemporaries to write some fine examples of political and social analysis. Generations of students have been misinformed about Gustave Flaubert's novel *L'Education sentimentale [Sentimental Education]* (many editions). It is not a novel *about* 1848 – two-thirds of it is concerned with the July Monarchy, and its subject is the romantic, emotional and political education of a young man. However, its third section does include some vivid descriptions of events in 1848. Victor Hugo, *Choses vues: souvenirs, journaux, cahiers, 1830–46*, ed. H. Juin (Paris: Folio, 1972), and *Choses vues: souvenirs, journaux, cahiers, 1847–48*, ed. H. Juin (Paris: Folio, 1972) are two extremely valuable records of Hugo's reactions. Karl Marx, 'The Class Struggles in France, 1848–50' in *Surveys from Exile*, ed. D. Fernbach (Harmondsworth: Penguin, 1977), pp. 35–142, also reproduced in many different editions – one of Marx's first attempts to write history, and still interesting in this light, but less useful as an analysis. Pierre-Joseph Proudhon, *Idées révolutionnaires* (Antony: Tops/Trinquier, 1996) and *Confessions d'un révolutionnaire* (Antony: Tops/Trinquier, 1997) – two recent reprints of Proudhon's confused but lively reactions. Alexis de Tocqueville, *Souvenirs* (Paris: Folio, 1978): a masterful essay by an intelligent and observant conservative critic of the Revolution.

– Notes –

1. Alphonse de Lamartine, 'Quel ministère faut-il au pays?' in *La Politique et l'histoire* (Paris: Imprimerie Nationale, 1993), p. 297.
2. Peter Amann, *Revolution and Mass Democracy: the Paris Club Movement in 1848* (Princeton: Princeton UP, 1975), p. 17.
3. Roger Magraw, *A History of the French Working Class, Vol. I* (Oxford: Blackwell, 1992), p. 121.
4. Peter McPhee, *The Politics of Rural Life: Political Mobilization in the French Countryside, 1846–52* (Oxford: Oxford UP, 1992), p. 61.
5. Victor Hugo, *Choses vues: souvenirs, journaux, cahiers, 1830–1846* (Paris: Folio, 1972), p. 334.
6. Figures from Charles Tilly and Lynn Lees, 'Le Peuple de juin 1848', *Annales ESC* 29:5 (1974), 1061–92 (p. 1063).
7. AN, BB/18/1460, letter dated 19 January 1848, discussing the past two years.
8. AN, BB/18/1460, letter dated 21 February 1848.
9. Lamartine, *Politique*, p. 74.
10. Christine Guionnet, *L'apprentissage de la politique moderne* (Paris: L'Harmattan, 1997), p. 150.
11. Hugo, *Choses vues 1847–48* (Paris: Folio, 1972), p. 94.
12. Pierre Joseph Proudhon, *Les Confessions d'un révolutionnaire* (Antony: Tops/Trinquier, 1997), p. 63.
13. Paguerre, 24 October 1847 banquet at Chartres (Eure-et-Loir), AN, BB/30/296. Details concerning the campaign taken from John J. Baughman, 'The French Banquet Campaign of 1847–48', *Journal of Modern History* 31:1 (1959), 1–15.
14. Information in this paragraph is taken from AN, BB/30/296.
15. Figures for attendance are not available for all banquets: hence the statistical anomalies in this table.
16. See, for example, speeches made by Barrot and Dumont on 11 November 1847 at Valciennes (Nord), AN, BB/30/296.
17. Testelin in *L'Echo du Nord*, 13 November 1847, AN, BB/30/296.
18. 17 October 1847 banquet at La Charité (Nièvre), AN, BB/30/296.
19. Raimbault, 5 December 1847 banquet at Châteaudun (Eure-et-Loir), AN, BB/30/296.
20. Crémieux, 21 November 1847 banquet, AN, BB/30/296.
21. Marecal, reported on 4 November 1847, AN, BB/30/296.
22. Ballange, reported on 8 December 1847, AN, BB/30/296.
23. Odilon Barrot, *Mémoires posthumes, Vol. I* (Paris: Charpentier, 1875), p. 491.
24. Lherbette, 14 September 1847 banquet held at Soissons (Aisne), AN, BB/30/296.
25. 29 September 1847 banquet at Orléans, AN, BB/30/296.
26. Desseaux, 25 December 1847 banquet in Rouen, AN, BB/30/296.
27. AN, BB/30/296.
28. Barthy, Castres (Tarn) banquet on 5 December 1847, AN, BB/30/296.
29. Flocon, 30 December 1847, AN, BB/30/296.
30. Lamartine, *Politique*, p. 322.
31. 17 December 1847, AN, BB/30/296.
32. Maire, Orléans (Loiret), reported on 24 November, AN, BB/30/296.
33. Louchet, Le Mans (Sarthe) banquet, reported 13 August 1847, AN, BB/30/296.
34. Lamartine, *Politique*, p. 317.
35. Daniel Stern, *Histoire de la Révolution de 1848, Vol. I* (Paris: Charpentier, 1862), p. 81.

36. Ledru-Rollin, Chalon (Saône-et-Loire) banquet, 19 December 1847, AN, BB/30/296.
37. Alain Corbin, 'L'impossible présence de roi; fêtes politiques et mises en scènes du pouvoir sous la Monarchie de Juillet' in A. Corbin, N. Gérôme and D. Tartakowsky (eds), *Les Usages politiques des fêtes* (Paris: Presses de la Sorbonne, 1994), pp. 77–116 (p. 115).
38. Barrot, *Mémoires, Vol. I*, p. 470.
39. Jean Baptiste Gobert, Committee of Enquiry, 20 May 1848, AN, BB/30/296.
40. Boissel to the Committee of Enquiry, 20 May 1848, AN, BB/30/296.
41. Barrot, *Mémoires, Vol. I*, p. 506.
42. Edme Nicolas d'Heurle to the Committee of Enquiry, 19 April 1848, AN, BB/30/296.
43. Jean Baptiste Delestre to the Committee of Enquiry, 19 May 1848, AN, BB/30/296.
44. Circular in AN, BB/18/1474.
45. Jacques Richard to the Committee of Enquiry, 12 April 1848, in AN, BB/30/296.
46. Tilly and Lees, 'Peuple', p. 1062.
47. Poster dated 21 February 1848, AN, BB/30/296.
48. Letter to the Foreign Ministry, in AN, BB/30/296.
49. Georges Duveau, *1848: the Making of the Revolution*, trans. Anne Carter (London: RKP, 1967), p. 25.
50. Commission of Enquiry, 8 and 10 April 1848, AN, BB/30/297. The *Chant du Départ* was composed to celebrate the fifth anniversary of the taking of the Bastille in 1789. Its chorus was: 'The Republic calls us, we must know how to win, or learn how to die; a Frenchman must live for her; for her a Frenchman must die.' See François Moureau and Elisabeth Wahl (eds), *Chants de la Révolution française* (Paris: Livre de Poche, 1989) pp. 159–63.
51. Hugo, *Choses vues*, p. 291.
52. Léon de Malleville, Commission of Enquiry, 20 May 1848, in AN, BB/30/297.
53. Hugo, *Choses vues*, p. 290.
54. Pierre Guyon, Tribunal at Laon (Aisne), 14 May 1848, in AN, BB/30/297.
55. Léon de Malleville, Commission of Enquiry, 20 May 1848, in AB, BB/30/297.
56. Lamartine, *Politique*, p. 328.
57. Roger Gould, *Insurgent Identities: Class, Community and Protest in Paris* (Chicago: Chicago UP, 1995), p. 35.
58. Amann, *Mass Democracy*, p. 42.
59. Amann, *Mass Democracy*, p. 33.
60. Amann, *Mass Democracy*, p. 35. The analysis which follows owes much to Amann's detailed research.
61. Amann, *Mass Democracy*, p. 67.
62. Gustave Lefrançais, *Souvenirs d'un révolutionnaire* (Paris: Futur Antérieur, 1972), p. 42.
63. Proudhon, *Confessions*, p. 244.
64. Amann, *Mass Democracy*, p. 162.
65. Amann, *Mass Democracy*, p. 107.
66. Amann, *Mass Democracy*, p. 187.
67. Amann, *Mass Democracy*, p. 196.
68. Athanase Coquerel, *Rapport fait au nom de la Commission chargée de l'examen du projet de décret sur les clubs* (Paris: Imprimerie de l'Assemblée Nationale, 1848), pp. 3–4.
69. Joan W. Scott, *Gender and the Politics of History* (New York: Columbia UP, 1988), p. 101.
70. Felicia Gordon and Máire Cross, *Early French Feminisms* (Cheltenham: Edward Elgar, 1996), p. 62.
71. Claire G. Moses, *French Feminism in the Nineteenth Century* (New York: State University of New York, 1984), p. 142.

72. Coquerel, *Rapport*, p. 9.

73. Alexandre-Auguste Ledru-Rollin, *Discours divers et écrits politiques*, Vol. II (Paris: Germer Baillière, 1879), p. 18.

74. Proudhon, *Idées révolutionnaires* (Antony: Tops/Trinquier, 1996), pp. 74–5.

75. George Sand, *Politique et Polémiques* (Paris: Imprimerie Nationale, 1997), p. 534.

76. Daniel Stern, *Histoire, Vol. II*, p. 36.

77. Lamartine, *Politique*, p. 386.

78. Hugo, *Choses vues, 1847–48,* p. 318.

79. Hugo, *Choses vues, 1847–48*, p. 105.

80. It could be argued that the elections of September 1792 constituted the first experiment in male democracy. However, the difficult political circumstances of this period discouraged the mass of the male population from voting; therefore these elections were only a very partial implementation of the principle. See Isser Woloch, *The New Regime* (New York: Norton, 1994), pp. 60–112 for further details.

81. Maurice Agulhon, 'Préface au *Manuel Républicain de l'homme et du citoyen, 1848* de Charles Renouvier' in his *Histoire Vagabonde*, Vol. II (Paris: Gallimard, 1982), pp. 49–67 (p. 55).

82. George Fasel, 'The French Elections of April 23, 1848', *French Historical Studies* 5:3 (1968), 285–98.

83. Figures from Gould, *Insurgent Identities*, p. 49.

84. Tilly and Lees, 'Le Peuple', pp. 1069–70.

85. Victor Hugo, *Napoléon le Petit* (Neuilly-sur-Seine: Saint-Clair 1975), p. 242.

CHAPTER 7

Peasants, Socialism and Order: 1848–51

The tiny village of Sost (Haute Pyrénées), 900 kilometres away from Paris, did not hear of the proclamation of the Second Republic until 29 February 1848. When news arrived, the Mayor told his fellow citizens to remain calm, but he was interrupted by a municipal councillor who shouted 'there are no more mayors, and so no more orders to obey!'. Circulars arrived from the prefecture, but these were ripped into shreds by one François Manent, who threw them in the mud and then jumped on them, declaring that 'there are no more chiefs, everyone is free!'.[1]

Across France, March and April 1848 were marked by many such strange events. Tensions and frustrations which had been repressed for months, years, even decades, suddenly burst into the open. Forests were invaded, châteaux burnt, looms smashed and grain exports halted by crowds. Minority groups were subjected to violence. In Alsace, near France's eastern borders, the homes and shops of Jewish people were attacked.[2] In Lyon, workshops employing foreign workers (usually Italians) were destroyed.[3] In north-eastern regions, Belgian migrant workers were attacked.

These actions were widespread. During the first months of the Republic some eighteen thousand troops were mobilised to prevent forest invasions, and another fifteen thousand to quell anti-tax riots.[4] Significantly, as the new Justice Minister noted, these forest invaders and anti-tax rioters invoked the Republic to justify their 'pillage and violence'.[5] The simple proclamation of the Republic was seen to legitimate popular action against longstanding enemies. It would therefore be wrong to see the Republic as actually creating these movements: hostility to forest laws, to taxes and, unfortunately, to Jewish and other minorities had existed long before 1848. The Republic was understood as a space within which previously forbidden actions were now legitimate. As confused and bewildering as these actions appear, they do reveal a popular counterpart to the utopian republicanism of Lamartine, Ledru-Rollin and Sand. Here, in broad outlines, was the people's Republic.

In the months which followed, many of these naïve rioters and happy revellers were disappointed. The Republic did not mean an end to taxes: on the contrary, it meant the forty-five centimes land tax. It did not mean the collapse of social hierarchy, nor the end to forest laws. Many gave up their dreams, voted for conservative candidates in April 1848, and then turned to Louis-Napoleon in the December 1848 presidential elections; but for some, republicanism was not an ideal which could be forgotten. As the moderate, conservative Republic of 1848 became the distinctly right-wing Republic of 1849–51, some kept alive another vision: that of a Republic they labelled '*la belle*' (the fine), '*la bonne*' (the good), '*la rouge*' (the red) or '*la sociale*' – the Social Republic. In this chapter, we will examine this popular republicanism.

– I. PARTICIPANTS –

There were four examples of mass male democracy during the Second Republic:

1. the legislative elections of April 1848
2. the Presidential elections of December 1848
3. the legislative elections of May 1849
4. the referendum of December 1851.

On each of these occasions, the department of the Pyrénées-Orientales demonstrated a clear preference for republican politics, and often for left-wing republican politics. In the elections of April 1848, some ninety-five per cent of the votes cast in the Pyrénées-Orientales went to republican candidates.[6] In the December 1848 Presidential elections, Louis-Napoleon was the victorious candidate in the Pyrénées-Orientales, but he did not win the crushing majority which he gained in the rest of France.

Table 7.1: Votes cast in December 1848 Presidential elections[7]

Candidate	Total votes (in millions)	Votes in Pyrénées-Orientales
Louis-Napoleon	5.4m	14 420
(Bonapartist)	(74.2%)	(47.61%)
Cavaignac	1.44m	6 089
(Conservative-Republican)	(19.5%)	(20.12%)
Ledru-Rollin	0.37m	8 771
(Radical Republican)	(5.0%)	(28.96%)

Table 7.1 shows the large proportion of votes won by Ledru-Rollin, the left-republican candidate, in the Pyrénées-Orientales – almost six times the national average.

This left-leaning tendency was reinforced in the May 1849 General Election.

Table 7.2: Results of the May 1849 general elections[8]

Political grouping	No. of Deputies	Percentage of votes in France	Votes in Pyrénées-Orientales
Party of Order	450	53%	2 000 (3.3%)
Démoc-Soc	220	35%	20 000 (63.3%)
Moderate Republican	80	12%	–
Legitimist	–	–	8 200 (25.2%)

As usual, a word of caution needs to be issued against the figures in table 7.2: elections were not fought by well-organised, nationally-based political groupings. There were still local differences in forms of politics: in the Pyrénées-Orientales, the legitimists maintained a degree of independence from the Party of Order, whereas elsewhere their candidates joined this coalition. However, the most significant point is, once again, the high left-wing vote in the Pyrénées-Orientales, in which the 'Démoc-Socs' (democratic-socialists) were the majority tendency. Across France, the moderate republicans who dominated Republican politics in 1848 were replaced by left-republican groupings. The winning party was the conservative 'Party of Order' coalition.

Louis-Napoleon's *coup d'état* took place on 2–3 December 1851. His forces expected resistance in Paris. In the capital, some twelve hundred people revolted against his attack on the constitution: of these, four hundred were killed in battles with troops.[9] However, the strongest resistance developed in rural districts in southern and central France. In all, nine hundred communes rebelled, of which one hundred were sites of armed resistance. One prefecture and twelve sub-prefectures were briefly seized, and there were thirty armed clashes between rebels and troops. This vast insurrection involved approximately one hundred thousand people: of these, some seventy thousand were armed, and twenty thousand took part in clashes with troops.[10] In the Pyrénées-Orientales there were some ten thousand demonstrators. Following the insurrection, a thousand were arrested, and 692 were eventually condemned.

Our last test of the Pyrénées-Orientales' politics is the December 1851 referendum which Louis-Napoleon held to gain national approval for his *coup d'état*.

Table 7.3: Referendum results, December 1851[11]

	Yes	No	Abstention
Votes in France	7 440 000	640 000	1 500 000
(in millions)	(77.65%)	(6.69%)	(15.6%)
Votes in Pyrénées-	27 598	3 397	14 556
Orientales	(60.54%)	(7.46%)	(31.95%)

The Pyrénées-Orientales produced one of the lowest 'yes' votes in France. Fourteen other departments were more hostile. Some of them were other 'red' departments, like the Var in the south-east, but the most hostile were the monarchist departments of the west, such as La Vendée, Morbihan and Loire-Inférieure.[12] Many anti-Bonapartists who felt too intimidated to vote 'no' abstained: significantly, the Pyrénées-Orientales showed a high rate of abstentions.

Why did the Pyrénées-Orientales exhibit this long record of radical sympathies? To some extent, it comes as a surprise. No reform banquets seem to have been held in the department in 1847.[13] In April 1848, the Club of Clubs sent out 276 delegates to encourage republican candidates in the elections. Only one was sent to the Pyrénées-Orientales, and he did little.[14] The department was clearly not led into left-wing commitments by Parisian politicians but rather the reasons for its radicalism were internal.

The Pyrénées-Orientales are on the eastern edge of the Pyrenees, next to the Mediterranean coastline. The department is shaped like a long triangle, with one short edge running north–south along the coastline, and its point stretching westwards along the Pyrenees. Its capital, Perpignan, is near the coast. To the south, beyond the Pyrenees, lies Spain; to the north, the department of the Aude. The traditional agricultural practice of this area was polyculture: the multiplying of products – olives, grain, goats, sheep, fruit – to reach the security of self-sufficiency. In the nineteenth century, its economy was changing. Small forges were set up in the forests in the south and west. The most important innovation was vinegrowing. By 1850, 48 000 hectares in the department were devoted to vines and 44 500 to cereals.[15] Vine production was market-orientated: it connected individual families to wider regional, national and even international markets, and involved them in discussions about economic policies. The vine was a labour-intensive plant, which could be grown on poor soil that would not support grains. Its success encouraged peasants to move from the isolated hill valleys in the west, and to settle in the plains to the east. Such economic developments also encouraged a steep rise in population.

Table 7.4: Population of Pyrénées-Orientales, 1801–51[16]

Date	Total population	Population of Perpignan
1801	110731	10415
1851	181955	21783

Catalan influence was strong in the Pyrénées-Orientales; until 1659, the area had effectively been 'North Catalonia'. After that date, it became the French province of Roussillon. Despite Louis XIV's pro-French policies, Catalan remained the most common language spoken in the towns. Even in the 1830s, people still used the insulting Catalan term '*gavatx*' to refer to northerners in the rest of France, and most church services were conducted in Catalan.[17]

Like many southern departments, the Pyrénées-Orientales comprised of large villages and small towns: a rural landscape very different from the *bocage* of the Vendée (see Chapter 4). As Peter McPhee notes, in this department, the best term for the typical rural dweller would be 'villager' rather than peasant, for the cultural and emotional centres of rural life lay in the villages and not the fields.[18] These dense, concentrated villages resembled towns in the vibrancy and richness of their communal cultures, while many of the small towns resembled villages in their close connections with agricultural life. Even in Perpignan some 18.6 per cent of the adult population worked in the fields in 1846.[19]

– II. Events –

Early in 1848 republican political culture was discovered by the mass of the population. Demonstrations, such as that watched by Sand (see document 6.3), expressed an optimistic sense of social solidarity, uniting all French people. The planting of Liberty Trees in squares or at crossroads, a practice from the First Republic, was revived. Priests would bless the tree, symbolising the union of republican and Catholic idealism. Speeches would celebrate the event, drawing the audience's attention to the lessons to be learnt. A tree would live longer than the people who planted it: it represented the transcendental nature of the Republic, something which was bigger and greater than the lives of individuals. It also marked out a space for future ceremonials.[20] (See document 7.1.)

The elections of 23 April 1848 were a crucial test which the republicans failed. In principle, they were to be open, honest elections in which any man could stand as a candidate. Ledru-Rollin, serving as the Minister of the Interior, proclaimed that 'the time of tricks and lies is over'. However, within that commitment was an assumption that it would be inappropriate for non-republican candidates to compete in these elections. Therefore, the Commissars of the Republic, who briefly supplanted the prefects in March and April 1848, were instructed to intervene against such unwelcome candidates. Ledru-Rollin warned his Commissars that 'if the doors of the Assembly are opened to men with an ambiguous commitment to Republicanism and an ambiguous morality, then we are heading for anarchy'. [21]

Other republicans shared Ledru-Rollin's doubts. Some, such as the veteran revolutionary Blanqui, would have preferred to see a revolutionary dictatorship. Many considered that there was a case for delaying the elections while the nation was 'republicanised' through propaganda tours and, in the long term, through a reformed schooling system. Others had doubts about parliamentary democracy. Proudhon, in a dramatic phrase, considered that universal (male) suffrage was 'the most certain way of making the People lie'. He explained: 'universal suffrage ... is an atomistic sort of theory through which the legislator, incapable of making the people express the unity of their essence, asks them to express their opinions one by one.'[22] His words reflect a common republican assumption that their politics should be unitary: Proudhon argued that parliamentary elections would destroy this supposed political unity.

The elections were held on Sunday, 23 April 1848. The Provisional Government did not consider that the thirty-six thousand mayors of France's communes could organise them efficiently. Many were illiterate, others simply incompetent. Thus, voters had to walk to their local cantonal town, which might be five, even ten, miles away. The Provisional Government chose a Sunday in the hope that Catholic conservatives would be persuaded to go to church rather than to the polls. In the event, they were disappointed: in many communes, priests led their parishioners from the church to the electoral booth, and along the way gave them advice on how to vote. (See document 8.2.)

In one sense, these elections were extremely successful. About eighty-four per cent of adult males voted: a much higher proportion than the ten or fifteen per cent who had voted in the democratic elections of 1792, thirty-five per cent more than the proportion voting in the 1996 Presidential Elections in the USA, and more than ten per cent higher than participation in the 1997 British General Elections. Old right-wing candidates from the Orleanist governments were decisively rejected, while liberals, members of the Dynastic Opposition and republicans were generally successful. Despite the success of some left-wing candidates, these elections were disastrous for the left republicans.

Following the dissolution of the National Workshops in Paris in June

1848, there were further experiments in 'Republicanising' economic organisation. Government funds were made available for producers' co-operatives. Strict tests were imposed: in Lyon, out of seven groups which applied for funding, only two were accepted. Furthermore, few of these co-operatives survived into the 1850s.

Table 7.5: State-subsidised co-operatives[23]

	Created in 1848	Surviving until 1856
Co-operatives in Paris	30	9
Co-operatives in the Provinces	26	5

Police surveillance ensured that these co-operatives did not become bases for radical working-class republicanism.

Labour militants had been frustrated in the elections, their clubs had been stripped of their powers, and they had not been given the opportunity to put their economic ideas into practice via co-operatives. In the autumn of 1848 they returned to the methods which had triggered the February 1848 Revolution. On 17 October two thousand guests attended a banquet in the working-class quarter of La Poissonnière, in north-central Paris. They paid a fee of one franc, and heard speeches from Proudhon, Leroux and Greppo. Other banquets were held: there was a 'patriotic' banquet at Doujon (Allier), a 'democratic' banquet at Autun (Nièvre), and a 'fraternal' banquet in the Cher.[24] While these isolated meetings hardly add up to a movement, they carried a poignant symbolic weight, which the increasingly conservative state authorities understood all too well. Repressive police action stopped these meetings. In the highly contested politics of the Second Republic, the slow construction of a rival centre of authority to the government was not possible.

A more promising initiative was taken by seventy-five radical deputies in November 1848. They formed the 'Republican Solidarity' organisation, which could be considered 'the first attempt to organise a national political party in France'. By January 1849 it had offices in sixty-two departments, some 353 branches and a national membership of approximately thirty thousand.[25] This grouping marked the start of the 'Démoc-Socs', or Democratic Socialists. In the brief time in which it was allowed to be active, two lessons were clearly learnt: first, if republicans were to win elections, they needed to win the rural vote and, above all, the peasant vote. Second, to gain these allegiances, republicans had to offer a social reform programme. Republican Solidarity was formally banned on 29 January 1849, when conservative deputies argued that it amounted to a revolutionary conspiracy. This ban demonstrates the problems faced by republicans: they were fighting to persuade a politically inexperienced electorate to accept radically new ideas at a time when increasingly authoritarian and conservative governments were seeking to 'restabilise' French society.

In 1849 the political geography of the republican left changed. In April 1848, left-wing votes had been concentrated among the skilled workers and the lower-middle classes of the bigger towns and cities, mainly in the northern third of France. In the May 1849 elections, they gained the bulk of their support from rural departments in the south-east and centre, concentrated along the Mediterranean coastline and through a long stretch of departments running up the Rhône river to the centre of France. In the Pyrénées-Orientales, an impressive network of Démoc-Soc organisations developed. These distinctive features were noted by the Public Prosecutor, the chief legal official of the region, based in the city of Montpellier (Hérault). 'You have sent me to a region which is like nowhere else in France', he wrote to the Minister of Justice. 'Two departments in particular – the Hérault and the Pyrénées-Orientales – have a distinct identity.'[26]

What was so unusual about the Pyrénées-Orientales? The answer given by the Minister of Justice might have been that it was marked by extreme administrative instability. Between February 1848 and January 1849, no less than eleven prefects were successively appointed to the department.[27] 'In effect, there is no regular authority', complained the new Republican Prosecutor when he arrived in Perpignan in January 1849. 'No court, no chief of police, no prefect, no cooperation from the Prefecture, no mayor, and no municipal councillors.'[28]

The reason for this instability lay in the strength and organisational ability of the department's republicans. The last deputy of the Orleanist regime to be elected in Perpignan was Arago. While his politics were relatively moderate, he had pioneered populist forms of political culture. His 1846 campaign had created a loose network of militants across the department. In February 1848 they acted decisively. They seized control of the Perpignan town hall and dismissed Orleanist officials. This was not the isolated action of an activist minority: in the following general elections, the department voted decisively for republican candidates. Perhaps more significantly, this anti-Orleanist move was repeated at local level. Between July and September 1848, local elections were held in all French communes. Across France, some fifty-five per cent of the old Orleanist mayors were re-elected. In the Pyrénées-Orientales, only twenty-four per cent of them survived.[29]

This lively republican political culture thrived in the department's clubs and cafés. In March 1851 the Public Prosecutor told the Minister of Justice 'of all the towns in my region, Perpignan is the one with the most clubs'. He identified fifty-eight clubs.[30] Twenty-four of these were in or near Perpignan; others were grouped around the city. It was precisely in these areas that the resistance to Louis-Napoleon's *coup d'état* was concentrated in December 1851. The fifty-eight clubs contained almost six thousand members – approximately one-sixth of the department's electorate according to the electoral register of April 1848.[31] Usually members paid between 0.5 and one franc per month subscription to join, and, as far as can be seen, the clubs were only open to men.

The Public Prosecutor divided the clubs into three categories – non-political, red and conservative (whether Party of Order or legitimist). To these, he added a sub-category: philanthropic clubs which provided assistance such as medical insurance to their members, and which could be either red or conservative in character.

Table 7.6: Types of clubs in the Pyrénées-Orientales in 1851

Political allegiance	No. of clubs	No. of members
Red	19	2 337 (39%)
Conservative	9	1 925 (32%)
Non-political	30	1 761 (29%)
Total	58	5 997 (100%)

Table 7.7: Sub-category of philanthropic clubs in the Pyrénées-Orientales in 1851

	No. of clubs	No. of members
Philanthropic	8	2 137

The largest single category was the non-political clubs. However, these had relatively few members; less than a third of all club members belonged to them. The largest number of people belonged to the red clubs. There were not many conservative clubs but, as table 7.8 shows, some of them, particularly those with a philanthropic function, had very large memberships.

The non-political clubs were essentially leisure facilities. They provided 'a place for relaxation for workers and honest farmers. They drink and gamble more cheaply and peacefully than they would in a cabaret.'[32] The red clubs had a significantly different function: they were centres of discussion and organisation. Only eight of the fifty-eight clubs were registered as subscribing

Table 7.8: Average membership of clubs

Clubs	Average membership
Conservative	240
Red	137.47
Non-political	60.7
All philanthropic clubs	267.1
Red philanthropic clubs	184.25
Conservative philanthropic clubs	350

to journals. Seven were red clubs and the eighth was non-political. Some details have been preserved about the red club at Sournia, a cantonal town in centre of the department, in April 1849.

Table 7.9: Membership of the red club at Sournia (Pyrénées–Orientales)[33]

Profession	Adult male population	Club members
Labourers	174	78
	(57.0%)	(63.4%)
Farmers	32	16
	(10.5%)	(13.0%)
Artisans	55	22
	(18.2%)	(17.9%)
Officials	13	1
	(4.2%)	(0.8%)
Businessmen	4	3
	(1.3%)	(2.5%)
Liberal professions	5	1
	(1.6%)	(0.8%)
Soldiers, others	22	2
	(7.2%)	(1.6%)
Totals	305	123
	(100%)	(100%)

Table 7.9 compares the membership of the red Démoc-Soc club (column 3) with the town's adult male population (column 2). The figures in column 2 reflect the economy of the department. The majority of working men might have owned some land, but they earned the bulk of their income by working for others: principally for the thirty-two farmers. About one-fifth are artisans and, as this is a cantonal town, there are also a handful of merchants, officials and professional people. Column 3 allows us to see which groups were more likely to join the Démoc-Socs. The labourers and farmers are over-represented: this suggests that they strongly supported the club. The artisans are represented in the club in proportion to their numbers with the com-

mune, while the officials (who may well have been dependent on state patronage) are almost entirely absent. Although this is a small sample, it is still significant to see that most of the businessmen joined. This suggests that the club was not appealing to 'backward' sectors who were rejecting modernisation, but to the best-educated who were participating most fully in the new economic forms, principally commerce connected to the wine trade.

The red clubs were centres of political organisation and political authority. For example, in February 1849, a red club in Prades (a sub-prefecture to the west of Perpignan) organised a ceremony to mark the anniversary of the February 1848 Revolution. The Captain of the Prades National Guard mobilised his men, not to oppose the ceremony, but to act as a guard of honour to accompany it.[34] He was reprimanded for his activities by the Republican Prosecutor in Perpignan. A year later, the Démoc-Socs of Prades had not lost any confidence. On 24 February 1850, the acting mayor and his councillors left the church in a group, then gathered together in the square to shout, three times, 'Long live the Republic!'. 'During the whole day, the cabarets and cafés were full. At 5pm the Mayor sent out a message by the Town Crier that all good Republicans should illuminate their houses.' Eight hundred people gathered in the town square to celebrate and to sing republican songs around the Liberty Tree, including the Marseillaise and 'Ça Ira'.[35] The sub-prefect called out the police to disperse them. The crowd refused to move, and shouted at the police, ending each slogan with a cry of 'Ça Ira!'. Eventually, twenty people were arrested.[36]

Clubs like those in Sournia and Prades grew up in small market towns and cantonal centres in 1849 and 1850. On market days they became centres of propaganda, spreading their ideas to the countryfolk: men like the 'red' grocer in Illes would distribute 'drinks and propaganda' to his customers.[37] Minor officials, such as mayors, forest guards, rural postmen and primary school teachers, could also act to spread the ideas of the Démoc-Socs and they were closely watched by the authorities.[38] Between February 1850 and December 1851, forty-seven mayors, twenty-three assistant mayors and thirty-seven primary school teachers were dismissed from the department's 228 communes.[39]

The strength of the Démoc-Socs even affected judicial procedures. The Republican Prosecutor noted that the statistics for trials with juries seemed to show that this was almost a crime-free department, for there were only six such trials in 1850. In reality, the judicial administration was reluctant to appeal to juries, for they knew that such bodies would be unwilling to convict Démoc-Socs.[40] At times, the Public Prosecutor seemed to despair: 'this department seems destined to be continually agitated'.[41]

These conservative republican authorities faced two problems: one was the great strength of the Démoc-Socs; the second, the department's right-wing, the Carlists, as legitimists were known in the Pyrénées-Orientales. 'In the Roussillon region, almost everyone is either a White or a fanatical Red', wrote the Public Prosecutor, 'there is only a tiny minority of moderates.'[42] The large conservative–philanthropic clubs were often headed by old monarchists, rather than 'moderate' republicans from the Party of Order. Their conspicuous sponsorship of such institutions provoked a red backlash, instead of creating calm.

In some rural towns, the tensions between the Démoc-Soc 'reds' and the Carlist 'whites' was such that the slightest gesture seemed enough to trigger a violent conflict. In Elne, south of Perpignan, on Sunday 6 May 1849, there was a procession outside the church. Girls dressed in white and girls dressed in red argued as to who should lead the procession. While these colours were the 'traditional' colours of Mediterranean Catholic culture, in the charged atmosphere of 1849 they had acquired a new significance. The girls' argument immediately became 'the object of a political struggle', involving monarchists and republicans, and requiring police intervention. Three men were badly wounded.[43]

Following the conservative victory in the May 1849 elections, legislation restricted the clubs. In some areas, these laws were successful. Radical activities were curtailed in the well-policed cities, but the little towns of the countryside were better able to resist such repression. Démoc-Socs looked for other means by which they could organise. One possibility was to make use of the still-legal Mutual Aid societies which provided their members with basic insurance against unemployment and sickness. Looking once more at the list of clubs drawn up by the Public Prosecutor in 1851, one wonders how many of those thirty 'non-political' clubs were actually covers for Démoc-Soc organisations.

Faced with judicial repression, Démoc-Soc organisation changed. They could not confront the authorities in the open. Some adopted underground techniques of organisation, for which there were many sources of inspiration. These included the *Charbonnerie* groups of the 1820s, masonic and *compagnonnage* sub-cultures and, in some parts of Mediterranean France (such as the Gard), older Protestant traditions. In the Pyrénées-Orientales in particular, the experience of Catalans as a minority within a dominant French culture may also have inspired the Démoc-Socs.

These secret societies took the name of 'Montagnard', the term used for the radical faction in the Revolutionary parliaments of 1793–5. In areas where these societies were strong, often there was a surprising – and suspicious – calm. The Public Prosecutor realised this. 'They are organising secretly with more courage than ever before' he commented. 'They are not organised in big societies which would be too large to hide, but in groups or cadres in which the members are classified, positioned, organised, almost numbered, with great cleverness. They are ready to follow, as one man, their chiefs.'[44]

Judicial repression produced another counter-move from the Démoc-Socs. Peter McPhee, in his detailed analysis of the Pyrénées-Orientales, notes this shift.

> Politics became more strongly embedded in popular culture, not only to escape from the grasp of a repressive bureaucracy, but also to respond to the impatience and the hopes which circulated in the villages. Because of the erosion of civil liberties, provincial Republicanism after 1849 had to turn to the events of local life in order to express its ideas and organise its supporters.[45]

In other words, rather than destroying the Démoc-Socs, state repression transformed them into a different sort of movement. If formal organisation was increasingly difficult, they could still use *in*formal expressions of political commitment.

The Démoc-Socs' retreat into popular culture led to some near-farcical measures. In October 1850 the Prefect banned all clothes and objects which 'had a political aim or which could serve as a symbol'.[46] The Liberty Trees were obvious targets and were cut down in November and December 1850; but more trivial symbols were also politicised. On 6 February 1851, there was a dance in St Estève, just outside Perpignan, to celebrate the local saint's day. As this was a well-known red commune, three policemen watched the dancers carefully. They noticed that one dancer wore a red ribbon in his buttonhole, and forcibly removed it. This annoyed the dancers, who chased the policemen, assaulted two of them, and threw the third into a canal. In the evening the Republican Prosecutor, the Prefect and a column of infantry arrived in the village: they made two arrests and suspended the Mayor. As they left, stones were thrown at the soldiers. And all because of a red ribbon at a dance ...[47] From December 1849 to December 1851, dances, songs, symbols and processions were forbidden or curtailed in forty of the department's 228 communes.[48]

This entry into popular culture affected the Démoc-Socs in another way: the legal clubs and the illegal Montagnard secret societies were nearly entirely male in their memberships. However, women could participate almost as fully as men in the mixed arena of popular culture. The Démoc-Socs' resilience in 1850–1 depended on wide, deep support from entire communities, involving men and women, young and old. It has to be stressed that the Démoc-Socs were not actually choosing these new political forms, but were being driven into them. They survived not because of the cleverness of their tactics, but because their ideas and ethics met with a ready response from a broad majority of rural people in some areas.

Late in 1851, the Démoc-Socs were still confused about which tactics to follow. While they had formed the Montagnard secret societies, and while many of these were armed, it was unclear whether they were planning a revolt. Different schemes co-existed in an uneasy compromise. Most pinned their hopes on the forthcoming elections in May 1852, in which they considered that the now well-organised republican left would secure a clear victory. If this victory was denied to them by either conservative deputies or by the President, Louis-Napoleon, then the Montagnard societies would be mobilised. This compromise policy failed to end tensions between the electoral and insurrectionary wings of the movement.

The *coup d'état* of 2–3 December 1851 came as a surprise. On 3 December, posters announcing the seizure of power by Louis-Napoleon were displayed in Perpignan. A crowd variously estimated as between two hundred and eight hundred gathered during the morning, and demonstrated outside the Prefecture. They were dispersed by soldiers. Over the next three days, the Montagnard societies were mobilised. Across the Pyrénées-Orientales, some ten thousand people may have demonstrated against the *coup d'état*, concentrated in the vine-growing belt around Perpignan. There were some armed clashes, but by 7 December the Démoc-Socs had realised that, across France, there had not been massive resistance. They were alone, confronting armed soldiers who were prepared to use their weapons. Under these circumstances, they dispersed.

The Pyrénées-Orientales were placed under martial law, and the referendum of 21 December 1851 was held while soldiers patrolled the streets of red communes, police and soldiers hunted for Démoc-Socs resisting arrest, and local administrations were purged. In total, 101 mayors and deputy mayors, plus fifty-six councillors, were dismissed from the department's 228 communes, and some 692 people were condemned in special courts.[49]

– III. POLITICAL CULTURE –

The Second Republic was a period of transition in left-wing thinking: older Republican ideas from the 1790s co-existed with newer ideas concerning the political role of the proletariat.

A key term in political debates was 'association'. During the period of 'utopian' Republicanism, in March and April 1848, many republicans believed that through 'association' all France's economic ills would be cured. When Hugo stood for election in the by-elections of June 1848, he was asked to comment on the ideal of 'association', 'which will save the Republic and make mankind into a family of brothers'. Hugo responded by comparing 'association' and 'society': 'In the last analysis, what do these two words stand for? ... The same idea: fraternity.'[50] Hugo denied that the term 'association' had any specifically new meaning. For him, it was merely a synonym of the older republican term of 'fraternity', an ideal to encourage a sense of unity. Such attitudes were typical of middle-class republicans. '"Assocationism" was all things to all men', observes Magraw, 'and for some bourgeois leaders it implied social reform without class conflict.'[51]

For many working-class radicals, the term had a different meaning. Corbon, a member of the Catholic-Socialist team who had edited the *Atelier* journal since 1840, argued that association was 'the great need of our epoque'. He was not proposing a vague social ideal, but a form of economic organisation which would alleviate the evils of competition, and inspire workers with a 'new moral ideal'.[52] In part because of Corbon's careful arguments, the moderate Republican Government agreed to support co-operatives (see table 7.5 above). However, within these governmental discussions there was always a fundamental ambiguity: did 'association' mean the harmony of rich and poor, as understood by Hugo? Or did it mean the autonomous organisation of workers, outside of the control of the government and ruling class? This second interpretation was more likely to be supported by working-class radicals.

Working-class militants had been attracted to Blanc's ideas concerning the partnership of the Republican state with a network of worker-controlled associations, according to which the state would supply capital and organise contracts, while leaving the day-to-day management of workshops to self-managed co-operatives. These concepts inspired many debates in the Luxemburg Commission, but were impossible to put into practice after the conservative victory in the May 1848 elections.

As governments grew more conservative in 1848–9, so working-class ideas developed. There was a series of attempts by radicals to organise their economic projects *outside* parliament. Jeanne Deroin, a feminist-socialist, sponsored a Union of Associations, which claimed the support of 104 co-operatives in November 1849.[53] While the government tolerated non-political co-operatives, it was hostile to attempts to radicalise them.[54] Radical associations rarely survived long: Deroin's Union was broken up by a police raid on 29 May 1850, during which Deroin herself was arrested.[55]

Some militants realised how 'association' could become a trap. They pointed out that the schemes accepted by the government merely allowed an élite of skilled workers to preserve their relatively comfortable positions, while ignoring the plight of the unskilled majority. One such radical was Jean Drevet, employed in the National Workshops in 1848, and transported for his participation in the June 1848 rebellion. In a short text published in 1850, he called for an inclusive working-class socialism, through which the techniques of association – by which he meant workers' co-operatives – would be extended throughout society.[56]

The most prestigious working-class theorist in this period was Pierre Joseph Proudhon (1809–65). Proudhon had worked in a printshop; he was almost entirely self-taught, and his ideas had both the originality and the idiosyncratic qualities of someone educated outside orthodox schools. His first work was entitled *What is Property?* (1840), in which he argued, in a phrase that has since become famous, that property was theft. In this work he also declared himself to be 'an anarchist'. This was the first time that the term 'anarchist' had been used in a positive sense; prior to 1840 it had simply meant a destructive person, or a vandal. In fact, Proudhon's ideas were less revolutionary than these eye-catching slogans suggested. He defined 'property' as objects or possessions which one owned but did not use: in other words, a farmer who ploughed his own field was not a property-owner, but a farmer who rented out his field was. In the same vein, even Proudhon's 'anarchy' was less terrifying than it first sounded. His social and political ideal was the independent family enterprise, whether farm, shop or firm. 'Anarchism', for Proudhon, meant allowing these families to live without authoritarian direction from Church and state.

He rejected the plans of utopians like Fourier and Saint-Simon. In his confrontation with Fourier's thinking, a mean-minded misogyny was revealed in Proudhon's thinking: the independent family was to be represented to the outside world by its male head; any attempt to limit this literally patriarchal power was to be resisted. Proudhon opposed all proposals to liberate women.

Throughout the Second Republic, Proudhon produced a steady stream of articles, pamphlets and full-length books. All seem to have been written in a hurry: they lurch wildly from dramatic slogans ('universal suffrage is the most certain way of making the People lie'), through sustained, almost lyrical polemics, to frankly dull, hair-splitting expositions of Proudhon's clumsy understanding of Hegelian dialectics, and arrogant dismissals of his rivals. One is left with an impression of several strong, but not necessarily coherent, themes. First, Proudhon placed the concept of 'the people' at the centre of his thinking: the revolutionary coalition of enlightened professionals, lower-middle-class and working-class militants should be preserved. Secondly, within his writing, there was a quasi-Catholic, moralistic approach to politics. He repeated arguments about Orleanist corruption, but his moralism was also directed at the population at large. Proudhon had a pessimistic attitude to human nature, quite unlike the utopians he opposed. If he rejected big institutions, it was because he suspected that all people had within them a tendency to corruption. The long-term solution to the problem of political corruption was simply to prevent anyone from holding power.

From this idiosyncratic point of view, Proudhon attacked the happy dreams of the 'utopian' Republic. He argued that the Government had replaced the spontaneous, benevolent, revolutionary action of 'the people' with its authoritarian rule. As by definition no government could be revolutionary, this meant the end of the revolution. 'Fear of the People is a disease shared by all those in authority; for those in power, the People are the enemy.'[57]

Proudhon developed a quite different ideal of 'association' from the state-centred schemes put forward by Blanc and the Luxemburg Commission. 'It is only ever despite himself, and because man can do no other', he wrote, 'that he enters into association with others.'[58] Instead of a state-run economy, Proudhon proposed a version of market capitalism, in which independent families would be loosely federated to each other. Rather than thinking in terms of workers' co-operatives, Proudhon understood 'association' as the creation of banking and credit facilities for small farmers and workshop owners.

There was some real point of contact between Proudhon's concepts of economic reform and the proposals of the Démoc-Socs in 1850–1. To gain rural support, the Démoc-Socs had to offer the broad mass of peasants social reforms. These farmers were angry about government policies: partly about the forty-five centimes tax, but also about more long-standing grievances. Small farmers who switched to cash crops were competing on a far wider scale than ever before, with very little government support. Tax reform, credit facilities and an expansion of schooling were all policies which made immediate sense to them, for such measures would enable them to compete more effectively. The Démoc-Socs did not merely discuss this type of programme. In 1849–51 they also adapted their message to their audience. Skilled writers such as Pierre Joigneaux worked to teach peasants that socialism was 'not something frightening'; their writings 'offered pragmatic solutions to endemic problems'.[59] When new press laws made it difficult for Démoc-Socs to publish papers, they turned to printing pamphlets and almanacs.

Démoc-Socs represented an ethic of mutual aid. The true Republic would be a society without middlemen, in which independent producers voluntarily helped each other. They presented their peasant supporters with a distinctive interpretation of history, arguing that the legitimists and Orleanists had exploited rural France, without benefiting the mass of the people. In their place, the Démoc-Socs offered a type of moral and economic renaissance of rural society, in which its true worth would at last be realised. This ideal certainly resembled Proudhon's thinking, for it implied a rejection of authoritarian controls, whether from the state or from the big landowners. 'The more precise the economic demands of the Montagnards', writes Margadant, 'the more they resembled the anarchist ideal of a free village community, emancipated overnight from the power of the state'.[60]

– IV. LEGACY –

After 1851, the Démoc-Socs were forgotten for more than a century, their ideas caricatured by the victorious Bonapartist authorities. When the republican movement revived in the late 1860s, in opposition to the Second Empire (1852–70), it wished to stress its commitment to legality and constitutional rule. The memories of the peasant insurrectionaries of 1851 were embarrassing, and they were rarely recalled. It was not until the social histories of the 1970s that the scale of the peasant insurrection became clear.

Therefore, the most immediate legacy of peasant socialism was antisocialism. The existence of the Démoc-Soc movement gave the Party of Order a political target around which it could orientate its propaganda and political culture. Table 7.9 lists some of the expressions used by the Montpellier Public Prosecutor to describe the Démoc-Socs in his region.

Table 7.10: Terms used by the Montpellier Public Prosecutor to describe Démoc-Soc and Montagnard groups, 1848–51

Date	Expression
July 1848	'the makers of disorder'
December 1849	'Socialists'
	'the Reds or Montagnards on one hand, the Whites or moderates on the other.'
March 1850	'the most perverted and ignorant class'
May 1850	'anarchist propaganda'
	'anarchic doctrines'
July 1850	'the exalted party'
October 1850	'the anarchic party'
November 1850	'the red party'
December 1850	'the anarchists'
April 1851	'demagogy'
August 1851	'demagogues'
November 1851	'the demagogic party'

In general, the Prosecutor chose not to use the terms which the Démoc–Socs themselves devised; normally he devised his own euphemisms. Why? The answer is probably that he did not consider the Démoc-Socs to be part of the 'acceptable' range of political movements. To accept their representation of themselves would have implied that he accepted them as a legitimate political movement. Instead, the Prosecutor's words suggest that their political culture needed to be decoded and reclassified in order to be understood. His terms suggest that they represented something fundamentally unacceptable; rather than political leaders engaged in constructing something, they were merely 'makers of disorder' or 'anarchists' (understood in pre-Proudhonian terms). In other words, their politics were fundamentally destructive. Their existence as a significant movement was based on their appeal to unworthy elements: to 'the most perverted and ignorant class', a sector which should not be represented politically. Above all they were 'demagogues', or rabble-rousers. Their politics were based on an appeal to passions, they were 'exhalted', rather than rational. Such terms, which formed the common vocabulary of both the Party of Order and the conservative authorities, reveal how the political space opened up in February 1848 had shrunk. (See document 7.3.)

The Public Prosecutor's response was to oppose Order to anarchy. The Pyrénées-Orientales would be cured by a healthy injection of authority. 'There is no region of which it would be more appropriate to say "all they're asking for is to be governed"', he argued.[61]

The key argument produced by the authorities in the Pyrénées-Orientales was that they represented the values of civilisation against the anarchy of the Démoc-Socs. When one evaluates the Démoc-Socs' record, it is clear that the authorities' argument was a hollow one. The Démoc-Socs were supported by some of the most modern elements of French society; in particular, the market-sensitive vine-growing villages. The backbone of their support came from middle-aged, married men, concerned about the future of their families. Rather than opposing the development of French society, the Démoc-Socs asserted a rival version of modernity, in which the facilities of the state would be used to help the lower classes, and to strengthen their communities. Such ideas, while vague, constituted the basis of mid-nineteenth-century socialism. When compared with the bombast, authoritarianism and the aggression of the Party of Order, it is difficult not to conclude that it was the Démoc-Socs, and not the Party of Order, who represented civilisation.

– V. DOCUMENTS –

– DOCUMENT 7.1: FÉLIX PYAT'S SPEECH AT THE PLANTING OF LIBERTY TREES IN BOURGES (CHER), 2 APRIL 1848 –

Pyat, a left-wing republican, used this occasion to present key themes of republican political culture to a provincial audience.

Citizens,

This festival is definitely not a vain, sterile spectacle from which you will learn nothing. It is not like those festivals under past kings. It is the Festival of the People, and it is as rich and as simple as they are; it is a Festival of Agriculture, of Industry, and of the Arts; it is a festival for all of you peaceful heroes, you who fight the soil and conquer the harvest, who create order by your wealth, and property by your labour. This is well-deserved praise for your long suffering, this is a consecration of your new rights, it is a Festival of Work, which will be the only monarch in the future, whose sceptre will be the horn of plenty.

The Government has given you your place of honour, because you have had your share of effort. It has called on all of you, for the first time, to join together in this great civic act, alongside your officials, under the auspices of the God of your fathers, to plant with your hands this Tree, the symbol of the alliance of Man and Nature, of France and Liberty.

Plant it in our old Gallic soil, in this earth which is like a breast of the Motherland, in this soil of Bourges ...

The Republic, like this young tree, will take root in the soil, it will reach out to the sky, it will defy the winds and storms. Yes, it will always stand upright, despite the efforts of our enemies. I swear to you, Citizens from all around, to you National Guards, the defenders of the interior, to you soldiers, our champions abroad, you will defend it against everything. Soon, thanks to you, it will grow protecting branches, big enough to cover in its shade the children of the nation and to nourish them with its fruits.

Long live the Republic!

Source: AN, BB/30/333

– DOCUMENT 7.2: SOCIALISM IN THE CAFÉ –

This passage, from a Démoc-Soc paper, shows how Republican political culture was becoming rooted in the daily life of rural France. It discusses the Démoc-Socs' reaction to state repression, and shows their sense of an increasingly polarised society.

Three men seated around a table terrify you; the reading of a newspaper in a public space makes you shiver. We don't want your petty-spirited police tyranny. Village cabarets are *our* salons. We talk of our crops and of the Republic. Those who have read the newspapers tell us what is in them. Those for whom every day is a Sunday don't understand what it is to celebrate the weekly day off. And just because we want to go to the café with the locals, with the mayor and the deputy, because we drink a couple of glasses of wine to console ourselves for drinking only water during the week, because our tongues wag a bit faster than usual, your policemen come, and prosecute the café-owner. No, no, enough of that! It's gone beyond a joke.

Source: *Feuille de Village*, 20 March 1851, cited in Roger Magraw, 'Pierre Joigneaux and Socialist Propaganda in the French Countryside, 1849–51', *French Historical Studies* 10 (1978), 599–640 (632)

– DOCUMENT 7.3: THE VOCABULARY OF ORDER –

Victor Hugo's *Napoléon le Petit* was a stinging personal attack of the lies and deception used by Louis-Napoleon to achieve power. This passage describes parliamentary debates within the Second Republic: while clearly Hugo intends to caricature the reactions of the right-wing deputies, there is more than an element of truth in his observations.

[The Party of Order's leaders] discovered how to turn their innocent colleagues' minds: it was as if they implanted in them a new type of dictionary in which all the words used by democratic speakers and writers were immediately translated: for 'humanity' read 'ferocity'; for 'universal well-being' read 'upheaval'; for 'Republic' read 'terrorism'; for 'socialism' read 'pillage'; for 'fraternity' read 'massacre'; for 'the Gospel' read 'death to the rich'. In this manner, when a left-wing speaker said, for example, 'We want the end of war and the abolition of capital punishment' these poor people of the right clearly heard him say 'We want to burn everything and kill everyone'. After such a speech, which addressed issues such as liberty, universal peace, and well-being, to be gained by work, harmony and progress, you could see the representatives [of the right] get up from their seats white-faced. They were not sure whether they had been guillotined, and they reached for their hats in order to find out whether they still had their heads.

Source: Victor Hugo, *Napoléon le Petit* (Neuilly-sur-Seine: Saint-Clair, 1975), pp. 61–2

– VI. FURTHER READING –

On the Second Republic, see the 'Further reading' in Chapter 6.

The best work on rural history during the Second Republic is Peter McPhee, *The Politics of Rural Life: Political Mobilization in the French Countryside, 1846–52* (Oxford: Oxford UP, 1992). To this should be added Ted W. Margadant, *French Peasants in Revolt: the Insurrection of 1851* (Princeton: Princeton UP, 1979), a slightly older work which opened up the whole question of peasant politics.

There are few studies specifically on the Pyrénées-Orientales. Of vital importance is Peter McPhee, *Les Semailles de la République dans les Pyrénées-Orientales, 1848–52* (Perpignan: L'Olivier, 1995). John M. Merriman has written an excellent study of politics in Perpignan: 'Quartier Blanc, Quartier Rouge: Cultural Marginality and Popular Politics in Perpignan' in his *The Margins of City Life* (Oxford: Oxford UP, 1991).

Francis Demier, 'Les ouvriers de Rouen parlent à un économiste en juillet 1848', *Mouvement Social* 92 (1982), 3–31 is a vivid study of one of the first working-class communities to oppose the Republic. Mary L. Stewart-McDougall, *The Artisan Republic: Revolution, Reaction and Resistance in Lyon, 1848–1851* (Gloucester: McGill Queen's UP/Sutton, 1984) discusses the

growth of a republican left in Lyon. J. Gaillard, 'Les Associations de production et la pensée politique en France (1852–1870)', *Mouvement Social*
52 (1965), 59–84 concerns the decline of workers' associations during the
Second Empire. (On working-class political culture, see 'Further reading' for
Chapter 3.)

Bernard H. Moss, 'June 13 1849: the Abortive Uprising of French Radical-
ism', *French Historical Studies* 13 (1984), 390–414 discusses the movements
of left republicans in Paris. Roger Magraw, 'Pierre Joigneaux and Socialist
Propaganda in the French Countryside, 1849–51', *French Historical Studies* 10
(1978), 599–640 presents a well-written study of rural socialist propaganda.
Peter Sahlins, *Forest Rites: the War of the Demoiselles in Nineteenth-Century France*
(Cambridge, Massachusetts: Harvard UP, 1994) does not concern the Second
Republic, but it is an imaginative and thought-provoking study of rural
politics in the early nineteenth century.

There has been an extended debate among historians concerning the
nature of suffrage during the Second Republic which I have not been able
explore fully here. Different perspectives can be found in the following essays:
Maurice Agulhon, '1848, le suffrage universel et la politisation des campagnes
françaises' in his *Histoire Vagabonde III* (Paris: Gallimard, 1996), pp. 61–84;
Melvin Edelstein, 'La participation électorale des français (1789–1870)',
Revue d'histoire moderne et contemporaine 40:4 (1993), 629–42; Peter Jones,
'An Improbable Democracy: Nineteenth-century Elections in the Massif
Central', *English Historical Review* 97 (1982), pp. 530–57 and his *Politics and
Rural Society: the Southern Massif Central, 1750–1880* (Cambridge: Cambridge
UP, 1979); Peter McPhee, 'Electoral Democracy and Direct Democracy
in France, 1789–1851', *European History Quarterly* 16 (1986), 77–96; Eugen
Weber, 'The Second Republic, Politics and the Peasant', *French Historical
Studies* 11 (1980), 521–50. Christine Guionnet, *L'Apprentissage de la politique
modern: les élections municipales sous la monarchie de juillet* (Paris: L'Harmattan,
1997) contains some fascinating and observant comments on the nature of
French political life.

– NOTES –

1. Mayor of Sost to Minister of Justice, 22 March 1848, AN, BB/18/1461.
2. Schroëngrun to Minister of Justice, 9 March 1848, AN, BB/18/1461.
3. Mary Lynn Stewart-McDougall, *Artisan Republic: Revolution, Reactions and Resistance in
   Lyon, 1848–51* (Gloucester: McGill Queen's UP/Sutton, 1984), p. 52.
4. Ted W. Margadant, *French Peasants in Revolt: the Insurrection of 1851* (Princeton: Princeton
   UP, 1979), p. 42.
5. 29 February 1848, AN, BB/18/1460.

6. Peter McPhee, *Les semailles de la République dans les Pyrénées-Orientales, 1848–52* (Perpignan: L'Olivier, 1995), p. 108.

7. Figures for all-France votes, Roger Price, *The Second French Republic: A Social History* (London: Batsford 1972), p. 220; figures for Pyrénées-Orientales from McPhee, *Semailles*, p. 144.

8. All-France results from Peter McPhee, *The Politics of Rural Life: Political Mobilization in the French Countryside, 1846–52* (Oxford: Oxford UP, 1992), p. 130; for Pyrénées-Orientales from McPhee, *Semailles*, p. 163.

9. McPhee, *Politics*, p. 227.

10. Margadant, *French Peasants*, pp. xvii and 8.

11. All-France results from McPhee, *Politics*, p. 245; Pyrénées-Orientales figures from McPhee, *Semailles*, p. 385.

12. Bernard Ménager, *Les Napoléon du Peuple* (Paris: Aubier, 1988), pp. 433–4.

13. None are listed in AN, BB/30/296. This is not to say that none took place, merely that police authorities did not see the Pyrénées-Orientales as a source for opposition.

14. Records in AN, C/940; see also McPhee, *Semailles*, p. 106.

15. McPhee, *Semailles*, p. 236.

16. Figures from Jean-Pierre Pelissier, *Paroisses et Communes de France: dictionnaire d'histoire administrative et démographique: Pyrénées-Orientales* (Paris: CNRS 1986).

17. John M. Merriman, 'Quartier Blanc, Quartier Rouge: Cultural Marginality and Popular Politics in Perpignan' in his *The Margins of City Life* (Oxford: Oxford UP, 1991), pp. 113–55 (p. 115).

18. McPhee, *Semailles*, p. 226.

19. Merriman, 'Quartier Blanc', p. 118.

20. Mona Ozouf, *La Fête révolutionnaire, 1789–99* (Paris: Folio, 1976), pp. 409–21.

21. Alexandre-Auguste Ledru-Rollin, *Discours divers et écrits politiques*, Vol. II (Paris: Germer Baillière, 1879), pp. 17–19.

22. Pierre Joseph Proudhon, *Idées révolutionnaires* (Antony: Tops/Trinquier, 1996), p. 44.

23. Figures from Stewart-McDougall, *Artisan Republic*, pp. 98–9.

24. Details in AN, BB/30/333.

25. McPhee, *Politics*, p. 110.

26. Public Prosecutor, 10 August 1851, BB/30/380.

27. McPhee, *Semailles*, p. 126.

28. Republican Prosecutor, 2 January 1849, BB/30/362.

29. McPhee, *Semailles*, p. 128.

30. AN, BB/30/391, 10 March 1851.

31. The May 1850 law which restricted the right to vote reduced the department's electorate significantly: Public Prosecutor, 29 November 1850, AN, BB/30/380.

32. Public Prosecutor, 10 March 1851, AN, BB/30/391.

33. McPhee, *Semailles*, p. 135.

34. 19 March 1849, AN, BB/18/1474.

35. Ça Ira was one of the most famous hymns of the 1789 Revolution. The title could be translated as 'it will come about' or as 'the day will come', and this line forms the repeated chorus of the song. Among other hopes, the song promises: 'Who is high, shall be made low; who is last, shall be first … the aristocracy will say "we are guilty" to the French people who have been kept silent … the true and the false will be distinguished'. A rather more violent version – which may well be the one which was sung in Prades – also promised that the aristocrats would be taken to the lampposts and hung, that there would

be no more nobles or priests, and that there would be equality. See François Moreau and Elisabeth Wahl (eds), *Chants de la Révolution française* (Paris: Livres de Poche, 1989), pp. 45–8.

36. Public Prosecutor, 27 February 1850, AN, BB/30/362.
37. Republican Prosecutor, 18 May 1849, AN, BB/30/362.
38. Public Prosecutor, 4 January 1850, AN, BB/30/380.
39. McPhee, *Semailles*, p. 284.
40. 6 May 1851, AN, BB/20/155.
41. 4 January 1850, BB/30/390.
42. 29 November 1850, AN, BB/30/380.
43. Public Prosecutor, 9 May 1849, AN, BB/30/362.
44. 9 April 1851, AN, BB/30/380.
45. McPhee, *Semailles*, p. 296.
46. Public Prosecutor, 14 October 1850, AN, BB/30/380.
47. Public Prosecutor, 8 February 1851, AN, BB/30/391.
48. McPhee, *Semailles*, p. 331.
49. McPhee, *Semailles*, pp. 396 and 379.
50. Victor Hugo, *Avant l'Exil* (Paris: Nelson, 1936), pp. 174–6.
51. Roger Magraw, *A History of the French Working Class, Vol. I* (Oxford: Blackwell, 1992), p. 173.
52. Corbon, *Rapport au nom du Comité des travailleurs sur la proposition Alcan ...* (Paris: Imprimerie de l'Assemblée Nationale, 1848), pp. 2–5.
53. Bernard H. Moss, *The Origins of the French Labor Movement, 1830–1914* (Berkeley: California UP, 1976), p. 44.
54. John Merriman, *The Agony of the Republic: the Repression of the Left in Revolutionary France, 1848–51* (New Haven: Yale UP, 1978), p. 51.
55. Felicia Gordon and Máire Cross (eds), *Early French Feminisms, 1830–1940* (Cheltenham: Elgar, 1996), p. 65.
56. J.-P. Drevet, 'Le socialisme pratique, 1850' in A. Faure and J. Rancière (eds), *La Parole ouvrière* (Paris: Bourgeois, 1976), pp. 396–426.
57. Pierre Joseph Proudhon, *Les Confessions d'un révolutionnaire* (Antony: Tops/Trinquier, 1997), p. 124.
58. Pierre Joseph Proudhon, *Idée générale de la Révolution au XIXe siècle* (Paris: Fresnes-Antony, nd), pp. 62–6.
59. Roger Magraw, 'Pierre Joigneaux and Socialist Propaganda in the French Countryside, 1849–51', *French Historical Studies* 10 (1978), 599–640 (607).
60. Margadant, *French Peasants*, p. 141.
61. Public Prosecutor, 22 July 1850, AN, BB/30/380.

CHAPTER 8

Bonapartism and Counter-revolution: 1851

This chapter analyses conservative opposition to the Second Republic. A key strand within this reaction was Bonapartism, a form of political culture which had begun as an official state ideology during the First Empire (1806–14). It did not die with the defeat of Napoleon Bonaparte in 1815, nor even with his death in 1821. Instead, as was shown in Chapter 2, it survived as a popular expression of anti-Restoration feeling.

In the last chapter, we saw that most people in the Pyrénées-Orientales welcomed the Republic. In this chapter we will examine the growing hostility to it in the northern department of the Somme, and the wider issue of the nature of Bonapartism.

– I. PARTICIPANTS –

The cult of Napoleon took the form of 'many different, and often contradictory, beliefs and ideas'.[1] In Chapter 2, we saw a Bonapartism of gossips and drunks, based on sensational stories – a ridiculous, incoherent political culture, but one which was still capable of scaring Restoration authorities and, perhaps, of providing the unschooled, ignorant people of France with an ideal which could inspire their resistance to the Bourbon monarchy.

Following the defeat of Napoleon at Waterloo in June 1815, the Restoration authorities repudiated Imperial political culture and encouraged the teaching of negative images of the Revolution. However, some Bonapartists attempted to defend Napoleon's legacy. A key work in this process was *Le Mémorial de Sainte-Hélène*, by the Count de Las Cases, who accompanied Napoleon into exile in 1815. His record of his conversations with Napoleon presented a sympathetic image of a wise, imaginative and progressive ruler, who was only defeated by treachery and the power of the British. (See document 8.1.)

A third strand of Bonapartism developed as a youthful, romantic belief. Just as some young people, disillusioned with the corrupt and cautious nature of post-Revolutionary politics, were attracted to utopian socialism (see Chapter 5), so others might be drawn to Bonapartism. There were several notable literary portrayals of this form of Bonapartism. Alfred de Vigny, a gifted novelist and a serving army officer, discussed it in his semi-auto-biographical *Servitude et Grandeur Militaires* [Military Baseness and Greatness], published in 1857. He described a young generation who, born in the first years of the nineteenth century, were 'fed on the Emperor's bulletins, and who always had an unsheathed sword before their eyes'. His father told him stories of war with Napoleon's armies, and so his 'useless love of warfare' was born. 'War was ominpresent in my school. The drum stifled the teachers' voices, while their books only spoke to us in a cold, pedantic language ... our cries of "Long live the Emperor!" interrupted Tacitus and Plato.'[2] When he met the survivors of Napoleon's 'Grande Armée' he considered that 'these men seemed to be the survivors of a race of giants who were dying out, one by one, forever'.[3] Vigny's account grows more intriguing as another theme emerges. He was not simply an admirer of Napoleon; his mental condition is closer to that of an addict, or of the victim of a religious cult.

> Bonaparte had infatuated me since childhood ... his glory was so violently strong in my head, that my brain had no room for anything else ... My father was no longer my master because I had seen his master, and it seemed to me that it was he alone who held all the earth's authority. What dreams of authority and slavery! What corrupting thoughts of power, which so easily seduce children! What false enthusiasms, what subtle poisons: what cure could ever be found for you?[4]

A similar evocation of the cult of Bonaparte can also be found in the person of Julien Sorel, the hero of Stendhal's magnificent novel, *Le Rouge et le Noir*, published in 1830.

Despite the Bonapartist sympathies which circulated among the poor, the army and the young, Bonapartism was poorly organised as a political move-ment. Napoleon's son, the Duke of Reichstadt, claimed the title of Napoleon II, but was a poor leader. His contacts in Paris were surprised by the Revo-lution of 1830 and played little active part in it. The revolutionary crowd shouted some Bonapartist slogans, but there was no effective political organis-ation to represent their sympathies. Reichstadt died in 1832.

Napoleon's nephew, Louis-Napoleon, became the Bonapartist pretender and engaged in a more active campaign to restore Bonapartist rule to France, following two strategies. One was to imitate Napoleon's 'Hundred Days', to arrive at the border, proclaim his presence and await popular sympathy. Louis-Napoleon attempted this strategy twice: at Strasbourg in 1836 and Boulogne in 1840. After the second attempt, he was arrested and imprisoned. He escaped from prison in 1846 and took refuge in London.

Louis-Napoleon's second strategy was more imaginative. He tried to reconstruct Bonapartism as a political ideology, thus moving away from the sentimental cult which had gripped young men like Vigny, and placing Bonapartism on a rational basis. In 1839, he published his *Napoleonic Ideas*, followed in 1844 by his *Extinction of Poverty*. Both works suggested a forward-looking, reform-minded politics, encouraging state intervention and concerned with social unity.

Louis-Napoleon's activities had one concrete result: they kept the Bonapartist cause alive during the years when it might have declined into a mere folk memory. An example of its power comes in a speech given by Victor Hugo in the Chamber of Peers in June 1847.

> In my opinon, when I see the decline of our morality, the reign of money, the growth of corruption, the invasion of the highest positions by the lowest of passions, when I see the miseries of this period, I think of the greatness of the past and I am, sometimes, tempted to say to this Chamber, or to the press: 'Let's speak of the Emperor. It will do us some good!'[5]

This vague association of Bonapartism with an ethical sense of national glory was relatively common during the July Monarchy, and arguably growing in strength in the 1840s.

During the Second Republic (1848–51), the north-east of France, known as Picardy, became the most Bonapartist region of France, as is shown in table 8.1.

Table 8.1: 'Yes' votes in the 1851 and 1852 plebiscites, in percentages[6]

	1851	1852
Somme department	87.0	82.9
Picardy region	86.3	84.9
All France	75.2	76.0

The plebiscite of December 1851 ratified the *coup d'état*, and the replacement of the Second Republic by the Second Empire was legitimated by the referendum of November 1852. The highest level of Bonapartist support in these plebiscites came from three departments: the island of Corsica, where Napoleon was born, the Aube, to the east of Paris, and the Somme.

The Somme was a much bigger department than the Pyrénées-Orientales: 570 529 people lived there in 1850. Its capital Amiens had a population of fifty-two thousand in 1851 and was the thirteenth largest city in France.[7] Textile industries, producing woollen and cotton cloth, employed some forty thousand people in Amiens. In the countryside commercial farming, which increasingly specialised in beet production, grew rapidly in the first half of the nineteenth century. The department's commercially orientated economy was integrated into the developing national market: the rail link from Amiens to Paris, which was completed in 1846, helped speed up this process. The Somme was dominated by its business élite. Highly Catholic, they co-existed easily with the remaining aristocrats and rural notables.[8]

During the July Monarchy the Somme's voters had elected seven deputies; under the Second Republic they elected fourteen.[9] In the 1840s they tended to return members of moderate Dynastic Opposition. Three of the department's deputies gave speeches to 360 banqueteers gathered for a reform banquet held in Amiens on 5 December 1847.[10] Odilon Barrot, the leader of the Dynastic Opposition, was also present. His parliamentary seat was in the neighbouring department of the Aisne, to the east of the Somme.

As an industrial and commercial department, the Somme was badly effected by the economic crisis of the mid-1840s. A telling indication of the depth of the crisis comes from crime figures from this period.

Table 8.2: Arrests for begging by the Somme gendarmerie[11]

Year	Numbers arrested for begging
1843	60
1844	201
1845	256
1846	242
1847	441

Charitable institutions were unable to cope with the numbers who had been thrown out of work by the economic crisis. Rural labourers and urban workers took to the streets, some tramping to other towns in the hope of finding work or charity, others simply begging from passers-by. Periodically, the police implemented the laws forbidding vagabondage, and so the arrest rate soared in the late 1840s.

– II. EVENTS –

The Revolution of 1848 produced a confused response in the Somme. The Paris government called for troops to be sent by rail from Amiens to Paris to fight the rebels. On 24 February, a thousand workers invaded the station to prevent troops leaving.[12] The town's National Guard and municipal council accepted the workers' actions.[13] However, there was little organised sympathy for the Revolution. The first Liberty Tree to appear in Amiens was not planted by the town's inhabitants, but by a group of five hundred Parisian railway workers on 30 March 1848. The Mayor and Public Prosecutor attended the ceremony, but afterwards the Public Prosecutor mused 'however praiseworthy the Parisian workers' behaviour may have been, it would be better if these demonstrations from outside were not repeated in our town.'[14] Such events only excited the town's workers and terrified the rich.

In April 1848 the Paris-based 'Club of Clubs' sent out 276 delegates into the provinces to try to encourage Republican voting: only one was sent to the Pyrénées-Orientales, but four went to the Somme. Their reports make fascinating reading and provide evidence about attitudes to the Second Republic.

On 3 April 1848 Mourier, from the left-leaning Club of Democratic Unity, was appointed as a delegate to the Somme. He arrived in Abbeville, a town in the north of the department, on 7 April 1848. He found that while electoral committees had been established in Abbeville, Amiens and the rural communes, they lacked any clear sense of political purpose. No list of republican candidates had been drawn up. Worse still, the obvious political ignorance of the working class meant that they were likely to be misled by the 'so-called republicans' who now emerged to claim political leadership. There was a general anger against the forty-five centimes tax, which suggested that it would be difficult to win votes for the Republic. The Somme, wrote Mourier, was 'far from being reactionary, but I have to fight against three major vices: the indifference and ignorance of the working class, the egotism of the master and merchant. In general, there is little patriotism.'[15]

Mourier's solution was to create a club which would unite middle-class and working-class republicans. 'If the population is left to itself, then we're lost', he warned.[16] A 'Club of the Workers' was established in Abbeville on 11 April, with the help of the sub-prefect, but Mourier then found it difficult to find a building in which they could meet. The local authorities were legitimists, and they refused to allow Mourier's club access to the large buildings they owned. The Club did not meet until 16 April, when two thousand people attended a meeting to question candidates for the next election.[17] However, rather than strengthening the local republicans, the meeting may have further confused the situation. Club members were willing to back legitimist or conservative candidates. They were 'luke-warm, indecisive', warned Mourier.[18] It was not until 23 April 1848 that he managed to draw up a list of six satisfactorily republican candidates for the Abbeville *arrondissement*: none of them were elected.[19]

Lefèvre was sent by the Club of Clubs to Amiens. He arrived on 3 April 1848. He was happy to see that a Liberty Tree had been planted, but found that little else was ready. There was no organisation to present republican politics to the people, only a strange sort of meeting place called, for no obvious reason, the Republican Club.[20] Lefèvre appealed to the workers' organisations to help him organise a club. He realised very quickly the obstacles he faced: the farmers were 'suspicious of ideals, and care little about the Republic or the monarchy'. Two days later, he had grown more pessimistic. The key problem which the republicans faced in the Somme, and which was absent in the Pyrénées-Orientales, was the existence of well-organised anti-Republican forces. In Amiens, they were grouped in the St Denis Club, organised by General Festhamel, who was close to Odilon Barrot's 'Dynastic Opposition'. They paid workers to attend their meetings, and this inducement was effective.

> [Amiens] is one of the most backward towns. Neither the National Guard nor the bourgeoisie have any sympathy for us. The popular element, which is the basis of our strength in Paris, has barely awoken. The [new] authorities must be strong, active, dedicated men, devoted to the Republic.[21]

While the region's Public Prosecutor was less committed to the Republic than Lefèvre was, his judgement was remarkably similar. 'Amiens … is very difficult to govern. On the one hand, the working class understand nothing; on the other, there is a complete absence of patriotism among the National Guard and the rich.'[22] In the Pyrénées-Orientales, the advent of the Republic had produced a wholesale transformation of administrative and judicial bodies. In the Somme there was continuity. The Public Prosecutor noticed this when he reported on 28 February 1848 that 'justice has not been interrupted'.[23]

The most serious example of anti-Republican feeling took place in April 1848. Ledru-Rollin had appointed Leclanché, a man with a reputation as a radical, as Republican Commissaire to the Somme. On 18 April there was a riot to prevent him from entering Amiens. Between twelve hundred and fifteen hunded men, bourgeois and workers, invaded the Prefecture. The republicans tried to organise a counter-demonstration, but could not find enough supporters. The National Guard refused to respond. Finally, Leclanché was revoked and left Amiens with cries of 'Leclanché, get out of town!' ringing in his ears.[24]

The election results of May 1848 demonstrate the accuracy of the delegates' assessments. None of the fourteen deputies who were elected was a committed Republican; four of them had sat in the last parliament of the July Monarchy. After the elections, Mourier summed up the reasons for the republicans' failure. The workers were weak and dominated by the bourgeoisie, who threatened them with unemployment if they voted republican. The priests and mayors of the rural communes supported the urban bourgeoisie, and encouraged the rural voters to oppose the Republic.[25]

Amiens remained restless in the summer of 1848. The economic crisis meant unemployment and poverty for many, and conflicts in the town's municipal workshops reflected, on a smaller scale, the conflicts in the Parisian National Workshops. On 29 April a dispute over pay resulted in barricades being built in Amiens. Eighteen workers were later arrested.[26] In May there was a three-day strike by a hundred railway workers calling for higher wages.[27] During this period, the Public Prosecutor was careful to ensure that the town's workers did not come into contact with Parisian workers.[28] There was no significant growth of a Démoc-Soc sub-culture in the Somme. Instead, when a crowd protested against a proposal to revive urban taxes, they shouted 'Long live the workers, long live Napoleon, down with the Constitution!'.[29]

In the Pyrénées-Orientales, local élites were divided between moderate republicans and Carlists. In that department, even the coalition of the Party of Order could not bring about their fusion. In the Somme, businessmen, nobles and landowners watched the news from Paris carefully, and drew the conclusion that this was the moment to forget their differences. According to the Public Prosecutor, 'they united to avoid anarchy, and to assure the rule of law'.[30]

The success of this strategy emerged in 1849. The majority of the deputies elected in the Somme in May 1849 were 'moderates' from the Party of Order. At the end of the year the Public Prosecutor could report that Amiens's fifteen thousand workers were patient and well-behaved. The reason for their change of attitude was obvious: the end of the economic crisis. The Public Prosecutor's attitude to the four papers based in Amiens *arrondissement* was revealing: one was republican, and had moved leftwards. It had been suspended. Of the other three, one was legitimist, and the other two were moderate. They were seen by the Public Prosecutor as 'devoted to the cause of order'. Socialist journals and pamplets, sold by hawkers, had been banned. The one possible source of trouble in the department was the prison at Doullens, to the north of Amiens, where a number of prominent political prisoners were held. The report ended with the upbeat phrase 'there is work, and everything is calm'.[31]

The Public Prosecutor's reports for 1850 tell the same story. The Somme was a quiet department. Near Doullens, there had not been 'a single arrest of a begger for a month'.[32] Hawkers and socialist cabaret owners were arrested, socialist newspapers prosecuted, and the return of economic confidence brought work and therefore 'calm'. Admittedly, it was not quite complete calm: the Public Prosecutor reported a red handkerchief tied to tree in Herbonnières, a socialist elected to a munipal council in the Montdidier *arrondissement* and a doctor distributing the Démoc-Soc *Feuille du Village* to locksmiths in Croix de Bailly.[33] However, compared to the organised presence of Démoc-Socs in Pyrénées-Orientales, these were petty incidents. A passage in the Public Prosecutor's January 1851 report sums up the situation.

> The peoples of all three departments [Somme, Aisne and Oise] are calm, more concerned with their work than with the political incidents which trouble the higher spheres. Industry and commerce are working as they should; the workers have the benefit of exercising a profession; if the small farmers are suffering from the low price of grain, at least the rural labourers have work, and can afford to buy basic foodstuffs.[34]

In the Pyrénées-Orientales, the continuing low prices for agricultural produce encouraged independent vine-growers to consider socialism. In the Somme, the powerful presence of conservative landowners prevented the small farmers and labourers from developing their own left-wing political culture. The one cloud on the horizon was the forthcoming parliamentary elections in May 1852. The Public Prosecutor seemed to think that these might result in a Démoc-Soc victory, and during 1851 his reports begin to drop hints concerning this prospect.

The early reports from 1848 reveal Amiens to be a socially divided town, with a militant working class that was not afraid of taking action: workers intervened in February 1848 to prevent troops being sent to Paris, and went on strike on several occasions. However, this simple sense of class division was not enough to produce a left-wing political culture. The local authorities pursued a deliberate policy of keeping the local workforce isolated from the radical Parisian workers. The economic recovery of 1849 was decisive: in simple terms, the workers associated the Republic with poverty, while Louis-Napoleon's presidency (which started in December 1848) brought them work.

Following the *coup d'état* of December 1851, fifty-eight people were arrested in the Somme (nearly a thousand were arrested in the Pyrénées-Orientales). Forty-five of these were quickly released without trial; only thirteen men from the Somme appeared in court.[35] During the referendum held to ratify the *coup d'état*, there was no alternative political culture to Bonapartism in the Somme.

From the earliest days of the Revolution, there had been isolated examples of spontaneous Bonapartist sympathies across France. For example, in September 1848, peasants in the Gironde (in the south-west) believed that if Louis-Napoleon was elected President, he would repeal the forty-five centimes tax and pay deputies' salaries out of his own funds.[36] Elsewhere, his name was shouted by rioters invading forests or refusing to pay taxes. Such incidents suggest an informal, 'folk' Bonapartism, based upon myths and legends.

However, despite this cultural presence, there was no national Bonapartist organisation. After the elections of April 1848, only three deputies could be described as Bonapartist.[37] On 4 June 1848 Louis–Napoleon stood in several by-elections. He was elected in four constituencies, even though he was still technically banned from becoming a deputy. What astonished many observers was his success in Paris, where he gained votes from the industrial working–class of the eastern suburbs. These elections revealed 'a popular, Republican Bonapartism, a vehicle for social aspirations in Paris, rural and more imperial in the provinces'.[38] Bonapartism was blamed, probably inaccurately, for working-class radicalism during the June Days.

In September 1848 there was a new round of by-elections: Louis–Napoleon won five of the thirteen contested seats.[39] His victory in the Yonne department was accepted, and on 11 October the law preventing him from sitting as deputy was repealed. On 26 October, he announced his candidature for the forthcoming Presidential elections. He gained three-quarters of the votes cast in the December 1848 elections. Once again, his success amazed most political commentators, who had been expecting Cavaignac, a moderate republican, to win. His supporters were delighted, and argued that the strength of his support demonstrated his right to represent the nation. 'Nobody … had mentioned the name of Louis–Napoleon Bonaparte', wrote one provincial Bonapartist, 'and yet this name was to be found in all honest hearts, whatever their opinions or the position in society to which they belonged. This name carried in itself harmony and reconcilation between all the country's children.'[40]

Republicans were confused by his victory. Sand considered that the people had voted 'like children, who obey their hearts more than others' reason'.[41] Proudhon, more observantly, argued that Louis–Napoleon's success was due to his status as an anti-candidate: people voted for him out of disgust with the other parties.[42]

– III. POLITICAL CULTURE –

One element of Louis–Napoleon's success was his ability to present different faces to different crowds: appearing conservative to frightened aristocrats; anti-bourgeois, republican and socially aware to workers, and anti-notable and progressive to peasants. Another factor was based on cold-hearted political calculations: he persuaded notables and aristocrats to accept him as the force which could be used to 'break' the Republic. Their 'guidance' may have persuaded many to vote for him: as in the elections of April 1848, many still voted as they were advised by their priests and social superiors. (See document 8.2.)

The key to his long-term success lies elsewhere. Following his election as President he chose a government based largely on old ministers from the July Monarchy, including Odilon Barrot. The various right-wing factions in the victorious Party of Order saw their priority as repressing clubs (June 1849), censoring the left-wing press and, finally (in May 1850), excluding almost three million men from voting. While their actions were certainly effective in pushing the Démoc-Socs out of the political arena, they failed to create an effective political culture to legitimate their actions: they simply spoke of the need for 'order'.[43]

Louis-Napoleon embarked on a quite different campaign, creating a new form of political culture, an anti-politics, setting out 'to project himself as the focus of national unity, over and above political parties'.[44] Like his uncle, he asserted his claim to represent the entire nation and not simply a single political tradition. He made fifteen different tours across France between 1849 and 1852, travelling for thirteen weeks in total, bypassing parliamentary procedures in this attempt to create a direct bond between himself and the French people.[45] (See document 8.3.) In 1850 he launched a campaign to modify a constitutional law which barred a president from serving more than one term. A total of 1.46 million people – 14.7 per cent of the electorate – signed petitions in support of this campaign.[46]

In the years 1850-1 differences between Louis-Napoleon and the Party of Order became clearer. One significant disagreement took place in June 1850. Louis-Napoleon proposed to enlarge anti-club legislation in order to restrict electoral meetings. This could have been used against legitimists and Orleanists as well as against Démoc-Socs. The Assembly refused the bill by 395 votes to 245.[47] This vote reveals a fundamental disagreement about the nature of political representation. The deputies of the Party of Order retained a loyalty to parliamentary representation and procedures. Their political ideal was essentially that of the pre-1848 July Monarchy: 'parliament would be an assembly of economically active men immune to the blandishments of both throne and "mob".'[48] Louis-Napoleon's political culture asserted a new principle: that rule by one man could better represent the nation than parliament. Through the use of plebiscites to consult with the people, it could even be qualified as a 'democratic' – although, as was seen in Chapter 7, the idea of a 'democratic' plebiscite being carried out in a department ruled by martial law is inherently contradictory.

– IV. LEGACY –

The establishment of the Second Empire in December 1852 left many tensions within Bonapartism. Even among the prefects there remained a variety of interpretations concerning the nature of the regime. James McMillan suggests that there were four principal forms of Bonapartism:

1. Old-fashioned conservatives, essentially Orleanists or legitimists who had 'rallied' to the regime.
2. Centre-right conservatives, who accepted the principle of manhood suffrage, and who saw the Second Empire as the appropriate instrument to manage it.
3. 'Authoritarian Democrats', who were often also anti-clerical. Such officials genuinely believed that the Second Empire would benefit the majority of the nation.
4. Anti-notable officials, who saw the Second Empire as a means to end the power of the old aristocracy in France.[49]

Given this variety of Bonapartisms, it comes as no surprise that Louis-Napoleon never attempted to create a Bonapartist party to represent his politics. Instead, the most important political symbol of his regime was the new national holiday of 15 August: the anniversary of Napoleon's victory at Austerlitz in 1805. This was first celebrated in 1852. Usefully, the date coincided with the Catholic festival of the Assumption, and so Bonapartist prefects could use this festival as a means to 'rally' conservative supporters. It was also hoped that it would overshadow any celebrations of 24 February, the founding of the Second Republic. Mayors were instructed to make every effort to ensure that the festival was a success: they were to organise parades by soldiers or firemen, distribute charity to the poor, instruct all officials to attend and arrange for games, bonfires, fireworks and dances.[50] No plebiscites were organised between 1852 and 1870: this annual festival was often treated as substitute for a political consultation, and the regime's success or failure read into it. It attracted most support during the late 1850s and early 1860s, when economic expansion and rising standards of living encouraged popular support for the Empire. However, even during this period, some prefects noted that the event seemed too stage-managed, too calm to be a real festival. Significantly, after 1864, many officials refused to participate.

In the 1830s and 1840s, Louis-Napoleon had attempted to recreate Bonapartism as a rational political ideology which could attract the willing support of French people. Despite his success in winning the support of the majority of the electorate in December 1848, December 1851 and December 1852, his success is still doubtful. As Marx recognised in his classic analysis of Louis-Napoleon's rise to power ('The Eighteenth Brumaire of Louis-Napoleon'), his success was as much due to the balance of conflicting forces which surrounded him as to any initiative of his own. Working-class voters wanted social reform and political liberties; peasants wanted a progressive ruler who would hold back the aristocracy; and bourgeois and aristocratic supporters wanted him to manage popular political cultures. In a department like the Somme, with a politically ignorant working class, and pragmatic, united conservative forces, Bonapartism thrived.

Louis-Napoleon also seemed to offer an alternative to the confusing and complex parliamentary procedures. The key concept of the opposition to the July Monarchy had been its accusation of corruption. Bonapartism presented a regime without parties and without corruption, in which one man represented the national will. In 1815, there was some genuine belief that Napoleon I was blessed with a mission to save France. Louis-Napoleon's rule was a hollow echo of this belief. However, the concept of the 'democratic dictator', who could represent the people better than the structures of parliament and parties, has remained a permanent feature within French, even international, political culture. It certainly re-emerged in Pétain's rule of Vichy France in 1940–4, and in de Gaulle's premierships of the Fifth Republic in the late 1950s and 1960s.

– V. Documents –

– Document 8.1: The hero's return, 1815 –

This passage, describing Napoleon's return to France in 1815, is typical of Las Cases' treatment. It suggests a massive popular movement, unified in its single-minded support for Napoleon: a movement which would not require formal representation through parliamentary structures, but instead communicated directly to its leader, the 'Liberator'.

> Before my return, all of France was already gripped by the same idea. When I debarked, my proclamation merely echoed the same feeling: everyone who read it [felt it expressed] what was in their heart. France was unhappy, I was its instrument. The sickness and the cure were in harmony. This was the key to this electric movement, unprecedented in history. There was no conspiracy: this spirit [*élan*] was everywhere. Not a word was said, but everybody understood. Entire populations ran to their Liberator's path. The first batallion which rallied to me was worth more than a whole army. I was carried to Paris. The existing government [the first government of Louis XVIII] and its officials just disappeared, like the clouds dissolve before the sun. And when I fell into the hands of my enemies [after Waterloo, in June 1815], I was not treated as the leader of an insurrection, but I was recognized as the sovereign of the whole of Europe. I had my title, my flag, and my army: I had fought my enemy.
>
> Source: Le comte de Las Cases, *Le mémorial de Sainte-Hélène*,
> two vols, ed. G. Walter (Paris: Pléaide, 1965), I, p. 370

– DOCUMENT 8.2: ALEXIS DE TOCQUEVILLE GOES TO VOTE, APRIL 1848 –

De Tocqueville was one of the most original and perceptive conservative thinkers of nineteenth-century France. In 1848 he divided his time between Paris, and his family home in the department of the Manche, in Normandy. The following passage has become famous as a description of peasants voting in 1848.

> On the day of the elections, all the voters, in other words, the entire male population over 20, met in front of the church. They all lined up, two by two, according to alphabetical order. I went to the place I was assigned by my name, for I knew that in a democratic country in democratic times, you must let the people lead, and not put yourself at their head. At the end of the line, the sick and the weak who wanted to follow were carried on carts. Only the women and children were left behind. In all, there were 170 of us. When we got to the top of the hill which looks over [the village of] Tocqueville, we stopped for a moment. I knew they wanted me to speak. I reminded this fine people of the seriousness of the act they were about to do. I advised them not to be distracted by anyone in the town who tried to trick them. They should march together, each in his place, until they had voted. 'Let no-one stop to eat or to dry himself (it was raining on that day)', I told them, 'until he has carried out his duty.' They shouted that they would do so, and they did. All of them voted at once, and I think that almost all of them were for the same candidate.
>
> Source: Alexis de Tocqueville, *Souvenirs*,
> ed. Luc Monnier (Paris: Folio, 1964), p. 158

– DOCUMENT 8.3: LOUIS-NAPOLEON'S PROCLAMATION, 1851 –

This short text demonstrates Louis-Napoleon's claim to a more direct and representative link to the people of France than that presented by parliamentary structures.

> Proclamation of the President of the Republic: an appeal to the People
> The present situation cannot continue. The threats to the nation grow with each day which passes. The Assembly [parliament], which ought to provide the strongest support for order, has become a centre of plots. Instead of making laws in the general interest, it is preparing the instruments of civil war, and threatening the power which I hold directly from the people. [The Assembly] is fomenting evil passions; it is menacing the stability of France. I have dissolved it, and I call upon all the people of France to choose between it and me.
>
> Source: Louis-Napoleon Bonaparte, 'Proclamation du Président de la
> République; appel au peuple', *Bulletin des lois de la République*
> *Française* 465 (1851), 988–9

– VI. Further reading –

On the Second Republic, see 'Further reading' in Chapter 6.

The best introduction to this topic is James McMillan, *Napoleon III* (London: Longman, 1991), which provides a clear and observant summary of Louis-Napoleon's rise to power.

Bernard Ménager, *Les Napoléon du Peuple* (Paris: Aubier 1988) is by far the most penetrating and convincing analysis of popular Bonapartism in the nineteenth century. Robert Gildea, *The Past in French History* (New Haven: Havard UP, 1994) includes a interesting section on Bonapartism. R. S. Alexander, *Bonapartism and Revolutionary Tradition in France: the Fédérés of 1815* (Cambridge: Cambridge UP, 1991) is concerned principally with the 'Hundred Days', but does also consider the issue of popular Bonapartism. Victor Hugo's changing attitude to Bonapartism is discussed in Keith Wren, 'Victor Hugo and the Bonapartist Myth', *European Studies Review* 10 (1980), 429–59.

Thomas R. Forstenzer, *French Political Police and the Fall of the Second Republic* (Princeton: Princeton UP, 1981) and John M. Merriman, *The Agony of the Republic: the Repression of the Left in Revolutionary France, 1848–51* (New Haven: Yale UP, 1978) both discuss the political culture of 'Order' which prepared the ground for Louis-Napoleon's rise. Anita R. May, 'The Falloux Law, the Catholic Press and the Bishops: the Crisis of Authority in the French Church', *French Historical Studies* 8:1 (1973), 77–94 considers the Church's response to the new political circumstances of the Second Republic.

There were many contemporary analyses of Louis-Napoleon. Victor Hugo, *Napoléon le Petit* (originally published 1853, various reprints) is a lyrical, passionate denunciation, while Karl Marx, 'The Eighteenth Brumaire of Louis-Napoleon' in D. Fernbach (ed.), *Surveys From Exile* (Harmondsworth: Penguin, 1977) is a well-argued analysis of the class forces which led to the rise of Louis-Napoleon. Emile Zola, *La Fortune des Rougons* (1871, many republications and translations) was written after the fall of the Second Empire. It presents an exciting account of a Bonapartist counter-revolution in the south of France.

There are a number of good studies of the Second Empire. Alain Plessis, *The Rise and Fall of the Second Empire, 1852–1871* (Cambridge: Cambridge UP, 1985) is probably the best introduction. Rosemonde Sanson, 'Le 15 août; fête nationale du Second Empire' in A. Corbin, N. Gérôme and D. Tartakowsky (eds), *Les Usages politiques des fêtes* (Paris: Presses de la Sorbonne, 1994), pp. 117–34 is an observant study of the new national day, while Bernard Leclère and Vincent Wright, *Les Préfets du Second Empire* (Paris: Gallimard, 1973) consider the Imperial administration. Matthew Truesdell,

Spectacular Politics: Louis-Napoleon Bonaparte and the Fête Impériale, 1849–1870 (Oxford: Oxford UP, 1997) considers the public presentation of Bonapartism.

After writing this chapter, I read Sudhir Hazareesingh, *From Subject to Citizen: The Second Empire and the Emergence of Modern French Democracy* (Princeton: Princeton University Press, 1998). It presents an incisive analysis of political debates during the Second Empire.

– NOTES –

1. R. S. Alexander, *Bonapartism and Revolutionary Tradition in France: the Fédérés of 1815* (Cambridge: Cambridge UP, 1991), p. 5.
2. Alfred de Vigny, *Servitude et Grandeur Militaires* (Paris: Garnier, 1965), pp. 7–14.
3. Vigny, *Servitude*, p. 127.
4. Vigny, *Servitude*, p. 140–3.
5. Victor Hugo, *Actes et Paroles: Avant l'Exil, 1841–51* (Paris: Nelson, 1936), p. 145.
6. Figures from Bernard Ménager, *Les Napoléon du Peuple* (Paris: Aubier, 1988), p. 432.
7. Marcel Roncayolo, 'Logiques urbaines' in M. Agulhon (ed.), *Histoire de la France urbaine*, Vol. IV (Paris: Seuil, 1983), pp. 25–76 (p. 54).
8. A. Jardin and A.-J. Tudesq, *La France des Notables* Vol. II (Paris: Seuil, 1973), pp. 152–4.
9. Information taken from *Almanach Royal et National pour l'an MDCCXLVII* (Paris: Guyot and Scribe, 1847) and *Almanach national annuaire de la République française pour 1848–1849–1850* (Paris: Guyot and Scribe, 1850).
10. AN, BB/30/296.
11. AN, F/7/2404; these figures relate solely to actions by the gendarmerie; they do not record other arrests by urban police forces in the department.
12. Cour royal, AN, BB/30/359, 24 February 1848.
13. Public Prosecutor, 2 March 1848, AN, BB/30/359.
14. 30 March 1848, AN, BB/30/359.
15. 8 April 1848, AN, C/940.
16. 11 April 1848, AN, C/940.
17. 16 April 1848, AN C/940.
18. 18 April 1848, AN, C/940.
19. 23 April 1848, AN, C/940.
20. 3 April 1848, AN, C/940.
21. 5 April 1848, AN, C/940.
22. 15 March 1848, AN, BB/30/359.
23. 28 February 1848, AN, BB/30/359.
24. Public Prosecutor, 18 April 1848, AN, BB/30/359.
25. 6 May 1848, AN, C/940.
26. Republican Prosecutor, 29 April 1848, AN, BB/30/359.
27. Public Prosecutor, 18 May 1848, BB/30/359.
28. 1 July 1848, AN, BB/30/359; 10 Feb 1849, AN, BB/18/1477.
29. 23 November 1848, AN, BB/30/359.
30. 18 May 1848, AN, BB/30/359.
31. 7 December 1849, AN, BB/30/371.
32. 5 February 1850, AN, BB/30/371.
33. 13 May, 10 October, 5 June 1850, AN, BB/30/371.

34. AN, BB/30/371.
35. 16 February 1852, AN, BB/30/399.
36. 22 September 1848, AN, BB/18/1460.
37. James McMillan, *Napoleon III* (London: Longman, 1991), p. 30.
38. Ménager, *Les Napoléon*, p. 96.
39. Ménager, *Les Napoléon*, p. 97.
40. Adrien Sariac, *Quelques méditations sur les souffrances de peuple et les seuls moyens propres à les soulager* (Auch: Foix, 1849), p. 21.
41. George Sand, *Politique et polémique* (Paris: Imprimerie Nationale, 1997), p. 563.
42. P. J. Proudhon, *Les Confessions d'un révolutionnaire* (Anthony: Tops/Trinquier, 1997), pp. 221–9.
43. Raymond Huard, *La Naissance du parti politique* (Paris: Presses de Sci Po, 1996), p. 104.
44. Robert Gildea, *The Past in French History* (New Haven: Harvard UP, 1994), p. 71.
45. Peter McPhee, *The Politics of Rural Life* (Oxford: Oxford UP, 1992), p. 226.
46. Ménager, *Les Napoléon*, p. 108.
47. Huard, *Naissonce*, p. 104.
48. Thomas R. Forstenzer, *French Political Police and the Fall of the Second Republic* (Princeton: Princeton UP, 1981), p. 31.
49. McMillan, *Napoleon III*, p. 57.
50. Rosemonde Sanson, 'Le 15 août; fête nationale du Second Empire' in A. Corbin, N. Gérôme and D. Tartakowsky (eds), *Les Usages politiques des fêtes* (Paris: Presses de la Sorbonne, 1994), pp. 117–34.

CHAPTER 9

The Commune of Paris, 1871:
socialism and republicanism

One of the most misleading statements about the Commune was that written by Engels in 1891. 'Do you want to know what [the dictatorship of the pro-letariat] looks like? Look at the Paris Commune. That was the Dictatorship of the Proletariat.'[1] This statement can be faulted for many reasons, not least its assumptions that the communards were motivated by a single purpose and that a class-based proletarian identity was central to their political culture.

The Paris Commune lasted for seventy-three days, from March to May 1871. During this short period, a semi-secret underground formed by clubs, conspiracies, meetings and sub-cultures emerged into the publicity of power. Rather than creating a single new political culture, the Commune drew on a rich variety of existing political traditions: Jacobinism, Proudhonism, working-class associational socialism, nationalism and feminism.

– I. Participants –

The key participants in this third Parisian revolt are already familiar to us: they were the same social coalition who fought in 1830 and 1848. In Louis Constant's neat phrase, the majority of the Communards were located at 'the crossroads of the artisans, the *compagnonnage*, the proletariat and the petty bourgeoisie'.[2] The most appropriate term for them is probably the eighteenth-century category of 'the popular classes', rather than the more modern category of 'working class'.

Industrialisation had not transformed the Parisian economy by 1871. Roger Magraw argues that this period marks the 'apogee' of artisanal pro-duction in Paris, and points to the persistence of small workshops: in 1848 there were 5.4 workers for every employer, in 1872 there were 4.8.[3] In many workshops, the bosses were barely any better off than their workers.[4] Parisian economic development often took the form which English commentators termed 'sweated labour', whereby de-skilling and a tightening-up of work discipline allowed the exploitation of poorly-paid workers. In particular, poor women worked twelve- and fourteen-hour shifts in 'unhealthy, unlit work-shops without air or sunlight'.[5] Trades such as clothing manufacture were particularly affected.

Jacques Rougerie, one of the greatest historians of the Commune iden-tifies the typical communard as a metal-worker or a builder. He was 'a rebel of the old style. He belonged to the first half of the nineteenth century, to the pre-history of the labour and socialist movement; he was clearly not a modern proletarian.' Despite attempts to tighten work discipline, he resisted strict controls. 'Poorly adapted to the new forms of work, he turned up late, took Monday off, and often Tuesday as well, complained, got drunk, went on strike, joined a union, and rebelled more than most workers.'[6]

Paris was a city which grew enormously during the Second Empire (1852–70).

Table 9.1: Population of Paris[7]

Year	Population
1831	785 866
1841	899 313
1851	1 053 261
1861	1 696 141
1872	1 851 792

In part, this growth was achieved by the incorporation of a ring of suburban communes, inhabited by a third of a million people, into the city in 1861. Paris had also experienced something more than a simple quantitative growth in numbers. Napoleon III appointed Baron Georges von Haussmann as Pre-fect of Paris in 1853. He redesigned the city-scape, adding some eighty-five miles of road to the 450 miles of streets within Paris.[8] This was a colossal enterprise: by 1871, fully one-fifth of the streets of central Paris were new. Over one-third of a million people had been displaced from their homes. At the height of the reconstruction, one in five of the workers in Paris were employed in the building trade.[9] The modern profile of Paris – its wide boulevards, the great department stores of the central quarter – all date from Haussmann's renovation.

The new city was cleaner, richer and better organised than the still-medieval Paris of 1830 and 1848. Travellers by carriages and trains arrived more quickly and found a wider range of more modern goods. Yet there were many critics of this process. The 'Haussmannisation' of Paris came to sym-bolise the rule of the Empire. 'It was ruthlessly done and took time, money, technical skill and incredible administrative ability.'[10] Politically orthodox bourgeois were concerned about its finance: Haussmann relied on loans more than previous urban planners had. Others objected that there was no consultation procedure, and no elected local authority had the power to oppose his rule. Rumours of corruption and the easy money won by speculators were rife: those who bought up old slum buildings along the sites reserved for the new boulevards could sell them at impressive profits. The popular classes were angry for other reasons. Alongside the new boulevards, rents soared. Overcrowding in central apartment blocks grew worse: many left the old central districts to settle in the new, under-equipped suburbs of Montmartre and Belleville, to the north and east. They felt a sense of loss, of dispossession as a result of Haussmann's innovations. Proudhon, in his last, uncompleted work, echoed this emotion (see document 9.1).

Further generalisations could be made about Parisians prior to 1870, but instead of discussing them collectively, let us meet some individuals from among their number. For this chapter, I have chosen four works among a flood of histories, autobiographies, studies and polemics. These do not 'represent' the half a million communards in any rigorously selected scientific manner; however, they do allow us to glimpse some of the passions and causes which gripped them.

Table 9.2: Four authors

	Date of birth	Age in 1871	Date of publication and/or writing concerning the Commune
Andrieu	1838	33	*c.*1880
B...	1838	33	1909
Lissagaray	1838	33	1876, second edition 1896
Michel	1830	41	1896

Jules Louis Andrieu wrote his *Notes to serve for a History of the Commune of Paris of 1871* while in exile in Britain during the 1870s. He died in 1881, and his work was not published until 1971. His title may look clumsy, but it was a standard nineteenth-century formula: Guizot, for example, termed his autobiography *Memoirs to serve for a History of My Time.* The formula implies a certain modesty: the author has produced something less than a full history. Andrieu explained that he could not describe himself as a historian as he was a politically committed writer, and could not be impartial about what he had seen.[11]

Andrieu came from the academic proletariat: that hoard of part-time, temporary teachers who collected in Paris. His father, a secondary school teacher, had hoped that Andrieu would enter the prestigious Ecole Polytechnique which would have prepared him for a career in the administration.

However, an accident with a pair of scissors blinded him in one eye and barred him from the Ecole. In 1861 he was employed by the Parisian municipal administration. He married in the following year and records proudly how hard he worked to provide for his wife and family: his income was 1 200 francs in 1861, and rose to 6 000 francs in 1870 (A.: 14). One extra source of income was an evening class which he taught. This followed the secondary school curriculum, and was designed to help adults who had only attended primary school. It was attended by 'illiterates, workers, small shopkeepers and commercial clerks' (A.: 22). This list of students is a good example of inter-class mixing: the élite of the working class attended the same classes as the petty bourgeoisie. Through this course he met members of the First International Workingmen's Association, which he probably joined. However, he was not politically active: he was worried that republican activism would result in his dismissal from the administration.

B... was the pseudonym adopted by Victorine Brocher. Her work has the most dramatic title of all four: the *Memoirs of a Living Corpse*, which refers to her escape from the repression which followed the Commune. She was wrongly reported to have been shot and so managed to avoid police searches. Her work is the most clearly autobiographical of the four, and was intended as the first part of a longer work. Significantly, her story stops with her escape in 1871. Before 1871, she worked in 'a high-class shop'.[12] Throughout the years before the Commune she was preoccupied by the health of her sons, and had the tragic misfortune to see her first son die in September 1868, and her second die in March 1871, at the age of fourteen months. She was active in the International between 1865 and 1868, but seems to have lost contact with it after moving house in 1868.

Prosper-Olivier Lissagaray is far better known than our first two authors. His *Histoire de la Commune de 1871* has become a standard text. Unlike Andrieu, he asserted his work was a history, rather than mere notes or memoirs, and from 1876 (the date of its first publication) to 1896 (its second edition) he occupied himself in re-editing and rewriting passages. His *Histoire* is the least autobiographical of the four, and we gain little impression of his personality through reading it. Other sources allow us to piece together his life: born into a solid bourgeois and Bonapartist family in the French Basque region, he proved to be an excellent classical scholar. A journey to the USA converted him to republicanism. He moved to Paris in 1860, initially following his literary interests, but growing increasingly active in the republican movement. A photograph of him taken in 1871 shows him sitting in a studied casual pose, with one arm curled round the back of chair. He is a handsome man, dressed smartly, with neatly cut hair and a moustache. His face has that rather glassy expression shown by most people in nineteenth-century photographs: they normally had to sit still for several minutes. Otherwise, he looks confident and relaxed, with a half-smile on his lips.

Our fourth author is Louise Michel. Her mother, a single parent, was a servant to an aristocrat in the Haute-Marne, to the east of Paris. She trained as a schoolmistress, but refused to serve in state schools under the Empire, for she was a republican. She moved to Paris in 1855, where she worked as a schoolmistress, wrote bad poetry and grew active in the republican underground. She may well have joined the First International before 1870. Her work has the simplest title of the four: *La Commune*. This provides an interesting contrast with the works by Andrieu and Lissagaray: they specify 'the Commune of 1871', presumably to distinguish it from the Commune of 1792. By doing so, they invite comparisons between the two. Michel's title suggests that, on the contrary, the Commune of 1871 was unique, its name speaks for itself and needs no qualification. Her work is not as autobiographical as Brocher's, but she does write mainly in the first person. It includes long reproductions of other documents, including posters from 1871, and extracts from previous histories. These allow the communards to 'speak for themselves', directly, without the mediation of a historian.

There are several photographs of Michel. Two from 1871 show her, like Lissagaray, sitting on a chair. Unlike him, she looks nervous: instead of folding her arms neatly, she clutches at her elbows. Her hair falls to her neck in long strands. No one could call her 'pretty', but there is a sort of tough symmetry to her features: in one photograph she stares out directly at the viewer, almost challenging. She looks younger than her forty years but, paradoxically, she also looks like someone who had experienced a great deal.

These four authors – a writer, a council employee, a schoolmistress and a shop-worker – illustrate the diversity of social support gained by the Commune. They represent an élite within the popular classes: perhaps more politicised and more literate than their poorer neighbours, but still affected by the same events and gripped by the same passions.

– II. EVENTS –

All four authors refer back to 1848. Andrieu discusses life under the Second Empire, and Brocher speaks at length about 1848. Both describe the political cultures they inherited through their families. Andrieu tells his readers proudly that there was not a single Bonapartist among his grandparents (they were either monarchists or republicans) (A.: 7). Brocher is particularly eloquent in her descriptions of post-1848 repression. She writes of the expulsion of her republican father and her schoolmaster from Orléans early in 1852. Her father had left 3 000 francs for his wife with a notary: this was seized by the

Bonapartist authorities, thus impoverishing the family (B.: 39). Brocher's schoolmaster's departure was particularly upsetting: he had been given only forty-eight hours' notice, and in that time 'he aged 10 years … He hid himself behind one of the station pillars in order to hide his tears' (B.: 46). Through-out the 1850s, while she was a teenager, she was conscious of another world of political exiles, based in Brussels and London. Her political interests, awoken in 1848, were stifled by the repression of the 1850s: 'Orléans was crushed, not a single known Republican remained' (B.: 53). More briefly, Michel also situates the origins of the Commune in feelings inherited from 1848: she writes of 'a twenty year old anger' directed against the Empire.[13]

All four authors lived in Paris in the 1860s. Surprisingly, only one of them mentions Haussmann's redesign of the city. Brocher notes briefly that 'the town was turned upside-down by Haussmann; life was miserable, business was depressed, and rents were rising' (B.: 73). Andrieu does not directly describe the rebuilding of Paris, but, unusually, has a word of praise for Haussmann, noting that he was one of the rare Imperial administrators who would will-ingly accept republicans in his staff (A.: 69–70).

Rather than discussing Haussmann's remaking of Paris directly, all four authors refer to the cultural context created by Imperial rule. Michel talks of the Second Empire as 'a terror-stricken night' (M.: 13). Both Andrieu and Brocher write of the struggle to live morally during this period. Brocher, on arriving in Paris in 1862, was shocked by the culture of poverty in which the poor were trapped in a vicious circle of alcoholism, misery, suicide and prosti-tution. 'Words such as honour, virtue, faith meant little to these disinherited people: they were empty words, with little sense' (B.: 62). Andrieu saw similar dangers for any talented young man who could easily be drawn into corrupt journalism or corrupt politics (A.: 12–13). Both Andrieu and Brocher express their opposition to the Empire in moral terms.

Liberalising measures were passed in the 1860s. In June 1868 a new law permitted the discussion of economic and social matters in public meetings. A crude political sociology lay behind this measure: as the liberal middle class grew more critical of the Empire, Napoleon III appealed to the working class for support. In Paris, between June 1868 and August 1870, there were 993 'non-political' meetings, 310 electoral meetings and ninety-four meetings to discuss the plebiscite of May 1870.[14] The first meetings were studied, gentle-manly affairs, in which well-meaning economists and philanthropists tried to lecture to the popular classes. However, their tone soon changed moving from the middle-class centre to the working-class suburbs, and adopting an aggressive tone of opposition to the Empire, the industrialists and the rich.

Again, surprisingly, our four authors have little to say about these meetings. Michel does not mention the meetings at all. Lissagaray notes in passing the 'fever' of the public meetings in the winter of 1869–70, but does not describe them in detail.[15] Andrieu, the municipal clerk, was reluctant to attend any opposition meeting; however, his evening class for workers could, loosely speaking, be seen as part of this movement of popular intellectual and cultural self-help. Brocher alone speaks at greater length about political meetings. Following the birth of her first son in 1864, she decided to become politically active (see document 9.2). In 1865 her son grew ill: she learnt of the First International through the doctor she visited. The organisation opposed the socialism of the united workers to 'patriotism, chauvinism and the parish-pump mentality' (B.: 68) and held meetings twice a week. Brocher forced her husband to go with her, knowing that if he did not attend, he would drink their money away in a café. They supported a co-operative greengrocer run by Internationalists, which collapsed in 1868. However, although Brocher attended the closed meetings of the International, she never attended a public meeting – apparently she did not consider them suitable for women (B.: 190).

All four authors record their impressions of a different atmosphere developing in the final months of the Second Empire. Michel, anticipating the declaration of the Republic on 4 September 1870, records that the Republic existed in Paris before it was proclaimed (M.: 83). Andrieu was convinced that the Second Empire was so corrupt that it would fall under its own weight. 'I confined myself to educating myself and others, trying to create, while under the Empire, the Republic in myself and around me, and to spread it quietly' (A.: 31). Lissagaray cites an amusing detail: in September 1869 building works surrounded the Tuileries Palace. A large poster announced 'no entry to the public'. Someone scribbled beneath this 'they get in sometimes' – a reference to the invasion of the Tuileries in February 1848 (see document 6.2) (L.: 37).

In some parts of France there remained strong support for the Emperor: the north-east was particularly loyal. Between 300 000 and 500 000 people gathered to cheer Napoleon III when he visited Lille (Nord) in 1867; 150 000 in Beauvais (Oise) in 1869.[16] Moreover, election results show that Bonapartism was gaining support in the rural areas during the 1860s. However, in Paris, the Empire was growing less popular. The public meetings were one aspect of this growing opposition movement, but there were other important indications: the reviving memory of 1848, the success of oppositional papers such as Rochefort's *La Lanterne*, and the election of republican opposition candidates in Paris in 1863 and 1869. The general trend of the declining popularity of the Empire was clear in election and plebiscite results.

Tables 9.3 and 9.4 show that while support for the Empire grew in the 1850s, there was a re-emergence of opposition during the 1860s.

Table 9.3: Election results, 1852–69 (all voting figures in millions)[17]

Date	Eligible to vote	Pro-Government votes	Anti-Government votes	Abstentions
1852	9.8m	5.25m (53.6%)	0.81m (8.3%)	3.61m (36.8%)
1857	9.5m	5.47m (57.6%)	0.66m (6.9%)	3.37m (35.5%)
1863	9.9m	5.30m (53.4%)	1.95m (19.7%)	2.71m (27.4%)
1869	10.4m	4.44m (42.7%)	3.35m (32.2%)	2.29m (22.0%)

Table 9.4: Percentage of 'Yes' votes in Imperial plebiscites, 1851–70[18]

1851	1852	1870
75.2%	76.0%	68.0%

It was in this context that Napoleon III launched his policy of liberal-isation. After the legalisation of strikes in May 1864, greater toleration was extended to the press in May 1868, the public meetings law was passed in June 1868, and an ex-republican opponent of the Empire, Emile Ollivier, became Prime Minister in January 1870. The plebiscite of May 1870 asked voters to approve this liberalisation. Table 9.4 shows that more than two-thirds of the population voted 'yes'; significantly, the greatest number of 'no' votes came from the bigger towns.

In the summer of 1870, Napoleon III revived another aspect of the Imperialist legacy: an aggressive foreign policy. In 1869–70 Bismarck – the Chancellor of Prussia – and Napoleon III fought out a complex diplomatic duel, involving ambassadors, royal proposals of marriage and leaked telegrams. At stake was which nation would dominate Europe. In July 1870, Napoleon III declared war on Prussia. This decision was not only driven by external pressure for the May 1870 plebiscite had shown growing opposition to the Empire. If liberal policies could not secure the loyalty of the majority, then perhaps an aggressive foreign policy would prove a better instrument.

At first, there was a spontaneous movement of support for the Emperor's decision. The First International's pacifist manifesto of July 1870 was clearly a minority gesture: elsewhere, the streets of Paris rang with the sound of the newly-legalised *Marseillaise* (B.: 90). On 14 July 1870, demonstrators marched down the boulevards, chanting 'To Berlin!' (L.: 48). But the war proved fatal for the Empire. The army was poorly organised, over-confident and out-numbered by the Prussian forces. Michel retells the story of the general who, when sent to the frontier, found only empty streets. He telegraphed back to his superiors 'where are my regiments?' (M.: 66). French forces suffered heavy defeats, and on 1 September 1870 Napoleon III was taken prisoner following the battle of Sedan.

On 4 September 1870 the Chamber of Deputies was invaded by a crowd of Parisians, including Brocher and Michel. Initially the deputies tried to argue for a non-political, caretaker regime, but, as in 1848, the crowd insisted on radical action. 'Nothing could resist this human wave' wrote Brocher (95). As she heard Gambetta proclaim the Third Republic at the Hôtel-de-Ville, it seemed like her childhood dream was becoming real. 'I believed that everything was possible' (B.: 100, 104). Shouts of 'Long live the Republic!' rang out from the crowd. Michel records her sudden impression of the 'immense life-force' of this united movement (M.: 86). The twelve Parisian deputies, including the radical republican Rochefort, formed a Government of National Defence.

Three of our four authors seem reluctant to note a significant shift in their attitudes: initially anti-war in July 1870, by September 1870 they had become the most zealous of patriots. Brocher alone faces this issue honestly: 'I would have preferred that there had not been a war. However, as fate forced us to suffer it, we had to do everything to save France from foreign domination' (B.: 103). Memories of the first Republic circulated: a mass movement of volunteers had saved France from invasion at the battle of Valmy (September 1792). A new generation of volunteers, including Brocher's husband, joined the army in September 1870. 'They were convinced that the Republic could do what the Empire had not wanted – or was unable – to do' (B.: 105).

After her husband's departure, Brocher wanted to act for the Republic. 'I was gripped by an absolute need to participate in this fight. In one way or another, I wanted to be useful to my country!' (B.: 106). She eventually served as an ambulance woman with a National Guard unit.

The siege of Paris lasted from 19 September 1870 to 28 January 1871: it was the longest siege suffered by a major city in modern times, with the exception of Stalingrad in 1942–3. By January 1871, conditions in the capital were miserable. There was no firewood: all that remained was newly-cut green wood, which smoked so much that it stifled people. There was no milk. All that the poor could afford was adulterated bread, mixed with sawdust and other materials, which triggered off coughing attacks in those who ate it (B.: 108–9). On the streets, Brocher saw starving women who fainted with hunger (B.: 127).

Parisians had expected Trochu, the new commander of military forces in the city, to launch a '*guerre à l'outrance*', or all-out war. They were disappointed by the inactivity which followed. Confidence in the new government began to decline. Republicans argued that nothing had changed: it was like living under the Empire. 'The prisons were full, intimidation and informers were everywhere, and defeats were changed into victories on the posters' (M.: 108). In an effort to rally support, the Government of National Defence held a plebiscite in Paris, asking Parisians to approve its pursuit of the war.

Table 9.5: Voting in the 5 November 1870 plebiscite (L.: 67)

	'Yes' votes	'No' votes
Civilian males	322 900	54 000
Soldiers	237 000	9 000

This 'Bonapartist' tactic – the use of a plebiscite – confirmed the suspicions of the Republican left, who had demanded new elections of the capital's mayors.

The majority were reluctant to criticise the new government openly. Andrieu dismissed this attitude as a 'patriotic illusion' (A.: 61); Brocher was more understanding: the watchword of the people was 'stay calm; no disunity before the enemy' (B.: 117). Revolutionary demonstrations, posters and the near-revolts of 8 October 1870 and 6 January 1871 were only supported by a radical minority. On the other hand, the majority were learning another lesson. The difference between the rich élite, who ate in restaurants – which served rabbits, elephants steaks (from the zoo) and, eventually, rats – and the poor who starved in the streets was obvious; no precise sociological debates about proletarians, artisans and bourgeois were needed. While the Government spoke in terms of national unity, Paris was becoming a divided city. Moreover, the poor could justifiably feel that right was on their side: they formed the majority of the National Guard; they were not profiting from the war.

Intense political discussions thrived. 'Everything became a club; the street became a debating chamber' (M.: 125). Everyone was concerned about the pursuit of the war: everyone discussed the capability of the leaders. 'Reading the paper had become a vital necessity' (B.: 115). Radical republicans were suspicious of both the moderation of the Government of National Defence, and the continuing power of royalists and Bonapartists. Drawing inspiration from the First Republic, they developed 'vigilance committees' in each *arrondissement*. These had two functions: first, to watch over mayors who were not active in the war effort, and second, to rouse patriotic and republican feelings. These committees were centralised in a central committee: a body which included many Internationalists and trade unionists. Like the clubs, which they resembled, these committees were successful in creating a new ideal, critical of the government's performance. Michel remembered them fondly: 'There, you felt free: looking back to the past, without wanting to imitate 1793, and looking to the future without fearing the unknown ... There was the joy of feeling that you were in the right place: at the centre of an intense fight for freedom' (M.: 111). Lissagaray noted that 'if few precise ideas emerged from these frantic meetings, how many people drew inspiration from them!' (L.: 299). But compared with 1848, these organisations seem disappointing. Andrieu dismissed them: 'people went to clubs like they went to the theatre or café; they went for a night out' (A.: 53). In April 1848 there had been 200 clubs in Paris; in March 1871 there were only thirty-six.[19] While they were effective in creating a collective passion, they had the same weaknesses as the clubs of 1848: they lacked 'unity, discipline and secrecy'.[20]

On 28 January 1871 an armistice was signed between the French and Prussian forces. The leaders of both sides accepted that its purpose was to allow the election of a new government to negotiate the French surrender. This act came as a great shock to many Parisians, who had believed that Trochu would lead them to victory, and had accepted government pledges that Paris would be defended to the last man. Alongside the understandable fear of occupation, there was also an ultra-patriotism, usually republican in character, which insisted that France had not been defeated: it had been betrayed by a new government which feared popular military action more than it feared the Prussians.

The newly-elected Chamber of Deputies met in Bordeaux on 12 February 1871. Nearly two-thirds of the deputies were monarchists, and Thiers, a liberal Orleanist, acted as president. 'It was like being thrown half a century backwards' notes Lissagaray (L.: 93). The Assembly passed legislation which ignored the commercial and economic crisis in Paris: for example, it insisted that the moratorium on rents was ended. Many Parisian families were thrown into poverty, as the near-starvation conditions of the siege had hardly changed. 'And we live in a Republic!' thought Brocher (B.: 145). Parisians' anger had been stifled during the siege by the demands of national unity before the enemy: now it began to emerge openly.

On 18 March 1871 the regular army, commanded from Versailles (some fifteen miles west of Paris), attempted to seize artillery held by the Parisian National Guard. The artillery was defended initially by women (including Michel), who sounded the alarm. The National Guard was mobilised and the cannons were saved. Following this act, Thiers ordered the retreat of all governmental and military officials from Paris. In their place, the National Guard ruled Paris. 'The red flag flew from the Hôtel-de-Ville. Like the morning mist, the army, the government, the administration all evaporated' (L.: 118). The National Guard's first act was to organise new municipal elections to create a body to represent Paris.

Elections took place on 26 March 1871 and they were denounced as illegal by the Versailles-based national government. Although it was not immediately obvious, these elections created a chasm between Paris and Versailles. Lissagaray noted that many of the old Republicans of 1848 failed to participate (L.: 147). Only 227 000 out of 480 000 eligible voters participated in the elections. Voter participation was low for two reasons: many rich people had left Paris at the end of the siege, and many conservatives agreed with the Versailles government that the elections were illegal. Lissagaray is probably largely correct in noting that 'all the workers, all the far-sighted and generous members of the petty-bourgeoisie' supported these elections (L.: 134). Ninety-one councillors were elected: thirty-one either refused to take their seats or, having already been elected to the National Assembly, chose to sit at Versailles. On 16 April, a series of by-elections were held (Andrieu was a successful candidate), the addition of the new members creating an assembly of eighty-one members. Eighteen of them were middle-class, thirty were professional people, and thirty-five were craftsmen. Lissagaray gives a good description of them : the majority were 'petty-bourgeois, employees, accountants, doctors, teachers, lawyers, publishers' (L.:172). In a literal sense, this was far from the 'dictatorship of the proletariat' proclaimed by Engels. However, over one-third of the Commune's representatives were craftsmen: it is difficult to think of another representative body from any period of European history which contained so many workers. Their average age was thirty-eight: much younger than the average age of those who sat at Versailles.[21] Within their body, two organised political groups were represented: thirty-two were Internationalists,[22] and between eight and eleven were Blanquists.[23] Furthermore, fifteen members of the Council were Freemasons.[24]

Some mayors and deputies tried to mediate between the Council and the Versailles parliament. However, by 30 March 1871, fighting started between the National Guard and the Versailles-based army. Paris was under siege once more. With few exceptions, the communards proved incapable of organising an adequate defence of their city. Brocher's description of the National Guard unit in which she served was probably not unusual: it was not 'organised, dressed, equipped or armed' (B.: 159). Many communards were aware of their oncoming defeat: Andrieu told the municipal employees that 'victory was impossible' (B.:70). However, the Versailles army advanced slowly, leaving time for a new Paris to emerge.

The Commune Council passed several social reforms. On 16 April it allowed trade unions to take over abandoned workshops and reopen them as co-operatives. Ten such institutions were immediately established, and by 14 May there were forty-three working co-operatives in Paris. On 20 April, it accepted a bakery-workers' petition calling for an end to night-work. On 30 March the separation of the Church and state had been decreed; this was followed up in a more piecemeal fashion in May, with the gradual secular-isation of both girls' and boys' schools. The communards' reforms of girls' schooling suggested a repudiation of the Proudhonist legacy, which stressed domesticity as the key female virtue. Several organisations for women were created: in most cases the initiative for these came from outside the Com-mune Council, but it is significant that its members accepted them. Women served the Commune in auxiliary military roles such as running ambulance services; some – such as Michel – also became active soldiers.[25]

All four authors note the special role played by women during the Com-mune. However, surprisingly, our two female writers have less to say than the two men. Michel entitles one chapter of her work 'Women of the Commune', but in this short section she does little more than cite names of some prominent female communards (M.: 257–9). Brocher only recounts how she met Michel on 21 May and was invited to join her group of female activists (B.: 190). The two male writers are far more lyrical: Andrieu praises the instinctive socialism of the female communards (see document 9.4), Lissagaray their spirit of devotion (L.: 216).

The reasons for this difference in treatment is obvious: the books by Michel and Brocher are in themselves feminist. In a society where women were denied political rights, merely by writing they are asserting their right to intervene in politics. For this reason, there was no need to include specific sections on women and the Commune. Andrieu and Lissagaray, while both more or less sympathetic to reforms of women's political status, still saw this issue as only one among many.

A new ethic of unity was created in Paris: 'The unity of a bee-hive, not of a barracks' (L.: 149). This new identity was noted by all our authors. 'An irresistible current of fraternity carried the city … A fever of faith, devotion and above all hope' (L.: 146, 198). Brocher remembered that 'in those times I did things of which I would never have believed that I was capable; an excitement transformed my being; inspired by an ideal, I was stronger than ever' (L.: 185).

Following continual retreats by the National Guard, the Commune Council voted through an exceptional measure on 1 May 1871. By forty-five votes to twenty-three, it decided to create a 'Committee of Public Safety' which would centralise the political powers held by the Commune. (In 1793–4, the first 'Committee of Public Safety' had been responsible for the organisation of the Terror.) This measure was openly opposed by a minority of the Commune (including Andrieu), and made public the disagreements within the Council.

On 22 May Versailles forces entered the west of Paris. All attempts at military co-ordination broke down. The communards returned to their homes and, in a desperate last measure, built barricades like their parents had done in 1830 and 1848. The Versailles forces showed no mercy: as they advanced eastwards, they shot prisoners and suspects. In the fighting and cannon fire, many buildings caught light. The Versailles forces invented the figure of the *pétroleuse*, the female petrol-bomb thrower, to explain these fires, and shot many women whom they suspected of this crime. Approximately twenty thousand communards were killed in the last days of the Commune, possibly more. The last barricades, near the Père Lachaise cemetery in north-east Paris, collapsed on 28 May 1871. Brocher managed to escape and, exhausted, walked back to her mother's home. As she entered the block, she met a baker. Shocked, he stuttered: 'That's not you, you're not Mrs Brocher, you've been shot!' (B.: 215). Michel was captured and sent to New Caledonia; Andrieu and Lissagaray both escaped to Britain.

Between 1871 and 1875, 38578 men, women and child Communards were put on trial. Of these, 10137 were found guilty.[26]

– III. POLITICAL CULTURE –

Many French people retained their republican sympathies throughout the Second Empire. Significantly, when the *Marseillaise* was officially encouraged in 1870, Parisians had no difficulty in remembering its words. However, during the 1860s, it became clear that republicans were drawing different lessons from the legacy of the Second Republic. One strand of republicanism – to be discussed in Chapter 10 – emphasised constitutional legality, and demanded the return of orthodox parliamentary government. Their conception of the Republic centred on its political structure: they were suspicious of attempts to build an extra-parliamentary movement. Like Emile Ollivier, some of them were prepared to compromise with the liberal Empire of the late 1860s. Others, sometimes labelled Jacobins, refused to rally to the Second Empire, but shared the same conception of the Republic as a political form.

Andrieu distanced himself from this moderate, constitutional Republicanism. For him, this was a moral choice: he saw the republican journalists, politicians and lobbyists of the 1860s as betraying the cause for which he fought. Lissagaray compared the constitutional republicans and the First International. While he does not appear to have joined the International, he was impressed by their members. At the trial of their leaders in May 1870 he noted that their speeches revealed 'the newness of their ideas, the clarity and the eloquence of a working-class world' (L.: 46). The old republicans of 1848 were not able to respond to the ideas of this new working-class élite (L.: 32).

While all four authors consider that there were major differences between constitutional republicanism and more radical forms of politics, none of them provide clear political criteria for this distinction. Were there none? Is a recent history of the Commune right to conclude that 'radical republicanism represented more a state of mind than an organised group'?[27] To answer this question, let us examine three examples of radical political culture: the First International, Proudhonism and the Blanquists.

Despite the International's connection with Karl Marx, who, based in London, acted as its secretary from 1864 until its demise in 1872, it was not an ideologically coherent body. Constant notes that most of its French members 'had not even heard the name Marx'.[28] It was not a tightly organised grouping of militants: Rougerie describes it as forming a 'popular intelligentsia', gathering together the best-educated and most confident members of the popular classes.[29] On three occasions between 1868 and 1870 there were mass arrests of its leaders, which somewhat stifled its political discussions. Within its ranks some supported the old, Proudhonian strategy of workers' co-operatives, while others, sometimes called collectivists, thought in terms of a communally-organised form of socialism. Many of its members, such as Brocher, were not concerned about these debates.

The International was not growing before the Commune. In Paris in January 1870, there were thirty-three sections, plus three co-operatively-run cafés. In March 1871 there were twenty-eight sections. During 1870 its total membership was less than one and a half thousand. Its most important audience was among the trade unionists of Paris. In early 1870 there were approximately one hundred trade unions based in Paris. Sixty of them were affiliated to the Federal Centre of Workers' Societies – a group created with encouragement from the International – and, of these, twenty were directly affiliated to the International. The total audience for the International's ideas and discussions was between twenty thousand and thirty thousand.[30] In other words, while this group was important as a centre of education and organisation, it was not a mass movement and it was not capable of leading the popular classes of Paris into revolution.

The most prestigious political theoretician of the extra-parliamentary left was Proudhon. He was the most frequently cited author in the public meetings, partly because of his ideas, but also because of the particular symbolic resonance which surrounded him.[31] Proudhon was the living symbol of working-class self-emancipation, and his followers took pride in the difference between his rough-hewn, dogmatic, aggressive political statements and the more polished, academic speech of the constitutional republicans. From Proudhon's confused ideas, most of the communards drew the basic conceptual framework for their political expressions. His two last works were crucial in this respect.

In his *Principles of Federalism* (1863) he proposed a political system which represented almost the opposite of the Empire: a system based upon the voluntary federation of villages, towns and cities, joined together for their mutual aid. In 1863 he was approached by a group of sixty workers who called for working-class candidates to stand in the forthcoming parliamentary elections, thus dividing the republican opposition along class lines. Proudhon was, by 1863, a convinced anti-parliamentarian, and had previously, in 1848, recommended the alliance of the working class and middle class. However, he was intrigued by the sixty workers' initiative, and in his *On the Political Capacity of the Working Classes* (1864) he sympathetically debated some of its implications. He argued that since 1789 France had been divided into two classes of 'waged workers and owners-capitalists-entrepreneurs'.[32] He considered that the initiative of the sixty workers marked the political maturity of the working class, and that henceforth workers should represent themselves. Such points suggest that Proudhon was moving away from the loose, associational socialism which he had proposed in 1848-9, and towards a class-based form of socialism. However, significantly, Proudhon never finished this work, and throughout it there are signs of his reluctance to accept a class-based vocabulary: the very title of the book referred to the working class*es*, not to the working *class*, suggesting that for him the workers did not form a united social grouping.

The principal ideological challenge to Proudhon came from Auguste Blanqui (1805–81). Blanquists acquired a reputation for militancy in the 1860s (A.: 29, 49). Their principal historian sounds a sceptical note: although the Blanquists gained the 'reputation for being the most zealous defenders of the French revolutionary tradition', this reputation was as much due to their manipulation of myth and ritual as to their record as activists.[33] Blanqui started to organise his followers during the 1860s. The first groups were composed of students; later, artisans joined. Initially they ignored the International: the focus of their activities was to prepare for the overthrow of the Second Empire. In 1867–70 they were formed into ten-member cells and given military training. There may have been three thousand members in Paris.[34] They were present at the political funerals in the late 1860s, at which they marched in paramilitary formation. On 14 August 1870 a small group of Blanquists attacked a fire station in La Villette, in the north of Paris, looking for arms. One fireman was killed. This action, while ridiculous in itself, brought them to public notice: all four of our authors record the attack in their works, although none of them voice sympathy for it. Blanquists were active again in the succeeding months: on three further occasions they attempted to lead Parisians into revolutionary action.

The Blanquists' beliefs combined elements of classical republican theory with socialism. They identified themselves with Hébert, an anti-clerical militant who was eventually executed by Robespierre's Committee of Public Safety in 1794. They argued that the population of France was not yet ready to vote freely for a Republic: the only way that the Republic could be instituted was through a revolutionary dictatorship. However, they also combined elements of class analysis in their theories, arguing that the Republic would mean the end of the exploitation of the poor by the rich. In 1870 they began to enter the International, thus causing further ideological confusion within its ranks.

The ideas of Proudhon, the First International and the Blanquists did not provide a clear programme for the Commune. The differences between these political cultures were frequently ignored: in the Club de la Révolution, few participated in debates between Blanquists and Proudhonians during 1870, and the two groups were pushed into an alliance by the force of events.[35] The communards did not write an equivalent to Marx's *Communist Manifesto* or Lenin's *State and Revolution*.[36] However, this does not mean that they had no ideas: they were guided by 'the collective memory of the revolutionary tradition' stretching back to 1789.[37] Furthermore, many of them – such as Lissagaray – had participated in the public meetings of 1868–70: here they had heard, and probably joined in, the criss-crossing political currents which made up the 'complex, shifting reality' of Parisian oppositional politics.[38] In other words, the Commune was certainly an improvised work, but its themes were improvised along certain established and well-understood lines.

So far we have seen the various political currents which formed the political cultures of the communards. How can we sum these up? What is the broader picture?

Some authors – for example, Michel and Engels – asserted a fundamental political unity as the basis for the Commune. This is a difficult argument to maintain. It is clear that the Commune Council was not united, and many commentators have noted the range of political cultures represented on it. Gustave Courbet, the painter, was elected to the Commune Council in the April by-elections. He considered that 'the majority were old-fashioned, classic, traditional republicans who lacked spontaneity, while the minority were very modern, having a sort of pacifist mysticism which they turned into a cult, which was represented by two words: labour and worker.'[39] Rougerie adopts a more subtle approach: he refuses to see the Commune council divided into two factions, and instead suggests that it was dominated by Proudhonian ideas on federalism and association during its first weeks, when it considered social reforms, and then turned to Jacobin concepts of organisation when faced with outright warfare.[40] This perception of developing clusters of beliefs is probably as accurate and realistic a summary of the Commune's politics as is possible.

– IV. LEGACY –

The Commune was not dominated by a single political *philosophy*, but it did produce a rich and startlingly clear collection of political *images*. Michel's description of the proclamation (document 9.3) is clear: 'There were no speeches, just a great shout, once, of "Long live the Commune!"'. An orthodox republican could certainly sympathise with some of the features which Michel describes: the people, the armed citizens, the phrygian caps, the memory of 1793, the invocation of the Republic ... Such features might suggest that the Commune was backward-looking, drawing its imagery and ideas from the tradition of the French Revolution of 1789. However, there are also new ideas, principally the red flags and red sashes. Lissagaray in his description of the scene emphasises the same point: 'the flags before the platform were mostly red, although some were tricolours: all carried red ribbons, symbolizing the arrival of the people' (L.: 151). Elsewhere, Brocher notes the importance of this colour: 'universal suffrage had legalised the rioter's red flag' (B.: 160). Red became the official colour of the Commune, its symbol of revolt against the tricolour Republic.[41]

This choice of colour is significant. While the communards never managed to produce an articulate political argument to explain their revolt against the Third Republic, their political actions and expressions clearly show their opposition. At the heart of this opposition was their concern with the working class. While Andrieu was no socialist, even he noted that the International represented 'the most important section of the Republicans, the workers' (A.: 54). Against all sociological logic Lissagaray consistently describes the communards as workers and proletarians. We can see here the same paradox that was noted in Chapter 3: the proletarianisation of industry had not yet arrived in France, but the concept of the proletariat enabled a wide range of social groups to make sense of their condition. They felt that their subordinate status was being constructed in terms of economic class and – whatever their economic condition – they identified their struggle with that undertaken by the proletariat.

All four authors also refer to another key concept: the Paris Commune was an explicitly municipal revolt: 'a free Paris in a free France' (B.: 160). In Michel's words, in 1871 'Paris breathed!' (M.: 198). For many, the key issue was not social revolution or socialism, but the recreation of Parisian municipal liberties. Following the two decades of imperial centralisation, even this simple demand carried heavy political implications with it. This was the revenge of those who had been 'Haussmannised' against their masters.

Compared with the Bonapartist tobacco pouch of the 1820s and the slogans shouted by the crowds of 1848, the communards made use of more sophisticated instruments of political expression. As well as participating in meetings and discussions, they printed posters and read newspapers. In this respect, despite all the indications of continuity with past struggles, their political culture was markedly more modern.

In the 1870s little was said publicly about the Commune. For much of this decade, government and administration were controlled by monarchists; it was dangerous to revive this memory. However, by 1880 the Third Republic was controlled by republican groups: they passed an amnesty for all those convicted for crimes committed during the Commune. Very quickly, a cult of the Commune began to grow, marked by an annual pilgrimage to the Père Lachaise cemetery on 18 March.

Different groups drew contrasting lessons from the Commune. For anarchists, this was a federalist, decentralist revolt, whose defeat revealed the true nature of state tyranny. For Marxists, it was a proletarian revolt, whose defeat showed the need for a properly organised workers' political party. A third strand, more properly French, took from it the idea of 'municipal socialism': as the industrial working class did not form the majority of French society, the best hope for socialists was to capture town halls, and to introduce step-by-step reforms from these bases. Lastly, there were persistent attempts by the far right to co-opt the Commune as an anti-republican revolt. In May 1938 a delegation from the fascistic paper, *Je Suis Partout*, attempted to participate in a ceremony to commemorate the repression of the Commune.[42] Far from simply being the 'dictatorship of the proletariat', the Commune inspired a contradictory variety of political traditions.

– V. DOCUMENTS –

– DOCUMENT 9.1: PROUDHON LOOKS AT HAUSSMANN'S PARIS –

The passage expresses the feeling of dispossession which many felt following Haussmann's redesign of Paris. The importance of the racist vocabulary in the last lines should not be exaggerated: racism was never the basis of Proudhon's political thinking. However, it is an indication of another form through which this sense of dispossession could be articulated.

> [In 1863] a hidden agitation started in Paris, which recalled the movements of 1830 and 1848 ... Ah! cried those who claimed to lead the movement, this is no longer the new, boring, exhausting town of Mr Haussmann, with its straight boulevards, its gigantic mansions, its magnificent – but deserted – quays; with its sad river, which carries nothing but stones and sand; with its railway stations which – having replaced the ports of the old city – have destroyed its function; with its squares, its new theatres, its new barracks, its tarmac, its legions of roadsweepers and its awful dust; a town populated with English people, with Americans, Germans, Russians, Arabs; a cosmopolitan town in which you know longer see a native. This will be the Paris of the old days, whose ghost can be seen in the lights of the stars, shouting 'long live Liberty!'.
>
> P. J. Proudhon, *The Political Capacity of the Working Classes*, pp. 9–10

– DOCUMENT 9.2: VICTORINE BROCHER BEGINS HER POLITICAL STUDIES –

This passage illustrates another form of politicisation: Brocher validates a feminine political culture, in which maternity stimulates political activity, and in which women play a privileged role in preserving political memories.

> On 14 January 1864 my first son was born. More than ever, I felt the need to become involved in my country's events. Of course, I wanted to raise my child myself. to give him everything which his needs demanded of me.
>
> I had a son, [so] I wanted to know everything about what was going on around me, so that I could teach him in turn; I wanted him to breathe a bit of my soul.
>
> I had kept some friends from the old times [from 1848]. We wrote to each other, we exchanged ideas about society. I wrote regularly to my [exiled] father and to those friends who were loyal to us. In a word, like the vestal maidens of ancient Rome, we kept alive the sacred flame.
>
> Source: B..., *Souvenirs*, p. 63

– DOCUMENT 9.3: LOUISE MICHEL ATTENDS THE PROCLAMATION OF THE COMMUNE, 28 MARCH 1871 –

Michel's description suggests that this event was almost theatrical in its mobilisation of symbols. She emphasises the unity of purpose of all Communards.

> The proclamation of the Commune [at the Hôtel-de-Ville] was magnificent: it was not a festival; it had all the dignity of a sacrifice. You could tell that the elected officials were ready to die ...
>
> There was a sea of armed people, their bayonets pressed as closely together as corn in a field ... The drums sounded: among them were the two great drums of Montmartre which had awoken Paris on the night of the entry of the Prussians into Paris, and on the 18 March ...

This time the church bells were mute. Cannon fired regularly, saluting the Revolution.

As the bayonets paraded past, they dipped in front of the red flags, which were grouped round the bust of the Republic.

At the top, there was an immense red flag. The battalions from Montmartre, Belleville, La Chapelle had put phrygian caps* on their flags: they were like the sections of 93.

In their ranks were soldiers from all the armies who had stayed in Paris: there were infantrymen, marines, gunners, zouaves.

The bayonets were pressed more tightly together in the surrounding streets. The square was full, looking more than ever like a field of grain. What would the harvest be?

The whole of Paris was there. The cannon were sounding regularly.

On the stand stood the Central Committee [of the National Guard], each wearing a red sash ...

There were no speeches, just a great shout, once, of 'Long live the Commune!'

* According to Republican legend, when slaves in Ancient Rome were released, they wore a phrygian cap to mark their new status as free men.

Source: Michel, *Commune*, pp. 192–3

– DOCUMENT 9.4: ANDRIEU PRAISES THE WOMEN OF THE COMMUNE –

All commentators on the Commune refer to women's political activities. This passage shows that even sympathetic men were not necessarily feminists, and that the concepts of clearly different male and female psychologies were respected by many Communards.

Women do not understand anything about politics. They are prisoners in society, protected within households, they have nothing to gain from men's freedoms. But, their instincts, and their upbringing leads them to be socialists. [They are moved by] the feelings of pity and the revulsion against injustice which inspires the best of them, by their continual dealings with money. They are also *communalistes*,* because their family concerns lead them to consider local issues. For these reasons the Commune gained many passionate female supporters from all classes of society. Women gives up lost causes less easily than a man; they are attracted by the drama of great disasters.

* ie believers in local self-government

Source: Andrieu, pp. 120–1

– VI. FURTHER READING –

On the Second Empire, see the 'Further reading' section in Chapter 8. On republicanism, see 'Further reading' section in Chapter 10.

The best introductory work is Stewart Edwards, *The Paris Commune, 1871* (London: Eyre and Spottiswoode, 1971). Edith Thomas, *Louise Michel* trans.

Penelope Williams (Montréal: Black Rose, 1980) is a well–written, lively biography which also serves to introduce key political issues.

The four texts used for this chapter were: Jules Andrieu, *Notes pour Servir à l'histoire de la Commune de Paris de 1871* (Paris: Maspero, 1984); Victorine B..., *Souvenirs d'une morte vivante* (Paris: Maspero, 1976); Louise Michel, *La Commune* (Paris: Stock, 1978); Prosper Lissagaray, *Histoire de la Commune de 1871* (Paris: Maspero, 1983).

More detailed analyses of the Commune can be found in the following works. Everything written by Jacques Rougerie is highly recommended: of particular interest are his: *Le Procès des Communards* (Paris: Gallimard, 1971); 'L'AIT et le mouvement ouvrier à Paris pendant les événements de 1870–71', *International Review of Social History* 27 (1972), 3–102; and 'Sur l'histoire de la Première Internationale', *Mouvement Social* 51 (1965), 23–46. Martin P. Johnson, *The Paradise of Association: Political Culture and Popular Organization in the Paris Commune of 1871* (Michigan: University of Michigan Press, 1996), stresses the role played by political organisations, and argues that a coherent political agenda lay behind the Commune's revolt. Alain Dalotel, Alain Faure and Jean-Claude Freiermuth, *Aux Origines de la Commune: le mouvement des réunions publiques à Paris (1868–1870)* (Paris: Maspero, 1980) is a detailed and well-researched analysis of the public meetings movement; parts of this work are translated in Adrian Rifkin and Roger Thomas (eds), *Voices of the People: the Politics and Life of 'La Sociale' at the End of the Second Empire*, trans. John Moore (London: RKP, 1988). Gay Gullickson, *Unruly Women of Paris: Images of the Commune* (Ithaca: Cornell University Press, 1996), is an excellent analysis of both the historiography surrounding the Commune and of women's participation in it: it is essential reading. Also on women's history, see: Eugene Schulkind, 'Socialist Women during the 1871 Paris Commune', *Past and Present* 106 (1985), 124–63 and David Shafer, 'Plus que des ambulancières: Women in Articulation and Defence of their Ideals during the Paris Commune', *French History* 7:1 (1993), 85–101. Two useful local studies of a radical and a moderate *arrondissement* are presented by Robert Wolfe, 'The Parisian "Club de la Révolution" of the 18th *arrondissement*, 1870–71', *Past and Present* 39 (1968), 81–119 and Robert Tombs, 'Prudent Rebels; the 2nd *arrondissement* during the Paris Commune of 1871', *French History* 5:4 (1991), 393–413. Marx's *Civil War in France* is a rushed essay; essentially a justification of the revolt and a denunciation of the savagery of the repression. Rather more interesting is the interview with Marx published in the *World* – both texts can be found in David Fernbach, *The First International and After* (Harmondsworth: Penguin, 1974). Eugene Schulkind (ed.), *The Paris Commune of 1871: the View from the Left* (London: Cape, 1972) is an excellent collection of translated texts from the Commune, and also includes a selection of left-wing essays on the Commune. Madeleine Rebérioux, 'Le mur des fédérés; rouge, "sang craché"' in P. Nora (ed.), *Les Lieux de Mémoire* Vol. I (Paris, 1997), 535–58 is a sensitive essay on the memory of the Commune.

The Commune has also been analysed and debated by urban historians. David Harvey, *Consciousness and the Urban Experience* (Oxford: Blackwell, 1985) is a detailed Marxist analysis of Haussmannisation; Roger Gould, *Insurgent Identities: Class, Community and Protest in Paris from 1848 to the Commune* (Chicago: University of Chicago Press, 1995) a critique of Harvey's work. Anne-Louis Shapiro, *Housing the Poor of Paris, 1850–1902* (Madison: University of Wisconsin Press, 1985) details the conditions of the working class in the new suburbs. Maxime du Camp, *Paris: Ses Origines, Ses Fondateurs et Sa Vie jusqu'en 1870* (Monaco: Rondeau, 1993): an enormous work, begun in 1870, which provides a wealth of details on the administration of Paris. The best analysis of Haussmannisation can be found in the work by the art historian T. J. Clark, *The Painting of Modern Life: Paris in the Art of Manet and His Followers* (London: Thames and Hudson, 1990).

There have been a number of excellent studies of working-class history and politicisation in this period. Among others, the following are particularly recommended: Joan W. Scott, *The Glassworkers of Carmaux: French Craftsmen and Political Action in a Nineteenth Century City* (Cambridge, Mass.: Havard University Press 1974); Michael P. Hanagan, *The Logic of Solidarity: Artisans and Industrial Workers in Three French Towns, 1871–1914* (Urbana: University of Illinois Press, 1980) and *Nascent Proletarians: Class Formation in Post-Revolutionary France* (Oxford: Blackwell, 1989); Judith G. Coffin, *The Politics of Women's Work: the Paris Garment Trades, 1750–1915* (Princeton: Princeton University Press, 1996); Michelle Perrot, *Workers on Strike: France, 1871–1890* (Leamington Spa: Berg, 1984).

There has been a flood of works on the late nineteenth-century growth of socialism in France. Pierre Joseph Proudhon, *De la Capacité Politique des Classes Ouvrières*, two vols (Paris: Le Monde Libertaire, 1977), and his *Du Principe Fédératif et de la nécessité de reconstituer le parti de la Révolution* (Anthony: Tops/Trinquier, 1997) give an insight into pre-1871 French socialism. Proudhon's influence is considered by Maria Fitzpatrick, 'Proudhon and the French Labour Movement: the Problem of Proudhon's Prominence', *European History Quarterly* 15 (1985), 407–30. Sudhir K. Hazareesingh, 'Defining the Republican Good Life: Second Empire Municipalism and the Emergence of the Third Republic', *French History* 11:3 (1997), 310–38 considers the left-wing and republican debate on municipal self-government. Geneviève Prosche, 'La "Dérive" réformiste du socialisme muncipale ou "possibiliste"', *Revue historique* 577 (1991), 121–32 discusses the development of 'municipal' socialism after 1871. Patrick H. Hutton, *The Cult of Revolution-*

ary Tradition: the Blanquists in French Politics, 1864–1893 (Berkeley: University of California Press, 1981) is the only full-length study of the Blanquists.

The opposition to the Commune deserves a chapter in itself. Paul Lidsky, *Les Ecrivains contre la Commune* (Paris: Maspero, 1982) considers the hostile literary reaction to the Commune; Robert Tombs, *The War Against Paris, 1871* (Cambridge: Cambridge University Press, 1981) is principally an analysis of the military campaign.

Most historical information available on the internet is extremely simple. One notable exception is the following website devoted to images from the Commune: http://www.library.nwu.edu/spec/siege [North-Western University collection].

– NOTES –

1. Friedrich Engels, 'Introduction to *The Civil War in France*', in Karl Marx and Friedrich Engels, *Selected Works in Three Volumes*, Vol. II (Moscow: Progress, 1977), p. 189.
2. Louis Constant, 'Preface' to Victorine B..., *Souvenirs d'une morte vivante* (Paris: Maspero, 1976), p. 1.
3. Roger Magraw, *A History of the French Working Class, Vol. I* (Oxford: Blackwell, 1992), p. 221.
4. B..., *Souvenirs*, p. 101.
5. B..., *Souvenirs*, p. 61.
6. Jacques Rougerie, *Le Procès des Communards* (Paris: Gallimard, 1971), pp. 131–4.
7. David Harvey, *Consciousness and the Urban Experience* (Oxford: Blackwell, 1985), p. 64.
8. Roger V. Gould, *Insurgent Identities: Class, Community and Protest in Paris from 1848 to the Commune* (Chicago: University of Chicago Press, 1995), p. 73.
9. T. J. Clark, *The Painting of Modern Life: Paris in the Art of Manet and His Followers* (London: Thames and Hudson, 1990), p. 37.
10. Harvey, *Consciousness*, p. 75.
11. Jules Andrieu, *Notes pour Servir à l'histoire de la Commune de Paris de 1871* (Paris: Spartacus, 1984), p. 1. (Future reference for this work will be given in the text, and marked as 'A.'.)
12. B..., *Souvenirs*, p. 78. (Future reference for this work will be given in the text, and marked as 'B.'.)
13. Louise Michel, *La Commune* (Paris: Stock, 1978), p. 18. (Future reference for this work will be given in the text, and marked as 'M.'.)
14. Alain Dalotel, Alain Faure and Jean-Claude Freiermuth, *Aux Origines de la Commune: le mouvement des réunions publiques à Paris* (1868–1870) (Paris: Maspero, 1980), p. 43.
15. Prosper Lissagaray, *Histoire de la Commune de 1871* (Paris: Maspero, 1983), p. 39. (Future reference for this work will be given in the text, and marked as 'L.'.)
16. Bernard Ménager, *Les Napoléon du Peuple* (Paris: Aubier, 1988), p. 148.
17. Alain Plessis, *De la fête impériale au mur des fédérés* (Paris: Seuil, 1979), p. 209.
18. Ménager, *Les Napoléon*, p. 432.
19. Raymond Huard, *La Naissance du parti politique en France* (Paris: Presses de Sciences Po, 1996), p. 141.
20. Martin P. Johnson, *The Paradise of Association: Political Culture and Popular Organization in the Paris Commune of 1871* (Michigan, University of Michigan Press, 1996), p. 30.

21. Stewart Edwards, *The Paris Commune, 1871* (London: Eyre and Spottiswoode, 1971), pp. 183–206.
22. Rougerie, 'L'AIT et le mouvement ouvrier à Paris pendant les événements de 1870–71', *International Review of Social History* 27 (1972), 3–102.
23. Patrick H. Hutton, *The Cult of Revolutionary Tradition: the Blanquists in French Politics, 1864–1893* (Berkeley: University of California Press, 1981).
24. Edwards, *Commune*, p. 298.
25. On social reform, see Edwards, *Commune*, pp. 249–76.
26. Rougerie, *Procès*, pp. 17–22.
27. Johnson, *Paradise*, p. 21.
28. Constant, 'Préface', p. ii.
29. Jacques Rougerie, 'L'AIT', p. 65.
30. Rougerie, 'L'AIT'.
31. Dalotel et al., *Origines*, p. 231.
32. Pierre Joseph Proudhon, *De la Capacité Politique des Classes Ouvrières*, two vols (Paris, 1977), Vol. I, p. 59.
33. Hutton, *Cult*, p. 1.
34. Hutton, *Cult*, p. 30.
35. Robert Wolfe, 'The Parisian "Club de la Révolution" of the 18th *arrondissement*, 1870–71', *Past and Present* 39 (1968), 81–119 (p. 88).
36. The nearest equivalent to an agreed manifesto was the 'Declaration to the People of France'. This is reproduced in a slightly edited translation in Eugene Schulkind (ed.), *The Paris Commune of 1871: the View from the Left* (London, 1972), pp. 149–51, and in French in Rougerie, *Procès*, pp. 151–5. However, this document was principally the work of a Proudhonian journalist, Pierre Denis; it was not widely discussed by the Council (see Edwards, *Commune*, pp. 217–18), and is dismissed by Lissagaray (L.: 210).
37. Johnson, *Paradise*, p. 12.
38. Dalotel et al., *Origines*, p. 117.
39. Rougerie, *Procès*, p. 76.
40. Rougerie, *Procès*, p. 155.
41. Johnson, *Paradise*, p. 217.
42. Madeleine Rebérioux, 'Le mur des fédérés; rouge, "sang craché"' in P. Nora (ed.), *Les Lieux de Mémoire* Vol. I (Paris: Gallimard, 1997), pp. 535–58.

CHAPTER 10

Republicanism Recreated: 1870–1900

A distinctive image can be found on the back of all modern French coins. It shows a tall woman, dressed in a simple flowing dress, striding barefoot through a field. Her hair is loose and falls down her shoulders. She wears a Phrygian cap. Her strong left arm clutches a bag containing seeds, which she scatters across the field with her right hand. The rising sun can be seen on the right side of the picture. This design, entitled *The Sower*, was produced by Oscar Roty in 1895.[1] His picture is not a portrayal of late nineteenth-century France: agricultural techniques were far more advanced than the primitive technique that Roty has depicted, and women's clothes were more cumbersome than the simple shift featured. So, if this is not a portrait of a prominent political woman of the 1890s, who has Roty drawn?

– I. PARTICIPANTS AND EVENTS –

Roty's picture was a celebration and an affirmation of a revolution in political culture which was implemented without bloodshed or civil war. A series of decisive elections in the late 1870s allowed republican groups to seize control of the state from the monarchists.

Table 10.1: Republican deputies, 1871–7[2]

Date of election	Republicans elected
February 1871	*c.*150–200
February–March 1876	340
October 1877	321

Their key victory was the general election of 1876. After this date, the republican groups certainly encountered some problems: Chapter 11 will examine a deep crisis which beset the republican state in the last years of the nineteenth century. However, at general elections from 1876 to 1936, the French electorate consistently returned clear majorities of republican deputies.

– II. POLITICAL CULTURE –

What programme did these victorious republicans offer their voters? Before answering this question, we must recall once more the fractured state of French politics. The first organised mass parties did not emerge until the late 1890s. Republican groups in the 1870s and 1880s were usually small networks, centred on single dominant personalities. Many only came alive once every four years to fight elections. Their political ideas were still expressed through loose, participatory political cultures, in which journalists, novelists, songwriters, playwrights and artists (like Roty) were as important as political leaders in forming ideas.

Roty's image of *The Sower* was an eloquent expression of republican aspirations, reflecting the developments in republican political culture during the mid-nineteenth century. His picture followed the accepted symbolic codes of French republican art. The ancient Republics of Athens and Rome had made use of female figures to symbolise civic virtues: and so, consciously imitating this tradition, French republicans of the 1790s invented the figure of Marianne, a fictional peasant woman, to represent their Republic. Even Roty's placing of Marianne in a stylised rural setting was commonplace. It suggested that the process of the 'Republicanisation' of France was a natural, organic process of growth, rather than a political battle. The original aspect of his image is the action of the central female figure: she is sowing. This action suggests the educational work of the Third Republic which, through its schools, cultural societies and festivals, was attempting to sow the seeds of a deep and long-lasting republican culture in France.

However, this image can also be read in a number of different ways. It could be argued that the picture was a manifesto for a sexual revolution: the key figure is a broad-hipped woman. Her loose clothes and bare arms suggest a sexual theme in Roty's design. The fertility of the field she sows is compared to her own fertility: her biological ability to produce a new generation of republican children. Such issues were to assume greater importance in the last years of the nineteenth century and the first decades of the twentieth century, when social scientists and commentators noticed that the population of France was stable. Today, this would be seen as desirable: in the late nineteenth century it was a cause for concern, and was often interpreted as a sign of national degeneration.

In evoking these images of fecundity and sexuality, Roty's design suggested a revolution in cultural attitudes. Anti-clerical republicans argued that

Catholic culture was based upon sexual repression, and that it provoked unhealthy obsessions. The Church had made sexuality shameful, and had constructed a series of taboos around puberty, menstruation, procreation and pregnancy; the Republic would create a new, 'sexually-positive' culture, in which the romantic, sensual and emotional intimacy of individual couples would not act as an antisocial force which disrupted social cohesion but, on the contrary, would form the basis for a unified, harmonious society. Republican ideals would not only shape the nature of government: they would become the inspiration for new forms of family life. In Judith Stone's words, marriages were to become 'miniature Republics'.[3] The emotional warmth which drew together husband and wife would then be reflected in the love of parents for their children (see document 10.1). These were not ideas which romantic republican couples discovered for themselves: they were publicly paraded by politicians and writers in their speeches. For example, speaking at the death of Louis Blanc's wife, Victor Hugo commented: 'He was her glory, she was his joy. She fulfilled that great [yet] humble function of women, which is to love.'[4]

Written works from the mid-nineteenth century echoed these loving, sensual themes. For example, Gustave Droz's *Monsieur, Madame et Bébé* (1867) celebrated the intimacy of a flirtatious, loving couple. Jules Michelet, a prominent republican historian, turned to a new range of subjects in the late 1850s, and produced works on issues such as *Love* (1859) and *Woman* (1860), which discussed the social and political issues associated with family life. These works attempted to break with the older, censorious, Catholic tradition of condemnation of sexual attitudes, and proposed either a benign celebration of sexuality, or – at least – argued that social problems concerned with sexual issues could be solved through the correct application of a rational social-scientific policy.

These ideas formed the basis for a 'new' republicanism which, while drawing inspiration from the First Republic (1792–1804) and Second Republic (1848–52), was also distinct from them. The First Republic now seemed too dependent on an aggressive militancy, while the Second was too utopian and too confused in its attitude to socialism and property rights. In their place, the Third Republic was, ideally, to be based on a federation of independent, emotionally secure, property–owning families. While there remained a current of idealistic anti-capitalism within republican political culture, it did not find expression in the form of economic reforms such as workers' associations. Instead, the inherent individualism in free market capitalism was to be controlled in two ways, from above and below. From above, the Republican state was intended to represent the collective interests of the citizens, teaching them through its schools their shared duties and collective, patriotic, interests. From below, the family was intended to form an oasis of harmony, in which co-operative, collective ethics were to be expressed through the reign of women in a stable domestic setting. Between these two, it was argued, the anarchic individualism of free market capitalism would be contained and controlled.

This quiet, contemplative republicanism was nurtured in the French villages, cafés and dining-halls in the 1870s.[5] In this decade, there were no official celebrations of 14 July, and following the revolutionary disturbances of the Commune, monarchist governments and provincial prefects sternly forbade republican political demonstrations. Instead, on 14 July, there were private, even semi-secret, banquets to celebrate the memory of past Republics and the ideal of the future Republic. In the early 1870s these were often small groups of male friends who met in private houses late in the night. After the electoral victories of 1876–7 their banquets were held more publicly. Attendance grew, and the participation of citizens in this celebration identified them collectively as supporters of the Republican cause. As a rule, only men attended, and by the 1880s, these events quickly changed character, becoming more focused instruments of political propaganda for prospective republican candidates.

It was to the republicans' advantage that their opponents were divided. Bonapartists, Orleanists and legitimists could not agree about which day should mark the annual national holiday, while, after some discussion, the majority of republicans happily accepted 14 July as the central date in their political calendar. The destruction of the Bastille, celebrated in this anniversary, proved to be a good basis for republican propaganda: they cheered the invasion and demolition of this political prison, whose very name seemed to symbolise all the arrogance, violence and intolerance of the backward, pre-Revolutionary, *ancien régime*. An example of this can be found in a speech by Victor Hugo to the Senate.

> The fall of this Bastille was the end of all Bastilles. This citadel's collapse meant the collapse of all tyrannies, all despotisms, all oppressions. It was the deliverance, the enlightenment of the whole world from the darkness. It was the dawn of Man. The destruction of the evil edifice meant the construction of Good. On that day, after a long torture, the great, honourable Humanity arose, with his chains under his feet and his crown on his head.[6]

Such impassioned, idealistic sentiments were repeated by republican candidates a thousand times over in elections in the late nineteenth century: as Roger Thabault, in his description of his hometown Mazières-en-Gâtine (Deux-Sèvres), quietly notes 'the Republican party emphasised ideas, the Conservatives material interest.'[7]

In the west of France, Catholics and monarchists refused to accept 14 July as a national holiday. Occasionally there would be violent confrontations; more often anti-republicans would simply ignore the festival, marking it only by placing a Catholic statue or religious object on their balcony, so that republican crowds could see their disapproval. In some areas, such tactics successfully intimidated republicans: in the commune of Landevant (Morbihan), some 130 of approximately three hundred registered voters had supported the republicans in the elections of 1881. However, in 1882, only twenty-four participated in a banquet to celebrate the 14 July, and only eight were present in 1883.

In the 1880s, as the festival gained determined municipal backing from a new generation of republican mayors, it grew more elaborate. The morning was spent in the inauguration of new statues of republican saints: Voltaire, Diderot, Gambetta, Hugo ... Speeches would be made, reminding the crowds of the significance of the commemorated figure, and of his contribution to the development of republican culture. In areas which had elected anti-clerical mayors, priests would be sternly reminded to sound their church bells to mark the anniversary. Bigger towns might stage a military parade. At midday, a banquet would be held, in which, as in 1847–8, lengthy toasts were declaimed. The *Marseillaise*, which had once more become the national hymn in January 1879, was sung. If the mayor was sympathetic, the banquet might be held in the largest municipal building, probably the schoolhouse. Then, in the afternoon, concerts, plays and dances would be organised, which would last into the evening. (See document 10.2.)

As the republicans came to power in more town halls, so republican symbols multiplied. In the 1860s, Bonapartist mayors had conspicuously displayed photographs of Napoleon III. The Republican governments wanted to continue this tradition of political symbolism, and offered republican mayors photographs of the new Republican President, Jules Grévy, who was elected in January 1879. However, these new mayors preferred to order busts of Marianne to mark their ascent to power, and the final end of monarchism and Bonapartism as political forces. The production of cheap busts of Marianne developed into a lucrative trade for stonemasons.

The political framework created by this new Republic suggested a degree of power for women: the harmony of the female-dominated domestic sphere would 'balance' the competition of the male-dominated economic sphere. Such ideas were eloquently captured by Michelet in a passage in his work *The People* (1846) (see document 10.3). Here, Michelet suggests a cultural opposition between the male-dominated world of work, which was dirty and strenuous, and the world of femininity, symbolised by this young wife in her white dress. Her husband adopts a rational, calculating approach to his workshop, reminiscent of Dickens's figure of Gradgrind. Her attitude is quite different: she sees human beings, not numbers. While her husband's approach results in conflict, hers produces harmony: like a member of the royal family, she glides gracefully through the troubled region. Significantly, she shares with the workers a sense of suffering, and can identify with them on this basis. (In later works, Michelet depicted women as permanent invalids, and wrote in an obsessive, voyeuristic, manner about menstruation.) There is a strange, discordant note towards the end of passage: Michelet mentions the presence of young *female* workers; but if the world of work is a quintessentially *male* area, why are they here? Michelet supplies no answer, but it could be argued that the ideals which he has depicted are class-based: only certain rich women are able to approach the ideal femininity which he admires. Most working-class women had to work for at least part of their lives. In Michelet's eyes this could mean that they were 'un-sexed': they did not possess essential attributes of female identity. Arguably, the task for a future republican regime was to 'return' them to their proper place.

Republicans assumed that men and women possessed fundamentally different psychologies. Their vision of social harmony was based on the compatibility of these two natures, not on the recasting of a female culture in a male form. In order for woman to perform her proper social and cultural role, she had to be 'liberated' from the domination of the Church, and to be educated to accept republican political culture. For this reason, a series of laws between 1881 and 1886 introduced a slow secularisation of girls' schooling. This measure took a long time to be enforced thoroughly: as late as 1906 there were still sixty-year-old Catholic teachers at work in some state girls' schools. However, a programme of educational and social reform had been stimulated by the republicans' coming to power.

Another consequence of the republicans' commitment to the encourage-ment of loving, intimate domestic couples was their acceptance of the need to reform divorce laws. Divorce had first been introduced into France in 1792, and henceforth was seen as a republican measure. It was limited by Napoleon, and then abolished in 1816 by the Restoration. Because republicans considered that every marriage should be based on the voluntary association of two loving individuals, they could not accept the idea that husband and wife should remain legally bound together when the warmth and intimacy of a marriage had disappeared. A limited form of divorce was reintroduced in 1884, and in turn was supplanted by a more liberal measure in 1906.

Other issues proved more difficult to solve. On occasion the republicans' respect for family life and property rights could prevent them from enacting effective reforms. Problems associated with housing conditions in Paris provide a good example of these weaknesses in Republican political culture. At first sight, statistical enquiries suggested that conditions of life were improving for the population of Paris.

Table 10.2: Death rates in Paris[8]

Dates	Death-rates in Paris, per thousand
1861–65	25.7
1896–1901	19.1

However, these statistics do not represent accurately the health of city's population. Following the Haussmannisation of Paris, workers were pushed out to slums and shanty towns to the north and east (see Chapter 9). Land speculation continued during the nineteenth century, pushing rents up, and thus forcing working-class families to live in more and more crowded conditions. More precise analyses showed how these conditions adversely affected life in working-class areas.

Table 10.3: Differentiated annual death rates in Paris, 1896[9]

Areas	Death rate per thousand
very poor *arrondissements*	22.84
poor *arrondissements*	20.74
comfortable *arrondissements*	17.12
wealthy *arrondissements*	13.44

Moreover, problems associated with ill-health were not located simply in the slum areas: diseases such as cholera and typhoid could spread from the poor to the rich *arrondissements*.

How was a reforming republican administration to solve this problem? In the long-term, the only viable solution was to produce legislation which would destroy old, unhealthy houses, and enforce the building of new houses. A form of medical inspection was needed to investigate conditions in individual households, and to form the basis of legal action against landlords. However, this implied challenging the property rights of both tenants and owners. Some medical reforms were reluctantly introduced in February 1902; but as for the second aspect – the building of new houses – the Republican authorities refused to accept that the free market could not solve the problem by itself. To intervene would amount to a challenge to the 'freedom' of autonomous families of tenants and landlords to negotiate a solution. As a result, Paris remained surrounded by a ring of slums and shanty towns until after the Second World War.

On occasion, the republicans' gendered vision of freedom could stimulate reforms. The growing concern about the stagnation of French population levels led republicans to consider measures which would encourage parents to have more children. In particular, in a remarkable gesture, both Catholics and republicans voiced concern and sympathy for single mothers. Initiatives were taken to help them: first by private charities, then by municipalities, and finally by powerful national associations. Concerned philanthropists such as Paul Strauss co-ordinated welfare bodies. While always acting in the name of 'the family', it was significant that their small army of *dames visiteuses* showed no respect for the privacy of the single mothers they visited. Motherhood had become a 'national duty'; in the service of this ideal, well-meaning philan-thropists were entitled to patronise and direct wayward women.[10]

These piecemeal initiatives and institutions were finally codified in a 1904 Law on 'assisted children' which also made clear the ideological assumptions behind these republican initiatives. Where there was a viable family unit, the republican state had to respect the rights and freedoms of the father. How-ever, when mothers had been abandoned by husbands or lovers, then the state was entitled to intervene, to act as a type of replacement patriarch. There were also situations in which women could be seen by republican legislators as having been *effectively* abandoned. For example, with a few minor exceptions, the Republican governments accepted that the individualistic logic of *laissez-faire* capitalism should dominate the workplace: workman and employer were supposed to negotiate with each other as free individuals. However, 'women were not citizens'; in the eyes of republican legislators, they did not possess the necessary civic and political qualities which would allow them to negotiate their contracts.[11] Under these circumstances, the Republican state intervened to protect women from exploitation. Laws passed in 1892 and 1900 established limitations on women's and children's work.

– III. LEGACY –

This idealistic, often sentimental, cult of vaguely-defined but deeply-held republican values formed the basis for the republicans' political culture in the late nineteenth century. Every four years, it was mobilised to draw in voters' support for republican candidates at elections. Furthermore, the new political culture can be said to have literally transformed the towns, cities and villages. The range of powerful symbols produced was quite astonishing. Even the smallest village mayors took the trouble to direct the engraving of the letters 'RF' (République Française) on to their municipal buildings. In Paris, a number of remarkable monuments were produced: the magnificent statue of Marianne who towers over the Place de la République, the Statue of Liberty, which was constructed in Paris and then shipped out to the USA, and the Eiffel Tower, which was built to commemorate the centenary of the 1789 Revolution.

After the First World War, this Republican political culture aroused less excitement. It is often said by historians that the last time that Marianne went into battle was during the Liberation of France, in 1944, as the groups of the Resistance rose against the Nazi authorities. Perhaps so, but I wonder if Marianne will soon return for another combat: since the 1980s, efforts by left-wing and anti-racist groups to co-ordinate action against the neo-Fascist National Front have met with little success. In the face of the Front's slow but relentless growth, there are signs that its opponents are reviving the older Republican imagery as a rallying point for their campaigns.

– V. DOCUMENTS –

– DOCUMENT 10.1: FATHERS AND SONS –

Gustave Droz's *Monsieur, Madame et Bébé* was one of the best-sellers of the late nineteenth century. Between 1866 and 1884 121 editions of this work were published.[12] Through a mixture of short fictional sketches and friendly advice, Droz sketched out a new ideal of family life. This passage, addressed to fathers, shows how unrealistic some of our clichés about 'Victorian' families can be. However, there is an sting in the tail in the last paragraph which shows how Droz was still concerned with the construction of paternal authority.

> There is nothing inevitable about love. Children's affection has to be won and deserved; it is a result, and not a cause, and gratitude is the beginning. At all costs, your baby must feel grateful. Don't expect that he'll understand your care for him, your dreams for his future, the months that you paid for his wet-nurse, and the dowry which you're amassing. That sort of understanding needs a type of complex calculation of which his little brain isn't capable, and social concepts which he won't yet have mastered. He won't even realise how affectionate you feel for him. Don't be surprised, don't call him ungrateful. First of all you must make him understand your affection: he must appreciate it and understand it before he can respond to it. He must know the notes before he can sing the tune.
>
> The little man's recognition at first will only be an egotistical calculation, spontaneous and uncomplicated. If you make him laugh, if you make him happy, he'll want you to do it again, he'll hold his little arms up to you and shout 'again!'. And the memory of the pleasures that you've given him will stay in his mind. Soon he'll

say 'nobody makes me as happy as daddy does: he throws me up in the air, he plays hide and seek, he tells me stories!' And soon his gratitude will grow, like a 'thank you' comes from the lips of someone you've made happy.

So, learn how to make your child laugh ... In doing this, your paternal authority will lose some of its austere prestige, but you'll win that deep, long-lasting power that comes from affection. Your baby will fear you less, but he will love you more. Where's the harm in that?

Gustave Droz, *Monsieur, Madame et Bébé* (Paris: Hetzel, 1867),
from the chapter on 'Fathers and Babies'

– DOCUMENT 10.2: CAMILLE PELLATAN ATTENDS THE 14 JULY –

Camille Pellatan was to become Minister of the Navy in 1902–5. In the 1880s, he was a left-republican, or 'radical'. This passage captures the idealism and exuberance which republicans could feel about their festival.

Garlands were linked with other garlands, triumphant arches stretched across the roads. [One saw] statues of the Republic, bright decorations shining everywhere. The crowd rushed by without panic down all the main roads, past the national colours which were displayed everywhere. Here, there were three young girls, each dressed in one of the three colours of the flag, walking hand in hand; there, one saw little children dressed in red, wearing Phrygian bonnets. Decorations were placed in the squares, fairs held throughout the town: a thousand little details arising from the cooperation of a whole people. Processions crossed the town, accompanied by brass bands. Then, as night fell, the town was lit by millions of lights, brightened by coloured lanterns, while fireworks flowered in the sky, mixing with the stars, and the dances of the squares. Everywhere there was a serene joy, and the light of this town festival lit up the night sky like a great dawn ... This was the 14 July of the Republic.

Source: cited in Maurice Agulhon, *Marianne au Pouvoir: l'imagerie et la symbolique républicaines de 1880–1914* (Paris: Flammarion, 1989), p. 149

– DOCUMENT 10.3: MICHELET, FEMININITY AND CAPITALISM –

Jules Michelet was a respected and popular history professor. Following his dismissal from his post in 1852, he turned to writing an imaginative series of less specialist works. This passage is from one his first 'non-specialist' works. It illustrates the moral idealism that often accompanied republican commitments.

It's absolutely certain that workshop-owners would be a lot more humane if their families, which are often very charitable, were less separated from manufacturing. I can recall a touching example, full of grace and charm, which I witnessed. The master of a workshop obliged me by offering to guide me around his workshop, and his young wife wanted to accompany us. At first I was surprised to see her, with her fine white dress, consider this journey across the wet and dry areas of the workshop (not everything is clean or pretty in the manufacture of the finest products), but then I understood the reason why she faced this purgatory. Where her husband wanted to see things, she saw people, souls and even tragedies. Without her saying anything, I understood that as she glided through this crowd, and sensitively took note of all the thoughts – I won't say 'hateful' thoughts, but let's say the worried, perhaps envious thoughts – which were fermenting there. Along the route, she distributed fine, well-placed phrases being – for example – almost tender to a poor young girl. The young lady, who was unhealthy herself, cared greatly for the young girl's suffering. Several people were touched by her: an old worker, who thought her tired, offering her a chair with a charming quickness. The younger workers looked more down-hearted; she, who saw all, said a word and chased away their clouds.

Michelet, Le Peuple (Paris: Flammarion, 1974 [1846]), p. 118

– VI. Further reading –

The best textbooks on this period are: R. S. Anderson, *France, 1870–1914* (London: RKP, 1977) and Jean-Marie Mayeur and Madeleine Rebérioux, *The Third Republic from its Origins to the Great War, 1871–1914*, trans. J. R. Foster (Cambridge, University of Cambridge Press, 1984).

Issues of gender politics are discussed in a number of works. Elinor A. Accampo, Rachel G. Fuchs and Mary Lynn Stewart (eds), *Gender and the Politics of Social Reform in France, 1870–1914* (Baltimore: John Hopkins UP, 1995) is a magnificent collection of essays, which are essential reading for anyone interested in this period. Accampo's introductory essay is particularly impressive. James McMillan, 'Clericals, Anticlericals and the Women's Movement in France under the Third Republic', *Historical Journal* 24 (1981), 361–76 is a well-written and provocative denial of the republicans' claim to liberate women. Steven C. Hause with Anne R. Kenney, *Women's Suffrage and Social Politics in the French Third Republic* (Princeton: Princeton UP, 1984) discusses the difficult formation of feminist political culture. Sharif Gemie, *Women and Schooling in France, 1815–1914: Identity, Authority and Gender* (Keele: Keele UP, 1995) and Jo B. Margadant, *Madame le Professeur: Women Educators in the Third Republic* (Princeton, Princeton UP, 1990) are both social histories which examine Republican political culture through the issue of schooling. Rachel G. Fuchs has produced a number of excellent works on the treatment of single mothers. These include: *Poor and Pregnant in Paris: Strategies for Survival in the Nineteenth Century* (New Brunswick, New Jersey: Rutgers UP 1992), 'Morality and Poverty: Public Welfare for Mothers in Paris', *French History* 2 (1998), 288–311 and 'The Right to Life: Paul Strauss and the Politics of Motherhood' in Accampo et al., *Gender and the Politics of Social Reform*, pp. 82–105.

Republican politics have been analysed by a number of authors. Pamela

Pilbeam, *Republicanism in Nineteenth Century France, 1814–1871* (London: Macmillan, 1995) is a good introduction to developments in republicanism during the mid-nineteenth century. Philip Nord, *The Republican Moment: Struggles for Democracy in Nineteenth Century France* (Cambridge, Mass., Harvard UP, 1995) is a more demanding work on the growth of a republican opposition to the Second Empire. Katherine Auspitz, *The Radical Bourgeoisie: the Ligue de l'enseignement and the Origins of the Third Republic* (Cambridge, Cambridge UP, 1982) is a detailed case study of a key pressure group. Peter J. Larmour, *The French Radical Party in the 1930s* (Stanford, California: Stanford UP, 1964): while, as the title suggests, this work is concerned with the 1930s, it does contain an extremely powerfully presented analysis of the ideas of Alain, a key republican political philosopher (Chapter 2, pp. 60–77). Claude Nicholet, *L'idée républicaine en France* (1789–1924) (Paris: Gallimard, 1994) discusses political philosophy. Sharif Gemie, 'Politics, Morality and the Bourgeoisie: the work of Paul Leroy-Beaulieu (1843–1916)', *Journal of Contemporary History* 27 (1992), pp. 345–62 discusses republican attitudes to free-market capitalism. Sanford Elwitt, *The Third Republic Defended: Bourgeois Reform in France, 1880–1914* (Baton Rouge: Louisiana State UP, 1986) is a well argued series of essays on key republican political writers. Y. Lecouturier, 'La pénétration de la Republique dans le bocage calvadosien (1848–1924)', *Annales de Normandie* 28 (1978), 241–57 and Roger Thabault, *Education and Change in a Village Community: Mazières-en-Gâtine, 1848–1914*, trans. P. Tregear (London, 1971) are both useful local case studies of the process of 'republicanisation'.

Recently, historians have been turned away from an analysis of republican political ideas to examine the symbols and images used by the republicans. A pioneering contribution to this discussion were two works by Maurice Agulhon, *Marianne into Battle: Republican Imagery and Symbolism in France, 1789–1880*, trans. Janet Lloyd (Cambridge: Cambridge UP, 1981) and *Marianne au Pouvoir: l'imagerie et la symbolique républicaines de 1880–1914* (Paris: Flammarion, 1989). Deborah Silverman, *Art Nouveau in fin-de-siècle France* (Berkeley and Los Angeles: California UP, 1989) is a detailed study of cultural politics. A number of essays in P. Nora (ed.), *Les Lieux de Mémoire* (Paris: Gallimard, 1997) are also very useful. In Vol. I see the essays by Girardet, Ory, Mona Ozouf, Jacques and Mona Ozouf, and Vovelle, and in Vol. III, that by Mona Ozouf. Charles Rearick, 'Festivals in Modern France; the Experience of the Third Republic', *Journal of Contemporary History* 12 (1977), 435–60 is a beautifully written essay which vividly captures the nature of the republican festival. Olivier Ihl, 'Convivialité et citoyenneté: les banquets commémoratifs dans les campagnes républicaines à la fin du XIXe siècle' in A. Corbin, N. Gérôme and D. Tartakowsky (eds), *Les Usages politiques de la fête aux XIXe–XXe siècles* (Paris: Presses de la Sorbonne, 1994), 137–57 is a detailed study of republican banquets. Emile Zola, *Docteur Pascal* (various editions): a novel written in 1893 to complete the famous *Rougon-Macquart* cycle. It captures many of the hopes and worries of the republicans.

There are a number of good political biographies containing chapters which usefully illustrate the manner in which the republican political system worked. See, amongst others, Patrick Gourlay, *Charles Daniélou (1878–1953): Itinéraire politique d'un Finistérien* (Rennes: Presses Universitaires de Rennes, 1996) and J. F. V. Keiger, *Raymond Poincaré* (Cambridge: Cambridge UP, 1997).

– NOTES –

1. See Deborah Silverman, *Art Nouveau in fin-de-siècle France* (Berkeley and Los Angeles: University of California Press, 1989), pp. 176–8 for both a reproduction of this design and a commentary on it.
2. R. D. Anderson, *France 1870–1914: Politics and Society* (London: RKP, 1977), p. 164.
3. Judith Stone, 'The Republican Brotherhood: Gender and Ideology' in Elinor A. Accampo, Rachel G. Fuchs and Mary Lynn Stewart (eds), *Gender and the Politics of Social Reform in France, 1870–1914* (Baltimore: John Hopkins University Press, 1995), pp. 28–58 (p. 35). I have found this essay extremely useful.
4. Victor Hugo, *Depuis l'Exil*, Vol. I (Paris: Nelson, nd), p. 385.
5. The evidence and arguments presented in the next paragraphs are drawn from: Olivier Ihl, 'Convivialité et citoyenneté; les banquets commémoratifs dans les campagnes républicaines à la fin du XIXe siècle' in A. Corbin, N. Gérôme and D. Tartakowsky (eds), *Les Usages politiques de la fête aux XIXe–XXe siècles* (Paris: Publications de la Sorbonne, 1994), pp. 137–57; and Christian Amalvi, 'Le 14 Juillet: du *Dies irae* à *Jour de fête*' in P. Nora (ed.), *Les Lieux de Mémoire*, Vol. I (Paris: Gallimard, 1997), pp. 383–423.
6. Victor Hugo, *Depuis l'Exil*, Vol. II (Paris: Nelson, nd), p. 149.
7. Roger Thabault, *Education and Change in a Village Community: Mazières-en-Gâtine, 1848–1914*, trans. P. Tregear (London: RKP, 1971), p. 182.
8. Ann-Louise Shapiro, *Housing the Poor of Paris, 1850–1902* (Madison: University of Wisconsin, 1985), p. 79.
9. Shapiro, *Housing*, p. 79.
10. Rachel G. Fuchs, 'The Right to Life: Paul Strauss and the Politics of Motherhood', in Accampo et al., *Gender and Politics*, pp. 82–105 (p. 90).
11. Mary Lynn Stewart, 'Setting the Standards: Labor and Family Refomers', in Accampo et al., *Gender and Politics*, pp. 106–27 (p. 116).
12. James McMillan, *Housewife or Harlot? – The Place of Women in French Society, 1870–1940* (Brighton: Harvester, 1981), p. 35.

CHAPTER 11

Political Anti-Semitism and the Dreyfus Affair, 1894–1906

Towards Fascism?

On 5 January 1895 Emile Zola, a prominent writer, watched a strange ceremony. In the cold morning light he joined several thousand spectators crowded round the railings of the Ecole Militaire courtyard. They were there to watch the terrible sight of the formal military degradation of Captain Alfred Dreyfus. The ceremony began at nine a.m. Dreyfus's insignia – the stripes on his trousers, the buttons on his coat, the braid on his cap and sleeves – were torn away. The crowd was hostile, and shouts of 'Kill him! Kill him!' were screamed as his clothes were torn. The climax of the ceremony was the public breaking of Dreyfus's sword.

On 22 December 1894 seven judges had found Dreyfus guilty of passing military secrets. His lawyer had protested about the manner in which the trial was carried out: he had not been allowed to see a secret file of documents which had apparently persuaded the judges to find him guilty. Their verdict was damning and few dared to challenge their unanimous decision.

Zola felt upset as he watched the ceremony. Dreyfus shouted out, again and again, 'I am innocent!'. The contrast between this isolated man and the concentrated anger of the threatening crowd moved Zola, and he considered making the dramatic situation the basis for a story. However, Zola never wrote his story and, until 1897, he considered that Dreyfus was guilty, as did most of the French population. In January 1895, nobody who watched the degradation ceremony could have guessed that the verdict reached at Dreyfus's trial would initiate one of the greatest political confrontations in French history.

– I. Participants –

In 1895 only Dreyfus's immediate family and his defence lawyer challenged the unanimous guilty verdict. By 1898 the verdict was debated by a growing number of writers, independent politicians and other activists: it had grown into 'the Dreyfus Affair'.

The Dreyfus Affair excited many. In this sense, Léon Blum, the socialist Prime Minister of France in 1936, can be seen as typical. He was a passionate supporter of the cause of Dreyfus's innocence, and later recalled that 'life no longer counted for my friends or for me. We would have sacrificed ourselves … for what we considered to be truth and justice.'[1] Blum, alongside a number of other writers and politicians, joined the loose grouping which became labelled the 'Dreyfusards'. Their beliefs were a relatively simple restatement of the republican ideas which were examined in Chapter 10.

Opposed to them was an equally heterogeneous grouping, who acquired the label of 'anti-Dreyfusards'. In this chapter, we will concentrate on this new political culture, which challenged and subverted the norms of republicanism.

Older perceptions that 'France was split by the Dreyfus Affair' are simply exaggerated. The people of the small towns and villages were rarely actively involved. The details of the Affair were too complex and difficult for them to follow. Despite the presence of 'Gyp' (a female writer) in the anti-Dreyfusard camp and Louise Michel (a little reluctantly) in the Dreyfusard camp, most of those involved were men. Lastly, while one or two confrontations did mobilise working-class people (principally the republican rally at Longchamp, near Paris, on 11 June 1899), workers showed only patchy interest in the contest between Dreyfusards and anti-Dreyfusards. Rather than 'splitting France', the Dreyfus Affair divided a community of middle-class newspaper readers.

Before we study the ideas and beliefs which developed during the Affair, we need to understand the social context in which it arose.

The process of the 'republicanisation' of the Third Republic was often traumatic, and the republicans' political victory left many embittered. Between 1877 and 1882 seventy-nine of the eighty-three prefects were replaced. The judiciary was similarly purged: 1 763 magistrates out of 2 148 were dismissed, as were 2 536 out of 2 941 JPs.[2] Even the most humble, most minor officials could suddenly find themselves faced with new problems. Two small-scale examples will illustrate how quickly structures changed. The first is drawn from the south-western department of the Gironde, in 1875, when monarchists still dominated the Republic's government. Dupont, a schoolmistress in a small rural commune, faced a dilemma. A good friend of hers, a doctor, had recently died. Normally, one might expect that she would have willingly attended his funeral. However, he was a freethinker, and his will had specified that he wanted a secular funeral. Was it proper for a schoolmistress to attend such an event? Dupont did attend, but carried a prayerbook in her hands during the secular service, and conspicuously knelt to pray after the burial. She considered that she had properly balanced her personal obligations and her professional duties: the bishop of the Gironde disagreed and called for her dismissal. Eventually she was suspended for six months.

In 1879, in the southern department of the Drôme, a different type of dilemma faced a Catholic schoolmistress. The Government was now headed by republicans. When one of the department's deputies died, he specified in his will that he wanted a secular funeral. She discussed this incident with her schoolgirls, and told them 'he lived like a dog and he's been buried like a dog'. The next day, their parents complained, and the schoolmistress attempted to deny her acts. However, her pupils provided evidence against her: she had spoken her words as part of a dictation exercise, and copies of her comments were to be found in the schoolgirls' books. The republican administration showed no sympathy for her: the school inspector and prefect condemned her actions, and she was promptly dismissed.[3]

In neither case were these women seeking to act in a politically provocative manner: both were following what they understood to be the moral conventions of their society, both made mistakes in trying to navigate their way through these norms. What their cases reveal is how easy it was for minor officials, for ordinary people, to make such errors, and suddenly to find themselves humiliated, ostracised, and even unemployed, when a few months previously they had apparently possessed a secure position and an attractive future.

During the late nineteenth century, many sectors of French society were experiencing economic problems which they, rightly or wrongly, blamed on the government. From approximately the mid-1870s to the mid-1890s there was a long period of stagnation in the French economy, primarily revealed by declining or stagnant prices, and persistent unemployment. Economic rivalries often took a particularly bitter tone. An example of this type of rivalry is the hard-fought contest between southern wine producers and northern spirits producers for domination of the domestic market. Initially the vinegrowers seemed to be in the stronger position: they stressed the 'healthy' and 'natural' qualities of their product against the artificial, 'industrial' nature of the northerners' spirits. They even managed to persuade the Academy of Medicine to issue a 'warning' to all drinkers in 1872: it declared that a safe, moderate level of alcohol consumption was one litre of wine per day.[4] However, the vinegrowers were then disadvantaged by the spread of the phylloxera virus which devastated vineyards in the 1880s. The introduction of new American vines saved the vinegrowers in the 1890s, when they were hit by a new problem: chronic overproduction.

The battle between wine producers and spirit merchants certainly had a political dimension. It involved lobbying the Chamber of Deputies, and resulted in several laws, usually ineffective, being passed to protect the vine-growers' interests. The crisis in wine production provoked an angry mass movement in southern departments. In May and June 1907, 170 000 demonstrators protested in the streets of Perpignan and 500 000 in Nîmes. However, this movement retained a 'self-consciously apolitical' character. One manifesto of the demonstrators declared that 'we are those who love the Republic, those who detest it and those who couldn't care less'.[5] These rural people were suspicious of urban political movements and, while willing to voice their own concerns, were reluctant to follow urban leaderships.

Other economic contests were more openly politicised. In 1867 a new municipal abattoir was built in La Villette, a northern suburb on the edge of Paris. In keeping with the economic ideals of its reformist, republican mayor, stalls in the abattoir were rented out to independent butchers. Municipal regulations prevented any wholesaler from acquiring more than two stalls. The butchers were colourful figures in the area: they could easily be recognised by their bloody aprons and their clogs. They formed a tight-knit community of male workers who, after work, ate and drank together. Near La Villette was a quarter populated by Jews. They bought their meat from kosher butchers, who slaughtered cattle according to Jewish religious customs. The majority of the La Villette butchers disapproved of such methods and their organisation condemned them. In 1891, the municipality ended the restrictions on multiple ownership of stalls, and so provoked protests from the butchers' organisation. They put forward an economic argument: the municipality had a duty to protect the small independent butchers from their domination by the rich. However, during their successful campaign, outside political groups urged them to stress another theme: that of anti-Semitism.[6]

Three examples have been cited: the schoolmistresses who were caught out by the rapid political changes in the 1870s; the vinegrowers, suffering from a series of economic and agricultural problems in the late nineteenth and early twentieth century; and the butchers of La Villette, proudly defending their independent commercial status. Such incidents may seem disparate and unrelated: however, they share common features. They show that the late nineteenth century was not a settled era. The 'Great Depression' was not much more than a stagnation in prices, but it did spread a sense of insecurity. The advent of the Republic had not solved France's economic and social problems: indeed, as was seen in Chapter 10, the republicans' blinkered loyalty to free market economics often prevented them from acting effectively. All three of these examples show cases in which orthodox republicanism was unable to act as a vehicle for grievances.

In the last years of the nineteenth century several new political cultures developed, all aiming to put right the problems left unaddressed by the cautious republican administrations. For some, the answer was to be found in the traditions which had motivated the communards. During the 1880s a number of small socialist parties were created, and in 1892 the Fédération des Bourses du Travail (Federation of Trades' Councils) was organised. The French labour movement (the trade unions and trades councils) was largely dominated by anarchists by the late 1890s. As can be seen in table 11.1, while socialist organisations were certainly growing in numbers and influence during the 1890s, they represented only a minority of the working class.

Table 11.1: Socialists' electoral performances, 1893–1902. (The total number of deputies in the Chamber grew from 576 to 586 in this period.)[7]

Year	Votes	Deputies
1893	598 000	49
1898	888 000	57
1902	875 000	48

The socialist and anarchist left did not monopolise the legacy of the Commune: other strands, its republicanism, its nationalism, were taken up by rival groupings.

Many workers were loyal to republican political culture, and still hoped that a genuinely radical republican government would act to end the poverty and exploitation they experienced in their work and homes.

Lastly, some Catholic political groups took steps to break their long-running association with the monarchists. This movement, initiated by Pope Leo XIII in 1892, was known as the *ralliement*, for it marked the 'rallying' of Catholics to the Republic. Some *ralliés* aimed to work with moderate republicans, and to create a strong, pluralist, centre party; others were more in sympathy with the socialists, and intended to build an ethical, anti-capitalist movement.

All these tendencies were represented in the sprawling, confused movement led by General Boulanger from 1886 to 1889. (Unfortunately, for reasons of space, we cannot discuss this movement in detail. See 'Further reading' for other sources.) Initially, Boulanger seemed to be merely a figurehead for national pride: this was the man who would stand up to Germany. However, in rallies and meetings other themes quickly emerged. Boulangism represented a new sort of anti-republicanism: one which was *not* based on the Catholic or monarchist oppositions, although it might draw support from these groups; and one which was based on mass mobilisation. The movement began to decline rapidly following Boulanger's flight to Brussels in April

1889 and his subsequent suicide. Forty-two candidates were elected as Boulangists in the elections of autumn 1889.

The political situation in France in the 1890s was tense. Economic depression and structural political changes had created a sense of insecurity across society. New political groups – socialists, anarchists, *ralliés* – were challenging easy assumptions about the Republic's ability to represent 'the people'. Both the apparent strength of Boulangism prior to the elections of 1889, and the surprising breakthrough by socialist candidates in 1893, were reminders of the fragility of the Republic.

It was in this context that the Dreyfus Affair unfolded.

– II. Events –

There are two dimensions to the Dreyfus Affair: first, the personal tragedy suffered by Alfred Dreyfus, and second, the wider political and social conflicts between the Dreyfusards and anti-Dreyfusards. In this chapter we are more concerned with the second than with the first: none the less, in order to understand the case properly, we need first to examine Dreyfus's experience.[8]

Dreyfus came from an intensely patriotic, republican, French-Jewish family. They were typical of the group which Pierre Birnbaum has labelled 'the State Jews' (*les Juifs d'Etat* – the term does not translate easily into English).[9] These were Jewish families who had been resident in France for centuries. Prior to 1789, they had been kept apart from the rest of society: a range of laws had prevented them from taking up political positions or certain economic functions. In 1790, they were offered full French citizenship. Many Jews welcomed the chance to participate in the political life of their nation: some began to work for the lower grades of public administration. In the course of the nineteenth century, a few successfully gained important positions: for example, Ernest Handle was appointed Prefect of the Nord in 1871. A handful of others followed in the 1880s and 1890s. For most of them, their 'Jewish-ness' was a private matter: in public they were first and foremost republicans.

Alfred Dreyfus was a good example of this republican-Jewish culture. Aged thirty-five in 1894, he had followed a brilliant military career in the artillery service. His intelligence, his success and also his Jewishness were resented by other officers. In September 1894 a note, recovered from the German embassy, seemed to indicate that secrets were being leaked by a French officer. Suspicions quickly focused on Dreyfus. Press rumours began on 31 October 1894, but it was the anti-Semitic *Libre Parole* that transformed the story into front page news on 1 November 1894. The nationalist and anti-Semitic press put pressure on the Minister of War, General Mercier, to act. A trial, held on 19–22 December 1894, found Dreyfus guilty. In April 1895 he was sent to Devil's Island, in the South Pacific.

Initially the campaign for a retrial was led by Alfred Dreyfus's brother, Mathieu. A patriotic Jew, like his brother, Mathieu was unwilling to criticise the authorities. When he was approached by Bernard-Lazare, an anarchist and a Jew who had recognised the dangers of the development of anti-Semitism in French society, Mathieu was delighted by his offer to help, but dismayed by the revolutionary, unpatriotic tone of Bernard-Lazare's writing. Unlike Mathieu, Bernard-Lazare recognised that this case was not a result of a judicial error, but had been caused by the growth of anti-Semitism in French society.

In 1896 a diligent new officer was appointed to the War Office: Colonel Picquart. He was given responsibility to answer Mathieu Dreyfus's first questions. On reviewing the evidence, and particularly the 'secret' file which Dreyfus's defence lawyer had never been allowed to see, Picquart began to doubt the judges' verdict. Nothing actually proved Dreyfus's guilt. Picquart could see that the handwriting on the note taken from the German Embassy was similar to that of Dreyfus, but certainly was not an exact match. In October 1896 Picquart's superiors became aware of his doubts, and they moved him from his post. In his place Colonel Henry was appointed, and began to forge evidence in order to substantiate the accusation of Dreyfus's guilt.

By 1897 the Dreyfusards finally began to win converts. Mathieu had (reluctantly) allowed Bernard-Lazare to publish a pamphlet on the case and a copy was sent to all deputies and senators. Most of them ignored it. Many patriotic and conservative Jews were annoyed by it. They wished to maintain their full, uncritical loyalty to the French state: pamphlets such as that written by Bernard-Lazare were potentially embarrassing. However, some converts to the Dreyfusard cause were made. Auguste Scheurer-Kestner, a conservative Protestant republican, who was a life senator, was persuaded by their arguments. He came from the eastern province of Alsace-Lorraine: he had many Jewish friends, and as a Protestant was also aware of the prejudices in French society. Lucien Herr, a reformist socialist who worked as a librarian in the prestigious Ecole Normale Supérieure also joined the Dreyfusards. He was a useful contact, for he used his position to spread socialist and Dreyfusard ideas throughout the school. Others, such as Emile Zola, Jean Jaurès (a socialist leader), Joseph Reinach (a Republican, Jewish deputy) Octave Mirbeau (an anarchist novelist and writer) and the young Marcel Proust (later to write *A la recherche du temps perdu*) followed.

The Dreyfusards identified the real author of the note found in the German Embassy: Major Esterhazy. The handwriting on the note resembled his writing far more closely than that of Alfred Dreyfus. Questions about the Affair were asked in the Chamber of Deputies. On 4 December 1897 Prime Minister Méline attempted to stifle further debate by stating: 'There is no Dreyfus Affair'. On 10–12 January 1898 Esterhazy was tried. After three days of court proceedings, the judges took three minutes to find him innocent.

This caused despair among the Dreyfusards. It was in this context that Emile Zola published his now-famous letter 'J'accuse ...' in the Dreyfusard daily *L'Aurore* [The Dawn]. This letter accused the Ministry of War of a systematic cover-up, and challenged the President of the Republic, Loubet, to act. Over 200 000 copies were sold. His letter sparked off a furious reaction. There were anti-Semitic riots in fifty-five towns. Twelve of these riots were almost rebellions: they lasted for two or three days and involved mobs of violent demonstrators. Over 150 shops were ransacked and two Jews were killed.[10]

General elections were held in April 1898. Most candidates were reluctant to address openly the issues raised by the Dreyfus Affair. The four most committed pro-Dreyfusard candidates were all defeated, and a group of about twenty anti-Semitic anti-Dreyfusards were successfully elected. They took their seats on 1 June 1898, shouting 'down with the Jews!'. However, the overall composition of the Chamber had changed little, and there was still no single dominant party.

In August 1898 Jaurès, a prominent socialist leader who had lost his parliamentary seat in the April elections, began to publish a series of well-argued articles in his *Petite République* daily. Concentrating on technical issues of handwriting and legal procedure, he demolished the case against Dreyfus, and provided convincing evidence that the documents produced by Colonel Henry were forgeries. Henry was held in jail, awaiting trial. On 31 August 1898 he committed suicide. This event was probably the turning-point in the Affair. Henry's suicide could mean only one thing: that he acknowledged his guilt. If this was so, then the Ministry of War's case against Dreyfus collapsed.

The anti-Dreyfusards were organising their forces. Jules Guérin took over the Ligue Antisémitique française early in 1897, and made vigorous efforts to expand it. Déroulède revived the old League of Patriots: an organisation which had originally been republican in the early 1880s, had drifted into Boulangism in the late 1880s, and had decayed in the early 1890s. Déroulède turned it into an organisation of civilian support for the army, and clearly hoped to draw the army into a military intervention against the Dreyfusards. (See document 11.1.) He attempted to subvert an army unit based in Paris on 23 February 1899, but the commanding officer refused to listen to him.

On 31 December 1899 the Ligue de la Patrie française was launched. This was not a mass organisation, but rather a grouping of intellectuals, formed to counter the growing prestige of the Dreyfusards' campaign.

One result of this increasingly well-organised anti-Dreyfusard network was more violence on the streets of Paris and other big towns. This reached its peak on 4 June 1899 when an aristocratic anti-Dreyfusard attempted to attack President Loubet at the Autieul horse races, near Paris. On 11 June the Dreyfusards, anarchists and socialists responded by organising a massive popular demonstration at Longchamps which drew large crowds of workers.

Meanwhile, a retrial had been organised for Dreyfus in the Breton town of Rennes. The trial lasted from 7 August until 9 September. By a majority of five to two, the judges once again found him guilty. Rather than risk further violence, President Loubet intervened, and offered Dreyfus a pardon. It was not until July 1906 that he was finally found innocent.

These judicial decisions marked an uneasy victory. It remained unclear who had actually won. The anti-Dreyfusards were angry as Dreyfus had been released, but the Dreyfusards were disappointed: the judicial reviews had been extremely cautious, and the type of libertarian revolution in political culture for which they had been working had not come about. The ultimate victors were not so much the Dreyfusards, as the *anti*-anti-Dreyfusards: those who opposed the street violence and noisy politics of the anti-Dreyfusards, without sharing the Dreyfusards' libertarian ideals. Much of the later literature written by Dreyfusards expresses a sense of disillusion with the Affair and its results (see Further reading).

– III. POLITICAL CULTURE –

Anti-Dreyfusards saw the Affair as a type of revelation, from which they could diagnose the state of France. The growth of the heterogeneous Dreyfusard coalition confirmed their worst fears. Who joined the coalition? – the political minorities, the unassimilated, the foreigners and degenerates. Against these strangers, the anti-Dreyfusards defended their ideal of French-ness. An example of how the anti-Dreyfusards reasoned on these matters can be found in the writing of Maurice Barrès, a noted intellectual and writer. After some hesitation, he joined the anti-Dreyfusards. He argued that the Affair had become a test of nationhood. According to Barrès, the only reason that Zola defended Dreyfus was because Zola was not properly French, but really Venetian.[11]

Anti-Dreyfusard political culture was caught between two conflicting images. On the one hand, even the anti-Dreyfusards had to concede that the Jewish presence in France was small: one poster printed by anti-Semites in

1898 talked of the Jews as 0.3 per cent of the French population.[12] (In fact, this was probably three times too large. Official figures record 45 000 Jews in France: they constituted only 0.11 per cent of the French population.[13]) On the other hand, this tiny minority seemed to possess astonishing powers: the same poster spoke of their 'omnipotence'. What mysterious force did they possess? What pulled the disparate Dreyfusards together? The anti-Dreyfusards invented a frightening myth: behind the Dreyfusards lay a sinister conspiracy, which they termed the 'Syndicate'. It was backed by Jewish finance, and Jews from 'Poland, Vilna, and Lithuania' were being taxed to provide money for an international Dreyfusard campaign.[14] This 'Syndicate' aimed to ruin France. By 1899, when public opinion was moving against the anti-Dreyfusards, they developed a new interpretation of the Affair. The central issue, the anti-Dreyfusards argued, was not Dreyfus's innocence or otherwise, but the future of the army. Their campaign aimed to defend the honour of the army from the vilification organised by this mysterious syndicate. (See document 11.1.)

At the centre of the anti-Dreyfusards' political culture was anti-Semitism. This was not a new theme to French politics. Images which expressed hostility to Jews had been common in France since before the Revolution. There was the old folk-tale of the Wandering Jew, condemned to walk the world until Christ's Second Coming. Within Catholic religious culture, there was a particular stress on the role of the Jews in the death of Christ: a theme present in many Easter sermons. Alongside these old myths were more recent memories and rumours, often centred on the role of Jews as moneylenders in pre-1789 France. In times of economic crisis, some particular hostility developed against these minor commercial figures: as was seen in Chapter 6, there was some anti-Semitic violence during the 1848 Revolution in eastern departments. These old hatreds and bigotries had become fossilised in French culture, to the point where socialists and republicans would use the image of the Jew as a type of sloppy shorthand for corrupt forms of capitalism or moneylending. Zola's prominent role in the Dreyfus Affair is curious: one of his novels in the famous Rougon-Macquart cycle, entitled L'Argent [Money, published in 1891], contains a number of anti-Semitic images, including the stereotypical cliché of two Jewish brothers, one a master of international commerce, the other a rather badly drawn portrait of a Marxist revolutionary. Both are implicitly distinguished from a native, French form of commerce. If Zola had died in 1896, it is likely that he would have been remembered as a precursor of anti-Dreyfusardism, rather than as a defender of republican liberties. This unthinking use of anti-Semitic images was regrettably common, but it should not be exaggerated: Zola, for example, never made anti-

Semitism the basis of his thinking or writing. However, these clichés had made most French people familiar with hostile images of Jews before the Dreyfus Affair.

During the 1880s and 1890s, two developments changed French anti-Semitism. First, as a result of violent persecution in eastern Europe, many Jews fled the countries in which they had settled, and took refuge in western Europe. They were joined by Jewish refugees from Alsace-Lorraine, which came under German control after the French defeat in the Franco-Prussian war (1870–1). These Jews were very different from the 'State Jews' described by Birnbaum. Often the new arrivals could not speak French; they dressed differently, and they followed a more visible and public form of religious ritual. In other words, while the Jews who had been settled in France for centuries were often growing increasingly integrated into French society and culture, these new immigrants and refugees were quite different.

The dual presence of these two types of Jews was the trigger for the anti-Semitic revival in the late nineteenth century: anti-Semites simply could not accept the concept of these *different* forms of Jewish-ness. Their hatred was directed at the 'State Jews', but their caricatures and polemics made use of images of the new immigrants.[15]

The second development was the conscious reworking of anti-Semitism. In the words of its most important ideologist, Edouard Drumont, anti-Semitism was 'an economic and social question'.[16] The new anti-Semitism of the 1890s was secular; it did not oppose Christians to Jews. It was used as a means to understand economic and social conflicts (see document 11.2) and, ultimately, it provided the aggressive nationalists of the 1890s with a way of defining 'French-ness': French-ness, that is, as opposed to Jewish-ness.

Drumont (1844–1917) had worked for the Parisian municipal administration in the 1860s, and for a succession of minor papers in the 1870s and 1880s. One of his first books was entitled *Mon Vieux Paris* [My Old Paris] (1879). It was a nostalgic evocation of an idyllic community which had thrived in Paris, before the railway and the department store, before Haussmann and the Commune. Originally a republican, in the 1880s Drumont was drawn towards Catholicism. His life changed in the mid-1880s. His wife had been seriously ill for some time and in 1885 she died. Following her death, he threw himself into writing a massive two-volume, thousand-page long work, entitled *La France Juive* [Jewish France], within which over 3 000 names were cited.[17] The work quickly became a best-seller: in its first year of publication, over 100 000 copies were sold. In twenty-five years it went through two hundred editions; more than one million copies were sold before the First World War. Significantly, its last re-edition was in 1941, during the Nazi Occupation of France.[18]

It is difficult to see why this work was such a success. Jean-Paul Sartre, the existentialist-Marxist philosopher and novelist, re-read it after the Second World War. His judgement captures the nature of the book: it was 'a collection of revolting and obscene stories'.[19] *La France Juive* is a relentless, monotonous compendium of hate-filled images; inaccurate, distorted and fundamentally false. Why then did so many people read it?

One response is to question whether those who bought it did actually read it. Its thousand pages would have been tough going for a semi-literate worker or peasant. It seems likely, as Michael Burns suggests, that it was often bought as a type of status symbol, to sit on cottage shelves alongside the Bible (often the only other book in the house).[20] It is difficult to imagine that many would have read the book from cover to cover. Instead, its readers were more likely to have treated it as a compendium, within which they could find the message they sought. As Willa Silverman notes, 'in *La France Juive* Drumont gives every reader a reason to hate something about the Jews'.[21] This encyclo-paedic quality is probably the key to the book's success. Peasants could have mulled over his protests about rural usury and high-priced land markets; small shopkeepers could have read his tirades against department stores; Catholics could have enjoyed his stories of the republicans' betrayal of France, and so on.

Not all initial responses to *La France Juive* were positive. The royalist pre-tender, the Comte de Paris, was horrified by the work, which he considered to be journalistic trash.[22] Many republicans still understood anti-Semitism as an essentially Catholic attitude, and refused to accept Drumont's polemics, understanding them as another attempt to modernise Catholicism.

However, *La France Juive* captivated many readers. Léon Daudet became a prominent anti-Dreyfusard. Writing during the First World War, he could still remember the publication of *La France Juive*. On that day, he walked round the arcades surrounding the Odéon theatre, watching the buyers queuing, and then walking away with one volume in their pocket, another open in their hands.

> I was confronted by a new issue: that of a race which had been invaded. Drumont's words shone as if they were burnished gold, he wrote with a deep sense of tragedy which today I can still hear ringing out, in one chapter or another, of *La France Juive*, like an alarm to the nation ... Among the students, there was a sympathetic interest. We admired the bravery of this isolated man who attacked all the powers of money.[23]

Elsewhere, Daudet reveals another aspect of Drumont's success: 'he loved his readers, and spoke to them in a good-natured and friendly way, which made his blows against his enemies seem yet more terrible.'[24] Just as Drumont idealised the 'old' community of *Mon Vieux Paris*, so in his writings he attempted to create a sense of community among his readers.

A detailed account of the sensation of reading Drumont can be found in Georges Bernanos's work, *La Grande Peur des bien-pensants* (1931). The title of this work is difficult to translate, but let us begin by describing Bernanos's ideas. Bernanos was a Catholic who felt contempt for the manner in which the Church had compromised with the Republic. He hated the moderate Catholics, the 'bien-pensants', the God-fearing, who would not fight for their faith. In the 1930s he was one of many right-wing intellectuals who were fascinated by Fascism, but who wished to reassure themselves that it was an integral part of French political culture. It was in this context that he rediscovered Drumont, who created 'the Great Fear' of the God-fearing. Drumont's ideas were well-rooted in French political culture, argued Bernanos: the French people of the 1920s and 1930s, whether they knew it or not, were sons or grandsons of readers of *La France Juive*.[25] Bernanos, who was born in 1888, was not able to remember the initial reception of *La France Juive*, but as early as 1908 he was a militant member of the far right and it was in this context that he learnt of Drumont.

Bernanos recalls the same quality of Drumont's work that was noted by Daudet: 'it was like a conversation between friends' (Bernanos, 1931: 33). However, there were other themes which Bernanos also admired: this was a work which could terrify and impassion as well as a work which could suggest friendship.

> *La France Juive* is surely one of the most virulent works which has ever been written, formed by a crafty, insidious lyricism which acted on the imagination like fertiliser on a seed. For a moment, for a short moment, our people were hit by this free word, and their flesh stung under its red-hot brand (Bernanos, 1931: 176–7).

In other words, Bernanos is saying that it is a violent work, and even the anti-Semitic reader would be shocked by its hatred and virulence. However, the book was successful because it was violent, not despite. It worked best on 'simple people' who understood its message 'summed up in a few essential, simple, violent images' (Bernanos, 1931: 186).

Bernanos sees in Drumont's work an assertion of the 'human' qualities of honesty, simplicity and naïvety, which are contrasted to the malign, artificial qualities of the Jew. Naïvety becomes a key concept in Bernanos's appreciation of Drumont's work. *La France Juive* is praised as a 'naive work' (Bernanos, 1931: 163). Drumont is motivated by a 'naive genius' (Bernanos, 1931: 164); the French people have a 'naive adoration' for the army. 'This is how the victor sounds, this is his savage laugh, his celtic laugh which is – alas!

– always a bit naive' (Bernanos, 1931: 181). Bernanos argues that Drumont's work is not a rational, academic theory. It comes from his 'guts' (Bernanos, 1931: 45). The circle of simple, honest friends created within Drumont's 'naïve' writing is contrasted to a threatening outside world, full of clever Jews who know how to take advantage of the naïve good nature of the French.

Bernanos's records allow us to see, first, why Drumont was a successful writer but, second, why anti-Semitism grew as a political movement. It gave a voice to those who felt neglected or humiliated by the new Republic; it allowed them to protest over issues which the old right, the monarchists and Catholics, had not addressed. However, it did this without drawing the anti-Semite into a fundamental critique of their society. Stephen Wilson's discussion of anti-Semitism among servants is well-worth considering at this point.

> They dared not attack, probably they would not have thought of attacking, employers and masters as such, but they could safely vent their resentments against Jews, and Jewish employers; for this attack did not fundamentally confront or undermine the institution of [domestic] service, but merely allowed these resentments, which it necessarily generated, to express themselves in a harmless way.
> [Anti-Semitism had a] general function of providing an illusory critique of the social system. [26]

Sartre noted similar qualities in anti-Semitism. It roused anger against individuals, not institutions: it promised that simply by destroying a malignant presence, a harmonious society would be created.[27] Instead of demanding a searching analysis, instead of making critics define themselves as critical individuals, anti-Semitism provided an 'easy-thinking' route to protest, 'a short-cut to intelligence, to knowledge'.[28]

La France Juive was a bestseller. Drumont made a number of attempts to build on his success. He intervened in the September and October 1889 general elections, encouraging candidates to adopt anti-Semitic policies: some members of the declining Boulangist movement listened to him. In the municipal elections of December 1889, some councils were contested by candidates of the Ligue Antisémitique de France (or LAF: sometimes also listed as the 'Ligue Antisémitique française'), an organisation started by Drumont. However, by 1892 the LAF had declined into little more than a fan club for its flamboyant aristocratic leader, the Marquis de Morès, who renamed it 'Morès et ses amis' (Morès and his friends).

Drumont tried another initiative. In 1892 he started a daily paper, *La Libre Parole* [the Free Word]. This proved to be more successful: by 1894 it was selling 200 000 copies each day.[29] While most of these sales went to cities, its success influenced another paper – *La Croix* [the Cross] had been created by the Assumptionist Order in 1883. It was published in the form of different editions for particular departments, and – due to the co-operation of many priests – it reached far into the rural world. It grew steadily more anti-Semitic in the 1890s. In 1895 its Paris-based national edition sold 170 000 copies.[30]

These papers were not exceptional in their encouragement of anti-Semitism. They were followed by the Bonapartist *Autorité* and by *L'Intransigeant*, edited by the ex-communard, Henri Rochefort. Other mainstream papers followed this pattern, and so, as the Dreyfus Affair grew in political importance, most readers still relied on anti-Semitic papers for information and analysis. In February 1898, when anti-Semitic riots broke out across France, only about 3.7 per cent of the newspaper-reading public were buying a pro-Dreyfusard paper.[31]

One of the most revealing examples of anti-Semitic politics was the publication of *Indicateurs des Juifs*. These were small handbooks which claimed to list all the Jews living within a certain area. Three were published in 1898.[32] They were based on the myth of the Jewish conspiracy: the *Indicateurs* aimed to clarify this mystery. 'The occult power of the Jews has been revealed to everyone, but the importance and the breadth of this power, which is so fatal for our country, is unhappily still unclear.'[33] Their editor, Philippe Sapin, would send announcements to all the people he had classified as Jews, telling them of his forthcoming publication and their entry in it. (It should be remembered that this was a time of growing anti-Semitic violence.) When those listed wrote in to protest, Sapin delighted in publishing their letters and his sarcastic, dismissive response. (See document 11. 3.)

A successful newspaper editor, Drumont was also a successful parliamentary candidate in the elections of May 1898, when he won one of the Algerian seats.[34] However, he was not a successful political leader. Bernanos considered that Drumont's election marked the end of his political life: 'Henceforth the great man was at the mercy of parliamentary intrigues, and he died at their hands' (Bernanos, 1931: 308–9). A number of other leaders attempted to direct the anti-Dreyfusard and anti-Semitic cause in 1898 and 1899. One of the most ambitious of these was Jules Guérin.

In the 1880s, Guérin had tried to run a theatre and to start a business. Both ventures had failed, leaving him with debts and unresolved courtcases. He took refuge in the anti-Semitic movement, and in 1892 was charged with the organisation of the LAF.[35] Originally he had been a follower of Morès and following the latter's death in 1896, he re-formed the LAF. By studying this organisation we can learn more about the practical, daily politics of the anti-Semites.

Drumont remained the nominal leader of the LAF in 1897, but Guérin effectively controlled its activities. A police report from 1899 noted his domination of the organisation. The LAF was 'the personal work of Guérin'. He was its 'absolute master'.[36] When he left France to visit Algeria, the LAF was like 'a body without a soul'.[37]

Arguments developed between Guérin and Drumont and by June 1898 the rupture between the two was common knowledge. One could see their rivalry from a political perspective: Drumont tended to be Catholic and conservative in his ideas, while Guérin picked up a radical, even revolutionary, rhetoric. This could also be seen as a difference in tactics: Drumont favoured confronting the government through his paper and the group of anti-Semitic deputies, while Guérin aimed to build a noisy and threatening street presence. Guérin was certainly more successful than Drumont in making contacts with left-wing groups, such as Rochefort, some Blanquists, and even the anarchist group associated with the *Révolutionnaire* paper.

Guérin was not consistent in his political commitments. By April 1898 he was accepting money from the new royalist pretender, the Count of Orléans. The money flowed in: an initial grant of 100 000 francs, followed by regular monthly payments of between 20 000 and 30 000 francs. Finally, another grant of 300 000 francs was paid to Guérin to finance his new headquarters in the rue de Chabrol, which were opened in March 1899.[38] As a result of this support, the LAF took a favourable attitude to the Pretender. In February 1899, speeches by the Count of Orléans could be read in Guérin's *L'Antijuif*. This illustrates the absurdity of anti-Semitic politics: the 'revolutionary' Guérin, attempting to prove his radicalism in order to outshine the 'conservative' Drumont, was actually being financed by the most conservative political grouping in France.

Rather than accepting the words of anti-Semites at face value, and seeing them as dedicated – albeit mistaken – idealists fighting for a cause in which they believed, it is more appropriate to remember Zeev Sternhell's comments: 'anti-Semitism had become a lucrative business, a trade which could provide for its men'.[39] The difference between Drumont and Guérin was principally about status and influence. This involved a debate about *styles* of political culture, but raised very few questions about political principle.

Guérin tried every method possible to rival Drumont's influence. His first initiative was to professionalise the organisation of the LAF. In 1897 he created sections in each Parisian *arrondissement*, and encouraged their creation in the provinces. An elaborate system of monthly passwords was devised to guard against the threat of infiltration. In August 1898, with the benefit of royalist finance, Guérin started his own weekly paper, *L'Antijuif*, which was intended to rival Drumont's *Libre Parole*. By January 1899, 120 000 copies were printed of each issue, although only about 65 000 of these were actually sold.[40]

Guérin's initiatives met with some success. Police reports estimated that in April 1897 there were only 385 members of the LAF. By August 1899, this figure had risen to 54 000, of whom 10 000 lived in Paris.[41] Following Guérin's re-organisation of the Ligue, they acted as a group of militants, ready to be mobilised for any demonstration by a system of messengers.[42] Guérin achieved some success in drawing in a heterogeneous mixture of support: at his meetings royalists, Bonapartists, Catholics, Boulangists and socialists 'were all united under the leadership of Guérin in opposition to Dreyfus'.[43] When this coalition grew too broad, Guérin solved the problem by forming sub-groups of liberals, republicans and socialists within the LAF.[44]

Guérin encouraged LAF militants to appeal to working-class people,[45] and attempted to imitate socialist and syndicalist methods of organisation. In August 1898 he announced the formation of the 'Mutual Society for the Protection of National Labour'.[46] This was to form the basis of a non-socialist Trades Council. While some workers did attend his meetings and follow him on demonstrations, the only sustained working-class support came from the butchers of La Villette, who formed Guérin's unofficial bodyguard during this period.

In May 1899 Guérin announced a new initiative. In opposition to the 'Grand Orient', the leading masonic organisation in France, Guérin proposed a 'Grand Occident de la France', or GOF. This venture appealed to the anti-masonism which many anti-republicans felt. A police spy attending a GOF meeting in May 1899 reported that some officers, lawyers, butchers, clerks and a few workers attended.[47] Its headquarters were in the rue de Chabrol, where it offered members free medical consultations, free legal advice and the use of a library and shooting gallery.[48]

Rumours about a new *coup d'état* were circulating in Paris: Déroulède's attempt to subvert an army unit in February 1899 added substance to these fears. When Dreyfus was sent to Rennes for his retrial in August 1899, the police decided to take preventive action against any possible conspirators. Many nationalist, royalist and anti-Semitic leaders were arrested early in the morning of 12 August. Guérin escaped arrest and barricaded himself in the LAF headquarters in the rue de Chabrol. Rather than forcing their entry, the police decided to starve him out. Guérin did not surrender until 20 September. This siege allowed the police to take stock of the real strength of LAF support.

> There is a large number of LAF members in Paris, but most of them are quiet people, who – while profoundly anti-semitic – would not endanger their lives or give up their liberties. The GOF has, at most, fifty people at demonstrations,

including the butchers. As Jules Guérin is not there to lead them, they do not know how to march, and they do not trust those who want to act as their leaders.[49]

The widespread publicity which the siege brought quickly revealed that the LAF was little more than a circle of Guérin's friends. His claims of an active membership which numbered thousands were clearly exaggerated.

During its three years under Guérin's leadership, the LAF was pushed through a number of different projects. First, Guérin aimed to create a tightly centralised organisation, willing to engage in street violence. In the 1890s, such organisations usually took the name 'ligue', although in earlier decades this term had referred to peaceful pressure groups, such as the Ligue d'Enseignement [The Teaching League], created in 1866. The new right-wing *ligues* of the 1890s relied on 'an appeal to the emotions, a cult of the leader, and brute force'.[50] While they were certainly innovative, they failed to present the solidity and purpose of the modern mass political party.

Second, Guérin consciously imitated the tactics of the labour movement. He made a specific appeal to workers, and offered LAF members immediate benefits for joining and a strategy for the long-term defence of their economic interests.

Third, in the form of the GOF, Guérin tried to create a counter-Freemasonry: an élitist network of people with influence, who would be able to sway political events without mass mobilisations.

Lastly, the 'siege of Fort Chabrol' can be seen as Guérin's imitation of the Commune. Without the benefit of a coherent political culture or a deep-rooted social movement, his stand looked farcical.

When these initiatives are examined together, we are left with an impression of the simple opportunism of Guérin and the LAF. This was not a movement with any form of political consistency: it lurched from cause to cause, pulled by money, stimulating hatred, with no long-term strategy.

– IV. LEGACY –

During the 1890s there seemed a possibility that anti-Semitic groups would succeed in creating a revolutionary, anti-republican coalition, uniting nationalists, monarchists, and socialists, based on the idea of 'anything, rather than the Jewish Republic'.[51]

There were many debates within left-wing groups over their attitude to anti-Semitism, and many discussions between such groups and anti-Semitic organisations. Occasionally, such discussions were fruitful: one could cite Barrès's paper, *La Cocarde*, as an example of a successful fusion of political cultures. However, this was short-lived. While both socialists and anti-Semites might rage against the corruption of capitalism, they analysed it in different ways and proposed radically different solutions. Barrès, for example, could not accept the idea of the proletariat as an active agent of their own liberation.[52] Conservative monarchists were interested in new anti-republican movements and could be persuaded to finance them. However, these old-fashioned groups were openly cynical about the ideas proclaimed by these new right-wing rebels. Monarchists retained their own way of understanding politics. Equally, left-wing groups kept their own ideas. For example, Emile Pouget, an experienced syndicalist propagandist and editor of the dogmatically working-class *Père Peinard*, always refused to work with Drumont – not because Drumont was anti-Semitic, but because he was a Catholic.[53]

Debates aiming to unite these various strands in a single anti-Dreyfusard electoral coalition in 1898 proved extremely difficult. Left-wing anti-Semites wished to appeal to socialists and republicans, meaning that contacts with royalists had to be kept secret.[54] No single organisation to represent all these strands of opinion was created in 1898. A further attempt to found a 'Republican Nationalist Party' in 1900 involved discussions between the Ligue de la Patrie Française, the Ligue des Patriotes, anti-Semites, and the 'French Socialists' led by Rochefort. Once again, monarchists were not formally included in these debates, and the party never had more than a paper existence.

During the Dreyfus Affair, socialists and republicans realised the re-actionary implications of anti-Semitic and racist concepts. After 1900, the occasional use of anti-Semitic concepts which had appeared in the left-wing press was slowly dropped.

The Dreyfus Affair permanently changed the nature of right-wing political culture, marking the turning-point between what can be termed the 'old' and 'new' right. The old right was best represented by the monarchists: they believed that because they represented social and political élites, they had a 'natural' right to rule. They were uncomfortable in running parliamentary campaigns, or in devising political strategies based on mass mobilisation (see Chapter 4). The 'new' right was represented by the *ligues*. Their politics were based on mass protest; they accepted that the twentieth century was to be an era of mass politics, and their goal was to mobilise forms of social solidarity in the service of an anti-republican, anti-democratic revolt. For this cause they were willing to make use of violent methods. There is, of course, a paradox here: the anti-Dreyfusards, enemies of democracy, were often able to make better use of the weapons of democracy than its avowed defenders were.

In place of the Republic, and its individualistic political culture based on one man, one vote and the free market, the new right sought to build a stable system of mass politics on forms of collective identity. Bernanos identified 'family, order, province and profession' (Bernanos, 1931: 176) as the appropriate bases for a stable society, and Barrès wanted a government which would 'restore the blocs' which made up the nation.[55] Such ideas, coupled with the anti-Dreyfusards' use of violence, are clear precursors of the Fascist ideologies of the twentieth century.

A long-term consequence of the Affair which affected all political traditions was the generalisation of more professional political parties.[56] As the Dreyfusard Daniel Halévy noted sadly, even an anti-militarist party still needed a tough leader.[57] Three new centre-left and centre parties were created in 1901, followed in 1905 by the creation of the SFIO (Section Française de l'Internationale Ouvrière – the French Socialist Party), led by the Dreyfusard Jaurès. Voting in the Chamber of Deputies slowly grew more disciplined.

The centrist republican groups had been extremely worried by the rise of the new right during the Dreyfus Affair. They determined to keep the right wing out of power by attacking what republicans still considered to be the base of right-wing power: the Church. The formal separation of the Church and state was enacted in December 1905. To pass this legislation the centre republican groups needed the support of the socialists. There was a precedent for this: in June 1899 Waldeck-Rousseau had included the socialist Millerand in his cabinet. The new, more strictly organised, parliamentary groups allowed clearer negotiations between centrist republicans and socialists. Although socialists did not formally enter the government, the parliamentary 'Bloc des Gauches', which united left-of-centre republicans and socialists, allowed them to participate in the drafting of legislation. However, there were clear limits to the themes on which republicans and socialists could agree: republicans were still reluctant to accept anything which would compromise the free market. For this reason, the formation of the Bloc des Gauches tended to encourage anti-clerical measures, such as the separation of the Church and state, and to discourage social reform.

The most profound lesson of the Affair was about the nature of democratic political culture. The republican interpretation of democracy was certainly limited: it excluded women from the political sphere, enforced a single concept of national culture, was individualistic, reluctant to acknowledge the importance of collective interests, and rested on the idea of a self-selecting élite guiding the nation. None the less, it did encompass a commitment to civil liberties and human rights. A genuinely popular republicanism could have created a deep commitment to a democratic, libertarian political culture, supported by educational institutions, and inspired by values of toleration and solidarity. The Dreyfus Affair shows that these values were not widely respected in France. Many Dreyfusards saw themselves as a scientific, rationalist élite, working to limit the fury of the mob. The anti-Dreyfusards and anti-Semites had successfully subverted the weapons of parliamentary democracy and – tragically – the first lesson in democratic politics for many French people came through the hate-filled, violent, mystifying rhetoric of the anti-semites.

– V. DOCUMENTS –

– DOCUMENT 11.1: AN ANTI-DREYFUSARD DEFENDS THE ARMY –

Déroulède was originally a French patriot who wanted to see energetic measures taken to return the provinces of Alsace-Lorraine to France. Towards this end, he created the Ligue des Patriotes in 1882. In this passage, he suggests that the army is a more representative institution of French nationhood than parliament.

LONG LIVE THE ARMY!

'Long live the Army!' ... Long live what is the best and purest in today's France: the spirit of service, of discipline, of solidarity, of the nation! Isn't this simple slogan, which is heard from the military review to the barracks' doors, also a condemnation and a blow against all these seedy politicians?

The army is modest and quiet: perhaps she doesn't understand the national pride and patriotic faith that the People place in her? ... To help us shake off the yoke of sects and cliques, does she still hesitate to cross the lines marked down by a Constitution which has usurped all power and violated all rights? Let yesterday's cries, let today's acclamations assure and enlighten her. The people is with her: let her be with the People!

I ask her, I beg her to avenge the Nation, to serve and save the Republic which is being dishonoured, the France which is being killed ... After all ... if the army doesn't start to march with the people, she will have to fire on them, and to get shots back from them. There'll be deaths on both sides, deaths of Frenchmen. Is that what my critics want, those who accuse me of wanting to build the union of the Army and the People?

There is no other solution to the crisis we're going through. The union which I'm calling for will give birth to liberty: it's the only possible way out that's quick and avoids blood. For twenty years our worthy soldiers have been policemen for deputies against France; now they're becoming policemen of France against deputies.

Paul Déroulède, Speech to the League of Patriots, 16 July 1899
Source: Raoul Girardet (ed.), *Le nationalisme français: anthologie,*
1871–1914 (Paris: Seuil, 1983), pp. 176–8

– DOCUMENT 11.2: ECONOMIC ANTI-SEMITISM –

This leaflet illustrates how anti-Semitic themes were used to explain economic conflicts. The author contrasts the 'real' and 'honest' nature of French commerce with the adulterated nature of the goods which, he claims, the Jews are selling. It is worth noting the broad spectrum of groups which he calls on to act: arguably, many of these people would normally have been politically passive.

Notes from a small shopkeeper of Caen
An appeal to his fellow citizens

To all of you, to workers, employees, shopkeepers, share-holders, people of Caen of all conditions, to all of you who realise that your interests are in jeopardy.

Do you know what's the cause of this evil?

Yes, you know it!

It's the monopolist [*accapeur*]!* It's the Jew!

The monopolist, with his big store, exploits hundreds of trades in the same space without paying taxes on them. He has an unfair advantage.

He crushes and ruins the small shopkeepers, by his unlimited and often illegit-imate competition, which affects you far more than you think!

Look around you! Think about what's going on! How many interests have been hurt! How many useless purchases! Don't let yourself be fooled by the label 'Bon Marché'!** What tricks it covers! What deals! Each day, how the cloth is stretched, pulled, enlarged! What ingredients are used, what glue, what weights – all to make this junk feel rich and look good.

Look at these goods after they've been in the rain, after they've been washed, after they've been in the sun. You can see how they've shrunk, how they're twisted, how they're ruined. The buyer is left empty-handed, but the cash-till in the big Jewish store is full.

Workers! Remember that this so-called 'bon marché' is usually based on lower-ing your wages.

Patriots! Bear in mind that usually behind all these great stores there is cosmo-politan, anti-French finance.

They're stealing your money and your savings, and this money doesn't come back as a gentle shower on you and yours. The benefits make a few big Jewish financiers rich to the detriment of the small and medium businessmen who cannot fight anymore.

Landlords, share-holders! What are you going to do with your buildings when businessmen close the shops which you've deserted in our towns?

Workers, employees, agents, commercial travellers! You don't need much intelli-gence to understand that the more they suppress the middlemen, the less you will be needed; the more business and industry is concentrated in a few hands, the fewer jobs there'll be: this is as clear as day.

French women! You usually do the shopping. The weapon to fight the mono-polist, the Jew, is in your hands.

Wives and daughters of shopkeepers, housewives, bourgeoises, charitable ladies, nuns: you're making the Jew rich. The Jew who drives your fathers and husbands into ruin, the Jew who – thanks to his sense of solidarity – invades everywhere, and throws your sons onto the streets.

You're letting this Jew live, oh daughters of France! And now, this Jew, with the money that he's stolen from us, has decided to organise a syndicate to save the traitor Dreyfus, who sold the blood of your brothers, from his well-deserved punishment.

The Jew stands before you: your enemy and your master. His strength comes from his sense of solidarity, which he only uses to gain money.

This is what you don't accept!

You'll oppose French solidarity to this Jewish invasion which wants to submerge us.

Buy only from the shops of Caen, from Frenchmen!

Ladies, lead by your example.

Everyone, workers, shopkeepers, share-holders, clerks, and so on, in your own interests, don't buy anything from these BIG MONOPOLISTIC STORES! BUY NOTHING FROM THE JEWS!

* This word could also be translated as 'hoarder'. It was a politically charged word, which had been used frequently during the French Revolution.

** The title of one of the first big department stores in Paris: also a phrase meaning 'a bargain'.

Source: AN, F/7/12643; handed out on the streets of Caen, 27 December 1898

– DOCUMENT 11.3: SAPIN'S REPLY TO REINACH –

The deputy, Joseph Reinach, wrote to protest about Sapin's *Indicateur* and its effects. Reinach asked him to consider its effects on the 'thousands of small, modest Jewish workers'. This phrase seemed to infuriate Sapin: his polemical reply shows that the anti–Semites lacked any sense of the sociological reality of their country and reveals how they were using the concept of 'Jew' to create an illusory distinction between 'good' and 'bad' capitalism.

> Can you show us any Jew who has ever worked the land? A Jew who has worked metal or cut wood? Can you show us a Jew who has ever gathered together stones and built a house for himself?
>
> No, Monsieur le député, you cannot show us this, for the Jews are too lazy to labour at such difficult tasks. They leave all that to the Christians, to the *Goyim* as you call them in the synagogue. When the *Goy* has worked hard and above all when he has saved, that's when the Jew 'works' ...
>
> Workers? – The Jews! No, tell us that they are braggarts, dealers, speculators, sharks, hoarders, tight-fisted employers [*affameurs*], yes, all you like, but *never* workers!
>
> Source: Philippe Sapin, *Indicateur des Juifs* (Lyon: Sapin, 1897), pp. 56–7

– DOCUMENT 11.4: MIRBEAU'S APPEAL TO THE WORKING CLASS –

Octave Mirbeau was a prominent anarchist writer and journalist. He became a Dreyfusard in 1897. He was disappointed by the apathy of the working class for the Dreyfusard cause, and frustrated by the caution of many socialists – particularly Jules Guesde – in facing the issue. This passage, from the principal

Dreyfusard paper, is part of a wider debate between socialists. Guesde's argument, which Mirbeau rehearses, was that Dreyfus was a bourgeois, and his fate was nothing to do with the working class. Mirbeau's reply is twofold: first to assert that an injustice which hurts one person can potentially strike anyone, and, second, to show how the Dreyfus Affair was raising wider questions.

They tell you:

'This Dreyfus Affair has nothing to do with you and there's nothing in it for you. What's the injustice which Dreyfus suffers got to do with you? What's it to you that he suffers in pain and anger, down there, on his island? If he didn't commit the crime of which he's been accused, for which he's been condemned to the most terrible of tortures, so what? He's committed crimes against you, some of them terrible: he's rich, he's an officer, and so an eternal enemy. If he's suffered injustice, then this amounts to justice for you ... Everything's fine ... Walk on, proletarian, and if you feel like it, sing as you walk.'

This is the generous advice given to you by Mr Guesde, and he knows what he's talking about. He's a rigorous logician, so they say, and he's got a fine beard. As well as all these social humiliations which means that Dreyfus deserves, if not your hatred, then at least your indifference ... Guesde almost added this: on top of everything else, because he's a Jew, Dreyfus doesn't deserve your pity ...

And haven't you said to yourself:

'That's what people are like, after all! It's always the same story!' ... Indifferent, you recite this lesson to those who are getting excited: 'Who cares what they say or do? They're bourgeois fighting between themselves. It's nothing to do with us ...'

Well, you're committing a crime, you as well, not only against this unfortunate man who's suffering, but also against yourself, because the two of you are linked.

When injustice strikes a living being – even if he's your enemy – you get hit as well. By injustice, Humanity's split into two. You must heal it, ceaselessly, by your efforts and, if you're rebuffed, do it by force, if necessary. In defending him, who's been oppressed by every brutal force, by all the passions of a declining society, you're defending yourself in him, you're defending your people, your right to freedom and to life, which is such a fragile conquest! Tomorrow, you'll be hit once again.

Look where this Dreyfus Affair has led us.

Today, it's more than a terrible misfortune which has hurt an innocent. It's grown, and because of all the accumulated lies which we've uncovered, it's become a question of life and death for a whole people. This is history – *your* history – which is being made. Because of this, we can see that the army has been fatally shaken – not in the principal of national defence, which we'd want to strengthen – but in its old and tyrannical constitution, which doesn't contain our modern liberties, nor our modern customs. The army, such as it is, is no longer a safeguard, it's a danger. Who applauds it today? The Caesarians★, who only dream of bloody riots. Who does it rely on? The anti-semites, who only dream of pillage. When, on those days of furious madness, someone shouts 'Long live the army!', they're also shouting 'Death to something!'. Those two cries are, from now on, linked. Openly, admiringly, those who applaud the army, tell us that it's ready to massacre, it's impatient to kill. The army has become the rallying point of all savage hatred, of all barbaric appetites, of all violence. Is this intentional? I couldn't say … Has it been done fully? Definitely …

We've arrived at the decisive moment at which either the army … adapts to the new environment in which we've evolved, or we submit to its seditious domination.

Well, I say we won't submit!

* Caesarians: those who believe in the political authority of the army.

Source: Octave Mirbeau, 'To a proletarian', *L'Aurore*, 8 August 1898
(in Pierre Michel and Jean-François Nivet (eds), *L'Affaire Dreyfus*
[Paris: Séguier 1991], pp. 74–80)

– VI. FURTHER READING –

The best introduction to the Dreyfus Affair is Eric Cahm, *The Dreyfus Affair in French Society and Politics* (London: Longman, 1996): a clearly written and dramatic account of the Affair. There is no easy introduction to the politics of the anti-Dreyfusards: the recent biography by Willa Z. Silverman, *The Notorious Life of Gyp: Right-Wing Anarchist in fin-de-siècle France* (Oxford: Oxford UP, 1995) could be a good starting place, as could Chapter 7 of Brian Jenkins, *Nationalism in France: Class and Nation since 1789* (London: Routledge, 1990).

There are many well-written analyses of issues raised by the Affair. Stephen Wilson, *Ideology and Experience: Antisemitism in France at the Time of the Dreyfus Affair* (Rutherford: Fairleigh Dickinson University Press, 1982) is an exhaustive social history: his chapter on the Henry subscription is particularly insightful. Michael Burns, *Rural Society and French Politics: Boulangism and the Dreyfus Affair, 1886–1900* (Princeton: Princeton UP, 1984) analyses changes in rural political cultures. His work is critically assessed in Nancy Fitch, 'Mass Culture, Mass Parliamentary Politics, and Modern Anti-Semitism: the Dreyfus Affair in Rural France', *American Historical Review* 97:1 (1992), 55–95. P. Birnbaum (ed), *La France de l'Affaire Dreyfus* (Paris: Gallimard, 1994) is a wide-ranging selection of essays on social and political themes. The essay by Yves Lequin, 'Dreyfus à l'usine? Le silence d'une mémoire' in this volume is a thought-provoking study of that most difficult of topics: apathy. Christian Delaporte, 'Images d'une guerre franco-française; la caricature au temps de l'Affaire Dreyfus', *French Cultural Studies* 6 (1995), 221–48 studies the cartoons and images produced by the anti-Dreyfusards and Dreyfusards: it is worth consulting for the drawings alone. Philip G. Nord, *Paris Shopkeepers and the Politics of Resentment* (Princeton: Princeton UP, 1986) is not a study of the

Dreyfus Affair, but does provide a detailed, sensitive analysis of a group from which the anti-Dreyfusards drew support.

The far right has attracted great historical interest in recent years. William Irvine, *The Boulanger Affair Reconsidered: Royalism, Boulangism, and the Origins of the Radical Right in France* (Oxford: Oxford UP, 1989) is a well-written examination of the relationship between Boulangism and monarchism; Patrick H. Hutton, 'Popular Boulangism and the Advent of Mass Politics in France, 1886–90', *Journal of Contemporary History* 11 (1976), 85–106 addresses the issue of the socialist potential within Boulangism. Zeev Sternhell, *La Droite Révolutionnaire, 1885–1914: les origines françaises du fascisme* (Paris: Seuil, 1978), and 'Barrès et la gauche: du boulangisme à *la Cocarde* (1889–1895)', *Le Mouvement Social* 75 (1971), 77–130: two works by a controversial historian who claims to identify an indigenous French Fascist tradition. While one may disagree with his conclusions, no one could deny Sternhell's ability to piece together the elements of far-right thinking. One of the best criticisms of his work is: Jacques Julliard, 'Sur un fascisme imaginaire: à propos d'un livre de Zeev Sternhell', *Annales ESC* 39:4 (1984), 849–59. Michel Winock, *Edouard Drumont et Cie: Antisémitisme et Fascisme en France* (Paris: Seuil, 1982): a penetrating series of essays. Jean-Paul Sartre, *Réflexions sur la Question Juive* (Paris: NRF, 1954) is a deftly argued dissection of anti-Semitism. Patrick H. Hutton, *The Cult of Revolutionary Tradition: the Blanquists in French Politics, 1864–1893* (Berkeley: California UP, 1981): Chapter 7 of this work documents the Blanquists' decline into the far-right. Benjamin F. Martin, *Count Albert de Mun: Paladin of the Third Republic* (Chapel Hill: North Carolina UP, 1978): a biography of the man who led the *ralliement* movement. On anti-Semitism and the old right, see J.-M. Mayeur, 'Les congrès nationaux de la "démocratie chrétienne" à Lyon (1896–97–98)', *Revue d'histoire moderne et contemporaine* 9 (1962), 171–206. Lastly, on the difficult topic of defining Fascism, Gilbert Allardyce, 'What Fascism is Not: thoughts on the deflation of a concept', *American Historical Review* 84 (1979), 367–98 is a challenging polemic.

There are a number of revealing and interesting anti-Dreyfusard texts. Two edited collections provide a broad selection: John S. McClelland (ed.), *The French Right (from De Maistre to Maurras)* (London: Cape, 1970) and Raoul Girardet (ed.), *Le nationalisme français: anthologie, 1871–1914* (Paris: Seuil, 1983). Léon Daudet, *Souvenirs et polémiques* (Paris: Bouquins, 1992) is an autobiographical memoir which concentrates on literary figures and journalism. Maurice Barrès, *Scènes et doctrines du nationalisme* (Paris: Juven, nd) is a more serious attempt to set out the political philosophy of the new right. Georges Bernanos, *La Grande Peur des bien-pensants: Edouard Drumont* (Paris: Livres de Poche, 1969), is a fascinating evaluation of the reinvention of anti-Semitism.

Patricia E. Prestwich, *Drink and the Politics of Social Reform: Antialcoholism in France since 1870* (Palo Alto: Society for the Promotion of Science and Scholarship, 1988), and Laura Frader, *Peasants and Protest: Agricultural Workers, Politics, and Unions in the Aude, 1850–1914* (Berkeley: California UP, 1991) are two well-researched works which evaluate the interplay between the economics, politics and culture in the Third Republic.

Pierre Birnbaum, *Les Fous de la République: histoire politique des Juifs d'Etat de Gambetta à Vichy* (Paris: Seuil, 1992) and 'Grégoire, Dreyfus, Drancy, and the rue Copernic: Jews at the heart of French history' in P. Nora (ed.), *Realms of Memory: the Construction of the French Past* (New York: Columbia University Press, 1996), pp. 378–423 are two pioneering works on French Jewish history. Philip G. Nord, *The Republican Moment: Struggles for Democracy in Nineteenth-Century France* (Cambridge, Mass.: Harvard UP, 1995): Chapter 4 outlines the changes in Jewish religious institutions during the mid-nineteenth century. Good starting-points for studying the experience of immigrants are Marie-Claude Blanc-Chaléard, 'L'habitat immigré à Paris aux XIXe et XXe siècles: mondes à part?', *Mouvement social* 182 (1998), 29–52 and Gérard Noiriel, *Le Creuset français: histoire de l'immigration XIX–XX siècle* (Paris: Seuil, 1988). The latter has a particularly forcefully argued methodological introduction.

Within this chapter, I have said little about the Dreyfusards' political culture. However, they have left a lively collection of memoirs. Octave Mirbeau, *L'Affaire Dreyfus*, eds Pierre Michel and Jean-François Nivet (Paris: Séguier 1991) and *Combats Politiques*, eds Pierre Michel and Jean-François Nivet (Paris: Séguier, 1990) are two collections of short fictional and non-fictional texts by a gifted polemicist: the second collection details Mirbeau's shift from anti-Semite to Dreyfusard. Octave Mirbeau, *Le Journal d'une femme de chambre* (Paris: Livres de Poche, nd) is an unusual novel written during the Affair: it gives an insight into anti-Semitic popular culture. Further information on Mirbeau can be found in: Pierre Michel and Jean-François Nivet, *Octave Mirbeau: L'imprécateur au cœur fidèle* (Paris: Séguier, 1990). Emile Zola's texts on the Affair are collected in *L'Affaire Dreyfus: La Vérité en Marche*, ed. Colette Becker (Paris: Garnier Flammarion, 1969). Léon Blum, *Souvenirs sur l'Affaire* (Paris: Folio, 1981) and Daniel Halévy, *Regards sur l'Affaire Dreyfus* (Paris: Fallois, 1994) are memoirs which give poignant descriptions of the idealism which motivated the Dreyfusards. Georges Sorel, *La Révolution dreyfusienne* (Paris: Trident, 1988 [1906]) and Charles Péguy, *Notre Jeunesse* (Paris: Livres de Poche, 1969 [1910]) are rather more ambivalent texts: both seem to consider that the Dreyfusard movement actually failed.

Richard D. Sonn, *Anarchism and Cultural Politics in fin-de-siècle France* (Lincoln, Nebraska: Nebraska UP, 1989) has only a brief consideration of the Affair, but does include a provocative description of French cultural politics during this period. Lastly, Maurice Larkin, *Church and State after the Dreyfus*

Affair: the Separation Issue in France (London: MacMillan, 1974) considers an important result of the Affair.

– NOTES –

1. Léon Blum, *Souvenirs sur l'Affaire* (Paris: Folio, 1981), p. 36.
2. William Irvine, *The Boulanger Affair Reconsidered: Royalism, Boulangism, and the Origins of the Radical Right in France* (Oxford: Oxford UP, 1989), p. 53.
3. Examples taken from Sharif Gemie, *Women and Schooling in France, 1815–1914: Identity, Authority and Gender* (Keele: Keele UP, 1995), pp. 155–6.
4. Patricia E. Prestwich, *Drink and the Politics of Social Reform* (Palo Alto: Society for the Promotion of Science and Scholarship, 1988), p. 38.
5. Laura Frader, *Peasants and Protest: Agricultural Workers, Politics, and Unions in the Aude, 1850–1914* (Berkeley: California UP, 1991), pp. 141–3.
6. Information on La Villette from Philip G. Nord, *Paris Shopkeepers and the Politics of Resentment* (Princeton: Princeton UP, 1986), pp. 382–91.
7. Information from R. S. Anderson, *France, 1870–1914: Politics and Society* (London: RKP, 1977), pp. 168–70. During this period there was no single socialist party. Many socialist candidates stood as 'independents'.
8. For the details of Dreyfus's experience, I have relied on Eric Cahm's useful work, *The Dreyfus Affair in French Society and Politics* (London: Longman, 1996).
9. Pierre Birnbaum, *Les fous de la République: histoire politique des Juifs d'Etat de Gambetta à Vichy* (Paris: Seuil, 1992).
10. Stephen Wilson, *Ideology and Experience: Antisemitism in France at the Time of the Dreyfus Affair* (Rutherford: Fairleigh Dickinson University Press, 1982), pp. 109–19.
11. Maurice Barrès, *Scènes et doctrines du nationalisme* (Paris: Juven, nd), p. 80.
12. AN, F/7/12643, poster entitled 'La Patrie en Danger', published several times in 1898.
13. Figure of Jews in France from Wilson, *Ideology*, p. 414; population estimate of 40.7m in 1900 from André Armengaud, 'Population in Europe, 1700–1914' in C. Cipolla (ed.), *The Fontana Economic History of Europe, Vol. III: The Industrial Revolution* (London: Fontana, 1973), pp. 22–76 (p. 29).
14. *La Libre Parole*, 5 February 1899.
15. Christian Delaporte, 'Images d'une guerre franco-française; la caricature au temps de l'Affaire Dreyfus', *French Cultural Studies* 6 (1995), 221–48.
16. Letter by Drumont in the *Bulletin Officiel de la LAF* [Ligue Antisémitique Française], 1 January 1898.
17. Georges Bernanos, *La Grande Peur des bien-pensants: Edouard Drumont* (Paris: Livres de Poche, 1969), p. 161.
18. Wilson, *Ideology*, p. 171; Michael Burns, *Rural Society and French Politics: Boulangism and the Dreyfus Affair, 1886–1900* (Princeton: Princeton UP, 1984), p. 124; Michel Winock, *Edouard Drumont et Cie: Antisémitisme et Fascisme en France* (Paris: Seuil, 1982), p. 37.
19. Jean-Paul Sartre, *Réflexions sur la Question Juive* (Paris: NRF, 1954), p. 53.
20. Burns, *Rural Society*, p. 126.
21. Willa Z. Silverman, *The Notorious Life of Gyp: Right-Wing Anarchist in fin-de-siècle France* (Oxford: Oxford UP, 1995), p. 78.
22. Irvine, *Boulanger*, pp. 168–9.
23. Léon Daudet, *Souvenirs et polémiques* (Paris: Bouquins, 1992), p. 97.
24. Daudet, *Souvenirs*, p. 494.

25. Bernanos, *Grande Peur*, p. 45.
26. Wilson, *Ideology*, pp. 136–7.
27. Sartre, *Réflexions*, pp. 50–1.
28. Wilson, *Ideology*, p. 152.
29. Wilson, *Ideology*, p. 173.
30. Wilson, *Ideology*, p. 206.
31. Wilson, *Ideology*, p. 88.
32. Wilson, *Ideology*, p. 117.
33. Philippe Sapin, *Indicateur des Juifs, 1898: Les Juifs dans toute la presse française, l'armée et la finance parisienne* (Lyon: Sapin, 1897), p. 2.
34. Algeria was defined as a French department in 1848: its deputies sat alongside French deputies in the Chamber of Deputies until 1962.
35. AN, F/7/12461, police report, 18 July 1892.
36. AN, F/7/12459, report, August 1899.
37. AN, F/7/12459, report, 28 April 1898.
38. Zeev Sternhell, *La Droite Révolutionnaire, 1885–1914: les origines françaises du facsisme* (Paris: Seuil, 1978), p. 226–8.
39. Sternhell, *La Droite*, p. 225.
40. Sternhell, *La Droite*, p. 228.
41. AN, F/7/12882, report, 2 April 1897; and AN, F/7/12459, report, August 1899.
42. AN, F/7/12882, police report, 2 June 1898.
43. AN, F/7/12459, report, August 1899.
44. AN, F/7/12464, police report, 20 January 1900.
45. AN, F/7/12459, report, 21 April 1900.
46. AN, F/7/12882, police report, 10 August 1898.
47. AN, F/7/12882, report, 12 May 1899.
48. AN, F/7/12882, GOF brochure, June 1899.
49. AN, F/7/12882, police report, 11 September 1899.
50. Raymond Huard, *La Naissance du parti politique en France* (Paris: Presses de Sci Po, 1996), p. 255.
51. AN, F/7/12464, police report, 12 December 1899.
52. See Zeev Sternhell, 'Barrès et la gauche: du boulangisme à *la Cocarde* (1889–1895)', *Le Mouvement Social* 75 (1971), 77–130.
53. Richard D. Sonn, *Anarchism and Cultural Politics in fin-de-siècle France* (Lincoln, Nebraska: Nebraska UP, 1989), p. 45.
54. AN, F/7/12464, police report, 1 March 1898.
55. Maurice Barrès, *Les Déracinés* (Paris: Livres de Poche, 1972), p. 255.
56. Raymond Huard, 'Aboutissements préparés et cristallisations imprévues: la formation des partis' in P. Birnbaum (ed.), *La France de l'Affaire Dreyfus* (Paris: Gallimard, 1994), pp. 87–119.
57. Daniel Halévy, *Regards sur l'Affaire Dreyfus* (Paris: Fallois, 1994), p. 118.

CHAPTER 12

Conclusions

Era of Revolutions: still current, as each new government promises to end it.

Flaubert[1]

In the last ten chapters we have met many memorable people. Among them are the frightened postmistress of Sisteron, complaining about Bonapartist propaganda left on the streets; Tournon, sitting in a café near the Spanish border, humming a Bonapartist song and fiddling with his tobacco pouch; a Parisian print-worker, throwing mud at the word 'royal' written over a monument; a Lyonnais *canut*, reading confirmation of the new tariff in *L'Echo de la Fabrique*; a mud-spattered, be-clogged Vendéen deserter, waiting for his mother to arrive with well-darned socks, a clean shirt and food; a female Saint-Simonian, appealing to textile workers to consider the organisation of their society; Prosper Enfantin, growing his beard and his hair in order to look more like an Old Testament prophet; a banqueteer, shouting his agreement to Ledru-Rollin's fiery speech; a young girl, with a red ribbon in her hair, getting ready to fight her white-ribboned enemy at the doors of a church; Alfred de Vigny, drunk on memories of the *Grande Armée* and the little corporal; Victorine Brocher, looking at her newborn son and thinking that she needed to learn more about politics; a republican banqueteer of the 1870s, sneaking through the lanes on 14 July to drink a toast to Marianne; and the sinister, manipulative Guérin, considering yet another model for the LAF to follow.

What qualities do these people and movements have in common? In each chapter, we have seen three forms of political language. The articulate, precise words of political philosophers are important, and their influence on and their inspiration to political movements has been noted. But, more often, we have concentrated on the mediators: the pamphleteers and journalists. These people connect the language of the people to the language of the philosophers: they are closer to popular movements, and more sensitively reflect their emotions and concerns. Above all, this book has concentrated on the 'ordinary people': not necessarily dedicated political militants, but people like Jeanne Mertet, who found that darning a pair of socks for her son had become a political act. Their shouts, slogans, gossip, songs and stories form the backbone of these great participatory movements of social transformation.

Over the century, these movements changed in important ways. Political protest – even *popular* political protest – grew more technically sophisticated. We can trace a line of development from Tournon's tobacco pouch, through the slogans collectively chanted in 1848, the papers read in 1871, to a quite abstract instrument like Sapin's evil *Indicateur des Juifs*. The focus moved from visual culture, through oral culture, to forms of print culture.

The forms directing these protests grew more elaborate. In part, this was a result of the 1804 Napoleonic Code, which formalised previous political restrictions, and banned all meetings and associations of more than twenty persons. Under these circumstances, it was inevitable that French political development was going to take an unusual form. During the first half of the nineteenth century, the dominant pattern was for small distinct centres of political life – normally papers or conspiratorial groups – to attract a wider but more nebulous following around them. The mid-nineteenth century saw a number of innovations: the trade union, the banquet, the club (1848 and 1870–1) and the public meeting (1868–70). All these institutions can be seen as instruments to draw more people into a more tightly defined political culture. In the late nineteenth century, the Ligues attempted to perform a similar function. However, despite a century of development, it is noticeable how antiquated the political tactics deployed during the Dreyfus Affair appear. The two principal political protagonists – Zola and Drumont – were both 'literary men', who owed their place in the public sphere to their ability to write. Despite the sensationalist images of the Affair 'splitting France in two', in reality it probably involved the active participation of fewer people than the insurrection of December 1851 (Chapter 7). The Affair was played out within the media, which provided its own evaluation of the Affair's importance to a new audience of newspaper readers.

There is another lesson to learn. The nature of politics was changing during the nineteenth century. What seems like naïvety in the early nineteenth-century movements is often really an innocence about politics and political ideals. In the late nineteenth-century, expressions of political commitment were not only growing more sophisticated, they were also more manipulative. In Chapters ten and eleven we saw both republicans and anti-Semites consciously and deliberately creating political ideologies: systems of beliefs which were intended as much to hide a social reality as to explain it. While these both involved mass mobilisation, both – in different ways –

avoided mass empowerment. Regrettably, we have to note that both these movements point the way to the dominant forms of political mobilisation in the twentieth century. The directness, the honesty which marked the earlier forms has been lost.

Aside from the provisions in the 1804 Napoleonic Code, what other explanations can be found for the path of the development of French political culture?

A common-sense answer would be to refer to the Revolution of 1789, and the turmoil which it left behind. However, this does not provide a complete answer: many other modern nations have experienced deep social revolutions (Britain, the USA, Russia, China, and so on), but France is the only nation in which one particular revolution seems to have triggered off a whole series of revolutions. Nor can it be argued that these nineteenth-century revolutions were part of a process to find a political equilibrium after 1789. As we have seen, new revolutions often mobilised different sectors of the population and raised new questions about authority relations.

The 1789 Revolution created a series of new political tactics and instruments (such as the club and the paper). It failed to motivate the mass of the population, but the revolutionaries were none the less more effective at communication than their counter-revolutionary rivals. When the monarchy was restored, it was not the result of a mass movement: it was imposed by the allies. During the Restoration monarchists attempted to end the influence of the liberals and revolutionaries. However, they proved incompetent at working within the new political framework which had been established by the Revolution. Under these circumstances, with or without Charles X's failings as a ruler, it was inevitable that there was going to be a conflict between (broadly speaking) a pro-1789 revolutionary camp and an anti-1789, counter-revolutionary camp. In other words, the series of nineteenth-century revolutions were not triggered by the Revolution of 1789, but rather were caused by the Restoration.

The Revolution of 1830 had an unexpected consequence: it legitimated the strategy of revolutionary action as a means of changing government. Instead of the gradual development of a consensual, governmental political sphere, within which opposing political traditions could peacefully debate (as happened in Britain), a quite different political framework developed in France. One element in this was the extended political and historical debate on the nature of the Revolution of 1789: while in 1814 Louis XVIII may have considered the Revolution as a mere hiatus in the 'normal' development of French society, by 1914 it had become understood as the great founding act of a new France.[2]

Excluded and marginalised groups participated in these political-historical debates, and the development of their political cultures was shaped by their evolving interpretation of the Revolution of 1789. Their strategies were based on the idea of organising outside of parliament and officially constituted power structures. Their debates and analyses often included a genuinely revolutionary dimension, in the sense by which Castoriadis defines the term: they called into question the existing structures of power, and they asserted different sorts of political culture which suggested more democratic visions of the relationship between citizen and power structure.[3]

In these radical alternatives to the dominant power structures we can hear more than an echo of Aristotle's concepts of the self-governing *polis* and the 'political animal'. By their very nature, these revolutionary movements stressed the values of civic participation in political decision-making. These mobilising ideas, these myths, circulated widely before each of the revolutionary moments. However, such ideals were not translated into the institutional practices of successive political establishments. Ideas of participation, of 'people-power', were put to use as ideologies to justify the rule of new élites; in the case of monarchist and anti-Semitic groups, they were deliberately manipulated to justify a strict social hierarchy. Furthermore, the forms of political cultures generated by these radical movements were often based on peculiarly limited notions of political participation. While women's activism certainly contributed to the rise of these radical alternative cultures, none of them argued clearly and consistently for women's formal political empowerment. Equally, most of them possessed a unitary vision of politics, suggestive of a centralisation of political power and a suspicion of regional variations or pluralistic ethnic identities.

While similar radical groups and alternative political cultures can be found in other modern nations, the unique quality of these French movements is the clarity of their visions. Their concerns lay bare the underside of political modernity: they give voice to the frustrations and the desires of those excluded from political power and exploited by economic oppression. They remind us of the limitations of contemporary understandings of democracy. For these reasons alone, they are worth remembering.

— FURTHER READING —

Jürgen Habermas, *The Structural Transformation of the Public Sphere: An Inquiry into a Category of Bourgeois Culture*, trans. Thomas Burger (Cambridge: Polity, 1992): a complex but thought-provoking analysis of the development of political cultures by a celebrated philosopher and social thinker. Pierre Birnbaum, *La France Imaginée* (Paris: Fayard, 1998): an essay on the difficulty with which French political thinkers approached concepts of political and cultural pluralism. Cornelius Castoriadis, *Le Monde morcélé* (Paris: Seuil, 1990) and his *L'Institution imaginaire de la société* (Paris: Seuil, 1975): two stimulating and provocative collections of essays on the nature of political power and democracy. François Furet, *Interpreting the French Revolution* (Cambridge: Cambridge UP, 1981) analyses how interpretations of the Revolution of 1789 changed during the nineteenth century.

– Notes –

1. Gustave Flaubert, 'Dictionnaire des idées reçues', in *Madame Bovary, L'Education sentimentale, Bouvard et Pécuchet suivi de Dictionnaire des idées reçues, Trois Contes*, preface by J. Perret (Paris: Bouquins, 1981), p. 776.
2. On the nineteenth-century reinterpretation of the Revolution, see Mona Ozouf, 'Liberté, Egalité, Fraternité' in P. Nore (ed.), *Les Lieux de Mémoire Vol. III* (Paris: Gallimard, 1997), pp. 4353–89.
3. See Cornelius Castoriadis, *Le Monde morcélé* (Paris: Seuil, 1990) and his *L'Institution Imaginaire de la société* (Paris: Seuil, 1975).

Glossary of Names and Movements

Numbers in *italics* at the end of each entry signify page references

Balzac, Honoré de (1779–1850): novelist and journalist. Liberal in the 1820s, supporter of the 1830 Revolution, moved to legitimism in 1831–2. Author of the *Human Comedy*, a multi-volume cycle of approximately ninety short stories and full-length novels. *36–7, 108–9*

Barrès, Maurice (1862–1923): nationalist writer and novelist. Elected as Boulangist in 1889. Anti-Dreyfusard. Author of the *Culte du moi* (1888–91), which raised questions about personal integrity, and *Roman de l'énergie nationale* (1897–1900) which celebrated a cult of nationhood. *228, 237–8, 239*

Barrot, Odilon (1791–1873): Orleanist politician. Led the 'Dynastic Opposition' in the 1840s, a grouping which called for the reform of the Orleanist monarchy. A supporter of Louis-Napoleon in 1849–50, Barrot later became worried by his anti-parliamentary politics. *118–19, 122, 125, 169, 171, 175*

Béranger, Pierre-Jean (1780–1857): poet and songwriter. Composed many extremely popular liberal, anti-clerical songs during the Restoration. *35–6, 90*

Bernanos, Georges (1888–1948): anti-Semitic novelist and journalist. Following the defeat of France by Nazi Germany in 1940, Bernanos wrote many articles and essays criticising German rule. *232–3, 239*

Blanc, Louis (1811–82): utopian socialist, writer. President of the Luxemburg Commission February–April 1848. Author of the *Organisation of Labour* (1839) which proposed state sponsorship of workers' co-operatives. *126, 127, 156, 158, 209*

Blanqui, Auguste (1805–81): republican and socialist conspirator; advanced a theory of revolutionary dictatorship. Blanquists were one of the best organised groups during the Paris Commune (1871): following Blanqui's death the movement split into a nationalist right-wing and a marxist left. *128, 147, 197–8*

Bonald, Louis de (1754–1840): counter-revolutionary author and philosopher; proposed the regeneration of France through a revival of Catholic values. *67*

Cabet, Etienne (1788–1856): utopian socialist, newspaper editor. Author of *Voyage en Icarie* (1840). *93, 97–100, 108, 128–9*

Charbonnerie: secret liberal political movement during the Restoration; attracted some sympathy from students and officers. *30, 97, 100*

Chateaubriand, François-René (1768–1848): royalist and Catholic writer and novelist. His *Génie du Christianisme* (1802) proposed a Catholic renaissance in France; his novels of the Restoration contributed to French romanticism. Despite his profoundly royalist commitments, he was a critic of Charles X. *15, 18, 22, 23, 24, 38–9, 65, 71, 72, 77, 78*

compagnonnages: organisations of workers. Originally created in medieval guilds, the *compagnonnages* were archaic by the early nineteenth century. *47, 48, 105*

Considérant, Victor (1808–93): politician and newspaper editor. Follower of Fourier, active during the Second Republic (1848–52). *95–6, 104, 126–7, 130*

Constant, Benjamin (1767–1836): liberal philosopher and politician, serving in Imperial and royal governments. Author of *La Liberté des Anciens comparée à celle des modernes* (1819). *35, 90, 100*

Corbon, Claude (1808–91): one of the editors of the Catholic-socialist monthly *L'Atelier*, which started in 1840. Member of the Constituant Assembly (1848–9): appointed a life Senator of the Third Republic in 1875. *156*

Courier, Paul-Louis (1772–1825): liberal pamphleteer and activist. His essays addressed the common concerns of ordinary people, and contributed to the rise of liberalism in the 1820s. *32–5, 90, 100*

Daudet, Léon (1867–1942): writer and journalist, anti-Semite and anti-Dreyfusard. *231*

Démoc-Socs: republican and socialist movement which developed during 1849–51. Crushed by the *coup d'état* in December 1851.

Déroulède, Paul (1846–1914): nationalist advocate of military strength, leader of the Ligue des Patriotes, anti-Dreyfusard. Twice attempted to launch a *coup d'état* in 1899. *227, 236, 240*

Drumont, Edouard (1844–1917): anti-Semitic journalist and editor of the *Libre Parole*. Elected to Chamber of Deputies in 1898. Anti-Dreyfusard. *230–3, 234, 235, 238*

Fourier, Charles (1772–1837): utopian socialist writer and philosopher. *93, 95–7, 103–4, 107–8, 157*

Gambetta, Léon (1838–82): radical republican. Member of the first government of the Third Republic, and head of government 1881–2. *190*

Guérin, Jules (1860–1910): anti-Semite and anti-Dreyfusard. Leader of the LAF, 1897–1900. *227, 234–7*

Guizot, François (1787–1874): liberal-conservative politician and writer; Orleanist. Supporter of the 1830 Revolution, but then opposed further social and political reform. Almost permanently head of government in the 1840s. *16, 30, 116–17, 123, 125*

'Gyp', pseudonym of Sibylle-Gabrielle de Riquetti de Mirabeau, Comtesse de Martel de Janville (1849–1932): novelist and journalist. Anti-Dreyfusard and anti-Semite. Wrote many witty, light novels based on dialogues. *221*

Haussmann, Georges-Eugène (1809–91): Bonapartist, director of the urban modernisation of Paris in the 1850s and 1860s, which set a model for other French cities. *183–4, 187, 200–1, 213*

Hugo, Victor (1802–85): novelist, playwright, dramatist, poet and politician.

Originally a royalist and Catholic follower of Chateaubriand, Hugo became a Republican, and grew more concerned about social issues. In exile 1851–70. Author of *Les Misérables* (1862). *15, 34, 35, 114–15, 117, 125, 131, 155–6, 162, 168, 209, 210*

Lamartine, Alphonse de (1790–1869): poet and head of the Provisional Government of the Second Republic. Idealist republican. *113, 115–16, 120, 121, 126, 131*

Lamennais, Félicité (1782–1854): Catholic writer. Originally an ultra-royalist during the Restoration, grew more critical of monarchism, and took up issues of social reform.

Ledru-Rollin, Alexandre (1807–74): republican activist, minister of the Interior in the Provisional Government of the Second Republic, Démoc-Soc leader. *118–19, 121, 126, 131, 133–4, 143, 146–7*

Legitimism: monarchist opposition to the July Monarchy (1830–48), refusing rule by the liberal Orleanist branch of the Bourbon monarchy.

Leroux, Pierre (1797–1871): utopian socialist and Catholic; writer and editor of *La Globe*. *91, 101, 106, 130, 148*

Maistre, Joseph de (1753–1821): counter-revolutionary writer and philosopher: proposed a Catholic revival of France.

Michel, Louise (1830–1905): republican, feminist and anarchist activist and writer; communard. *186, 188, 189–90, 192, 194, 198, 200, 201–2, 221*

Michelet, Jules (1798–1874): republican historian and writer. *209, 211–12, 216–17*

Mirbeau, Octave (1848–1917): journalist, playwright, and novelist; a Bonapartist and anti-Semite in the 1870s and 1880s, he moved dramatically to the left in the late 1880s, and became an anarchist. Dreyfusard. Author of *Le Journal d'une femme de chambre* (1899). *226, 242*

Orleanism: leading ideas of the liberal July Monarchy (1830–48), which proposed a form of constitutional monarchy.

Pouget, Emile (1860–1931): anarcho-syndicalist journalist and editor. *238*

Proudhon, Pierre Joseph (1809–65): writer and political activist; inventor of the term 'anarchism'; author of *What is Property?* (1840) and *On the Political Capacity of the Working Classes* (1864). *117, 129, 131, 147, 148, 157–8, 174, 196–7, 200–1*

Pyat, Félix (1810–89): republican and communard. *160–1*

Rochefort, Henri (1831–1913): editor and political activist. Member of the radical republican opposition to the Second Empire; supporter of the Commune; imprisoned in the 1870s; adopted an increasingly right-wing stance in the 1890s; anti-Dreyfusard. *188, 190, 234, 235, 238*

Sand, Georges, pseudonym of Amantine-Aurore-Lucile Dupin (1804–76): novelist, feminist and republican. Proposed an idealistic form of republicanism in the 1840s; disillusioned by the Second Republic (1849). *128, 131, 135–56, 174*

Saint-Simon, Claude Henri de (1760–1825): utopian socialist writer and early sociologist. *93–5, 106–7*

Thiers, Adolphe (1797–1877): liberal and Orleanist politician. Supporter of Louis-

Napoleon in 1849–50, but concerned by his rejection of parliamentary methods. Directed the military campaign against the Commune, and engineered the reluctant acceptance by Orleanist notables of the Third Republic (1870–1940). *19, 24, 26, 125, 192*

Tristan, Flora (1803–44): socialist and feminist writer and activist. Proposed and encouraged working-class self-organisation. *59–60, 104–6, 108*

Ultras, ultra-royalists: monarchist right-wing during the Restoration (1814–30). Became legitimists during the July Monarchy (1830–48).

Vigny, Alfred de (1797–1863): officer and Bonapartist writer. *167*

Villeneuve-Bargemont, Jean-Paul-Alban (1784–1850): social Catholic and legitimist writer and investigator; Prefect for various departments, 1812–30; Deputy 1830–1; author of *Christian Political Economy* (1834). *78*

Villermé, Louis (1782–1863): writer and social investigator; author of *The Moral and Physical Condition of the Working Classes* (1840). *46–7*

Emile Zola (1840–1902): republican novelist and writer. Author of the twenty-volume *Rougon-Macquart* cycle. Prominent Dreyfusard activist; author of 'J'accuse' (1899). *220, 226, 227, 228*